THE BELLS
OF THE
KREMLIN

THE BELLS OF THE KREMLIN

AN EXPERIENCE IN COMMUNISM

by Arvo Tuominen

Piltti Heiskanen, *editor*

Lily Leino, *translator*

with an introduction by Harrison E. Salisbury

University Press of New England
Hanover and London, 1983

UNIVERSITY PRESS OF NEW ENGLAND

Brandeis University	University of New Hampshire
Brown University	University of Rhode Island
Clark University	Tufts University
Dartmouth College	University of Vermont

Printed in the United States of America.

LIBRARY OF CONGRESS CATALOGING IN PUBLICATION DATA

Tuominen, Arvo, 1894–1981
    The bells of the Kremlin.

    Excerpts from 5 books and taped interviews.
    Includes index.
    1. Communism—Soviet Union—History—20th century.
2. Communism—Finland—History—20th century.
I. Heiskanen, Piltti. II. Title.
HX313.T86 1982   335.43′0947   82-17647
ISBN 0-87451-249-2

CONTENTS

PREFACE

WHILE IN Finland in the spring of 1982, a year after the death
of Arvo Tuominen, I visited Sanna Tuominen, one of the two
surviving sisters of the seventeen children in the family. Sanna
told me that, after the death of Tuominen's wife Lyyli, she had
seen Arvo at times lying on his bed looking up at the stars through
the window and wondering which of them was Lyyli's star, wink-
ing down to him. The two had always been very close to each other.

This was part of Arvo Tuominen's heritage from home. Eight of
his siblings had died young and after each death his mother had
consoled the tearful remaining children: "Look up to the heavens.
Each of us has his own star and our dead wink from there." Tuominen remained faithful to this heritage throughout his long life,
even through the years when he was Communist. "I have a direct,
automatic contact with God," he told me.

While the Moscow-Peking axis was still very strong, in the early
1950s, Tuominen predicted its breakup; as he put it, "it has a casting defect." His own brand of communism could not last because
of such "casting defects" as religion and basic decency in his character. "Even during my worst communist period I could not accept the communist rule of ethics: the end justifies the means," he
has written.

During the winter of 1939–40 I served as an officer in the Finnish
army, fighting the attacking Red Army. Most of the men in my
regiment were from the workers' district in Helsinki; many were
Social Democrats, and I assume some were Communists. It was a
difficult war and we had numerous casualties. Yet, I was not aware
of a single man who lacked the will to stand up and fight.

At that time Tuominen was still the secretary general of the
Communist party of Finland. He had 250 Soviet-trained saboteurs
and thousands of other Communists who followed his orders. The
impending attack of the Red Army had tested his faith in communism and found it wanting: he had given the order that there
was to be no sabotage; on the contrary, every Finnish Communist

was to fight for his homeland. "In this case," he had said, "the Soviet Union is the aggressor."

I met Tuominen for the first time in 1956 in Finland when he had just returned from his self-imposed exile, first in the Soviet Union and, later, in Sweden. I met him from time to time in the 1960s, but I did not really get to know him until the early 1970s, when I lived in Helsinki. I began to work on his books in 1974, after I had retired from the United States diplomatic service. I was then living in Austria but in 1974–76 I made five long visits to Finland to interview Tuominen. I taped many hours of talks with him, asked questions, updated, checked important points, and made good use of his remarkable memory.

The present volume contains material from five books by Tuominen and from the aforementioned tapes. Thus it is his book. My editorship consists, first, of selecting the material I believed to be of greatest interest to non-Finnish readers while maintaining a balanced picture of what Tuominen has to say and also considering his own views as to the most important parts. Second, I rearranged some of the material. Third, I asked Tuominen to clarify certain parts of the text and to expand and update others. But I have not changed in any manner the meaning of the text or even individual sentences. Here and there I wrote, in Tuominen's style, abbreviated passages as a bridge in place of the material I had eliminated. Only after his approval were they included in the book.

Most of the material is from the three autobiographical works Tuominen published during the years 1956–58. The first one was *Sirpin ja vasaran tie* (*The Way of the Hammer and Sickle,* Helsinki: Tammi, 1956) and the second *Kremlin kellot* (*The Bells of the Kremlin,* Helsinki: Tammi, 1956). The third one, *Maan alla ja päällä* (*Underground and Above,* Helsinki: Tammi, 1958), describes the time period between the two other books. By far the biggest part of the present book is from *Kremlin kellot.* The book also includes some material from the volumes *Myrskyn aikaa* (*During the Storm,* Helsinki: Tammi, 1970) and *Myrskyn mentyä* (*After the Storm,* Helsinki: Tammi, 1971), as well as the previously mentioned material from the interviews.

After the Finnish version was ready and approved by Tuominen it was translated into English by Ms. Lily Leino, an American with Finnish-born parents who has had a long career as a writer in both

English and Finnish and as a translator from Finnish into English. Because Mr. Tuominen wrote as he spoke, the book was full of colloquialisms and unusual political phrases that often made the translating difficult. In clarifying Tuominen's terminology I worked closely with Ms. Leino.

This is a book about the communist system, especially communism in the Soviet Union. But "I want to emphasize especially," Tuominen has written, "that my memoirs describe conditions and events during the height of Stalin's power. I do not speak of the present conditions in the Soviet Union which I do not know well and which may have changed much since the death of Stalin." Tuominen repeated this to me more than once.

In my view it would be wrong to assume that this is *only* a historical book. It is up-to-date to the extent that the Soviet leaders have chosen *not* to change the conditions since Stalin. While it is true, as Tuominen says, that the book describes the Stalin era, it is also true that the now less stern Soviet rule is still based on the same system.

Stalin was a big disappointment to Tuominen. He imagined that had Lenin lived, he would not have done many of the things Stalin did. For example, he was of the opinion that Lenin would not have attacked Finland because he "adored the Finnish people, especially the working class. There were in Sodom and Gomorrah a number of the righteous, but Stalin saw not a single righteous one in Finland" and therefore attacked.

One of my earliest childhood impressions was of the flashing and thundering of cannon, which I could observe from our shore of the Kronstadt Bay (a mile from the Soviet border), when Lenin's Red Army and the rebellious Kronstadt sailors, who had demanded basic democratic freedoms, dueled for two weeks. I also remember the many thousands of sailors fleeing to Finland over the ice and, a little later, less fortunate ones floating to our shore after the thaw. This was in 1921. Lenin had not found *any* righteous ones among the sailors who, a few years earlier, had helped him to power by storming the Winter Palace in Petrograd. Tuominen found Lenin's announced nationalities policy very attractive but chose to overlook the Red Army's attack on the Baltic countries, after they had declared their independence.

Thus Arvo Tuominen's wish "had Lenin only lived" was, in

my view, not very realistic and I think he knew it. He recalled Lenin's explanation to the Comintern Congress of 1920: "this is a *dictatorship* of the proletariat, a passing state of affairs, and in a dictatorship one must use force against one's own and against others." Tuominen renounced Stalinism but retained some of his infatuation for Leninism, partly because "it is difficult, especially for the Finnish character, to concede that one has erred." He seemed to reason: true, I misjudged communism but my error would have been less without Stalin.

There were a number of things that to a degree compensated for his disappointment in communism. He rejected the prime ministership of Finland—a quisling position, yet a tempting one—thereby showing that he was not an opportunist but more of a Finnish patriot than a Communist. Tauno Nurmela, former chancellor of the Turku University, in a book referred to Martin Luther before the Diet of Worms and to his famous phrase: "Here I stand and cannot do otherwise." "The entire Finnish nation stood like this in 1939," Nurmela wrote. "By so doing it saved its soul and independence. If one had to choose the one person among all the Finns who on that occasion most resembled the fearless Dominican monk and Wittenberg's learned doctor of theology, I would say without hesitation that it was Arvo 'Poika' Tuominen who by rejecting Stalin's offer returned to Finland, 'his spiritual fatherland.' " *

Highly satisfying for Tuominen was the fact that Finland's postwar policies moved closer to Tuominen's new way of thinking, so that the two met somewhere halfway. Perhaps the most conspicuous evidence of this was the friendship between Tuominen and President Kekkonen, who once as a young lawyer had assisted in sending the former to prison.

Satisfying, too, was the fact that Tuominen came out of it all with his life. That gave him the chance to write his unique inside story of communism.

P. H.

* *Minun isänmaani* (*My Fatherland,* ed. Simo Talvitie, Helsinki: WSOY, 1974).

INTRODUCTION

AN INCREDIBLE sixty-five years has passed since that unforgettable night in the Smolny Institute of Petrograd when a man almost unknown to the outer world and of little renown in Russia rose and proclaimed the establishment of a Soviet order. Few of those present in the hall of the onetime school for noblewomen could envisage what the words of Vladimir Lenin might portend. Most were simple peasants, workers, and soldiers whose drab greatcoats stank of tobacco, sweat, and the mud of trenches to whom Lenin's speech simply meant bread, land, and peace.

But even if the question had been put to Lenin's associates or to the bolshevik leader himself no answer could have been forthcoming that would have conveyed the drama, the tragedy, the dismal depths, the epic flights of heroism, the terror, the treachery, the sacrifice, the butchery, the cost in tens of millions of lives, the changes in human life that would flow from the events of that evening.

Today, more than half a century later, we probe and ponder, trying to discover what happened, why it happened, why it happened the way it did, who was responsible, and where the great dream—and great dream it was in the eyes of all those present at Smolny—went wrong. What changed the gold to dross? Who was the villain? What were the steps that led the utopian hopes of brilliant men and women, not only Russian men and women but those of a hundred nations and races, to such disaster as makes Dante's *Inferno* seem a mere childhood nightmare?

They are all gone now—Lenin, almost the first to die in January, 1924; Leon Trotsky murdered in 1940; Bela Kun, leader of the bloody Hungarian revolt, executed; Zinoviev, Kamenev, Bukharin, and Radek, Lenin's brilliant associates, killed in the purges of the 1930s with thousands of their comrades; the leaders of the Red Army, Tukhachevsky, Blücher, and the rest, mowed down in 1937–38; the great Chinese leaders, Mao Tse-tung and Chou En-lai, dead within months of each other; the list could go on for pages. Between the insatiable appetite of the purges and the sheer passage of years hardly an individual survives amongst the Russians except for the long-enfeebled Vyacheslav Molotov, once Stalin's closest henchman. Stalin, of course, went on March 5, 1953, followed soon after by Beria and most of his terrible police apparatus (as earlier generations of secret police had been wiped out to make way for succeeding generations).

The Revolution devoured its own—not only Stalin with his deadly purges but those involved in the revolutionary cause in other countries. Talmudism and casuistry have long since splintered and sundered the communist movements of country after country. The age of the survivors has come to an end. In 1981 Arvo Tuominen, a Finn, died. He was the last surviving member of the Presidium of the Comintern, the central apparatus established by Lenin and his cohorts in the aftermath of 1917 to lead the cause of world revolution.

The Comintern itself vanished with a stroke of Stalin's pen to further the Soviet cause in World War II. (Stalin turned its press and paper supplies over to the Moscow patriarchy so that a journal for the Orthodox Faithful could be published in accordance with a concordat he had signed with the church.) Even the Comintern's postwar successor, the Cominform, sturdy child of the Cold War, has gone the way of its predecessor, and the spreading cacophony of divergent communisms in recent years has made any pretense of a unitary world revolutionary center in Moscow more and more difficult to maintain.

How did it all happen? To answer this Arvo Tuominen leads us on a voyage of remarkable discovery, a voyage to a vanished land, a vanished era, the era of the birth of communism in Russia and in the world. Although he was not there precisely at its beginning, he came along soon enough, a sturdy Finn whose carpenter father wielded a hammer his whole life and whose mother's sole inheritance was the gleaming sickle that she swung with deft and energetic skill through the billowing Finnish fields of grain.

Arvo Tuominen was twenty-three in 1917. At twenty-seven he was co-opted to membership in the Executive Committee of the Comintern, and in 1921 in Moscow he met them all—Lenin, Trotsky, Bukharin, Zinoviev, Kamenev, Alexandra Kollontai, André Marty, the pleiad of fiery personalities who hoped to stir the embers of World War I into the flames of revolution. He did not meet Stalin then. Stalin was still invisible.

In 1933 at the age of thirty-nine, after spending nearly ten years in Finnish prisons for his communist activities, Arvo Tuominen went to Moscow where he joined Otto Wille Kuusinen, a Finnish Communist, resident in the Soviet Union almost from its formation, member of the inner circle of the Cominform. For five years Tuominen lived in the eye of the hurricane. These were the most deadly years of Stalin's purges. Tuominen and his wife lived through most of the period in the grey *Dom Pravitel'stva,* an early skyscraper apartment house across the Moskva river from the Kremlin in which were housed only the highest communist functionaries. One by one they watched as their neighbors vanished into the maws of Stalin's police.

Tuominen was present at the Comintern session at which Bela Kun, the fearsome Hungarian communist leader, was denounced, and listened silently as Kun sought by the force of his powerful oratory to turn away the accusations. He watched as Kun passed through the doors of the meeting room where two GPU men waited to arrest him. Tuominen was present at the 1936 trial of Zinoviev and Kamenev in the Hall of Columns in Moscow and puzzled with his wife as to why these men had confessed. He was at a resort in the Caucasus when the arrest and execution of Marshal Tukhachevsky and the other Red Army generals was announced. He still recalls his shock when high Communists shrugged their shoulders at the news and observed: "It's good that it happened this way."

Tuominen listened in silence as the leaders of the Polish Communist party, his colleagues in the Comintern, were denounced as spies and traitors and vanished. The same thing happened with the Lithuanian communist leaders, the Latvians, the Estonians, the Yugoslavs, the Rumanians, the Bulgarians, and many others. He stood by as thousands of his countrymen, Finnish Communists who had sought refuge in the Soviet Union and Karelian Finns, were arrested, imprisoned, or executed.

Finally in early 1938, Tuominen and his wife, by a stroke of remarkable luck and timing, managed to leave Moscow for Stockholm where Tuominen continued to function as secretary general of the Finnish Communist party. He did not break with Moscow but lived in a state of uneasy ambiance. Finally, November 13, 1939

Tuominen was ordered by the Comintern to return to Moscow to take the post of premier of the puppet Finnish government that the Soviet was setting up in preparation for the attack on Finland. He refused. A new order came through. This one from Stalin personally. He again refused. Stalin went forward with his plan. Finland was attacked. A Finnish "government" was established at Terijoki with Kuusinen at its head.

But Tuominen crossed the Rubicon. He broke with Moscow. He did not give up his leadership of the Finnish Communist party. Instead, he directed his comrades to support Finland's cause against the Soviet Union. Finnish Communists fought side by side with their countrymen in what Tuominen felt was their finest hour.

Years have passed. Tuominen gave up his Communist connections long ago. He stayed in Sweden until 1956 writing and working. Finally he returned to Finland, became the editor of the social democratic newspaper in Tampere, the city of his youth, served in Parliament, and dedicated himself to reconstituting the past in an epic series of books that have sold a record-breaking quarter of a million copies in Finland.

Little escaped his sharp eye and attentive memory concerning the life, the quarrels, the intrigues, the personalities that made up the fabric of his years in Moscow, his long service in the Comintern, his frequent presence in the Kremlin, his days in the raggle-taggle Hotel Lux on Gorky Street in Moscow that for years was the true home of the international revolution. He has not forgotten the plots that were hatched there, the incredible conflicts of personality, the love affairs and liaisons of the revolutionary personalities.

Tuominen was a Finn in the classic sense. He was thoughtful, stubborn, quiet, with an internal system of values that never ceased to clash with the end-justifies-any-means philosophy of the early international Communist movement and even more with the paranoia of the Stalin era. Yet, it was these stern, almost harsh characteristics that led him to stay in the ranks of the movement for as long as he did. Even though he was intimately aware of the falsity and deceit of the "cases" brought against his fellow Finns, he was slow to place in a similar category the sensational accusations leveled against the other communist leaders, including those of the Soviet Union itself. He protested unjustified charges leveled against the Finns but halted short of an open break because, as he felt, nothing would be accomplished unless he could bring his protest to the attention of the world—and this could not be done in Stalin's Russia. He offers no excuses for himself. He simply puts down in simple words what he did and what he felt. Others might have acted differently—and some did. But for himself this was the way it happened.

Thus, through the shrewd and realistic eyes of Tuominen we are presented with a record that is without parallel of the way things really worked within Russia's revolutionary center, first under Lenin and later under Stalin. Tuominen feels strongly that had Lenin lived the future of the Soviet Union would have been far different than it proved to be under Stalin—a conviction he shares with many of the early Bolsheviks. He does not address the question that has come more and more to the front in recent years—the question of whether Lenin did not clear the path that Stalin was able to follow.

The virtue of Tuominen's work lies not so much in its theory as in the author's reportage and observation. Here is the eye and ear of an insider in those distant times when so many of the world's radicals believed that the foundations were being laid down for a new world order in which man's inhumanity to man would vanish. Yet, one look at the quarreling, angry, competitive, jealous, hypocritical, intemperate, often alcoholic, sexually promiscuous, personally ambitious, selfish personalities that composed the chief revolutionary cadres provides a clue to their failure to reach the high goals that their words and supposed principles committed them.

The capitalists, commanders, and kings whom the revolutionaries opposed might be a cruel and intolerable lot, but the crowd that inhabited the dreary rooms of the Hotel Lux could match them chapter for chapter and verse for verse.

Much of Tuominen's attention naturally focuses on Finnish affairs and Finnish Communists. This is a striking asset for it enables us, despite our unfamiliarity with names and issues, to see the whole communist ethos operating in miniature. What happened to the Finns and the Finnish Communists is what happened to all the others. The Finnish Communist party and the Finnish leadership is simply a microcosm of what happened to the Communists in general. Tuominen provides an unforgettable portrait

of Otto Kuusinen, the Finnish communist leader, like himself a
survivor until very recent times. In essence Kuusinen was the classic
survivor. He lived all through the Stalin years at Stalin's side, turning his face away as Stalin and Stalin's police stripped away one
great section of the Finnish cadres after another. He looked on
impassively when Stalin shot Kuusinen's son-in-law and brother-in-
law and imprisoned his son who died soon after his release. He
would not even speak *of* let alone *to* anyone he thought might be
in trouble. He survived Stalin and went on to live out his years in
the politburos of Malenkov, Khrushchev, and even Brezhnev. He
was a voracious womanizer all his life, and he let his women vanish
one by one from his life, whether into Stalin's prisons or not made
no difference to him. Tuominen lived for years in Kuusinen's
apartment. He knew Kuusinen as well as any man can know another. He knew every flaw in his character and in the end could
even sympathize with him for, as Tuominen laconically pointed
out, what difference would it have meant if Kuusinen had stood
up to Stalin, had had principles that he believed worth fighting for?
Kuusinen simply would have vanished from the face of the globe
like his many comrades. Belief and principle had no part in Stalin's
world.

Kuusinen's way was not Tuominen's. Had he not managed to
get to Stockholm Tuominen surely would not have survived the
Stalinist thirties. In his career—and on this Finnish Communists
and non-Communists are as one—he never denounced a single
individual. This alone would have assured his passage into the
cellars of the Lubianka.

There is no other memoir quite like Tuominen's.

Harrison E. Salisbury

THE BELLS
OF THE
KREMLIN

THE WAY OF THE HAMMER
AND SICKLE

ONE OF THE customs observed in our home—one that puzzled
and sometimes irked us children—was that youngsters had to eat
their meals while standing at the table. The privilege of being
seated at mealtimes was attained only when one was capable of
regular income-producing work.

I never ascertained whether this system—by no means in general usage in our locality—was based on a desire to instill in the
children a respect for hard-earned bread or whether it was inherited
from my father's own home. I remember only the rather solemn
occasions, repeated every year or two, when father announced to
one of us that now he could sit while eating because that day he
had begun earning his livelihood at the carpenter's bench.

True, when one considers that our cabin had only three rooms—
on the left, the living room, on the right, father's carpenter shop,
and between them the kitchen—it would have been virtually impossible to fit into our living room a table large enough to seat
everyone. There would have been room when the family was still
small, but perhaps it was a question of my father's foresight.

When my father married, he began an independent life expressly
at the urging of his young wife. Until then he had been a stableman at a parsonage; now he became "Carpenter Tuominen." The
long evenings' putterings had blazed the way to a vocation: he
would become a carpenter. Having learned the trade with a master
carpenter, he built himself a cabin and, adjoining it, a small carpenter shop in the village of Kuotila in Hämeenkyrö, Western
Finland. In this cabin he lived and worked for nearly sixty years.
In it he sired seventeen children: seven from his first marriage,
which lasted twelve years, and ten from the second.

Over the years he became proficient at many other trades, serving as bricklayer, painter, glazier, or even builder, as needed. At
none of the trades was he a bungler, for he simply could not turn
out inferior work. Because of this versatility and conscientiousness

he earned enough to keep us going even in hard times; the family never actually went hungry, though we did want for many things. But his workdays, naturally, were long: from four or five in the morning until eight or nine in the evening.

Our family's comparatively comfortable circumstances were in large part a result of my mother's many skills. In the first place she was a splendid cook who could prepare delicious meals even from ingredients considered worthless by other housewives. Frequently she cooked for landowners on festive occasions, and then we children, too, could have a taste of her wondrous delicacies. She was also an accomplished weaver and seamstress. The whole family, including father, wore clothes that she had woven and sewn, and during our elementary school years we children often could pride ourselves on being better outfitted than many large landowners' children. Nor was mother's weaving and tailoring limited to her own family's clothes: scores of villagers were her customers.

To this day I have tried innumerable times to fathom when and how she managed to do everything: care for a huge family and a cow and in the summer work from twenty-five to thirty days for the landowners who pastured our cow and allowed us to grow potatoes. She never even seemed to be in a hurry. Part of the answer lies in the length of her days, for I never remember seeing mother in bed except when she was gravely ill. In the evening we children were lulled to sleep by the clack of the loom or the hum of the sewing machine, and the same sound echoed in the morning as we awakened.

My mother had the reputation of being a good reaper. She was a sturdily built woman with a strong back who as a young girl had learned the correct way to mow and reap. At harvest time the rye fields of our neighboring landowner, Kuukka, usually had a seven- or eight-row crew, with four reapers and a binder to each row. In addition to members of the family, the harvesters included nearby cotters and the landowner's tenant farmers, who worked by the day.

There was keen competition among the various groups, from first row to last. If my mother mowed in the so-called landowner's row, it always won. As a gleaner I followed the struggle with bated breath from early morn until late at night and when mother and I wearily dragged ourselves home my admiration was boundless.

Over and over again I reminded her that it was she who had won the competition.

When her fellow competitors observed that "Carpenter's Elina" truly was a remarkable reaper, my mother usually replied, "Nonsense, it's not my doing; it's just that I have such a good sickle. I received it as a legacy from my mother. It has a good blade, and my husband always forges and hones it very sharp. All the credit belongs to the sickle."

The sickle was the only inheritance she had received from her own mother; it symbolized the blessings and wishes for the future that my severely tried and long-suffering grandmother had wanted to give to her eldest daughter who, when but a child, found herself being reared by strangers. In handing over the tool, it were as though my grandmother had whispered the admonition that the sickle was not to be used carelessly to waste God's grain, for it was a good and beautiful sickle.

In addition to my mother's sickle, another object in my childhood home has remained indelibly in my memory: my father's hammer. That, too, had symbolic value for me: it represented a hammer in a moral sense and is associated with the memory of my father in the same way that the sickle is with my mother.

My father, as I have said, was a carpenter, but he was also a focal figure in the religious life of the community. He was of the orthodox evangelical persuasion, and those interpreters of the Word, clergymen as well as lay preachers, who were father's kindred spirits, usually came to our home immediately upon arriving in the locality. Then our father would allow himself an hour or two for discussion. Usually he sat in the shop at his carpenter's bench, rotating the hammer in his hand, and whenever the deliberation took a more emphatic turn he would hit the bench with the hammer as though to corroborate the matter.

Just as he had in religious matters, my father attained in secular affairs a certain position in the area as a dispenser of justice, a village judge. His unswerving sense of fairness and incorruptibility were well known. Landowners, tenant farmers, and cotters often dropped in to his shop to discuss their problems and to seek advice.

If someone tried to deviate from what was true and just, the hammer would smite the bench with startling force, and father's voice would rise to a falsetto: "You are supporting the wrong cause!"

His sympathy was wholly with the poor and oppressed, such as the tenant farmers, whose cause was of great concern at that time, but not even they received any support from him if they tried to gain their ends with methods which my father felt were not ethically sound.

I followed these discussions attentively, standing beside the carpenter's bench or sitting on the chopping block, and that banging of the hammer always had a solemn, otherworldly effect on me. Thus that tool was transformed in my mind into what might be called an ethical hammer that was an inseparable part of my father's resolute and unequivocal being. As the years have rolled by, the moral blows of my father's hammer have assumed an even deeper significance.

In roaming and "improving" the world, I have always noticed that I am bound to my childhood home by an invisible bond that in certain matters kept me from advancing as far as the ideology and doctrines to which I subscribed, or the explicit orders from above, would have demanded. It has impelled me to respect every person's and every group's religious beliefs and, even during my most zealous communistic period, prevented me from deriding religion or religious values, even though communist tenets as late as the 1930s declared religion to be one of communism's major enemies.

Religion, in communist phraseology, was "the original sin of petty bourgeois elementariness," something to be gotten rid of in oneself. I, however, was unable to do so, for to me it would have meant surrendering the basic ethical norms. Mother's sickle and father's hammer are the tools that to me symbolize justice, humanity, a better person, and, at the same time, a better world already on this earth. Those simple tools have been my guardian angels and mascots, and to them I often turned more or less consciously in the struggle against communism's hammer and sickle. For peculiar though it may seem, I had to struggle many times against communism, or, more specifically, against certain of its manifestations, particularly Stalinist practices. Those two hammers and sickles waged a continuous struggle within me for twenty years. Tightly though I tried to cling to mother's sickle and father's hammer, they often tended to lose out to the communist hammer and sickle, those emblems of power and violence.

Only a thorough knowledge of communist doctrines and fighting tactics can demonstrate to a faithful and dedicated adherent that inhumanity, injustice, and violence cannot be eradicated by these means but rather will be increased. The more I was able to familiarize myself with the true nature of communism—its practices, morality, and achievements thus far—the clearer it became to me that a better society or a new person could not be developed by following that path.

Thus communism's ornate hammer and sickle gradually began to symbolize for me destruction and ruin, while mother's sickle and father's hammer in all their simplicity came to represent the true, unfailing tools for creating a new and better world. After many an arduous struggle, I finally rejected absolutely and irrevocably the symbols of communist violence and adopted as my lodestar the constructive tools of my parents.

Although I had engaged in that struggle many times, it became dramatically decisive on the eve of the Winter War in the fall of 1939, when I was offered the post of prime minister in the Terijoki People's Government. In the tremendous conflict that raged within me during those dismal and ominous November days under pressure from the mighty communist hammer and sickle, my strongest and most dependable defensive weapons were my mother's sickle and my father's hammer, newly restored to their former strength and influence.

PILGRIMAGE TO COMMUNISM

IN THE AUTUMN of 1912, having reached the age of eighteen, I moved to Tampere* to learn carpentry, as my three older brothers had done before me. The work did not feel onerous though the day was ten hours long and during the greater part of the year

* An industrial city 100 miles north of Helsinki.

reached twelve hours with overtime. Despite the meagerness of my apprentice's wages, my income was satisfactory—compared to conditions in the countryside, it was downright good. My wages sufficed for food, clothing, and shelter better than those of many other apprentices since I didn't spend a penny on tobacco, alcohol, or even entertainment, except for theater.

Above all I was interested in studying and in activity at the labor organizations. Two or three days after arriving in the city I enrolled in the Workers' Institute, and for the next six years, the duration of my stay in Tampere, it was the place where I spent most of my leisure time. During those years there was hardly a lecture, or at least a lecture series, that I did not attend. One winter I was even able to listen to an entire series of forty lectures on the Finnish national epic *Kalevala*. In addition to attending lectures, I studied all the subjects then taught at the institute, among them spelling, bookkeeping, elocution, and even Swedish.

But perhaps even more educational for me than the institute was the club founded by some charter students and grandly called the "Saturday Society." The soul of this club was a kind of universal genius, a born philosopher and altruist, a hunchbacked man named Mauri "Masse" Lehtonen.

Represented in the Saturday Society were diverse characters and many ideological trends. I was drawn to politics, especially to world politics, and hence it became my task to keep the members of the society abreast of major political developments. The heyday of my specialty began with the approach of World War I in 1914.

Although we called it the Saturday Society, our club met almost every evening after the lectures either in the institute's offices or in the coffee shop at the workers' hall. There were many questions to be considered, and the day had to be extended into night. We kept abreast of all the changes at the front and with development in the war generally, like the veriest military experts. Although each of us had his own personal views on almost every matter, we were unanimous about one thing: we hoped for the defeat of Russia and the subsequent downfall of czarism, which in turn, we hoped, would result in Finland's independence.

During the years 1912–18 I participated enthusiastically and actively in a number of other organizations and supported many worthwhile causes, but I have mentioned the Workers' Institute and the Saturday Society in particular because they were the cultivating and educative forces that left the most significant impression: they were the universities of my youth. Since then I have had the opportunity of studying in many educational institutions, from the famous "University of Tammisaari" (a prison), where I "studied" for some ten years, to the highest political school in the communist world, the Lenin School in Moscow, but the Workers' Institute in Tampere nevertheless occupies its own special niche in my thoughts.

Although the atmosphere at this institution was free of communism, it was there that I was bitten by the political bug, particularly that of power politics. I had had some success as a political prognosticator, and this increased my self-confidence and guided my steps still farther along that path. Without these tools my life might well have been like that of my brothers, who faithfully followed the honorable trade taught us by our father and spent their entire lives at a carpenter's bench.

In 1917, about mid-March, the revolution came to Tampere. At that time a trainload of Russian marines arrived from Helsinki. Their first act was to cut off the brass tips of the gendarmes' aiguillettes; then they went to a restaurant where Russian officers from the nearby Lake Näsi fleet (there actually was such a command) were eating dinner. A red rosette was placed in front of each officer. Somewhat hesitantly the surprised diners, one after the other, fastened the rosettes to their tunics. Only the fleet commander—a rear admiral, or perhaps he was a full admiral—refused.

The leader of the marines thereupon pulled out a revolver, gestured with it and demanded, *"V golovu ili v grud'?"*—"In the forehead or in the chest?" With trembling hands the grey-haired admiral fumbled with the rosette and fastened it to the front of his tunic.

The events stemming from this ended all my plans of leading a peaceful life at a carpenter's bench.

In the elections of 1916, the Social Democrats gained a parliamentary majority, 103 seats out of 200, and Kullervo Manner, a Social Democrat, became speaker. When this parliament continued to function unhindered after the Russian Revolution in March 1917,

I, like almost everyone else in the labor movement, was enthralled by parliamentarianism. When Parliament then quickly passed such far-reaching laws as the eight-hour workday and new municipal laws, and when the freeing of tenant farmers and even the attainment of national independence seemed within reach after Parliament had passed the so-called Power Act, in which it declared itself to be vested with the "supreme authority" in Finland, parliamentarianism seemed to me to be the only saving faith.

At the Saturday Society, the young people's department of the labor union, and the Workers' Institute, we cheered and praised Parliament. We had dreamed of a socialist society as a devout Christian dreams of the Kingdom of Heaven and now had tangible evidence that this ideal could be realized step by step through parliamentary means.

Furthermore, Oskari Tokoi, a Social Democrat who had worked as a miner in the United States, headed the Finnish government. Incidentally, he emigrated to America in 1920 and spent the remainder of his life there, the last decades in West Townsend and Fitchburg, Massachusetts. He died in 1963.

But just then, in the early days of August 1917, when our admiration and praise for parliamentarianism had reached their apex, came the shocking news that Parliament had been dissolved. The dissolution was accomplished by the Russian Provisional government but, according to the inside information that reached us through many channels, the leaders of our bourgeois parties—or at least a considerable number of them—had hoped for it and had plotted with the Russians to bring about the dissolution. Regardless of the historical facts, we had sufficient reason then to believe the information. Certainly the leaders of the bourgeois parties made no attempt to oppose this obvious illegality.

The labor groups with which I worked, especially those with young people, were infuriated by the conduct of the bourgeoisie in dissolving Parliament and, above all, in seeking aid from Russia, a foreign power, and even relying on the use of its military forces, which we were then trying to banish from the country. After Parliament had passed the Power Act in due order and proclaimed itself the only legal supreme authority in Finland, the Russians, in our opinion, had no business here. Russia was a foreign power to us, and its intrusions in another power's affairs were seen as hostile acts. By the same logic, our anger at the bourgeoisie became increasingly bitter because of its continued fraternization with and reliance on this alien power.

But we were dissatisfied also with the leadership of our own party and our parliamentary group because of their vacillation and unclear position. Even as the party leadership gave the order to prepare for new elections, which it had labeled illegal, it explained that the old parliament was still in existence and was to be considered the only legal parliament. This kind of "double bookkeeping" was hard for me and for most of the party members to understand. The party and its leadership, on which the masses had depended, now began to lose its authority rapidly.

Butter riots, expropriations of food supplies, the besieging of city councils, municipal and other wildcat strikes, and their attendant violence began to be the order of the day. Contributing to this lack of discipline, which was assuming the nature of outright anarchy, were, naturally, many other prevailing factors: a critical food shortage; roaming battery workers unaccustomed to organized life and discipline; and the untrained masses which came pouring into the Social Democratic party and the trade organizations during those months by the tens of thousands. In addition to these determinants, a decisive role was played by the badly shaken faith of the workers' elite in parliamentarianism. They didn't have the firmness, or often even the desire, to control undisciplined elements and to demonstrate that only through the parliamentary, legal way could we manage our affairs and improve our conditions.

Although I did not belong to the most politically fanatical youths who rode the hobbyhorse of radicalism, my faith also began to be shaken. Defeat in the new elections—instead of 103 seats we now had 92—only increased our resentment and the desire to resort to extraparliamentary powers and measures.

On innumerable occasions, in our own clubs, we had reached the conclusion that we must be rid of the Russians, the sooner the better. But gradually we underwent a change of mind. We asked whether it was right, after all, that we scream "Russkies go home!" Couldn't we, too, use them to our advantage in dissolving Parliament or in some other dirty trick that required power and violence? When the situation in Russia during those early autumn months of 1917 appeared to veer ever more to the left, it increased our hopes that perhaps the workers, too, could engage in politics with the Russian soldiers.

I must emphasize that I have not even attempted here to conjecture what developments might have occurred had not the Social Democratic parliament been dissolved. I have merely described the feelings, opinions, and changes in mood at that moment. Subsequently, when the tide of historical events was already demonstrable, I frequently ventured a guess as to how a parliament with a workers' majority would have reacted to the bolshevik government that assumed power in Russia on November 7. Would the Social Democratic party and its leadership, already at that stage weak and tottering, have been able to preserve the ratified Power Act and Finland's absolute sovereignty, or would it—harking to the then so alluring siren songs ("Nations can be truly free and independent only by joining the great union of Soviet peoples")— have entered into such close cooperation with the bolshevik government as to lose the people's freedom and the country's independence?

Such a possibility could have existed and for the Finnish people, especially the working class, it would have meant even greater suffering than that which it experienced during the months and years subsequent to the dissolution of Parliament. We know well the road we have traversed; it has been burdensome and bloody, but the other road might have been even more difficult.

While working as a carpenter I had reported on meetings for the local social democratic *Kansan Lehti* (People's News). Its editors had kept an eye on my various activities and decided to name me an editorial apprentice. The position was open and there were many applicants, among them even a few university students, but the editors bypassed the others and offered me the job even though I hadn't applied for it.

Thus the carpenter became an editor, at a time when the editorial staff of every labor newspaper was like a front line command, where editorial apprentices and assistant editors were quickly made editors, even editors-in-chief, just as corporals can be molded rapidly into generals when war rages. When the civil war* erupted in Finland in January 1918, I, too, rose through every level of the editorial hierarchy at the *Kansan Lehti* within a few months; an assistant editor in January, I became the editor-in-chief in March. Of the seven editors the rest had departed for other jobs. Somehow I managed to get the paper edited in a city ever more tightly hemmed in by the Whites, until one day a hand grenade was tossed in through the window of the press's stereotype room. Some conquerors, with *Mausers* in hand, began clambering in after it. I realized then that editing had had its day and crawled under fire to an area that was still the scene of battle. That same evening, while engaged in defensive actions, I was taken prisoner and was transported with other prisoners of war to the railroad freight house already crowded with thousands of imprisoned men, women, and even children.

For me those days and nights in the Tampere freight house were not appalling, embittering, and mind molding because of the cold, hunger and other misery that I had to endure in that storehouse of horrors. They were appalling because I perceived that my ideal world, the world of my convictions, had utterly collapsed. Instinctively I realized that, having set forth on the revolutionary course of armed violence that had led to this disaster, the labor movement no longer could emerge unified and return to its previously espoused parliamentary course. With a child's faith I had linked the ideal of absolute justice inherited from my childhood home to the ideals and goals of the labor movement. Now that structure had collapsed.

A couple of neighbors' boys from my home town, who were wearing Home Guard uniforms and had fought on the side of the Whites, finally freed me, and at their suggestion I enlisted as a recruit in the Finnish army then being formed. Thus I managed to get out of Tampere, where many knew me. After my discharge in late autumn, 1918, I set off for Helsinki and once again began working as a carpenter.

The young man who now made his second entry into organized labor circles was no longer the idealistic, credulous youth who

---

* It was also a war for independence.

seven or eight years earlier had undertaken his first round in Tampere.

Actually, all the old values had failed. Until the age of twenty, I had believed that international social democracy, as manifested in the Second International, was powerful enough to prevent such cataclysms as a world war. My twentieth birthday was still a month away when World War I erupted and all Socialists everywhere popped back into their burrows like scared rabbits.

Thus it was natural that we, the young and impatient, craved something new. Continual reports from Russia told of the Bolsheviks' attempts to create a new world. The newspaper accounts were critical and even condemnatory, but on us Finnish youths who had suffered defeat in the civil war, Lenin's teachings and ideas had a powerful effect. After all, they impressed even some of the world's leading intellectuals, who looked for something from Lenin's endeavors that could not be achieved within the framework of old ideas.

The first step taken by the Finnish leaders of the rebellion after their flight to Russia in May 1918 was to "shed their old skin," as the communist leader Otto Wille Kuusinen put it.

In Petrograd* they had been lodged in the palaces of former fabulously wealthy merchants on the Kamennyi Ostrov and there, amidst the already faded and shabby luxury, they held peculiar, Freemason-like secret and semisecret conferences at which each person tortured and flogged himself to be cleansed of the opportunism of social democracy.

After a few weeks of flogging, Kuusinen, the shrewdest and most intelligent of the men, collected the results into a booklet titled *Self-Criticism*. In it Kuusinen indicated how social democracy, even in the revolutionary form that it assumed in Finland until 1918, was the most worthless of doctrines. While those old sins were confessed and it was shown that that path had even cost the revolution, the line of the future was being marked out. In other words, the way that the Lenin-founded Russian Communist party had taken: the dictatorship of the proletariat under the leadership of the orthodox Communist party. Municipal, cooperative, or par-

* Originally Petersburg, the city was renamed Petrograd in 1914 and Leningrad after Lenin's death.

liamentary activities, the trade union movement, and so forth, were seen as worthless and rotten; one should prepare only for the Russian-style armed revolution. That, summed up, was the content of *Self-Criticism*.

To take care of Finnish affairs, the Central Committee of the Finnish Social Democratic Foreign Organization had been formed, with its location in Moscow. Kuusinen's incomparable acumen—his best life insurance—was evidenced by the fact that he immediately sensed that the place to settle was Moscow, at the foot of the actual stairs of power.

In August 1918, Kuusinen and his pals set about forming the Finnish Communist party in Moscow, and after eight days of deliberation it began functioning on September 5, 1918.

The platform of the Finnish Communist party contained the basic resolutions that the party still has not disavowed. The first resolution began with the words: "Workers must energetically prepare for an armed revolution." Lawful activity was counterrevolutionary and served only to brake developments leading to the revolution; now was the time to form small armed groups that would appear on command and seize the power.

The formation of such armed groups and the banning of all public activity seemed absolutely senseless to me. Under these circumstances, the only possibility for even slightly improving the workers' wretched lot appeared to be the rousing of legal public organizations and functioning through them. And so I sent my respects to the emissaries and, through them, to the Finnish Communist party leaders in Moscow and Petrograd, informing them that their orders were absurd. We in Finland did not see any possibility at that time for continuing the revolution or for any armed appearances, and Russia seemed to be too preoccupied with its own civil wars to enable the Red Army to help us. I, for one, categorically refused to participate in any such armed groups.

The distemper that afflicted the Finnish Communist party during its early months was so grave that it might well have killed the patient. Kuusinen, who again was in Helsinki, led the actual frontline skirmishes. He soon realized that once more there was cause to undertake self-discipline, as the tactics devised at the founding of the Finnish Communist party by the party leadership—in other words, by himself—were obviously 100 percent wrong and ill suited to the situation. Even the most radical workers, on whose support the communist leaders had relied in building their heaven, drifted back in large groups to the public organizations being reactivated and brushed aside the armed secret organizations of the Finnish Communist party's agents.

In such a situation the only course for a wise general is to follow the army. General Otto Wille Kuusinen began issuing new slogans that I followed. In that way I became more and more the ideological hatchet man of Kuusinen and his staff and, at the same time, involved in a heated battle with the majority of the Finnish Communist party leadership in Petrograd.

The first new instructions that I received from Kuusinen were as follows: "Go ahead and join the Social Democratic party and the local unions, but only for the purpose of winning them back from the Tannerites." Väinö Tanner was the leader of the Socialists.

A further principle concerning the Social Democratic party was that, if the party could not be taken over from within, it should be disorganized and a new party formed.

We easily took over the Social Democratic Youth League. The capture of the Helsinki municipal organization, the focal and largest one in the country, was accomplished fairly quickly. In the same way we managed to take over most of the municipal organizations and party associations in northern Finland. At the same time we succeeded in taking over several newspapers. During one meeting, however, in attempting to capture a printing shop held by the Tannerites, Väinö Tanner threw me from behind the chairman's table which was on the stage to the wings, and otherwise, too, the entire effort came to naught. Likewise, at the Social Democratic Party Convention in the latter half of 1919, the Tannerites warded off our attempt to take it over by a two-thirds majority.

Now Kuusinen had reached what actually was his target. This was the time to put into effect the second part of his watchword: the disorganization of the party. Some six months later we founded a new party which was named the Finnish Socialist Labor party. I became its first party secretary. That fall, when we began publishing our own daily newspaper in Helsinki, *Suomen Työmies* (The Finnish Worker), I was made its editor-in-chief. In May 1920 the Finnish Federation of Trade Unions fell into communist hands and I became its vice-chairman.

That same year Kuusinen moved to Stockholm by an underground route. All the time we were in weekly correspondence with him. His couriers were chiefly Swedish women who came to me with suitcases bulging with English, French, and Swedish publications—mainly fashion magazines—with large blank areas. At the Socialist Labor party's offices we had a special iron with which we "pressed out the text." When the heated iron was run over the seemingly innocent margins of the pages, the text, written in a solution of alum or lemon, became visible. The same Swedish women carried our replies back; in emergencies we used our own couriers.

In February 1921 a courier once again brought me a fashion magazine. I ironed the text visible and to my surprise saw that the handwriting was Kuusinen's. He announced that he had received a letter from Lenin, who asked him to go to Moscow.

Lenin said that he was aware of the conflicts raging within the Finnish Communist party but disregarded them and guaranteed Kuusinen's inviolability. He hoped that Kuusinen would travel to Moscow as soon as possible because he was—as specifically stated in the letter—the only man within eyeshot who could help him at that time. The matter concerned the drafting of the Comintern's (Communist International) tactical platform.

Finally Kuusinen presented his own opinions, hinting that he was eager to go but (always the adroit tactician) that he was leaving the decision up to us, the frontline officers.

In my reply I expressed regrets that Kuusinen seemed to be in favor of leaving. But because we were not familiar with all the facts, because he was being summoned by such an exceptionally prestigious person, and because he himself seemed to be eager to leave, we dared not oppose it; we only hoped that he might thus be able to strengthen our sovereignty and protect us from falling into the clutches of the Finnish Communist party command in Petrograd.

We young Communists made that decision resentfully, suspecting that it would lead to difficulties. When I subsequently thought of that period—both during my Moscow years and now—I must say in a spirit of self-criticism that it was one of those turning points of the Finnish Communist movement by which history could have been guided in another direction.

Let us consider a hypothetical proposition: if we here—I at the forefront—had told Kuusinen that he could not leave, it is hard to say whether he actually would have gone. If he had, and if we had had the guts to say, "All right, we're sorry that you've gone, but we will no longer follow your advice and directions," what would have happened then?

One cannot say conclusively, but there is good reason to assume that this well-launched leftist labor movement would have continued to sail with the wind. Possibly even the authorities, in noticing that it had freed or was freeing itself of Moscow's embrace, would not have indulged in the bloodletting that they did in 1922, when the entire party committee was jailed, and in 1923, when the party itself was dissolved. Or, possibly, the development might have followed in the tracks of the Norwegian Labor party, which joined the Comintern but a few years later withdrew from it and returned to the social democratic lines.

Such a hypothesis is not unreasonable when one recalls that only a very small percentage of Finland's workers was then and is now Communist. Most of those now voting the Finnish Communist party ticket are simply embittered, traditionally grudge-bearing leftists, exasperated by existing conditions.

Without resorting to any mortification or self-criticism à la Kuusinen, I must say that among the biggest and most fateful errors that I have ever committed was my failure to have enough guts and brains to forbid Kuusinen's departure for Moscow.

The spell of Kuusinen, our bellwether, was so powerful that it didn't even occur to us to refuse attending the Fourth Party Congress of the Finnish Communist party. Our willingness was undoubtedly heightened by the fact that an invitation to the Comintern's Third Congress arrived at the same time.

I chose qualified representatives for the delegation, all Kuusinen men. On June 1, 1921, we left in small groups by a secret route over the Karelian Isthmus.

Kuusinen thus has shaped my destiny. It is quite probable that, had I not met Kuusinen, my development would have been considerably different. I would have become oriented toward the old Tampere revisionist social democratic line rather than the dangerous waters wherein a prison loomed from the very beginning.

During our first meetings, we held sharply contrasting opinions. Kuusinen had come to Finland in the belief that no labor movement was needed, only weapons. The revolution would continue. With the brashness of youth I said, "Nonsense, the world revolution will not continue; it will be limited to Russia at least for the time being, and if it does continue it will not do so in Finland at any rate for a long time to come. Every village here has its Home Guard; a revolution cannot be carried out here."

Kuusinen really did not make an impression on me at all; rather, he annoyed me. To me he was, in fact, no idol. But when I had attained several important posts in the party, he began to favor me more and more. I was quite pleased at being able to influence such a great theoretician, to be able to prove to him that a revolution could not be carried out in Finland. He was the first to accept my line.

LENIN'S MOSCOW

THE OPENING of the Moscow Congress was delayed by two weeks because of Kuusinen. It was his task to formulate the theses that would become the Comintern constitution. Kuusinen was an extremely able theoretician, undoubtedly one of the world's best in this particular field, in which he had to nitpick, splitting hairs and Marx's whiskers. He was very slow at his work; even on his best days he could complete only a few pages, often only a single or half a page. "Kuusinen doesn't write or do anything, he just plods along," observed Tuure Lehén, Kuusinen's son-in-law.

And so it was that the delegations that had been commanded to Moscow had plenty of time to inspect the city. Almost every day we dropped in on Kuusinen who took a short conversation break, drank black coffee, smoked cigarettes and then continued his plodding night and day. On the second or third visit we met a beautiful Russian woman, who moved about so familiarly that we expressed surprise. Kuusinen said merely that she was assisting him with the typing.

One day I received a message at my Tverskaya lodging house asking me to meet Kuusinen alone.

"Well, you see," he said nervously, "a certain unfortunate matter has come up . . ."

It seemed that the beautiful Russian had appeared one day for the purpose of becoming his assistant and had indeed been helpful since she was an educated girl and had a good knowledge of German, the language in which Kuusinen wrote his theses. Kuusinen had thought at first that one of Lenin's associates had sent the girl because of the difficulty and urgency of the work. But then he had begun to wonder at her helpfulness and agreeability, especially when she appeared at all hours to make coffee and do other small tasks. And then yesterday, as they had sat drinking coffee and a little something else, the girl had told him that she was on a more important mission than being simply his assistant or companion.

She had been in the service of the Cheka [the secret police] for a long time and had been given the assignment of becoming Kuusinen's girl friend in order to ascertain whether Kuusinen had informed on several Finnish Communists who had been arrested in Sweden and Norway. But now she was ashamed of having gotten into the whole thing.

The Cheka's methods are so devious that it was difficult to say whether the girl had confessed on her own initiative or on orders from above. The matter made Kuusinen very nervous, as it would have made anyone, since the shadow of the Cheka weighed heavily on all Russia. But necessity is the mother of invention.

"I've been thinking that you, who have come from Finland and are a focal figure there, could go to Lenin and explain the situation," Kuusinen said to me. "Sirola will accompany you as interpreter and assistant. I have already called Lenin and asked for an audience."

What a jolt! To go to Lenin and on such a mission! But protests were to no avail. I have forgotten to mention one fact. The delegation naturally had to have a leader, and I had assumed that Kuusinen or some other notable would be named to the post. But who should be named but Karl Ek, which was my pseudonym. And naturally the leader of the delegation had to attend to such muddles.

We had to wait a while at the outer gate; obviously Lenin had forgotten to leave word of our arrival, but quite soon the announcement that we could be admitted was relayed from the inner gate.

A few times we were asked to show our pass, but these inspections were child's play compared to the detailed investigations under the Stalinist regime. Then we were at our destination. From the door of the anteroom someone announced that comrades so-and-so had arrived. Everything was simple and uncomplicated; nowhere could one feel the ceremonial ponderousness of an Asian court.

Lenin's office was large and poorly furnished and certainly not luxurious: a few leather lounge chairs, a few straight chairs, and a large desk, worn and battered. He was sitting behind it but as we entered he rose and came to meet us. He greeted first Sirola, saying how happy he was to see him once more, and then turned to me. Sirola made the introduction, describing—if I understood correctly—my rapid rise in the Communist movement and concluding with the observation that, despite my youth, I knew my business.

Lenin remarked that age means nothing, urged us to be seated and went behind his desk. Sirola sat opposite him, I at the end of the desk.

The initial impression was disappointing. In my youthful innocence I had assumed that great men had to be impressive in looks and size. I am of average height—almost five feet, eight inches—but Lenin was considerably shorter. He also seemed quite worn and fatigued, with a sallow complexion and eyes a bit slanting, set like those of the Chinese. I don't remember their color but they were full of life; they sparkled in a special way already when he greeted us, and after exchanging only a few words one forgot the man's appearance and physical insignificance.

I concentrated on presenting my case as succinctly as possible. First of all, Kuusinen's affair of the woman who confessed to being a Chekist; Kuusinen's annoyance that Dzerzhinsky, the Cheka chief,* could have begun to suspect him; the nervous prostration that had prevented his working for the past twenty-four hours; my own conviction that the charge was baseless; my beliefs that Lenin himself must know Kuusinen's dependability and realize that the contention that Kuusinen could have lapsed into becoming an agent of the Swedish or Norwegian police was laughable.

---

* The Soviet state or secret police has been called in turn Cheka, the OGPU, the GPU, the NKVD, the MVD, and the KGB. The letters GPU represent Gosudarstvennoe Politicheskoe Upravlenie, or the State Political Administration. MVD means Ministerstvo Vnutrennikh Del, the Ministry of Internal Affairs. From "convenience and habit" Tuominen for the most part calls the institution the GPU.

I referred also to the time Kuusinen had spent as a refugee in Finland and how greatly he was respected by the Finnish revolutionary workers. The party whose secretary general I was—the Finnish Socialist Labor party—had been founded through Kuusinen's efforts. Finally, to obviate any remaining doubts concerning Kuusinen's revolutionism, I expressed regrets that we had not been able to join the Comintern when the party had been founded.

To that Lenin said, "The main thing is not whether the party has formally joined the Comintern. We already have parties in the Comintern that cannot be considered revolutionary. To my knowledge, the Finnish party is more straightforward in its revolutionism than they. No, young man, you should not be sorry."

I pursued the Kuusinen matter but Lenin cut me short, explaining that he was quite familiar with the dissension among the Finns but that he did not consider it serious in any way.

"Be good enough to tell Kuusinen that this is a trifling matter. I don't understand why some woman should have been sent to shadow him. I shall call Dzerzhinsky immediately, though I'm sure that he knows nothing about it—obviously some of Kuusinen's opponents have sicked some of the Cheka's minor officials on him. Therefore ask Kuusinen to continue his work in peace. The congress already is delayed because of him and it shouldn't have to wait much longer."

Here Lenin smiled and observed, "People always say 'Cherchez la femme?' and now a woman is trying to ruin our good work. First I manage, with great effort, to coax Kuusinen here from Stockholm, and then the man is made nervous . . . No, I know the emigrants. Even we had conflicts in our time. They're not worth taking dead seriously."

He seemed to be in a hurry to drop the subject. Although he did not actually make us feel that we had bothered him with a matter of secondary importance, that impression remained with us, especially since he so hurriedly began inquiring about conditions in Finland. It was flattering and at the same time almost shocking to realize how familiar he was with both the political and economic situations in Finland, as well as with the mentality of the Finnish people. Besides, he seemed to be genuinely interested in these matters. Many a Finnish emigrant leader was unable to ask the questions that Lenin put to us, particularly about the conditions of the Finnish workers, the relationship of the Social Democratic party to the bourgeoisie and the economic conditions, but he concentrated especially on our Socialist Labor party. He was familiar with its birth and position in the Federation of Trade Unions.

When I had described the successes we had had, the number of newspapers that we had taken over from the Social Democrats, the size of our membership and so forth, he expressed his thanks and satisfaction, as well as some compliments about the Finnish people in general and, particularly, its revolutionary proletariats. The tone of those, too, implied that Kuusinen's efforts to found the party had been worthwhile. When I repeated Kuusinen's statement that the Finnish revolution would be made on the Finnish, rather than on the Russian, side of the Neva river, it amused Lenin greatly and he said that that was correct: it certainly could not be made here.

Lenin's manner of speaking was very calm at the start of the conversation, but as we progressed his deep baritone rose a little as he asked sudden probing questions. If a reply tended to be long-winded, he would interject a brief remark or question as though to say, "To the point, to the point!" Later, at congresses and executive committee sessions, I observed that, whenever the speaker had digressed from the subject or rambled into too expansive explanations, Lenin's interjections would force the man closer to the heart of the matter.

It was one of the most nerve-racking quizzes that I have ever undergone and lasted over half an hour. But we had reason to depart satisfied; Sirola's nervousness had dissipated, and he was again full of life and enthusiasm.

I received a good grade from him: "Thank God you didn't drift into any prattling or needless explanations. Everything is fine now." Kuusinen felt the same way and was able to continue his plodding in peace.

I talked to Lenin for the second time during the early part of the congress. While preparing for our trip in Finland, we had decided to bring Lenin a slight token of our gratitude and esteem. After earnest and painstaking deliberation we decided—naturally!—on a Finnish sheath knife. We would have preferred a handsome and graceful knife made in Kauhava, but because the town at that time had no communist or, in our opinion, otherwise trustworthy knife factory or cutler, we had to relinquish the plan. The knife was to bear an inscription, and an unreliable cutler could have had us charged with high treason; in those times much lesser charges brought five or six years at hard labor.

However, a member of the communist underground railroad knew of a reliable cutler in Lapland, and he was given the honor of making the gift. Naturally, it proved to be a Lappish knife with a bone sheath and handle—quite elegant, actually, though it didn't please us nearly so much as a handsome knife from Kauhava would have.

As the leader of the delegation it was my task to present the gift and make the presentation speech. I sweated together a speech that was naturally checked by Sirola. To flank me I got two Finnish Communists, Rovio and Rahja, to assure impartiality: I represented the Kuusinen faction, Rahja the Mannerites, and Rovio was neutral.

Then one day in the Kremlin, as the session of congress was getting under way, Rovio sent a note by hand to Lenin, who was seated among the presiding officers, asking for an audience during the first intermission. Without any formalities, guards or messengers, Lenin at the very beginning of the intermission motioned us, already waiting in the corridor, to accompany him to the former czarist reception room next to the throne room. There we seated ourselves in a cozy corner and again without lengthy preliminaries came to the point immediately after exchanging greetings.

I made my brief speech from memory, and Rovio translated it sentence by sentence. The contents of the speech changed, however—and obviously to their advantage—due to Lenin's interjections. Despite Sirola's scrutiny, some exaggerations had remained, and these Lenin playfully deleted. The speech thus became something of a dialogue, with its undue solemnity eliminated. At the conclusion of the speech I presented the beautifully adorned Lappish knife on which were engraved the words, "To V.I. Lenin from the Finnish Communists."

I don't know to what degree the speech had hit the mark and impressed him, but the little gift seemed to amuse and please him, and he expressed his thanks for it briefly, remarking that he had done no more for Finland and its revolutionary workers' movement than what solidarity demanded of every revolutionary. At the same time he said a few kind words about the Finnish people, espe-cially the working class, and wished them a brighter future.

Right after the "formalities" had ended, another quiz began. As though continuing the previous visit, he inquired about conditions in Finland and especially about the delegates who had come to the congress from Finland; he was delighted that the front line was represented by such a large group. In an audience that lasted barely fifteen minutes, he squeezed an hour's worth of fact into that period.

He fastened the knife onto the upper pocket of his vest so that it was clearly visible when the jacket was open. There it dangled during many days of the congress and often we saw him on the dais take out the knife and sharpen his pencil or carve a stick. Then our delegation would whisper, "He's whittling with our gift again."

These two meetings, one of which lasted half an hour, the other a quarter hour, made a tremendous impact upon me. Outwardly Lenin was certainly not impressive: he seemed a quite ordinary, simple person. But even in that simplicity there was something. It was authentic. Secondary matters had no place in his life because he sought to reduce everything to clear, logical facts.

His speech almost always had a touch of the didactic, but he did not attempt to hatch fully realized theses. On the contrary, he plunged right in. He didn't try to impress his companions with shrewd and sage questions and explanations but astounded them with his simple, concretely relevant questions. He came to the point, met one half way, didn't allow one to evade and dodge. Afterwards, I have tried to clarify for myself what it was that created the impression of exceptional greatness; I have concluded that it must have been his unusual ability to penetrate both his fellow humans and the subjects under discussion. After exchanging a few words with him, I thought that he appeared to see through a per-son's intellectual self as an X-ray sees through the physical being. With one glance and two or three random thrusts he found out who you were and what you knew. It was useless to twist and turn and look wiser than you were.

Subsequently I had a chance to make comparisons. When speak-ing tête-à-tête, Stalin also was unassuming and direct, but the dif-ference was like night and day. In all matters, even small practical ones, Lenin probed with his questions for their background, their fundamental meaning, and did not leave even a secondary matter at the midway point. Stalin was direct in, shall I say, a too simple way; he had no passion for the truth, no such ability to extract what was significant from a person in a brief conversation. In talking with Lenin it didn't even occur to me to watch my language lest he get the impression that I was a dreadful opportunist or revisionist; still less would it have entered my mind that I could be liquidated for this. With Stalin one always had to keep one's tongue in the middle of the mouth. Lenin's open behavior was enough to dispel any such fear, and it is true that in Lenin's time, so far as is known, not a single one of his comrades, assistants, or party members was imprisoned or shot. Lenin proceeded from entirely different fundamentals than Stalin; namely, that the dictatorship of the proletariat should be applied to enemies and opponents and not to one's own comrades. He provoked discussion and debate among those around him, whereas Stalin tolerated only his own opinions, which were final. Lenin's forbearance toward his comrades was almost limitless.

He gave an example of this during the early days of the Soviet Union. When the Bolsheviks had decided to seize power, Zinoviev and Kamenev published the order in a nonbolshevik newspaper of that period, informing the world of what was coming. That was obvious treachery. Lenin berated both sinners, and it was taken for granted that they could have no future in a state led by Lenin. But having reprimanded them and thus returned them to the true Leninist path, he appointed both of them to high positions.

Preparations for the congress were made by an executive committee whose Finnish members were Kuusinen, Sirola, and Manner. Inasmuch as the committee could be expanded for this preliminary period to include national delegates, Kuusinen arranged for me, too, to become a member. Thus I first belonged to the Comintern's Executive Committee as a so-called "co-op member" as early as 1921.

It is needless, even impossible, to describe the excitement that tingled through a young Communist as he prepared to leave for the first meeting of the Executive Committee. Now he would have a chance to see all those great builders of the new paradise and the exploders of the old decaying world, who thus far had been merely sonorous names to him. The tension was heightened by the fact that Kuusinen and Sirola seemed totally unconcerned, though the meeting was scheduled to begin at three.

"We'll be lucky if it starts even at five," said Sirola. "It's the custom here."

Every meeting was at least two hours late. Lenin's arrival determined the starting time, and his desk calendar was filled with meetings.

The Executive Committee met in the throne room of the Kremlin, where the congress subsequently convened. There would have been occasion for historical reflections, to imagine the gold, silver, and jewel-bedecked uniforms that had filled these halls only five years earlier. The resplendent uniforms were flashing through the back of my mind when an odd type suddenly appeared in view: a frail little man—perhaps five feet four inches in height—wearing a threadbare black summer jacket that hung on him lopsidedly because its pockets were bulging with papers. The collar of his checkered, less than clean shirt was open, and that shirt also was visible through the worn seat of his pants.

"Hey, who's that hooligan?" I asked.

"Come, come," replied Kuusinen. "That's Bukharin."

Bukharin, author of *The ABC's of Communism*: the great theoretician! I had formed a picture from his books and articles of an orderly man with all buttons fastened. The disillusionment was great, but there was something engaging about him nonetheless. He came directly to greet Kuusinen, whom he had not seen in a long time and whom he had extolled in a eulogy;* then he greeted Sirola and even me.

He seated himself diagonally from us and in no time at all had drawn a caricature of Kuusinen, a really superlative one. He came over and showed it to us; on it he had written a witty reference to Kuusinen's "murder." He spent the entire time at that first meeting drawing caricatures of various people, supplying them with biting or amiable captions and showing them to the victims as well as to everyone else.

Bukharin gave life to the whole congress; he was a dash of color. Everything indicated that he felt well disposed toward Finns. Very often he would stop by to banter with Sirola and Kuusinen in

---

* In 1919 it had been rumored in Finland that Kuusinen had been shot while crossing the border into Sweden.

Russian and German. He was shrewd and, if need be, malicious as well, but generally his attitude was genially bohemian.

Then came a man whom I recognized immediately since his pictures were everywhere at the time: Radek, probably the sharpest pen in the Soviet government. He was now in Russia, therefore he wore a beard, a rather long one at that. It was said of Radek that he disguised himself when abroad by shaving his beard. He was slim but not tall, though somewhat taller than Bukharin. The only one of the bolshevik front guard who could be called tall was Zinoviev.

It was immediately apparent, however, that Radek was conscious of his position; his demeanor was angular and ironic, a warning against any heedless attack. He, too, came directly to greet Kuusinen, the lost sheep or prodigal son who, weary of wallowing in the mud of bourgeois pigs, once again had returned to the land of his fathers. Actually, up to then Kuusinen had met only Lenin, Zinoviev, and Trotsky. Sitting there between Sirola and Kuusinen, I effortlessly became familiar with many notables.

Trotsky—well! He was readily recognizable, if only by his bushy head of hair. But what a surprise he, too, was! One would have believed him, the flaming orator and creator of the Red Army, to be a man of some stature, but he seemed shorter even than Lenin. As able as he undeniably was, one soon noticed that he was also intellectually smaller than Lenin.

Lenin, Trotsky, and Zinoviev were the "big three" in those days. I had become acquainted with the third of the great ones immediately upon my arrival in Moscow, for he was the chairman of the Comintern, and it behooved me as leader of the Finnish delegation to greet him. His behavior was a trifle supercilious, a fact that did not sit very well with a young man. Of course, I already was prejudiced, because he was the one who accepted little favors from Rahja, such as food and drink that had been smuggled from Finland. Lenin certainly would not have accepted a single pound of butter from such sources, and I couldn't believe it of Trotsky, either.

But longer observation did not improve the picture. True, Zinoviev was a handsome, blackhaired man, but flabby and somehow reminiscent of a decadent aristocrat. He looked flaccid even sitting behind the chairman's table, with none of the erectness of

Lenin, Trotsky, or many others. Trotsky had hauteur, but it was strength; Zinoviev's superciliousness was a little like a spoiled child's defiance.

In looking back over the years at that assemblage in the throne room of the Kremlin, one realizes that a certain person is conspicuous by his absence. He was not conspicuous then because no one would have thought of asking for him—he simply did not belong among the great leaders. I knew of his existence since he was the commissar of nationality affairs at the Council of People's Commissars and as such had signed the Finnish peace treaty (the Treaty of Tartu), but more than that I did not know. He belonged to the Executive Committee, and the records show that he was present at its meetings as well as at those of the congress, but not once did he stand out from that dense crowd. Only the subsequent distortion of history has made him a great leader from the outset, a focal personality from birth. That man was Iosif Vissarionovich Stalin.

The foreign communist leaders naturally were overshadowed by the Russians. One of them, however, stood out immediately; stocky, buffalolike, a real fighter: he was the commissar and dictator to the hilt—Bela Kun, former dictator of Hungary. Although he wasn't taller than I, he viewed the world from a vantage point at least ten inches higher. If he somehow left the impression of an inflated frog, this surely was not the fault of the observer. Flanking him was Matyas Rákosi, one of the first secretaries of the Comintern and subsequently the vice-premier and strong man of Hungary.

The most noted foreigner at the third congress—even better known than Bela Kun—was the Frenchman, Marty, "Hero of the Black Sea." During the civil war the French government had ordered a certain squadron to aid Wrangel's counterrevolutionary troops in the Crimea. Marty was a senior seaman on the flagship and instigated a mutiny that frustrated the entire assistance plan. Naturally he was thrown into jail, but one didn't sit there very long for such sentences, and now he was free and in Moscow with a huge halo of heroism around his head. Hundreds of collective farms and factories dedicated to Marty sprang up in Russia.

Later during my years in Moscow I observed that he had only a mediocre intelligence but was sufficiently shrewd to remain silent and live on his reputation as a hero. He was a member of the Comintern's Presidium, even a secretary.

Finally Lenin arrived and the meeting could begin.

The first question on the agenda was the admission of the Czechoslovak Communist party into the Comintern. This huge party, with tens of thousands of members, had applied for membership, and Bela Kun had been delegated to ascertain its orthodoxy. He rose to give the results of his investigation in a flaming speech in which he denounced the party as predominantly social democratic, semi-bourgeois, and hardly communist at all.

Thereafter speaker after speaker rose to support Bela Kun. The official languages were German and Russian; translations were made into each. Bela Kun and the Czechoslovak leaders used German.

The matter was thrashed out for two days. Zinoviev opposed the move, Trotsky opposed it: if Czechoslovakia's petit bourgeois party, whose membership included peasants, artisans, factory workers, and minor officials in a confused mass, were allowed to join, it would ruin the entire Comintern.

The motions by the Czech leaders had an air of pettifoggery. When Bela Kun had the floor he grossly insulted the Czech leader Smeral, whose deputies retaliated by conceding that indeed they had been incapable of the exceptionally heroic stand made by Hungary (the Hungarian revolution had been lost, largely because of Kun's blustering)—they had merely offered slight resistance.

"When the police arrived to suppress the paper, Smeral could only throw himself on the floor, and the police had to carry him all the way to jail. It was the only resistance of which he was capable."

With Sirola's help I could easily follow the drama and my opinion was unequivocal: under no circumstances could such a party be admitted into the Comintern. The impressionable Sirola shared that view.

But Kuusinen remarked, "Well, now, let's not be hasty. Lenin hasn't spoken yet."

Lenin had merely made notes and listened attentively. Only when most of the others had had the floor did he rise to speak.

He was not a great orator as Russians go, not brilliant, glowing or dramatic, though his gestures were lively. His strength lay in his ability to get to the substance of matters. In a few sentences he summarized first Bela Kun's indictment and then the Czechs' defense. After that he characterized Smeral: a typical petit bourgeois attorney. What a superb stratagem on the part of an ink-slinging clerk, flinging oneself on the floor to be carried away by the police; what great heroism! The leadership of the Czechoslovak party was weak with such a man heading it. But its membership—laborers and working peasants, honest, decent people—as was evident from all that had been said, was made up of true revolutionaries.

And so it was that the only one to support the admission of the Czechoslovak Communist party into the Comintern was Lenin. Not with the Czech leaders' evidence but with his own material, perhaps obtained from others or gleaned from conversations. Point by point he examined the previous speakers' arguments and indicated that they were invalid.

And behold, after a few more speeches, everyone to a man, including Bela Kun, supported the admission of the Czechoslovak party into the Comintern.

The fear of losing one's life or of being placed on a blacklist played no part in the outcome. Speech was still free in the Soviet Union, so long as it followed communist lines; that was clearly evident at the congress itself. The shift to Lenin's viewpoint resulted from what could be called his special power: he argued magnificently, but at the same time he had a certain hypnotic talent for suggestion that induced one to believe even unproven claims.

That remark of Kuusinen's was typical of his adroitness, his sensitive nose, sixth sense, or what have you. With that nose he saved his own skin until he died of natural causes.

Typical of Lenin was the fact that the chastised Smeral remained his party's leader.

About two weeks elapsed from the scheduled start of the congress before Kuusinen ploddingly completed his theses.

"They're good," said Lenin, "but such classical, academic German. They should be in the contemporary language."

Kuusinen was given the assistance of the two Koenen brothers, who modernized the theses linguistically. To be on the safe side, Kuusinen even asked one of the brothers—Wilhelm Koenen, the older, as I recall—to present them at the congress, with the result that foreign works dealing with the Comintern often refer to the "Koenen theses."

When the theses had been read, Lenin took the floor, lauded Kuusinen and his competence, expressed his delight and in apt phrases let it be understood that Kuusinen was one of the few capable of such work. After his remarks the theses were approved, and Kuusinen was named secretary general of the Comintern.

Undeniably the most interesting of the speakers was Comrade Kollontai. There were many good reasons for this interest. In the first place, she was a really fine, trained, fiery orator, who was fluent in at least four languages. Second, though she lacked a year of being fifty, she was so expertly made up that she was passably pleasant to the sight. Third, it was she who most tenaciously tried to trip Lenin. And, last but not least, she was the originator of the waterglass theory.

The waterglass theory, in brief, holds that sexual intercourse with a man means no more to a woman than emptying a glass of water. Thus, a woman should have the right to go anywhere at any time with any man. This, however, is not the same as prostitution—far from it. This is precisely what would prevent prostitution.

A revolutionary thesis, indeed! It was on the verge of toppling the entire Soviet power. Lenin rose to condemn severely the waterglass theory and the sexual freedom that prevailed during the early days of the Soviet era. As it was, the whole affair remained simply a storm in a waterglass.

Another Kollontai stroke considered during the same congress was *rabochaia oppozitsiia,* the workers' opposition. The New Economic Policy (NEP), the partial restoration of individual capitalism that had been proclaimed by Lenin, had raised the hair of the most fanatical Bolsheviks and created the *rabochaia oppozitsiia,* led by Kollontai and the noted trade unionist Shljapnikov.

The discussion was opened by Kollontai who, in an hour's fiery speech in Russian, German, and French, attacked Lenin unscrupulously and acrimoniously. Lenin and his line were selling out the Russian Revolution—that was the gist of Madame's tirade. Lenin smiled throughout the speech and applauded whenever she succeeded in turning a particularly diabolical phrase.

Lenin rose to reply almost immediately and reacted to the at-

tacks quite humorously. "Comrade Kollontai," he said, "is weep-
ing for holy Mother Russia, saying that capitalists will be able to
despoil it with their franchises. She doesn't seem to comprehend
that that's how we're trying to save the Soviet power. I, on the
other hand, start from the premise that if we can preserve the
power by any means whatsoever, we have the possibility of can-
celing the capitalists' franchises and chasing them away. But if we
lose the power, soon the entire holy land of Russia will be one
huge franchise. Madame Kollontai's *rabochaia oppozitsiia* is not
concerned with the preservation of power. I am not concerned
with anything else."

The official history of the Soviet Union declares that, in the
struggle against the workers' opposition, Lenin was strongly supported by Stalin. Nothing was known of that at the time, however. At least publicly his support meant little, since he had
neither a big name nor noteworthy oratorical gifts.

The history of the Comintern is an opus unto itself that has yet
to be written. I shall content myself merely with giving the general impressions that a zealous young man received at his first major congress. Thus, I shall not comment on the checkered fortunes
of the German Communist party, though at that early stage they
had something in common with our own activities. Suffice it to say
that a general strike was proclaimed also in Germany and that a
revolution was attempted but failed.

This did not bring the party to its senses, however; instead, the
critics of the revolt, among them the party's former chairman,
Dr. Paul Levi, were ousted from the party. But Lenin, who could
smell an intelligent man from afar, announced to the committee
drafting questions on Germany for deliberation by the congress,
"It's true that Levi has become giddy-headed, but sometimes it's
better to be giddy than to have no head at all." And so Levi was
the leader of the second German party at the Moscow congress,
not that that brought much joy to Lenin.

For it was this rebel who brought up for discussion a matter in
which we Finns also had a certain interest: could the Comintern,
in the course of time, develop into an international organization
if its home were Moscow?

The answer of Levi and his companions was explicit: if the
Soviet Union finances the Comintern and maintains it in its own

capital, it will become a foreign affairs bureau of the Soviet Union.

This viewpoint gained support among the foreigners, and even Clara Zetkin defended Levi, though she belonged to the opposition party, but with the Russians' authority Levi's motion was crushed.

The matter was taken under consideration within the Finnish delegation, for the same fear had prompted us to resist external influence for years. Shouldn't we, too, try to bring about the transfer of the Comintern from Moscow to some neutral city in Europe, thus diminishing the direct Russian influence? To this question our emigrant Communists immediately retorted, "For God's sake, don't talk like that; it's downright heretical. Of course the interests of the Soviet Union and the world Communist movement are the same!"

Long discussions ensued. In our innocent lack of judiciousness we who had come from Finland still maintained that an increase in Soviet might would see the Comintern tied to Soviet political interests without any concern over whether they jibed with the interests of European workers.

I have recalled this discussion more than once over the past years. Even when holding positions of leadership in the Communist party I was constantly tormented by the suspicion that it probably would have been wiser to transfer the Comintern to another country, where it would not have been forced to promote the interests of the Soviet Union.

In 1921 we lived in an era of Lenin's idealism. True, by then Lenin already had seen some of his ideas collapse, among them the dictatorship of the proletariat. The aim had been for the workers and peasants to wield the power—in reality it had come to the point where some tens of thousands of party members ruled those millions. Instead of a dictatorship of the proletariat there was oligarchy, government by the few.

Bukharin has related that, in official sessions of the Central Committee, Lenin openly confessed that failure but consoled himself with the thought that when democracy is faithfully fostered within the party—even though dictatorship prevails in the country itself—and every party member has the right and the freedom to express his opinions and to further them by legal means, then, by continuously training new elements in the use of power, the country would move step by step from government by the few to government by the proletariat and from that, again step by step, to government by the people. So beautiful was Lenin's dream.

DIRTY LINEN IN PETROGRAD

WHEN Kuusinen, after his flight from the Finnish Communist party's tiny pen, had returned to Moscow's great sheepfold, the situation insofar as he was concerned could only be called humorous. He was a traitor, which in all organizations is a monstrous thing but in revolutionary organizations is the most monstrous of all. But sometimes the part can be greater than the whole. In other words, the shepherds in the tiny pen cannot always slaughter the chief shepherd's pet ram.

To continue the metaphor, we could say that Lenin's favor had caused respectable horns to grow on Kuusinen. Holding the Finnish Communist party's convention during or immediately after the Comintern congress had been his idea. His opponents, forced to reconcile themselves to this, certainly had no intention of capitulating without a struggle.

Already while we were in Petrograd, en route to Moscow, the Finnish Communist party leaders Manner and Rahja had noticed that the group I had brought along was unequivocally pro-Kuusinen. Rahja had utilized the duration of the Moscow congress to advantage and had imported a reserve group of more than twenty heads from Finland. For approximately a month it had been trained in the parish of Lempaala, near Petrograd, educated and pledged to the Manner-Rahja creed.

This bunch, collected from Finland to bolster the Manner-Rahja group, was of a much lower caliber than the pro-Kuusinen members, most of whom were party officials and newspaper editors. One of the ablest in the Manner group was a young man from Oulu named Antti Hyvönen, who later managed to clamber all the way to the central committee of the Finnish Communist party with Manner's support but who proved to be so immoral that he was expelled from that party as well as from the Soviet Union's Communist party.

He played no apparent role at this particular convention but had attempted to do so behind the scenes, asking for Manner's permission to shoot Kuusinen as an indication of his loyalty to Manner and Rahja. Manner, however, declined Hyvönen's offer. After World War II, when the Finnish Communist party was allowed to function in Finland once more, Antti Hyvönen became the assistant director of the communist Sirola Institute.

Shortly before the conclusion of the Comintern congress, we of the Kuusinen faction left Moscow hurriedly after hearing from our spies that Rahja already had marched his troops into Petrograd. For a few days we staged small skirmishes and charged the batteries until the arrival of the Comintern delegates, Radek and the Italian, Gennari, who was a member of the Comintern's Executive Committee.

It was then that we caught a glimpse of a Kuusinen characteristic that played its own part in his successful career. It is probably needless to point out that for one in his position merely to remain alive in the Soviet Union was in itself a successful career. So, when the dignitaries arrived, Kuusinen hastened to meet them at the gate, fawned upon them and made much of them with deep bows. Such behavior was disgusting to us. My closest comrades declared that, in their opinion, he was too servile toward the host country's representative.

Although Kuusinen's best assistants were women, once in a while they caused rather precarious situations. When he was in Finland in 1920, the biggest services were rendered to him by Aino Sarola, the wife of an engineer. She made herself literally indispensable to Kuusinen as a courier and liaison woman and later in other ways, too. As she dressed elegantly and was very attractive, it was no wonder her employer fell head over heels in love with her.

When Kuusinen moved to Stockholm and later to Moscow, Aino Sarola tried to get me to arrange a trip for her to the Soviet

Union. When I refused, Mrs. Sarola tucked a handbag under her arm and in low shoes and silk stockings began trudging through the Karelian marshes north of Lake Ladoga. After many adventurous days and nights, that persistent and resourceful woman had penetrated Soviet Karelia so deeply that she was stopped by the border guards or the Cheka only near Petrozavodsk. She claimed to be engaged to Kuusinen and to have come to Russia at the urging of Kuusinen to marry him. She was brought to Petrograd just in time for the start of our meeting. Kuusinen testified on her behalf and the Cheka relinquished her to Kuusinen, who installed her in our hotel, the Astoria.

Kuusinen's opponents raised a great fuss, declaring that the woman was surely an agent of the Finnish secret police. Kuusinen became alarmed, began obtaining statements about the woman's trustworthiness and even asked me to be a guarantor. But I knew that she had been associated with some questionable characters in Helsinki, and I refused to put my spoon into that soup. Kuusinen then quickly sent her to Moscow where she was kept in hiding until he could marry her. Once again a major congress was almost turned topsy-turvy because of a woman.

Anyway, the convention got off to a good and harmonious start, but then the mood changed and harsher words began raining down. They came in a veritable downpour. I have never heard such marathon speeches. Manner led off. His speech, which began at nine in the morning and ended only the following morning, set a record. Naturally we took meal breaks, and after midnight we even slept a little, but even so the speech lasted over ten hours.

For the most part the speech was a rehash of the conflict between the Manner and Kuusinen factions, but what made it interesting was its analysis of the opposition men, especially Kuusinen.

"I presume," said Manner, "that Kuusinen will want to claim that I, a minister's son, cannot be a proletarian or a revolutionary but I shall prove with historical evidence that a minister's son can indeed become a proletarian revolutionary, whereas the son of a typical petit bourgeois, a village tailor, cannot."

He had found examples to support his thesis from all over the world, and then he described a village tailor's position and trade. Tied to his employer, the tailor is servile and groveling on the one hand, but on the other has the petit bourgeois elementariness (Manner's favorite term) that continues elementally unto the third, fourth, and fifth generation. Kuusinen personified this.

Admittedly he is among the shrewdest and most intelligent men ever to have been in the Finnish labor movement, said Manner, but the question is not of shrewdness and intelligence but of whether a person actually can shed his old skin. Kuusinen has written *Self-Criticism* and in it flayed himself thoroughly, but all that is mere verbiage; he is revolutionary only in phrases. The man himself has not changed; he is still the same village tailor's son, a petit bourgeois whose head has further been turned by the fact that the village tailor's son has a master's degree. And that is why such a man is dangerous, very dangerous, to the revolutionary movement.

That was the main theme of the long, complex analysis of Kuusinen, which seemed to please the audience. Translators for Radek and Gennari alternated and, judging by Radek's face, that born cynic was enjoying himself greatly. The more malicious and insulting Manner's statements were, the more Radek beamed. What do you know, they're actually capable of it, he seemed to be thinking; these Finns aren't so stupid as I would have thought!

Kuusinen, too, had prepared a long speech, but next to Manner's marathon it remained a ten-thousand-meter run, if even that. It lasted five hours, but in the first place, he spoke slowly and, second, his hemming and hawing took up a quarter of the time. If one disregards that, Kuusinen's speech was, of course, more brilliant. He had firm foundations from which to strike: our convention majority, behind him the Comintern and his position as secretary general and, as an additional guarantee, the jurors sent by Lenin.

Generally speaking, a minister's son can become a revolutionary, conceded Kuusinen, but not in this instance. What is required is the shedding of one's old skin, and that Manner has never done. He came into the labor movement from the wrong end. He did not come in humbly and as a servant of the proletariat, he came in as a leader, to show that he was something. He immediately wanted to be Kullervo Manner, a head taller than others, not only in height but intellectually as well. Even at that point there might have been hopes of "skin shedding," but unfortunately just then he was elected speaker of the Finnish Parliament. And when the bourgeoisie and even some of us made the mistake of lauding him as a handsome speaker—and a certain methodicalness and formality made him a good speaker—the result was that he will always be a speaker. He is the speaker of a bourgeois parliament and can never be anything else.

That was the course followed by Kuusinen's analysis (naturally embellished with deviltry), and in passing he also sketched neat little caricatures of Manner's adjutants. Then he shifted to the heart of the matter, explained the origins of the dissension and in conclusion referred dramatically to us.

"Here we are, fighting and arguing, but these boys are making a revolution in Finland. Some of them have been in prison and after their release have founded a big new party. That's what they are now heading and they are the ones who should have the floor. We should keep our mouths shut, I as well as Manner and his phalanx. It's up to us to remain in the background and let them appear."

In his marathon speech Manner had been diplomatic enough to focus on and limit his personal attacks to Kuusinen. But in surveying the past year's events, he could not refrain from treading heavily on my doctrinal corns. He naturally sought to prove that all the instructions and orders issued by the Petrograd headquarters of the Finnish Communist party—in other words, by Rahja and himself—were sensible and right, whereas the activities undertaken by us resisters were obviously counterrevolutionary. He branded as downright criminal the fact that I had confiscated their proclamation of a general strike and had even labeled it a bourgeois provocation. I had naturally anticipated that attack and had tucked a weapon in my back pocket.

Shortly before our departure from Helsinki, Finnish Communist Hanna Malm had written a certain proclamation and, without showing it to us members of the inner circle, had attempted to sneak it directly into *Suomen Työmies*. I had already relinquished the post of editor-in-chief because I had other things to do than continually run to the Tampere city hall to answer the censor's charges, but the paper naturally remained under my supervision.

The proclamation was addressed to the peasants and declared, among other things, that the workers' lot was splendid compared to that of the peasants, who were robbed clean and left with nothing. A workingman could, after all, hide out from the tax collector, but a peasant's land and everything on it were subject to distraint. There was more like that, equally impossible.

I strictly forbade the publication of such a text, which raised quite a fuss. Hanna Malm sent her agent over to me to show a letter from Kullervo Manner. By that time Manner had divorced his wife and was having a fling with Hanna.

Among other things the letter said, "I'm surprised that Poika Tuominen didn't allow your proclamation to be published, for it's so good that I'm behind every word of it."* I had a copy made of that letter and sent the original back to Hanna with her representative.

Now when I began counterattacking Manner, I produced all the stupid orders that we had received from Petrograd and finally read Hanna Malm's proclamation. Then, looking out over the audience, I declared in the stentorian tones of a Roman tribune, "Comrades, you heard the kind of nonsense they've tried to feed us from here! Tell me, did I do the right thing in confiscating this proclamation or didn't I?"

The convention replied, as all conventions do when the proper mood has been reached, "You were right!"—"Such a thing couldn't have been published!"—"It's as hopeless and senseless as that strike proclamation!"

And one of the secretaries, a handsome and loud-voiced man named Leo Laukki, roared, "I tell you, if such a thing had been tried in America, the man would have been lynched like a Negro!"

The convention had had its say, and that was well and good, but I hoped for more: would Manner go into the net? After a few tense moments Manner rose and said that he was sorry not to have known anything about such a proclamation, that he was hearing

---

* In 1920 a newspaper columnist called him "Poika" (boy) Tuominen because he looked considerably younger than his twenty-six years. The nickname stuck, and in Finland he was generally known as Poika Tuominen to the end of his days. President Kekkonen addressed letters to him "Poika Tuominen, Tampere." A Tampere journalist wrote his biography and called it *Poika* (Raimo Seppälä, *Poika,* Helsinki: Tammi, 1981).

about it for the first time. And even he had to admit that there had been no alternative to confiscating the whole proclamation.

Then came my moment. "What do you think of a Finnish Communist party chairman who just swore that he saw nothing, yet in a letter written to Hanna Malm—a copy of which is in my hand—declared that he stands behind every word in the proclamation?"

I read the letter to the convention and worked up a mighty offensive, calling Manner a completely immoral man who lied even to the convention. Poor Manner could only rise, apologize and deplore that he actually had lied and tried to deceive the convention. This, of course, gave us a considerable advantage. The wrangling continued like that for about three weeks.

Manner worshiped elemental proletarianism greatly at this convention, which in itself was not surprising since his revolutionary mien was shackled by that ministerial family burden. Even the supporters whom he had recruited from Finland were, for the most part, crude laborer types whose every other word was an oath or a threat.

Rahja was the essence of such "elemental proletarianism." A more foul-mouthed person probably has never appeared anywhere in public. Presumably he was unable to say anything decently and without threats. He could begin comparatively calmly but soon would become excited and yell.

"Don't be so sure even though you do have an apparent majority, because you can't tell what will happen. We might even get more people"—as indeed they did—"and there are other ways of taking care of things."

As an example of these ways of taking care of things, he cited certain people who had been liquidated at his command. One man in particular he suspected and ordered his assistants to liquidate, requesting that they bring him the man's ears as evidence. "Lo, the ears came!"

Naturally this evoked a strong reaction even among Rahja's supporters. Manner, among others, expressed his regrets and added that Rahja could not be taken seriously. We Kuusinen men got a diabolical slogan to use whenever a factual discussion assumed a threatening tone: "Lo, the ears came!"

Radek and Gennari had followed our goings-on quite assiduously. About halfway through the convention, when the main speakers had already presented their cases and the actual ideological threshing had been concluded, Radek made a typically dazzling ("brilliant" is too mild a word) speech, in which he clearly supported Kuusinen's stand and lauded Kuusinen personally. Insofar as he could tell from the discussions and from what he already knew, Kuusinen's line was considered the better one by the Comintern and Lenin.

Radek's speech determined that Manner and Rahja no longer could even hope to achieve their major goal: Kuusinen's ouster from the Central Committee of the Finnish Communist party. But with their one-vote majority they still stubbornly tried to wield authority in the Central Committee. Finally we drew our bow to the breaking point and threatened to walk out. At that the Manner phalanx became distressed and eager for compromise.

Kuusinen stated the situation succinctly: "You take care of matters in Finland, I'll do it in Moscow. Rahja and Manner can do what they want in their own circle."

I became a member of the Central Committee as well as the director of the Finnish bureau. But before I consented to be elected, I set one condition.

When we had left Finland, the editorship of *Suomen Työmies* had remained in the hands of men who did not know how, or did not want, to be on their guard against the Mannerites. They allowed an idiotic pen name, "Mutteri,"* to run rampant on the paper's pages. "Mutteri" was Hanna Malm.

As the condition for my becoming a member of the Central Committee I wanted the authority to banish Hanna Malm from the country. Manner considered such hounding of a woman most inappropriate.

To that I replied, "This is not a question of Hanna Malm alone, but generally of people who are ordered to Finland to disorganize our plans."

Manner yielded and I was granted my wish.

* A nut for screwing onto a bolt.

Then we returned secretly to Finland by way of the wooded Karelian Isthmus. The journey had lasted over three months.

I began attending to my duties and first of all took steps to banish Hanna Malm from the country.

PROBLEMS OF COMMUNISM

THESE THREE MONTHS HAD, of course, been a time of overwhelming experience for me. During this period I had come to know the Soviet Union, that communist experiment in which a huge state was being guided for the first time according to procedures and policies previously unknown in world history.

But the Soviet Union was merely the beginning of the world revolution envisaged by Lenin and his school. Neither I nor probably any other participant in the Comintern congress doubted that the plan would be fulfilled in the very near future. We talked only of years, not decades. Lenin, too, believed that and so, apparently, did his entire school.

Germany, then struggling under the squeeze of the Versailles Treaty, was looked upon as the initial prize. The only island believed to remain for some time under capitalist domination was America. On the other hand, much was expected of Asia, since the slogan "Colonialism must end; Asia for the Asians" already appeared to be bearing fruit.

Although I was considerably disillusioned with the Finnish Communist party leaders as a result of my Moscow trip, my faith in Lenin and the ultimate triumph of communism was not shaken. On the contrary, having witnessed how socialism and communism were being built in Russia itself, I now had a solid foundation for my belief. I was, however, highly dubious about the possibilities of the Comintern. In my opinion, it could not become a true international organization of revolutionary workers because its home base remained in Moscow. "Whose bread you eat, his songs you sing."

Another matter, related in a way to the former and stirring greatly conflicting feelings within me as its nature became clear, was the morality of the Communists. It differed sharply from generally known and recognizable concepts of morality. Everything that you do for the good of the Soviet Union and communism is acceptable, hence morally right. That, in brief, is the nub of communist morality. It was difficult for me to comprehend and difficult to accept.

Also on the negative side was the dogmatic hair splitting that was practiced in the higher circles of the Comintern and especially on the upper levels of the Finnish Communist party. It was truly the arranging and examining of the hairs in Marx's beard, constant bickering about whether this or that saying was theoretically absolutely correct, in accord with the doctrine of Marx and Lenin. Those of us involved in practical work had proceeded from the belief that minor variations in nuance were not worth arguing about so long as we moved by and large in the right direction.

My feelings on returning home were thus mixed, and a similar mood seemed to prevail among the other participants in the convention.

One of the participants was the organizer of the Federation of Trade Unions, Frans Hiilos. He was an especially keen-witted man who kept clear of arguments at the meetings. Mostly he was interested in the theory of communism. He wanted to familiarize himself thoroughly with the Leninist-Marxist dialectic, and, at the same time, with Einstein's theory of relativity, which in those days was used to assist Marxism in the intensive dissemination of communist ideas.

It was thus only logical that the ideological hair splitting at the convention should affect him most deeply. Frans was sitting in a train somewhere between Pietarsaari and Kokkola, in northern Finland, when he became obsessed with the idea that every problem on earth could be solved by Marxist dialectics and the theory of relativity. Every solution, on the one hand, had to be examined in the light of the theory of relativity and, on the other, it had to provide, in the dialectical manner, a thesis and an antithesis and their resolution, a synthesis.

He jumped down from the train at the next station and continued his journey on foot. Aimlessly he followed a forest road and solved the problems confronting him. Beside the road was a house which at first glance seemed red. But was it actually red? Someone else might think it blue, for everything is relative, pondered Frans. A good Marxist, however, cannot leave the matter unclear, since it can be resolved the dialectical way. Red is thus the thesis and blue the antithesis. Their synthesis is, let us say, black. Good. The house, in other words, is black, possibly tarred.

Soon he came to a fork in the road, and since he was unfamiliar with the region, again had to rely on dialectics. The left road was the thesis, the right one the antithesis; the synthesis appeared naturally: he must go between the roads into the woods. While wandering around he dropped his bowler and instinctively was about to pick it up when logic intervened. The matter had to be considered. The thesis: pick up the hat; the antithesis: leave it on the ground. The synthesis also appeared: he kicked the hat away and continued on his journey bareheaded.

In this condition he was picked up by the authorities, who took him to Helsinki. Along the way he continued his stringent dialectics. As a result, he could neither remain seated in the train nor could he leave by the door. His solution was to smash a window with his bare fist and to try to get out that way. The hand was injured so badly that he carried the souvenir of this synthesis the rest of his life.

Because of his injury he was taken to the Surgical Hospital in Helsinki, where he continued his application of dialectics. After a few hours there he observed, "Well, here lies Frans Hiilos, whose mind is unbalanced. But who can guarantee that this actually is Frans Hiilos? The very thought might be ridiculous, quite impossible. This might just as well be Charles XII."

And so Hiilos was, for a while, the great Swedish warrior king, until he found that arrangement also too simple. Hiilos or Charles XII, the matter had to have a dialectic solution. The problem was so knotty that he was about to leave it to the theory of relativity. Finally, however, the dialectical weapons brought a clear victory: the synthesis was Mannerheim—Baron General Carl Gustaf Mannerheim.

The result was fortunate in that now he had family in the same building, for the head nurse at the hospital was Sophie Mannerheim, the general's sister. He asked to have his "sister" summoned, and when the head nurse arrived, Hiilos began chiding her fraternally but seriously.

"Sophie, Sophie, how can you keep your own brother in such an inferior room and so closely guarded?"

And Sophie, who had become aware of the patient's condition, replied, "So you're being guarded. Let's see if we can arrange for you to have better care."

All the while Hiilos knew that he was Hiilos and that he was merely enacting Charles XII, but, according to the Marxist-Leninist dialectic, he had to be Mannerheim.

After rest and care, Hiilos returned to his work at the Federation of Trade Unions and otherwise, too, returned to his former state—or perhaps not quite. Later in life he rather smiled at people who adhered zealously to doctrines.

If our frame of mind was confused and chaotic, the political arena itself seemed even more confused after our return home. Previously, from the founding of the Socialist Labor party in the spring of 1920, to the first half of the following year, we had had a clear political line, the so-called Kuusinen line, which was early Titoism or national communism. We proceeded on the assumption that a legal, public revolutionary party could function in Finland, thus making unnecessary a secret Communist party, the Finnish Communist party.

Nevertheless, we were in something of a quandary, since Kuusinen, our mentor and leader, had returned from his errant path to Moscow's bosom. He had become the Comintern's first secretary as well as Lenin's right-hand man in matters of international politics. While committing himself once again to the Comintern and the furtherance of Comintern policies, he simultaneously had committed to it the entire Kuusinen phalanx functioning in Finland. Thus we had no clear policy regarding our relationship to underground activity and to the Comintern. We now were obliged to endorse the Finnish Communist party, an illegal group to whose Central Committee I had been named at the party convention in Petrograd and of whose Finnish bureau I had even been made director.

Ahead of us now was the task of reconciling covert underground activity and public activity. Theoretically we had to accept, and in practice to attempt to apply, such statements as the following, then as now one of communism's most important tenets:

In countries still ruled by the bourgeoisie or by counterrevolutionary Social Democrats, the communist parties must learn systematically to combine legal activity with illegal. In such instances the legal activity must constantly be subjected to the real control of the illegal party.

Then there was this resolution regarding parliamentary work:

The Communist party does not enter this institution, Parliament, for the purpose of functioning organically but rather to assist the masses in destroying the machinery of government and Parliament itself . . .

Let every communist member of Parliament be aware that he is no legislator who strives for mutual understanding with other legislators, but a party agitator who has been sent into the enemy camp to execute the decisions of the party. A member of the Communist party is not accountable to the scattered groups that elected him but to the legally authorized or illegal Communist party.

A troublesome dilemma indeed.

In those days a certain communist plan, already in black and white, was attracting much attention: the projected incorporation of northern Finland, northern Sweden, and northern Norway into a special communist Soviet Republic of the North. The establishment of the Karelian Commune, headed by Dr. Edvard Gylling of Stockholm, was regarded as the nucleus of this plan. After Gylling, who was Scandinavian-oriented and who had good relations with the Communists in the Nordic countries, began governing the communist state in Soviet Karelia, it was decided that northern Finland, northern Sweden, and northern Norway should, at some opportune time, be forcibly incorporated into Soviet Karelia, which would thus be expanded into the Soviet Republic of the North.

I don't know how seriously the Communists in Sweden and Norway considered the idea, but the Finnish Communists and the leaders of the Finnish Communist party did harbor such a scheme, and it is also true that they received sympathy for their plan from Moscow's Kremlin. Just about that time Gylling published an article developing the idea of creating a Soviet Republic of the North. And Gylling certainly did not write it behind Lenin's back.

The subject was revived now and then and subsequently lay buried until after World War II—more precisely in 1947–48—when Finnish Communists again were given the task of studying the feasibility of a Soviet Republic of Lapland, into which the Lapps of Finland, Sweden, and Norway would be incorporated.

This idea probably originated with the great Stalin himself. He was vexed by the fact that even in this corner of the world he was not able to achieve the dream of the great Russian czars: clear access to the Atlantic, even though he had the Salla track built as the starting point for a highway to the Atlantic.*

Since 1918 there had been, in East Karelia, a provisional government of Karelia and Aunus which, with organizers from Finland, had instigated popular uprisings. In the summer of 1920 this government had moved to the Finnish side of the border and was highly active in fomenting all kinds of stirrings and disturbances with a view to creating an independent Karelia.

However, preparations for a major insurrection began only after the Treaty of Tartu between Finland and the Soviet Union, when the latter failed to grant autonomy to Karelia as the peace treaty stipulated. In that failure the Soviet Union did not adhere to its own Leninist policies of national self-determination, for according to them Karelia had every right to independence. At the Bolsheviks' All-Russian Party Congress in February 1917 it had clearly been stated, "All peoples who belong to Russia must be granted the right to free secession and the formation of an independent state."

I mention the Karelia case because it became fateful for me personally. When the news broke of Finnish troops crossing the border into Karelia and of battles there, the Socialist Labor party's Action Committee was harnessed to wage antiwar propaganda, as were our entire organizational machinery and press. We held large rallies in various parts of the country and published a proclamation in which the Finnish working people were urged to fight in defense of Soviet Russia.

In 1922 it was my belief—and I confess it truthfully—that if

---

* The track connected the railroad from Leningrad to Murmansk with the Finnish rail network, near the Arctic Circle.

war were to break out, Finnish workers should side with the Soviet Union. The Finns, in my opinion, were the aggressors. Thus,
siding with the Soviet Union then meant siding with the victim
of an injustice.

These views served as the grounds for my arrest on January 26,
1922. I was sentenced to the penitentiary and not released until
over four years later.

I have pointed out to President Kekkonen that his speeches
about the current relations between Finland and the Soviet Union
are almost word for word like the defense pleas I made at the
Turku Court of Appeals during my trial.

I asked him once, "I got five years. What are you getting?"

The president merely laughed and said, "Your text was correct;
it was just premature. One shouldn't talk even about valid things
prematurely," he observed playfully.

But by 1939, time had taught me that facts were not what I had
believed them to be in my youth, in the idealistic euphoria of
communism. When I was offered the post of prime minister in
the Terijoki government in 1939, I again had to make the choice
for the Soviet Union or for Finland; and after agonizing wrestling
with my conscience, my choice was clear. I had to defend Finland
and urged all Communists to do likewise. My position was manifest: Finnish workers must defend Finland when it is attacked regardless of the attacker. There was not the slightest doubt as to
who was the aggressor. The aggressor was the Red Army, and
Finland was defending its independence. The choice was thus
much easier.

But I also had come to realize fully that the Soviet Union was
not the fatherland of all workers, as I had believed in 1922. It
did not promote the cause of Finnish workers but of the Russian
nation and, above all, Russia's interests as a world power.

In 1922 a questionnaire was circulated in the Turku provincial
prison on whether or not a man engaged in the class struggle
should marry. I replied, half in jest, half seriously, that he should
not because a married man is a seed of dissension at the front and
that because he has a wife and children he cannot be ready at any
moment to look death in the eye. Obviously, however, I was not
truly dedicated to the class struggle since I didn't heed my own

advice—though I doubt whether any man, no matter how class conscious, is so fanatical that he wouldn't notice pretty young girls.

At any rate, near the end of 1920, I began to feel great interest in a young pig-tailed girl named Lyyli Kyllikki Rainio. While I was in prison she wrote to me often and kept me abreast of developments with her letters, which sometimes reached ten a month. When I was released in the spring of 1926, it seemed only natural for us to keep company.

The following year, after I had gotten a small apartment, I inquired cautiously whether we could move in together.

"Of course," replied Lyyli. "But first we must be married."

Fanatical Communist though I was, I was also sufficiently petit bourgeois to take that for granted. Naturally we had to be married, and so we were.

The marriage lasted over forty years, until Lyyli's death in 1968. During that time we experienced both fair winds and head winds, but whatever the situation we faced it together. Without her support I would not have pulled through until now.

In the summer of 1926 I became acquainted with a man named Yrjö Kaarlo Leino, in whose conversion to communism I played an important role. Because he became one of the most significant figures in Finland's postwar history, I shall skip ahead some twenty years to discuss his case briefly.

By 1944 Yrjö Leino was an important leader of the Finnish Communist party, partially because he had married Otto Wille Kuusinen's elder daughter, Hertta. He was the first overt Communist to be named to the 1944 Paasikivi government, where he was given the portfolio of minister for social affairs. A little later, when two more Communists were admitted to the cabinet, Leino was made minister of the interior.

But even powerful men come to the end of their rope, especially in the Communist movement. It happened to Leino in 1948. About a year later he came to see me in Stockholm, where I then lived, and over a period of four days told me about his term of office as minister of the interior and facts relating to it: how, during that term, he had been pressured from a certain quarter to make a clean sweep, how he was given not only hints and advice but outright orders to clear the way for people's democracy, how he was shown the manner in which real ministers of the interior—like Hungary's Rajk—function, and how he was taught, when he cited Finnish laws, that he was not the minister of the interior for the purpose of following old bourgeois laws but to create a communist society. Laws are changed, new laws are made in accordance with proletarian justice—and they are created by having the representatives of the proletariat, the Communists, take actions that are later ratified by legislation.

As is well known, Yrjö Leino's downfall occurred formally when Parliament in a majority decision gave him a vote of no confidence. When he made no move to leave his post despite that, President Paasikivi announced at a cabinet session that, inasmuch as a member of the cabinet in Finland must have the confidence of Parliament and Minister of the Interior Leino did not have it, he had no alternative but to relieve Minister Leino of membership in the cabinet.

But what actually were the forces which caused the downfall of this powerful man? The following is based on Leino's own account.

Early spring of 1948 was a time of uneasiness in Finland. The air quivered with the threat and fear of a Communist coup. In March a Finnish delegation was scheduled to leave for Moscow to negotiate a treaty of peace and assistance. Minister of the Interior Yrjö Leino had been named one of the delegates.

On the eve of departure, Leino left his residence and went to see General Aarne Sihvo, commander of the defense forces.

"General, you yourself know that the country is restless," Leino told Sihvo. "It has come to my attention that opponents of the friendship and assistance treaty are planning some kind of action these coming days. I also know that disturbances can be expected from the leftists. For that reason I have come to you, though giving instructions to the commander of the defense forces is not in the purview of the minister of the interior. You see, I'm afraid that Defense Minister Kallinen, who is a great man of peace, may not have noticed these portents of turmoil. I hope that the defense forces will maintain order throughout the land while the negotiations for the friendship and assistance treaty are under way."

That provided the decisive encouragement for Sihvo, who himself had taken tentative measures for controlling the situation. The army was on alert, an armored regiment had been brought to the outskirts of Helsinki, several ships had been stationed in positions of preparedness and certain roads were under surveillance. Now these measures received new emphasis, and the army appeared quite openly as an assurance of order.

The instituting of security measures and especially the seizing of arms from the reaches of Hautojärvi, the top Communist in the mobile police, so incensed the Communists that they ostentatiously sent a delegation of noted Communists to demand of Sihvo who had authorized such a provocative measure and to register a strong protest.

I have been told that Sihvo replied, "I am not responsible to you for my actions but because you are members of Parliament or otherwise persons in prominent positions I can tell you confidentially that everything has been done at the express urging of Minister of the Interior Leino."

That was an answer for which the delegation was unprepared. The previously demanding "prominent persons" withdrew silently from Sihvo's presence.

The negotiations were going on in Moscow at the same time. From the beginning it had been apparent that Minister of the Interior Leino was the focal figure among the Finns. Everyone else had to make way for this strong man. He was feted and honored by their hosts until, suddenly, a change occurred. The previously celebrated hero and respected negotiator was suddenly treated like thin air. No attention was paid to his statements; it was as though he had not spoken at all, and soon he himself realized the wisdom of remaining silent. The disapproval could not have been more obvious.

When Leino pondered the question he could only conclude that his instructions to Sihvo had somehow leaked to the Communists. Fear clutched at his throat, and sure enough, before long he was told politely that his eye disease required treatment in the Crimea or the Caucasus.

"An opportunity for such care has been provided for you," he was told courteously but firmly.

Leino was, in fact, suffering from an eye problem, a serious one, but he categorically refused. He feared that he would never return from one of "Stalin's sanatoriums."

By insisting vehemently and citing the need to return to his duties, he finally managed to leave for Finland. Leino's description of this flight was perhaps the most harrowing part of his tale. During the entire trip he was obsessed by the fear that something dreadful would happen before he reached Finland.

The downfall of a great minister of the interior thus, according to his own words, actually took place in Moscow because he had warned the army about the threat of a coup.

For my own part, I believe that Leino's tragedy lay in the fact that he tried to be a good Communist and at the same time a Finnish patriot.

The leaders of the Finnish Communist party continue to revile Leino but actually they should thank him for their lives. Had Leino not been a Finn, many of them would have gone the way of Rajk in Hungary, Slanski and Clements in Czechoslovakia, Kostov in Bulgaria, and incalculable thousands with them. Communism devours its children.

It was fortunate that, in its decisive moments, Finland did not have as its minister of the interior a remote-controlled man trained in Moscow who was wholly without his own will. Only the stubbornly strong Finnish nature of the communist minister of the interior prevented—in his own estimation as well—the Finnish Communist party from attempting a coup at a moment when it might well have succeeded.

TO STALIN'S MOSCOW

AS I MENTIONED PREVIOUSLY, I was released from prison in the spring of 1926, after which I was elected secretary of the Finnish Federation of Trade Unions. I wanted to lead the federation purely to further the Finnish trade unionists' aims. But there was a millstone: the leadership of the Finnish Communist party and behind it Moscow's Comintern and Profintern, the Red International Trade Union. At that moment the Finnish Federation of Trade Unions was particularly important to the Soviet foreign ministry. For that reason it was constantly—almost every week or at least monthly—being given foreign policy tasks that badly disrupted its practical work.

Before every international trade union congress, the Finnish delegates were coached to present the Soviet Union's propaganda demands of the moment. At the dictates of the Comintern and the Profintern, the Finnish Communist party leadership continuously sent outright orders on how we should hinder the activity of Väinö Tanner's social democratic government.

My leadership of the Federation of Trade Unions ended in April 1928 when I was again imprisoned. The grounds for the sentence were that, as secretary of the Finnish Federation of Trade Unions, I had maintained contact with the Soviet Union. It was also hinted that I had connections with the Finnish Communist party. For the most part the charges were valid and true, for I had tried my best to instill communist order in Finland.

After almost five years of imprisonment, I was paroled near the end of 1932. Immediately after my release I received a letter from Kuusinen in which he urged me to go to Moscow.

"By now you must believe that you will be repeatedly imprisoned there in Finland," he wrote. "The almost ten years that you have suffered should suffice. It's high time that you moved on to greener pastures."

My wife and I discussed the suggestion many times and clashed sharply, for she was vehemently opposed to it. It would simply be jumping out of the frying pan into the fire, Lyyli said.

But I didn't believe that. The thought of departure became a kind of open sesame to all my problems. When I stubbornly clung to the idea, Lyyli finally, though reluctantly, yielded.

I went secretly to Sweden and from there, in April 1933, by a Soviet merchant ship to Leningrad and thence to Moscow. I was now within sound of the bells of the Kremlin that had been calling me.

Kuusinen's chauffeur and magnificent car, as well as some members of the Finnish Communist party's Moscow office, were there to meet me. The car took me directly to the Soiuznaia Hotel on Maxim Gorki Street, where a large, attractive room had been reserved for me. The Hotel Lux was full and besides, Kuusinen didn't want to place me there because Manner, Hanna Malm, and a slew of other Mannerites lived there.

That same day the car took me to see Kuusinen. As befitted his rank—third or fourth secretary of the Comintern—he lived in the nationally known *Dom Pravitel'stva,* or "Government House." Kuusinen had reserved an entire afternoon for me so that he could review the situation and acquaint me with my coming lot.

Everything had been planned for me. I would remain in Moscow only long enough to watch the May Day festivities, then travel to a sanatorium to recuperate from the ailments acquired during my imprisonment. Now I had to concentrate all my energy on learning the Russian language; I had to learn enough to get along somehow on my sanatorium trip.

The thought of it brought on a nervous sweat, since I hardly knew the Russian alphabet and my aptitude for languages is not particularly commendable. But Kuusinen had it all worked out. He appointed his younger daughter Riikka to be my principal teacher; when Riikka tired or had no time, his elder daughter Hertta would take over.

"And remember that the instruction must above all be graphic," he said. "It's a new method and has proved very fruitful. Forget all the textbooks and formulas, like this!"

We sat there like schoolchildren, Hertta and Riikka and I, listening to father's lecture.

He walked slowly and purposefully to the door, seized the knob and said, *"Ia otkryvaiu"* as he opened the door.

After a long pause to see what effect it had on us, he said, *"Ia zakryvaiu"* and closed the door.

Admittedly the method was effective; in that single lesson I learned for all time how both to open and to close in Russian.

When I returned to the Soiuznaia late that night I had to woo sleep for a long time. Thoughts pursued one another through my head even to the borderline between wakefulness and sleep where the midnight bells of the Kremlin were pealing the "Internationale." I wondered whether they were ringing in happiness or misfortune for me and so dozed off.

I hadn't seen Kuusinen's daughters since my visit to Russia in 1927. Six years is a long time—or is for some. Hertta was now a different Hertta. Harsh experiences had changed the innocent, sweetly intelligent, playful young woman into what today is called a "hardboiled politician."

Riikka, too, had had her share of life's bitterness, but it had affected her differently. She had already dissolved her first marriage when she met a Bulgarian revolutionary student named Popov in Moscow during the early 1930s and married him. Around the time of my arrival in Moscow, Popov was being tried in the Supreme Court at Leipzig for the Reichstag fire in Berlin; the newspapers were full of the case in which three Bulgarians—Dimitrov, Popov, and Tanev—were charged with arson. Naturally, Riikka was disconsolate and wept now and then, for there seemed to be no hope of deliverance; the Bulgarian troika appeared doomed to be beheaded in the German manner in this conspiracy case staged by Hitler and Göring.

Riikka bore yet another heavy burden: she had been seriously ill with tuberculosis; one lung had undergone collapse therapy and, as I recall, so did the other. But it was as though these trying experiences had made her more sensitive than before, and she was quickly able to shake off her gloomy thoughts. She was an enchanting conversationalist, relaying gossip circulating in local circles and not hesitating to repeat even counterrevolutionary chitchat and jokes that people in politics would not have dreamed of circulating.

When she received the command from her father to teach me Russian, I could not have hoped for a more pleasant teacher. I have no flair for languages, and so I tried to take shortcuts, bypassing grammar. On those occasions Riikka tried to play the stern, firm teacher, but the real, warmhearted Riikka always won out, willing to try stretching the rules of grammar if only it would help me.

But on the occasions when Hertta took the reins, the teaching was tight and uncompromising; there were no digressions to nonessentials, no attempts to outwit the paradigms.

Kuusinen tried to make sure that his daughters did their duty and did not allow any idle talk. But six years had elapsed from our last meeting, and in that time so much had happened that he enlightened me whenever an opportune moment occurred.

After bringing me up to date on the conflict between Manner and himself, he shifted to a more important topic: developments within the Soviet Union and the Comintern. He spelled out clear guideposts: the head of the party was now Stalin; such men as Zinoviev and Kamenev were not worth mentioning, they were completely out of the game. He was absolutely sure of this. He knew something else as well: "Try not to refer very often to such old masters as Bukharin and Radek, for their stars, too, are fading."

This was complete news to me and certainly not welcome. I was especially taken with Bukharin, for in addition to a sharp mind and tongue he had deep compassion. Radek also was among my favorites and had been since I fell under the spell of his intelligence at the 1921 party congress when—with Kuusinen and Rovio acting as interpreters—I had talked with him more than any other congress participant. He was one of those scintillating persons around whom tales are spun. Kuusinen himself had told me earlier that Radek was able to dictate three articles simultaneously: pacing back and forth in his large office, he would dictate perhaps a political review to one typist, a cultural-political article to another, a satirical sketch to a third. Such tripartition of spirit seems impossible, but the same was said of Julius Caesar.

"True, Bukharin is the editor-in-chief of *Izvestiia* and Radek of *Pravda,* but their position really doesn't mean much," Kuusinen explained. "Actually, it's their downfall. They have been given such a responsible position the better to get evidence of their heresy. They have to write and pass on such volumes of public words that it will facilitate their hanging."

I looked at Moscow curiously to see the signs of the times. I had spent the summer months of 1921 there, a few days in 1927, about a week in 1928. Thus I had an impression of Moscow in the 1920s. In 1933 the city scene was noticeably different. Some new buildings had been erected, but the real change was in the traffic, which during the previous decade had been quiet. There were quite a few cars on the streets, some Russian but most of foreign make. In one respect the street scene had not changed for the better: clothing. The old-fashioned clothes of 1921 had been spruced up a bit during the NEP period; in fact, they had worsened since 1927.

Food was in extremely short supply. There had been a shortage in 1921 but on my next visits goods had been plentiful—they had even been in display windows—and people had said, "Buy this, buy that!" In the Moscow of 1933 what people said was, "You might be able to get some there . . ." and "I heard that you can get that there . . ." The shortage of goods was stupendous; only Torgsin, the store for foreigners, had anything available.

Friends asked me immediately whether I had any articles that might be taken to Torgsin, for it also accepted payment in gold objects such as watches, rings, and jewelry. The situation thus was not very encouraging, but I had not pictured anything better. Besides, I had lived in modest circumstances in Finland, too. All that was of secondary importance. I tried to concentrate on the most important, the essential fact: had this world changed conceptually, was it basically such as I had imagined it, was it precisely that for which it had been worth, and would be worth, making sacrifices?

And so, in exploring the conditions and studying the language and politics, time passed and May Day arrived. It has always been a great holiday in the Soviet Union, but during those years in particular the May Day parade was at its most impressive. It was well worth viewing, particularly since Kuusinen had gotten me a ticket for the row reserved for the Comintern Presidium, though at that time I had no position in the Comintern. The balcony of Lenin's mausoleum was reserved for members of the Politburo; I sat on the platform immediately below it. The festivities themselves have been described so often that it would be useless for me to waste good paper on them.

IN A SANATORIUM IN
THE CAUCASUS

THE DAY AFTER May Day a *putevka*—travel order—to the Frunze Sanatorium in Sochi was thrust into my hand, and Kuusinen himself came to the station to see me off. Naturally, the reservation was for the luxurious international car that was used by the Soviet elite, and fortuitously my compartment mate turned out to be a military man of high rank, whose collar tab bore two rhombuses—

in other words, he was a lieutenant general according to current grades, but in those days the army had not yet reverted to czarist ranks; he was a *komandir* and thus a division commander.

Kuusinen did not know him, but a man with such insignia had to be dependable, and so he introduced himself.

"Oh, yes, I know, I know!" smiled the *komandir* and was as charming as only a Russian at his best can be. "It's a great honor for me to meet such a famous person!"

During the conversation it turned out that the high-ranking soldier also was on his way to Sochi—not to my destination, true, but to the Red Army's officers' sanatorium. Kuusinen introduced me to him and explained that here was a man newly arrived from Finland who knew no Russian—perhaps Comrade *Komandir* would be so kind as to watch out for him until Sochi.

Comrade *Komandir* was enchanted at being able to perform a service for a Comintern secretary, and in fact he did take extraordinary care of me. He had a plentiful supply of food tucked away in his suitcase, for the army was well provisioned even during famines and officers especially so. In addition, we went periodically to the dining car, where it was out of the question that I should pay. Since I had had to travel in prison cars several times during recent years in my homeland, cars into whose tiny cells three and even four passengers were crammed, and whose chaperons differed considerably in appearance and behavior from the current one, the contrast was striking indeed. The scales tipped clearly in favor of the Soviet Union, my new fatherland.

Now I was on my way to a place about which every Soviet citizen dreams but few see. Sochi, Kislovodsk, Pyatigorsk, Essentuki, Zheleznovodsk, Gagra, Sukhumi—these are the names of small towns that he knows better than many considerably larger Russian cities. The small places are on the shores of the Black Sea or on the slopes of the Caucasus, and in them are spas at which princes and merchants had basked in their abundance and splendor, before the people seized the power. Now, of course, the people had the right to luxuriate and to relax their work-stiffened limbs, and those who managed affairs for the people made sure that the spas were well publicized. They even promised that if the people developed shock work to its utmost they would be able to enjoy all the delights.

Unfortunately, however, there weren't enough to go around, since the needs of the people's meritorious servants had to be met first. I too, stayed at spas for five summers.

These thoughts occurred to me only later. Then, traveling in the company of the friendly Comrade *Komandir,* I still had implicit faith and was exceedingly thankful to be allowed to see the wonders of the south—scenery that I could hardly have imagined.

True, certain events occurred that made me reflective. When we went to the dining car, I noticed that the curtains were drawn together tightly even in midday. I tried to part them but my chaperon hastened to stop me with *"Nyet, nyet!"* I noticed that the dining car personnel, too, made sure that the curtains were not opened. Comrade *Komandir*'s gestures and what I saw at the stations made me suspect the reason for such caution, and in Sochi I received a more detailed explanation. The stations were crowded with hungry people, mainly peasants, who broke the windows of the dining cars when they saw the elite sitting there eating. Nowadays everyone knows that the worst famine in the Soviet Union since the civil wars had begun in 1932, when the peasants refused to join collective farms and preferred to kill their cattle and horses. Those who were forced into the fields could accomplish little without draft animals and not nearly enough tractors were available then. Those not yet arrested loitered around the stations by the thousands, watching for an opportunity to move on to greener pastures.

I knew, of course, that there was want in my new homeland but I could not have imagined it to be as appalling as was evidenced in the masses of humans loitering about the stations, in the withered faces and hollow eyes, in the unfortunates so weakened by hunger that they could not stand. Even then I didn't comprehend fully how wretched their conditions actually were. When we occasionally stepped off the train to stretch our legs and I found myself drawn to those people in sympathy, my chaperon saw to it that I didn't touch them. In Sochi I was warned about the danger of getting spotted fever-transmitting lice from them. I needed that knowledge later, too, even in better times, as I crisscrossed Russia in my travels.

The most pathetic of all were the throngs of starving children— I soon learned the word *bezprizornye,* which means an abandoned, homeless child. The *bezprizornye,* who presented their own problem, traveled in armies, surviving better than the starving peasants, for they—these eight- to fifteen-year-old children—would form unscrupulous robber gangs that derailed trains, stole whatever they came across and did not hesitate even to murder. It was heartrending to see the smallest of them gather below the windows whenever the train reached a station, and with hands extended—sometimes making the sign of the cross—beg for a piece of bread. They could be found from the Moscow area all the way to the northern Caucasus perhaps because of the season, for the Russians themselves said that the *bezprizornye* moved with the seasons like crows; in the spring and summer they shifted to the north with the sun, and when summer faded into autumn they began their migration to the south.

One further fact that seemed odd to a newcomer: in Rostov some armed men boarded our car; two riflemen with fixed bayonets stationing themselves at either end. This soldierly action in peacetime amazed me, but my chaperon explained by various means that not only hungry peasants and swarms of *bezprizornye* roamed the Caucasian region but also large gangs of robbers who now and then would halt a train, rob it and even kill passengers. I don't know whether the regular cars were provided with four riflemen each, but at least the lives of us better folk were taken care of.

After several days we arrived at Sochi, the number one watering place in the Soviet Union. The Frunze Sanatorium bus was at the station to pick up those destined for that place, but my chaperon, Comrade *Komandir,* did not permit me to board it. Instead, he brought me there in a passenger car from the Red Army's sanatorium and took care of my registration personally.

Influence exists throughout the world, but nowhere does it mean as much as in the Soviet Union. When such a bigwig made a fuss about me—who knows what all he said!—it was reflected in the reception I got. I was surrounded by the respect and interest due a personage, and as my roommate I was given a high political commissar who assumed my guardianship from Comrade *Komandir.* I must mention, however, that I also had with me an exceptionally good recommendation from Kuusinen. When Kuusinen took care of a matter he usually did it thoroughly.

My life unfolded as pleasantly as a person who did not speak the language could possibly wish. The very next day after breakfast the guests at the sanatorium held a meeting in the garden to decide who should take this Finn under his wing. A university professor, an old party man who seemed to have considerable authority, volunteered to give me a half-hour lesson in grammar every day. A youthful, very attractive woman was designated to give me practical exercises. When we gathered together for the distribution of assignments, my progress was checked at the same time. No wonder that the listeners laughed when I uninhibitedly put forth my best efforts. Heaven knows what vulgarities I rattled off in my innocence, for at times the laughter must have carried across the Black Sea all the way to Turkey.

Thus the intervals between the daily sulphur baths—at the famous sulphur springs of Matshesta, some three miles from Sochi—the medical examinations and the rest periods were devoted to language lessons and recreation. For five successive years I spent five or six weeks each summer at a sanatorium, but this first two-month period was absolutely the most delightful. Later I spoke the language well enough to mingle more freely with the others, but at the same time it created certain inhibitions, and the Russian warmth and friendliness likewise did not bubble forth as profusely as it had toward a helpless monoglot.

By a pleasant coincidence, only a week later Eero Haapalainen and his wife arrived at the neighboring sanatorium that was dedicated to Lenin. Hearing about me, they immediately came over—less than a mile separated the sanatoriums—and thereafter Eero came daily to visit me and I to see him. He was an indispensable interpreter during the medical examinations.

Eero Haapalainen, the commander-in-chief of the Red Guard in Finland's civil war, had had a reputation as a rip-roaring boozer, but now he was completely changed, a man marked by disease. Vodka was generally not used in the sanatoriums or for that matter in the region as a whole, but it is hardly likely that he could have tolerated it anyway. He not only had a serious heart disease but had already had one cerebral hemorrhage that had incapacitated him for a while. Now he was in a fairly good condition, and subsequently I met him many times in Petrozavodsk, where he held important positions in the Karelian Soviet Republic. He lived long enough to be imprisoned and sent on the road of no return.

Of course I asked him immediately what the experiences during my journey there signified. Instead of rejoicing crowds at the stations cheering Stalin and me, there had been only wretched, starving, apathetic masses. How had the country come to such a pass?

Haapalainen tried to smooth things over. This is just temporary, he said. Next year it'll be a lot better and the following year, by and large, we'll have achieved the anticipated ideal society.

I got an even better interpreter some time later, when Kustaa Rovio, "Czar of Karelia," arrived at the Frunze Sanatorium and remained there to the end of my stay. He was an exceptional guide and interpreter and as a person one of the finest. My loneliness had disappeared; I was living in clover.

And why shouldn't I have been? Stalin's collectivization drive had resulted in a food shortage; bread and other commodities were scarce, but here in the big shots' sanatorium there was plenty of everything. Even the rooms were first-rate, by Russian standards, and the buildings were well constructed. The staff was large and well screened to assure the safety of our lives. All belonged to the GPU except perhaps for the cleaning women and the doctors. Although few of the doctors were party members, they were nevertheless politically trustworthy.

Kuusinen had enlightened me about this fact, too, by pointing out that only inferior doctors belonged to the party. Once in 1922 he had complained to Lenin about not feeling well and had asked, "Could you recommend a dependable doctor who is a party member?"

"Under no circumstances are you to go to such a doctor!" Lenin had cried. "We can't afford to lose you. You are still needed. Go see an old czarist-time specialist. Most of them are capable and even now do conscientious work. The party's doctor members are cutthroats, bunglers; that's why they've joined the party."

The physicians at Sochi thus guarded our bodies and souls against internal ruin. But in addition, holding down all kinds of assumed duties such as sports and outing instructors, were the GPU functionaries who closely followed the activities of their charges. Whoever entered the gate immediately came under the complete protection of the state.

I said that Sochi was number one among the watering places in the Soviet Union. That, like everything else under the sun, may be debated. At any rate, Sochi's advantages included the sulphur baths at Matshesta, which were excellent for heart disease and rheumatic pains. To what degree those who really needed help could benefit from them was another matter, since the upper classes kept Matshesta's bathtubs occupied. Second, Sochi had its "Riviera," which world travelers claimed to be fully equal to the real Riviera in natural beauty. Third, only a few miles from Frunze was the small private palace in which Stalin himself spent autumns. He arrived usually in October and remained until the festivities of November 7. At other times he would come only after the festivities and take care of his health until around Christmas.

These reasons account for Sochi's high standing. In the same area, just above Frunze and built into the side of the mountain, were the Red Army's huge sanatoriums. When the officers had swum in the Black Sea, an escalator returned them to their heights. A little beyond was the miners' handsome sanatorium to which the Stakhanovite shock-workers were admitted.

I have often been asked whether I met the cream of Soviet aristocracy at these sanatoriums. If by that is meant the finest whipping cream, the ten or twelve members of the Politburo, I must reply in the negative. Stalin stayed at his small palace; the rest, I don't know where. But the regular whipping cream enjoyed life in the same sanatoriums as I. Frunze and Lenin in particular were of the highest class, and especially exalted was the Stalin Sanatorium in Zheleznovodsk, on the side of the Iron Mountain, where I spent two summers. These mountain sanatoriums are not in the Caucasus itself but rather in the foothills, which are of volcanic origin and have many kinds of mineral springs.

Each sanatorium had its own garb, a hospital smock in which we went to drink mineral water or to attend concerts. The Stalin Sanatorium's was no fancier than the others, just an ordinary gray gown, but when it was observed among the others a rustle could be heard: a "chosen person" is amongst us! Those who did not wish to attract attention wore their own pajamas. This garment was, in fact, high fashion. In the afternoons, when we assembled for an outdoor concert after drinking mineral water, a third of the audience wore gaudy pajamas. The same was true at the evening concerts.

Also indicative of the special status of the Stalin Sanatorium was the fact that only about forty patients were admitted simultaneously, whereas many others might have four or five hundred, and its staff outnumbered the patients.

The residents of the community had no business in the sanatoriums, for a deep chasm separated them from the privileged class. Only those who had been given permission had the right to be in them; neither money nor honeyed words opened their doors. And when one belonged to these chosen best, as I did, the stay at the sanatorium included a free round trip, which, for security reasons, included the stipulation that the travel be first class. Society had to insure the lives of its elite members. Deification of the leader also resulted in deification of the leaders.

How things are now I do not know. Perhaps new winds have tempered class contrasts, bringing more social equality to the Soviet Union.

THE STALIN CANAL

AFTER RETURNING to Moscow from Sochi I went immediately to greet Kuusinen at the *Dom Pravitel'stva*. There, by a pleasant coincidence, I met the prime minister of Karelia, Edvard Gylling, who was visiting Moscow briefly.

When we had exchanged the latest news, he came right to the point.

"As soon as I heard of your arrival here it occurred to me that you would be a suitable man for Karelia," he said.

As a matter of fact, when I decided my fate by opting for Russia, I had thought of going to Karelia.

"Fine, I'll come gladly," I replied, "but I wouldn't care for any of your high positions. It would be good if you could arrange to get me a job as a bridge or track watchman."

Gylling looked at me seriously and observed, "Quite so; that's the kind of job I myself have wanted for a long time, since in many ways it would be the best. But, frankly speaking, the fact is that in this country people like you and me really can't have any other occupation than that of people's commissar or something comparable, or than be in jail or on the gallows. There is no alternative."

The words didn't sound at all pleasant, especially since there wasn't the slightest hint of playfulness in Gylling's tone. At that time I was not as familiar with the facts as I would be after a few years.

Kuusinen had listened to the conversation with his usual paternal smile and then broke in, "Well, now, what has Poika done to warrant his exile to Karelia? I've been thinking that he should remain here in Moscow, since people are badly needed for party work here."

Gylling flared up. "That's really terrible, that attitude of the Finnish Communist party! You hear how even Kuusinen betrays himself: only people who have done something wrong, who have failed elsewhere, are sent to Karelia. No wonder that all those incapable of work have accumulated there. Alcoholics have been sent there, and since they can't be taken care of in Petrozavodsk and there are no alcoholic treatment facilities, I've had my hands full. I've sent scores of drunkards to Uhtua and Kiestinki, where there's little chance of getting liquor. They're talented and skilled men, but all they do there is drink, making all kinds of excuses for sending people to Petrozavodsk to buy them liquor, and if they can't get any they distill it themselves."

Kuusinen only laughed at Gylling's sermon. Prime minister though he was, Gylling nevertheless was several rungs below Kuusinen in authority. Kuusinen's will always prevailed.

A few days later I traveled to Petrozavodsk, where my wife and I spent the rest of the summer as Gylling's guests. While at the sanatorium I had written to my wife, who had arrived in the Soviet Union several months after me, advising her to go to Karelia since that was my own objective.

Kuusinen had granted me the trip to Petrozavodsk as a kind of summer vacation until I would enter the Lenin School in mid-September. He deemed it best that I receive theoretical training at the highest political institute in the Soviet Union to strengthen my position and authority. Only then would I be qualified for the duties that he presumably was already planning for me.

My trip to Petrozavodsk occurred as opportunely as one could wish. History had been made in that region and I happened on the spot to view the drama as from the director's box.

Waterways have always been important because it is possible to transport more for less by water. Canals, which shorten distances, were being planned as soon as navigation had developed to any degree. The idea of linking the White Sea and the Baltic with a canal had glimmered in the minds of generations, especially since the numerous rivers and lakes of eastern Karelia actually encouraged the building of a canal. Czar Peter I is said to have moved the small warships of those days along chains of lakes from the White Sea to Lake Ladoga. During the last century the possibility of constructing a canal was studied many times, and finally, in 1914, the czarist government decided to start work on it; however, the project was dropped with the outbreak of World War I.

When the Soviet government undertook the task in the fall of 1931, the anticommunist world did not expect to hear of any results for a long time. The old saying, "Do it the Russky way," still held true in Russia, and if an achievement was announced it was usually sheer propaganda. Great was the amazement when, after less than two years, the canal was said to be by and large completed. After all, its length was about 140 miles—37 miles longer than even the Suez! It may be pointed out that there are 65 miles of excavated channel in the Suez Canal and only 29 miles in the White Sea Canal, but the Suez, which has no locks, was under construction for twelve whole years. The Panama Canal, built with American dollars, took seven years. No matter from how "bourgeois" an angle one drew comparisons, one had to admit that the construction of the White Sea Canal was a tremendous achievement.

My faith in communism's possibilities as the builder of a new and better world had in no way been shaken, but such proof of its creative strength was nevertheless welcome, since it once and for all negated its opponents' derision. When I arrived in Petrozavodsk in midsummer of 1933, the canal already was at such a stage that the first vessel could pass through it. The passengers were Stalin and his heir apparent at the time, Kirov—Zinoviev's successor as the ruler of Leningrad—as well as some notables from the Politburo, and it was on that voyage that the waterway received its official name: the Stalin Canal.

A few days later another voyage was arranged, this time for the directors of Leningrad's largest factories, high party bosses, and officers. Gylling and Rovio were among the invited, but Gylling was unable to accept and suggested that I accompany Rovio. Rovio made a few telephone calls to the upper echelons and got permission for me to go.

A whiff of history surrounded us already on the rail trip from Petrozavodsk to Karhumäki (Medvezh'ia Gora), as we were riding in a special Karelian government car that twenty years earlier had served the Russian imperial family. True, the history had a musty odor, must like the thick old velvet that was used even in the lavatory, where one sat as on a throne.

In Karhumäki we were welcomed by the chief of the local GPU— successor to the Cheka—who had been the overseer of the canal construction. Since the work was supervised by GPU men, the chief supervisor of the entire project was nominally Yagoda, but he had not visited the canal until now with Stalin. Considering the Russian manner of construction, the local boss lived in quite a luxurious two-story villa in the center of the town of Karhumäki, right near the station. Lodgings had been arranged for us there as Rovio was the highest chief of the Karelian party organization and, according to the Russian pecking order at that time, the top man in Karelia. He belonged to the expanded Executive Committee of the Soviet government, and such a man was somebody prior to the Stalin Constitution of 1936.

The invited guests even included Demyan Bedny, Stalin's court poet, who upon request—or demand—wrote hymns of praise to the peoples' leader. Apparently the post was profitable, since the over-sixty-year-old poet was quite corpulent and his twenty-year-old wife was exceptionally beautiful. An even more interesting acquaintance was one of the two top engineers accompanying us. It was he who had done the actual technical planning of the canal from the beginning. His name was Frenckell and his lineage went back to Finland.

We then moved to the dinner table, which, naturally, was typically Russian, with endless amounts of food. Russians don't practice moderation; there must have been enough to feed thirty or forty persons, though there may be no more than seven or eight diners, and eat one must lest one offend the hosts.

The GPU chief lectured at length to Rovio and me, who were not familiar with those matters, on the canal, its construction, and its political significance. The undertaking was unique in the whole world, he said, and the first even in the Soviet Union; the entire canal had been built with human material that cannot be utilized in the capitalist world: prison labor. An average of sixty thousand prisoners had worked the whole time: one man every ten feet on that 140-mile stretch. And thus was created a channel which, if deepened a little, could be used even by large warships.

Then he gave the floor to Frenckell and urged the engineer to tell his own story. Frenckell was fifty or perhaps a little younger, slim and calm, whose manner of speaking contrasted sharply with the Russian's bustling, ebullient style. He said that he had worked as a factory engineer and been arrested in 1929 in the so-called industrial saboteurs' case. He received the death penalty that was, however, commuted to ten years at hard labor—the maximum sentence a prisoner received in those days. He was sent to the infamous prison camp at Solovetskiye and had given up all hope when one day he was called in to see the camp commandant.

"You are known to be a skilled engineer. How would you, together with the other engineers here, like to undertake the planning of a canal between Lake Onega and the White Sea?"

He said that, to a prisoner condemned to die, such an offer at first seemed a mockery, but when the commandant proved to be serious, the offer also had to be taken seriously. After considering the matter briefly, he said that he consented and thereafter was given every opportunity to devote himself to the task.

I told him that it didn't seem natural for a saboteur condemned to death to undertake such a grandiose construction job for the Soviet Union. He said that he fully understood my skepticism, but that with his nature the challenge of such a gigantic task easily dissipated his depression and bitterness over the injustice he had suffered. The explanation seemed credible since the magnitude of the project undoubtedly had fascinated such a creative professional, despite the deep bitterness that he must have felt toward a system that had been about to destroy his life and had destroyed tens of thousands of his colleagues over the years.

The GPU chief tried to prompt Frenckell to give some recognition to Soviet prisons and remarked that this prominent communist leader from Finland—meaning me—had sat in the prisons of a capitalist country for ten years and undoubtedly could tell some harrowing tales. I took the floor and briefly enlightened them about the hardships and wretchedness of prison life in Finland. People died there, as two had in a recent hunger strike. This did not affect Frenckell in the slightest; he merely observed that prison conditions in every country are trying and harsh and drew no comparisons.

At that time he was the technical director of the canal *kombinat*, and his task was to plan hydroelectric plants at the larger waterfalls. A handsome villa near that of the GPU chief had been built for him, and he had received a full pardon during the construction of the canal, though the formal pardon had been granted only upon its completion. During Stalin's visit there the chief supervisor had received what was then the highest honor, the Order of Lenin. It had been bestowed on Frenckell as well, and he wore it stylishly on the breast of his tunic. With his splendid patent leather boots he looked for all the world like a high GPU officer. He told us that his family had arrived in Karhumäki several days earlier; now he was leading a happy life after his arduous years.

These reports and the GPU chief's superb hospitality made me highly interested in the great achievements. Above all, Frenckell's case had made a deep impression. A person who was hopeless from the viewpoint of the Soviet state had been dragged from beyond death's portals and given colossal work to do. Nowhere but in the Soviet Union could that happen!

When the court poet had retired to rest after the good dinner, or perhaps to write a new poem to Stalin or the GPU chief, and Frenckell and the other engineers had returned to their own villas, we three—Rovio, the GPU chief, and I—were left alone. Our host was in excellent spirits and eager to hear more about Finnish prissons. Life in them must be unbearable—was it possible that I had spent ten years in prison? I tried to ease matters by explaining that I hadn't spent them in one stretch but had been allowed to take a breather. He could not believe that anyone could spend ten years in jail and remain alive.

Since I had not the slightest reason or desire to gild prison conditions in Finland, I told him as much as I could without being unfair. My account left the impression that I had suffered an injustice.

He offered a consolation. "Don't worry, we've avenged you here, too. When you pass through this magnificent canal you will realize that it didn't come about effortlessly. Every prop pounded into the canal walls speaks of redress to those who have suffered unjustly; those beams edging the canal have been put in place with sweat and blood."

This concluding conversation no longer was as inspiring as the one during dinner had been.

As dawn broke the next day our festive journey began. The paddlewheel steamer *Karl Marx* had arrived from Leningrad to Povenets the night before, bringing with it ten more invited guests, the cream of this northern region. The steamer was quite spacious and its tidy cabins were most comfortable. At every lock a festal gateway had been built, decorated with bunting and garlands that also adorned the edges of the canal. The entire forty-eight-hour passage was one continuous flowery, gala affair. We paused at almost every lock for longer than required by the raising or lowering of the boat. A meeting was held, attended by a number of officials and workers, someone on the steamer made a little speech, and usually the local GPU chief described the achievements.

Only a very few dwellings were visible along the canal route and they were near the locks; there was not a trace of the workers' barracks for they, too, were farther back. Everything had been built of wood; cement had been used scarcely at all. One could not even imagine how many millions of trees had been used to line those long and deep canals with logs. And what logs they were, the straightest and thickest Karelian pine, all rounded and tarred! The locks also were wooden and operated manually. The intention was to operate them electrically but as it was now, four or five men cranked them by hand.

Along the entire route rivers and rapids and lakes had been deepened and straightened. One man-made lake took six hours to traverse. From Lake Onega it was all a series of ascents until we reached a high plateau with the greatly enlarged Lake Vygozero. It was many times larger than previously, and the Murmansk track had had to be moved almost twenty miles. The lake was surrounded by a forest from which 100,000 trees had been felled for logs. They were to have been moved to Sorokka for sawing but had already lain in the water for two years. Many of them undoubtedly had sunk, yet, as our boat passed through, others floated from shore to shore as far as the eye could see. Later I heard that most of them remained in Lake Vygozero as sunken logs.

The workers who actually had built the canal were nowhere to be seen, though it might be said of someone in passing that he had worked on the canal and was now a lock operator. GPU function-aries were numerous, and the majority of those in civilian clothes had been brought there later. The work force of 60,000 men had been removed completely, and when I inquired as to their present whereabouts I was told that many were on the Volga-Moscow canal.

As we began the descent to the White Sea, we met a Finnish man during a meeting at one of the locks. He was an American Finn, a lock operator, who wore relatively good civilian clothes and did not appear undernourished.* I made a speech in Finnish on that occasion, and Rovio translated it. After the speech the American Finn came over to see me. We were free to talk with whomever we wished, and since nobody seemed to notice that we spoke Fin-nish, we were able to chat undisturbed for quite a while. At first he warily told us how he and another American Finn had been sent as prisoners to Solovetskiye and then, a year and a half ago, had been brought to work on the canal. To his knowledge the labor force included many Finnish prisoners, some of whom were from America, the others Communists from Finland. At one time the sector on which he had worked had ten Finns, but only he and one other were still alive. He said that he had had a comparatively easy time of it during those eighteen months, which explained why he had survived.

Rovio and I urged the man to unburden his heart, and finally he did speak quite fearlessly, telling us that for at least the past year and a half this entire crew had lived in wretched temporary bar-racks during the winter and under the stars or in tents during the summer. The workers were divided into individual crews, each

---

* 5,000 to 7,000 Finns from the United States went to the Soviet Union, most of them during the depression years. In the early 1950s I met a few of them in New York. One young man told me that about five hundred of those who had not accepted Soviet citizenship had been able to return. "What happened to the rest of them?" I asked. "Bullet to the head and dirt into the mouth," he answered.—P.H.

under the surveillance of trustees. If so much as one prisoner escaped, the trustees knew that they themselves would be shot. There
were not many GPU guards. In his crew of several hundred men,
for example, there were only four or five uniformed GPU guards,
but for each ten prisoners there were two or three trustees. Because
these crews often penetrated the depths of the forests to fell and
strip the trees needed in building the canal, the GPU guards would
not have sufficed. Just enough food was given the men to keep
them alive, and the sanitary conditions were indescribable. Spotted
fever and typhoid raged, and scurvy was prevalent.

Then he told us a peculiar thing: the prisoners were divided
into three categories, and each group was allotted a different
amount of food for exactly the same work. He had belonged to a
group with relatively high food norms, whereas the other groups
had received less food for the same work. We asked what had determined this allocation. He explained that the death of destructive
elements—the intelligentsia and the worst kind of kulaks, farmers
characterized by Communists as having excessive wealth—was considered in no way undesirable for the Soviet state. On the other
hand, criminals and those sentenced for minor political offenses
were in a far more favorable position. The work norms were so
formidable that only the strongest could fulfill them. When the
norms were not met, food allowances were cut, and decreased food
in turn made one susceptible to infectious diseases. And once a
man entered the hospital barracks, it was like entering a cemetery.

The American Finn said with a little laugh, "It's pleasant for
you to pass through the canal and see the festive receptions at these
locks, but if you could go farther back it would be a different story.
You would see the bodies of thousands of forced laborers. They're
not even in regular graves, just buried like animals."

He did not sound especially bitter; in fact, he explained that the
most difficult times had been his stay in the Solovetskiye prison
and the first days at the labor camp.

"Now I'm in a better position. I'm being pardoned and freed,
and one can't be very bitter when the worst is behind one."

This conversation nevertheless dispelled much of the gala feeling
from both Rovio and me and diminished the favorable impression
created by the early part of the voyage. Thereafter we never again

made speeches at these meetings. They were not really mandatory.

We arrived at Sorokka, the end of the canal, and continued our journey to Kem. Not even Rovio, the "Czar of Karelia" and its long-time highest official, had ever been there. As a specialist on prison conditions, I wanted above all to investigate matters in that field, and so Rovio had obtained a permit for us to enter Solovetskiye. We contacted the GPU chief in Kem, who also was the assistant director of the Solovetskiye camp. By a coincidence, the head of the camp was in Kem just as we arrived.

He was visiting his assistant and said to us immediately, "You can't go to Solovetskiye after all. I know about your permit but unfortunately I must forbid your going because there's an outbreak of spotted fever and it wouldn't be healthy for you."

To no avail, we tried to assure him that we weren't afraid of spotted fever and that we had every intention of going there if there was no other obstacle. He was, however, ready to describe conditions at Solovetskiye as much as we wanted to know and furthermore, instead of Solovetskiye, he offered to allow us to familiarize ourselves with the prison camp at Kem, if we wished.

We spent one full day in the familiarization process, and that was more than enough. At that time there were said to be about eight thousand prisoners in the camp at Kem, and that was considered a small number. It was a kind of screening center to which prisoners were brought from Solovetskiye and through which others were sent there. Prisoners were sent from Kem to the various work camps, most of them in the Karelian forests, while those who had been brought here from other work camps were sent to Solovetskiye.

In Solovetskiye there were an estimated forty thousand prisoners. These numbers, like the Russians' numbers in general, were not to be considered accurate. I did feel, however, that these men tried to give as truthful a picture as possible since they wanted to show me in particular how enemies were dealt with in the Soviet Union and always would be.

When they learned at the beginning of our conversation that I was a prison expert, both GPU chiefs enthusiastically explained their system. They immediately stressed the fact that neither the camp at Kem nor the one at Solovetskiye was a correctional institution in the manner of youth and criminal prisons, where people were rehabilitated. No, those brought to these prisons were people for whom there was little hope.

The day which we spent at the Kem camp sufficed to prove that the prisoners themselves had no hope, either. The camp was like a living graveyard; the people were apathetic, had no desire to answer questions and seemed utterly without hope. When I watched the summer life at the Kem barracks—some of the prisoners were at work, others lay in their barracks or in the yard—I recalled the trying months in Finland during the summer of 1918. The worst prison camps were in Hennala and Tammisaari, but I had to admit that this camp was much worse even than those in Finland.

The only bright spot in the Kem institution was the youth camp filled with juveniles between the ages of twelve and sixteen. Conditions there were noticeably better, and the camp itself was separated in another part of the city. Cultural life of a sort was provided there to interest the viewer.

After we had concluded our visit and returned to the camp director's imposing home to relate our impressions of the day, neither of us could refrain from saying how terrible it all was. The people were all on the verge of death from starvation, and it was apparent that all were ill both physically and psychically.

The director said specifically to me, since he knew Rovio personally from an earlier time, "This is how it is here. As an old Communist, you tell me how they handle class enemies in a capitalist country. Isn't the objective there, too, to get rid of them? It would be useless to support and feed them; best just to get whatever use from them one can. These people here in the Kem camp and at Solovetskiye are the worst elements, enemies of society. In the first place, when the collective farms were being set up, all the kulaks were to be liquidated on orders of Comrade Stalin. Three million of them were arrested and brought to camps. Surely you don't imagine that these kulaks could become good Soviet peasants? Certainly not, at least not at this camp. If someone manages to leave here alive, he won't praise these conditions. The rest of the bunch here is also worthless, mostly members of the intelligentsia. It's sheer chance if we happen to get elements that might prove useful if they manage to survive. It's only natural that those here are allowed to perish. It's different with the young people; there's hope for them, even though they have followed a path of crime. The reasons for that were not political but something else. These adults are, without exception, such trash that it's best just to squeeze what one can out of them and then toss them into a hole."

He had been an overseer on the canal during much of the construction period and declared that the work force had contained very little material from which something would yet develop. Of those prisoners who survived to the end, those sentenced for criminal acts were pardoned, but those for political crimes were not, and he surmised that among the criminal prisoners there might be some who could even be useful to the Soviet Union.

The sum and substance of that ghastly recital was that, if we want to maintain the Soviet power, such elements must be imprisoned, and once they are imprisoned we cannot even think of keeping huge masses of people in camps for a score or more of years; it is only sensible and sound to put them to work digging canals and felling Karelian forests and to schedule the work in such a way as to get rid of them gradually.

After the war, when accounts were published of Germany's frightful camps, Buchenwald and others, with their gas chambers, I always saw in my mind's eye a picture of the Stalinist gas chambers which were even more diabolical, for everything possible was wrung from the people working on the canal projects, forests, and road construction jobs in the full knowledge that they would die there anyway. If someone somehow survived one work camp, he would not survive another. All the huge projects in the Soviet Union have been built with such labor, and in each case the average number of workers may have been annihilated several times. No one was able to provide precise statistics on the total number of lives expended on the construction of the Stalin Canal, but if figures were mentioned, they ranged from sixty thousand to two hundred thousand, all of whom perished. When one considers that sixty thousand people worked for approximately two years, and that most individuals did not survive for more than a year, these figures did not seem unreasonable.

Only then did I realize that this was all systematically planned. Prisoners had become one segment of the labor force in the Soviet Union, and the most grandiose works were constructed by them. After speaking to people at various places and watching the work with my own eyes, I knew that the phenomenon was not merely the manifestation of some GPU chief's zeal to destroy class enemies but a deliberate policy adopted at the highest levels of government.

Although this system had been in effect since Stalin became firmly entrenched, how was it that foreigners could be kept in the dark about it until Khrushchev finally revealed the truth in his speech of 1956? The answer is comparatively simple.

A prisoner who escaped from the horrors of such a work camp might well have given appalling accounts of his experiences, but they would not have been taken seriously on the assumption that either the embittered escapee is lying, or that newspaper reports were exaggerated. But what happens when the outside world arrives to see for itself?

Gylling and Rovio related that one of their most difficult administrative tasks had been a project they had had to undertake during the great world depression of 1931–32. In the Karelian forests almost all the timber was cut by prison labor. An uproar arose in England's House of Commons: England must not buy lumber from the Soviet Union because it is the product of slave labor. The British government appointed a three-member commission to investigate whether or not slave labor was used. When they departed, the Soviet Union was notified that a three-member delegation would arrive to investigate the matter.

Then a monstrous order came to the Karelian government from Kirov in Leningrad: within forty-eight hours all prison labor had to be removed from the route to be traveled by the commission and be replaced by as much free labor as possible. It seemed hopeless, since thousands of workers were involved. The removal of the prisoners was easy; they were driven so deep into the forest as to be inaccessible, but the acquisition of free labor was another matter. Where could enough people be obtained to give the impression of a real lumbering operation? Factories in Petrozavodsk, collective farms, and other sources of free labor were emptied.

Thus, when the commission traveled through the Karelian timber areas, it did not see a single slave laborer. The Englishmen were allowed to talk freely with the workers, each of whom could attest to the fact that he was a free person, come there from a factory or a collective farm, but not one mentioned when he had arrived.

It did not occur to the Englishmen to inquire about that, and even if they had, the workers had been coached to say that they had been at that particular site for years.

This feat was anything but easy to accomplish, and Gylling and Rovio received the thanks of the top Soviet leadership for their success. Not all the Soviet citizens were even aware that such a system existed. They knew only that millions of people had disappeared, that many of their relatives had vanished without a trace, but that was the extent of their knowledge, for they were not allowed to correspond with anyone who had been taken into custody; detainees were irrevocably dead to relatives. Thus, no one dared make inquiries; instead, everyone tried to forget and to dissociate himself from questionable relatives and acquaintances as soon as possible.

Under such circumstances one realizes why an "Iron Curtain" became essential, and why it was sealed almost hermetically in the mid-1930s. If a foreign worker had somehow been able to familiarize himself with even a fraction of that system he would have been aghast. If even a few of those millions of prisoners had been freed from the forced labor camps and managed to go abroad, what testimony it would have been against Stalin's system! Now and then someone did get out, but if he dared say anything about those conditions, his words were branded lies and he himself was labeled a tool of the capitalists.

Thus, day after day, it was possible to assert that Russia was a democratic country where the worker was free; a free state with no unemployment. Since this is one of the capitalist countries' greatest scourges, the significance of the propaganda is obvious: there exists one country with no unemployment. Had the truth been known, the world would have realized that there was no unemployment in the days of serfdom either, and that jails and prison camps were the Soviet Union's solution to unemployment.

A significant part of the Soviet Union's gigantic projects thus was created with slave labor, and even the so-called free labor force was no longer as free after 1938 as it had been prior to that, since not a single worker or official had enough freedom to change jobs at will. Thus, even those who were not in concentration camps were bound to their places of employment; every work camp was, in other words, a prison camp, and these came in various degrees of harshness, the worst kind being the Solovetskiye and Kem type, in which most of the prisoners were winnowed after only two or three years into the group doomed to perish.

Such was life in the Russia of Stalin's day.

THE LENIN SCHOOL IN MOSCOW

IN THE EARLY 1920s the Executive Committee of the Comintern founded the Lenin School in Moscow as a true communist institution of higher learning on an international scale. It began as quite a modest affair with perhaps several dozen students, then expanded year by year until it became an international political college with nearly a thousand students.

Over the years well over a dozen different sectors had been formed, the most important being the Chinese, German, French, English, and Spanish, the last of which included South Americans. The English sector included North Americans; the Scandinavian sector encompassed Iceland, Sweden, Norway, and Denmark. Italy, Romania, Yugoslavia, Greece, Bulgaria, and Czechoslovakia had their own sectors. The Finnish sector was fairly large, with about forty students at a maximum. One sector was missing, however: that of the Soviet Union.

In the largest courses—the Chinese, German, and Spanish—the number of students could be estimated at a hundred, perhaps even more. Since there were more than a dozen sectors, the total enrollment probably rose to around one thousand. The school never published a yearbook in which the pseudonymous students would have been listed or even their total number mentioned, and I did not try to find out on my own. It was not wise to poke one's nose into such matters. Excessive curiosity would have attracted undue attention.

The course lasted two years. It was presumed that the student had previous schooling, for example at the University of National Minorities of the West in Leningrad, the first training school for professional revolutionary cadres. But there were also those whose knowledge of spelling was found to be questionable upon their arrival. Spelling obviously could not be included officially in the curriculum at a college, but the problem was solved by having the brighter students tutor the semiliterate after hours.

At Kuusinen's initiative—naturally—an agreement had been reached with the administrators whereby my prison studies and other experience would compensate for the academic background that I lacked, allowing me to complete both courses within a year. Thus I accelerated the first-year course, transferred to the second course already before Christmas and in the spring of 1934 received a diploma as a graduate of the Lenin School after one year's study.

Upon completion of the course I became secretary general of the Finnish Communist party and a little later a member of the Comintern Presidium. From the fall of 1934 I also served as a regular lecturer at the school until 1936, when the course's male students were sent to Spain's so-called international brigade. My subjects were mainly the history of the Finnish labor movement and the trade union movement.

The primary subjects naturally were historical materialism, Leninism, and the history of the Soviet Union's Communist party. There was much emphasis on practical instruction, such as the technique of holding meetings and the tactics of taking over organizations.

In addition to the practical art of seizure, conspiracy was a continuing, regular subject. Specifically, students were taught how to do undercover party work, how covert recruitment takes place, how to use codes and so forth. Among those teaching coding was Hertta Kuusinen, Otto Wille Kuusinen's daughter, who had received special training at the corresponding section of the Comintern.

The technique of instigating revolts and organizing street riots and fights was always taught by Hertta's husband, Tuure Lehén, when he happened to be in town. A substitute took over whenever he himself was making revolts in other countries.

The training of Finns was considered highly important in the Soviet Union. According to the accepted theory, the failure of the 1918 revolt in Finland was due to the lack of trained revolutionary leaders. In the event of another revolution in Finland, there should be hundreds, preferably thousands, of them in reserve. To this end systematic and purposeful training had been under way since the beginning of the 1920s.

The first Finns, several hundred of them, were taught in Petrograd at the University of National Minorities of the West. Similar seats of learning were in Karelia. Besides the usual schools, there were many teachers' colleges and propaganda institutes at which some Finns always were being trained especially for Finland. In addition, Petrozavodsk had an "agricultural college" in which agriculture did not play much of a part but politics did.

In Petrograd there was also a military school whose student body was almost entirely Finnish, with only a few Estonians among them. It began functioning in the early 1920s and did not close until 1936. The number of Red commanders trained in this school rose into the hundreds. Naturally, politics was one of the subjects but the primary focus of the school was military.

When the Red Army attacked Finland in 1939, there were 250 saboteurs in the country, all trained in Soviet schools. Since I was still secretary general of the Finnish Communist party, they were at my disposal. I could have told them to blow up bridges, blow up factories, do this and that. But I told them just the opposite, that no one was to do anything like that; rather, that the country must be defended. There was, in fact, no sabotage in Finland during the Winter War.

A considerable part of the subjects and methods taught at the Lenin School were adopted in Finland after World War II by the Communists' Sirola Institute. It is an adaptation of the Lenin School, primped up a bit to make it acceptable to the ministry of education for government aid as a continuation school. Instruction on fomenting rebellions and taking over labor movements is concealed behind some other title.

The Lenin School was a highly unusual institution in that a revolutionary spirit, a true communist cadre spirit, had been implanted in it with great skill. Nevertheless, nationalism between the various sectors could reach such heights that at times there was danger of hand-to-hand combat. The students competed for three red flags, one given for academic achievement, another for physical culture, the third for intellectual achievement. Between 1934–36 the Finns won all three flags.

These achievements were duly noted at the meetings of the

Comintern Executive Committee and Manuilski or Dimitrov [president and secretary general of Comintern] had to concede that the same sector which achieved such outstanding results last year has renewed them this year. Nothing seemed to help. When Dimitrov became the Comintern's secretary general in 1935, he ordered the sector of his own country, Bulgaria, to win for the sake of its own honor and his prestige. The Bulgarians did distinguish themselves during the school year 1935–36 but nevertheless were not able to best the Finns.

Typically, when the competition was at its keenest in sports or culture, the big shots of the Comintern came to the aid of their sectors. Pieck and Florin and Ulbricht helped the Germans, Dimitrov the Bulgarians, Gottwald the Czecho-Slovaks, and Togliatti the Italians. Kuusinen, who did not often participate in such affairs, also came along faithfully; in the ski competitions he even helped to shape up the contestants, giving theoretical instruction and waxing the skis on the day of the event. There in the bitter morning cold he would bustle about on the slopes of Varpus Mountain or on the Moscow River.

Likewise, in the skating competitions, he would lend the good skates that he had gotten from Sweden to the defenders of Finland's honor and, because there were no qualified judges, join the rest of us in knavery to help the Finns against all others. On those occasions internationalism played a very small role in this international school. Nationalism was so rampant that we were often on the verge of scuffling, and once during a ski competition an actual fight was about to break out.

This was the reason. Since the Finns had won overwhelmingly the previous year, the Germans had gathered a special group of Austrian Alpine skiers with whom they expected to accomplish miracles. But to be on the safe side, they complained to the school administration that the Finns used the wrong method by compelling the competitors to start in pairs at half-minute intervals. They demanded a simultaneous start. We naturally resisted such a demand vehemently but then the school's directress, Kirsanova, called me in and declared that, in view of the many complaints, she was ordering the use of a simultaneous start—she herself knew absolutely nothing about skiing. This happened the day before the competitions.

Well, what could we do—a directive is a directive. There was still time to work out tactics with Kuusinen. The course was six miles and the snow was deep. Because the number of participants rose to well over a hundred, reaching the trail in the starting scramble would be decisive. Our people were ordered to ski for their lives to gain the lead, and in the morning we even made long parallel trails at the beginning. And so our sector's representatives rushed into the lead and then slackened their pace; when the German sector's competitors attempted to slog past through the yielding snow crust they failed because on the trail it was always possible to accelerate. There, on a two or three mile stretch, our people exhausted the Alpine heroes and almost all, girls as well as boys, arrived first at the finish line.

Naturally there arose a fearful commotion, the Germans protesting and howling that it was sabotage, which was a serious charge. But Kuusinen and I defended ourselves valiantly, declaring that, after all, they themselves had demanded it. If we had followed international rules this wouldn't have happened.

Whenever we became involved in altercations with the larger sectors we had a faithful ally: China. They—the Chinese—had not the slightest bit of envy. We fraternized with each other, attended their festivities and they ours.

From the viewpoint of the Finnish labor movement, many graduates of the Lenin School were not the most desirable types and were not even well informed on the various aspects of the Finnish labor movement. They were, however, the better informed on Russian and Comintern communism, whose objectives in Finland they were pursuing.

The most lasting school memories for both teachers and students involve certain extracurricular events and mishaps. Inasmuch as the institution was a boarding school, with the students of all sectors in residence, the teaching staff had more to do than merely take care of the scheduled classes. The students' private lives created all kinds of problems for the sectors' leaders despite the fact that the students were adults, their ages ranging from eighteen to over forty. Since the student body was about evenly divided between men and women, a natural lifestyle inevitably played its own part also in sexual matters. In the beginning the boys were domiciled in their own quarters, the girls in theirs, five or six to a room, but after the school was moved to the Varpus Mountain, to a newly completed building with double rooms, the boys soon began moving into the girls' rooms and vice versa. One of these instances deserves mention because of its uniquely human aspects.

Among our sector's youngest students was Martti Malmberg, whose pseudonym at the school was John Oderi, called simply Joni. He was certainly no luminary, and, in addition to his youth, he was quite nondescript. He had a complete lack of basic knowledge and a mumbling rapid speech of which he was constantly reminded by the teachers: "Say that again—no one can understand such mumbling." But he had special qualifications in the world of women, for he was a ladies' man who didn't limit himself to the girls in his own sector but, as an apparent expansionist politician, eyed the other sectors' girls as well. Amazingly enough, though his knowledge of languages was limited to his native tongue, he seemed to get along quite well in the foreign sectors also.

The students had been lectured many times on the need for precaution in sexual matters because of the great inconvenience that resulted if studies had to be interrupted every now and then as a result of love affairs. But Joni didn't take these lectures very seriously, freely continuing his open season on women. And so it happened that, after he had wooed Greta, the secretary of the Swedish sector, for a few weeks, poor Greta became pregnant. In those days it was possible to have an abortion—and this certainly wasn't the first time that such matters had been arranged at the school's hospital with the cooperation of the Finnish sector. Swedish-Greta's case was taken care of fairly effortlessly, though the head of the Swedish sector did reproach us, partly in jest, partly in earnest: "You send your youths to fish in foreign waters and now our sector is without a secretary." Furthermore, the matter was not resolved as usual by a few days in the hospital; complications forced Greta to spend many weeks there.

Our sector's leadership realized that Joni had to be enlightened to avoid a recurrence of such a mishap and urged to remain within the confines of his own sector. Moreover, shortly after the Greta case, a ban on abortions was instituted throughout the Soviet Union, so absolute that not even foreign students could obtain a special exemption; everyone was subject to Stalin's edict that an abortion could be performed only in an actual emergency after consulting with physicians.

Special lectures were now held for the students in which the virtues of precaution were stressed. And it must be conceded that the others did become much more careful. But not Joni. Unfortunately, he chose as his next victim—from his own sector, this time—young Mailis, a completely inexperienced girl. The inevitable happened to the poor girl and there no longer was the possibility of abortion. Mailis had to submit to childbirth in those wretched conditions—I say wretched, for in that respect they truly were trying and wretched.

Now the sector's leadership really had to take Joni to task. I especially recall the fuss made by Aino Pesonen, our sector's energetic and enterprising secretary, as she raged that it was simply terrible to have to spend all her time in straightening out Joni Oderi's amorous adventures. She had to arrange for hospital accommodations, and since the maternity hospitals were overflowing following the ban on abortions and a bed had to be found in some other hospital for a foreigner, an endless amount of paperwork was involved. Before even a minor permit could be obtained in Russia, scores of forms had to be filled out, and this was hardly a minor matter. Furthermore, one had to run around a city of millions inquiring where accommodations might be available. Finally Aino did manage to find a place, but the conditions were so woeful that Mailis's child did not survive long, dying of outright lack of care.

This was no longer an amusing situation. It was discussed seriously at many levels, but Joni just shrugged off the whole affair. Jukka Lehtosaari, who at that time headed the sector, and assistant director Lauri Gustafsson concluded that this fellow would hardly make a fighter or a disciplined worker for the Finnish Communist party's cadres.

But astonishingly, I subsequently noticed that this same Joni, Martti Malmberg, had achieved quite a high position in the upper echelons of the Finnish Communist party. Obviously the appraisal of the sector's leaders was all off base, unless the work of the Finnish Communist party administration in later years had concentrated—and that was possible—on precisely those areas in which Joni

Oderi's traits would be an outright asset in the shaping of a career.

At the Lenin School familial tendencies were directed toward furthering communism, as illustrated by another case involving the Swedish sector. There was even the deliberate maneuvering of love affairs.

In the Swedish sector there was a tall, slim, and handsome boy named Anton Strand, a real charmer. I met him for the first time at the school's sanatorium in the Crimea, where he was keeping company with a girl from the Spanish sector. The girl was exceptionally beautiful and shapely, and this handsome pair attracted much attention while strolling along the Crimean shore. Anton Strand wanted badly to marry the Spanish girl and filed an official petition with his sector to be allowed to marry her in accordance with Soviet law and later in Sweden. But the school's cadre section—in other words, the secret police of the Comintern—forbade it. The Spanish girl was not trustworthy, and hence such a marriage was deemed undesirable.

That was the end of that, and Anton brokenheartedly paced the corridors in his sector. But when the need is greatest, help is at hand. He noticed a very charming and well-educated girl in our sector—or matron, rather, for she had been married a long time and the marriage had gone on the rocks. This woman, Irja Nousiainen, now became the focal point of Anton Strand's emotions. They kept company but each asserted that they were not ardently in love.

Jukka Lehtosaari, who had been taking care of Finnish Communist party affairs in Sweden, then had the idea that perhaps the two could get married to each other. Our girl was not untrustworthy like the Spanish woman. If we could get our own person to become the wife of a Swedish party member who obviously was destined for a high party post upon his return home, it might be very helpful to us.

And so we set to work. I was given the task of sounding out Irja on the idea. At first she was not at all interested. As a veritable Soviet fosterling, she was apparently quite happy in the Soviet Union and had no yearning for the West.

She was, however, a sufficiently party-disciplined person to say, after I had explained the matter from the ideological viewpoint,

"*Vse ravno,* if the party interests demand it, I am ready to make any sacrifices whatsoever."

Anton Strand did not react to the idea quite that way. When the leadership of the Swedish sector suggested it to him he was fairly amenable—not so enthusiastic as he had been about the Spanish girl but still quite willing. Thus this party-political marriage was entered into, and in 1936 Irja traveled to Sweden with her Anton, supplied with documents attesting to the fact that they had been married in the Soviet Union. Subsequently the marriage was ratified according to Swedish law.

This was by no means the only marriage to be negotiated within the bounds of the Comintern and the Lenin School; during that period scores, even hundreds were arranged. For the most part they failed because they were shotgun weddings, but the marriage of Anton and Irja—later, Irma—has not run aground. I met this couple quite often when we were living in Stockholm; they are an especially fine and harmonious pair, have done excellent party work, and Irja has been helpful to the Finnish party in many ways.

Then there was the Pentikäinen case. Lieutenant Vilho Pentikäinen, who had served on the Finnish general staff, in early 1935 suddenly revealed himself to be a spy by deserting, driving his car to the border, and walking on the Karelian Isthmus to the Soviet side. The Finnish press wrote about it extensively; in the Soviet Union, of course, nothing was said about the event as was the custom.

A long time elapsed—at least six months, as I recall—and we party leaders no longer even thought about the matter. Then one day Sirola, who was the director of the Finnish sector at the Lenin School, came to me with a very mysterious air and said that he had just talked with a certain high official in the cadre section and had been told the following:

Pentikäinen who, since his border crossing, had been in the custody of the army's Fourth Section—in other words, the espionage and political division—had become superfluous. They had succeeded in pumping him of all he knew and thus had no further use for him. Furthermore, they declared that the man was unsuitable otherwise, too, since he had come to know one thing and another about their methods of operation in Finland.

Now they wanted to know whether the Finns could utilize him somehow, not by sending him to Finland but there in the Soviet Union, and asked specifically whether the Finnish party leaders could take him into the Lenin School or into some other school to be trained for special tasks. If the Finns didn't want him, they had no alternative but to get rid of him quietly.

Sirola, who was a sentimental person, told me the tale with horror and said that he feared the man's days were numbered unless we accepted him into the school. To me the idea seemed abhorrent and downright compromising, for though all kinds of extrapolitical subjects such as revolt instigation were taught at the Lenin School, it was nevertheless a political institute. Imagine enrolling a person having nothing to do with politics, not having been in any way on the roster of our party, the Finnish Communist party, being purely a spy. But Sirola could not have the man's life on his conscience and when we conferred with Kuusinen, he considered the matter for a while and then sided with Sirola.

Since it had been decided to accept Pentikäinen as a student in the Lenin School, Sirola and I began to coach him lest he betray himself by his actions. We assumed that the people's powers of perception were not sharp enough to recognize Pentikäinen despite the many photographs of him, especially since he claimed to be from a region in Finland where comparatively little political work had been done.

In addition, we agreed that he would not try to behave like a laboring man but would let it be understood that he was an office worker or a clerk with a somewhat better education than a common laborer. Over a period of several days Sirola and I gave him instructions on behavior and when he seemed ripe, he was given an assumed name like all the others and then enrolled in the school.

It must be admitted that he was a first-class conspirator. During his entire stay at the school he was a conscientious, good student who faithfully did his homework and other assignments, was not a chatterbox, did not boast about his knowledge in any field, remained modestly in the background and kept his secret in a superb manner. Judging by his traits he was definitely a first-class spy. During one whole year, from the fall of 1935 to the following spring, there was not the slightest cause for reproach in his behavior. I don't believe that a single one of the school's students found out that behind his pseudonym was the noted spy Penti-käinen.

Kuusinen and I—Sirola died in March 1936—kept an eye on his progress, and many times I wondered how the man could be used after the school ended and what his fate would be. But often matters take care of themselves, and this one did also.

By the time the spring semester had ended and the sector had made its so-called practice trips to kolkhozes [collective farms] and factories, the civil war in Spain was under way. So-called volunteers were sent from the Soviet Union by the thousands to join the international brigade. Activity at the Lenin School came to a halt, and it was made clear that all male students should leave for the front.

As the party secretary and one of the sector's teachers, I was given the task of proposing the action. The tone of the proposal made clear that departure was a party obligation, though formally it was emphasized that anyone who did not wish to go could report his reason if he did so immediately. Not one of the sector's male students wished to decline.

The matter was thus settled, and the following day the entire group was transferred to another school, where it was coached for the journey and given the necessary equipment. Military uniforms were not used, of course; everyone went in civilian clothes.

Before the transfer, pertinent instructions had been given at the school. Looking at those boys as they recited their oaths in small voices, I felt that except for one, none had his heart and soul in leaving—and who would want to leave once he is at an age to know what war is?

The only one whose glance and entire being revealed his willingness to go was Pentikäinen—he actually began to live again. For an entire year he had been oppressed by a nightmare, since he was sufficiently intelligent to realize that he was no longer needed. The army's Fourth Section did not need him; he also knew that the Finnish sector did not need him either, and that his future was at best uncertain. He lived a kind of shadow existence from day to day with a death sentence hanging over him. Getting into the war meant getting out of a dead end. And then he really began to live. The only time I saw his eyes shine and his bearing evince vitality was during the moment of registration.

When the address had ended, he was the only one who took me

aside, seized my hand and exclaimed, "This was a brilliant stroke. Life begins again!"

Thus he went to war in search of a new life.

HOME LIFE WITH KUUSINEN

UPON ARRIVING in Moscow, my wife and I first had stayed briefly at a hotel named Soiuznaia, in a room whose curtainless, almost street-level window reached to the floor and made living difficult especially when the lights were on, for curious pedestrians stared in as though at a display window until we managed to get curtains of white sheeting. After that we lived in a room especially reserved for us through the Lenin School.

In that manner we had spent almost a year in Moscow when Kuusinen, in the summer of 1934, suggested that we move in with him. He had a large empty apartment in which he lived alone and was eager to have us as his fellow lodgers. After divorcing Aino Sarola, a Finnish woman, he had married a Latvian-born woman named Palkina. By then he had had enough also of Palkina, gotten a divorce and wanted companionship.

We did not reply outright one way or the other, since the matter deserved some thought, and we felt it necessary to sound out others about the propriety of simply moving in with such a leader. I sought the opinion of Kuusinen's daughters, Hertta and Riikka, and they both—especially Hertta, who was quite vehement—advised us to drop the whole idea. True, the apartment was impressive and living there afforded many special privileges, but their father was difficult to get along with. He was very capricious; his lifestyle differed from that of other people; he could be charming and friendly for weeks, then sink into a kind of trance during which he would be unfriendly for weeks, and it would be difficult to know what was really on his mind. Then his fellow tenants would have a hard time. That was why they could not live with their father.

But Kuusinen persisted. He was one of those men who, having gotten an idea, almost certainly see it through. He returned time and again to the matter of our moving in with him, until finally we consented.

So we became Kuusinen's lodgers in *Dom Pravitel'stva*, "the house on the embankment." * At the time this building was among the largest in Moscow, completed in 1931 as I recall, and was located diagonally across from the Kremlin on the opposite shore of the Moscow River. It was a twelve-story colossus covering almost an entire block. How many thousands lived there I never tried to learn; curiosity was not good for one's health.

Thus this apartment, which had been reserved for Kuusinen already in the blueprint stage, had so much floor space that it would have sufficed even for a capitalist's family. But it was very badly planned. In addition, the rooms were absurdly large. For example, Kuusinen's study—though it probably had not been intended as such—would have been more than ample for a drawing or living room. Similarly, the room that we took over was needlessly spacious. In addition to these two rooms, the apartment had a comparatively small room between the study and our room, and beyond our room a large chamber in which Kuusinen slept. There was also a kitchen and a large foyer. In all, I would say that the apartment encompassed about two thousand square feet.

Dom Pravitel'stva had been planned as a model building, intended to be the last word in dwellings both as to elegance and comfort. Because it was designed and built especially for top government officials, it should have been tip-top in every respect. But during its construction and even before the roof was up, it was discovered that the building was on the verge of collapse, walls were crumbling, ceilings were falling, and so forth. The first generation of architects or group of planners was imprisoned and—so it was claimed—shot. The second, which attempted to salvage the work of the first, met the same fate. Only the third group of architects was able to complete the building and make it somehow habitable. Often in looking at the building we remarked that in this country people undoubtedly had been imprisoned and shot for lesser reasons than the designing and construction of such a building.

The apartment had only two closets, one with room for a few coats, the other tiny, with shelving so narrow that it was difficult to squeeze anything into it. The stairway, on the other hand, took

---

* The house is the locale of Yuri Trifonov's book by the same name.

up more space than even the grandest staircases in Western buildings, but the elevator at least deserved credit for functioning. As for the doors, sometimes they closed, sometimes they didn't, and the cracks admitted not only mice but slightly larger creatures as well; the windows were a little tighter; the floors had been intended to be the finest parquet, but almost every board was loose, and as one walked the boards rose gracefully underfoot and then clattered back into place. In this ostensibly luxurious apartment the appearance of water and drain pipes in full view several feet below the ceiling, as they are in the basements of Finnish buildings, was ridiculous. There they wheezed and rumbled and oozed and dripped.

The building was, of course, not intended as temporary housing but as a model of the way in which architecture in time would triumph throughout the land. It must be admitted that the constant repairs on the building improved it somewhat year by year. Floor boards were glued now and then and doors were repaired, and when we became familiar with buildings constructed later in the 1930s we found them to be vastly improved. Sabotage was talked about a great deal in the Soviet Union, but a more natural explanation was the architects' ignorance. Educated as they were in the Soviet era, they could not have gained experience in constructing modern buildings. And so the results were what they were: measurements and levels were inaccurate, foundations collapsed, and all the rest of the construction was more or less in accord.

This particular building had been planned by the state to the last detail, including the furnishings, which matched it in ugliness. Kuusinen's study contained an enormous sofa, long and broad and correspondingly ugly, while the desk in its hugeness would have been good enough for an "Iron Chancellor." The most important object, however, was quite unassuming in appearance: a card file.

Every system has its own secret weapon, and the Soviet system's is the card file. The GPU, the army's Fourth Section and the party's Central Committee have indexed millions of people, foreigners as well as Russians. For Kuusinen, a small file of several hundred cards sufficed. He kept track merely of the high political figures. Lenin and Stalin were followed alphabetically by the lesser bosses. It was his arsenal on the ideological front on which he worked. It contained whatever they had said that was favorable, apt, and felicitous about Marxism, Leninism, and Stalinism. But it also contained all those remarks that in Kuusinen's opinion were heretical—and that was its main function. Laudatory statements were rarely needed, for in those days only Stalin said anything good, but all the heresies of some Trotsky, Zinoviev, Kamenev, Bela Kun, Bukharin, and others were in that card file especially underscored, and when an individual lapsed into the danger zone, Kuusinen did not have to make inquiries at the GPU archives or the party's Central Committee. They might have provided shocking tales—true and false—about the heretic's private life, but such tales meant nothing to Kuusinen. He kept vigil over crimes that were against the "holy spirit," and these crimes were in his own card file. But the cabinet contained other things as well: notes on world literature along with his own poems that he occasionally was inspired to read to my wife.

The most conspicuous objects in Kuusinen's study, where he met visitors, had not been included in the government's plans. They were the exercise rings suspended from the ceiling. Every visitor immediately inquired their purpose, and Kuusinen explained that he couldn't keep in shape unless he used them every morning. That was true, except that he performed his vigorous morning exercises toward evening, since that was when he most frequently arose.

Life in this building was, to a considerable degree, loftily isolated, for it was difficult to get even one's best friends inside. In the first place, they were not anxious to come because of the numerous inspections and interrogations that admittance involved, but neither could just anyone be invited since admittance could have been denied despite the invitation. The building was controlled with an iron hand. Gatekeepers did not suffice. Every staircase also had a guard around the clock, and the guards in turn had a chief who examined every arrival. Each tenant naturally had his own permanent pass and, of course, was soon recognized by the guards, especially since there were not many tenants to each stairway. The apartments were so large that there were only two on each floor.

But if some stranger sought admittance to the building to visit us, for example, the guard would call his chief, who would inquire whom the stranger wished to see, then ask for his name and passport and thereafter call us to inquire whether we wished to receive such and such a person. If the reply was in the affirmative, the chief guard made out a pass for the visitor, who was often escorted to the door by the guard. In handing over the pass, the chief guard took the visitor's passport as security for the duration of his stay in the building. On the pass was noted that Comrade N. is arriving to see Comrade So-and-So at such and such a time—for example 10:12 A.M.—on that day. I would then receipt the pass, indicating that Comrade N. departed at 11:23 A.M. If this person had with him a parcel, no matter how small, or a briefcase or almost anything else, a special pass had to be written: Comrade N., who departed at 11:23 A.M., had with him such and such a parcel.

Such were the arrivals and departures. It was virtually a unique system, for though passes were used at hotels occupied by Comintern personnel—among them the Lux—the system was not nearly so stringent as at *Dom Pravitel'stva*.

The building's guards formed a good-sized company in the May Day parade. There were many staircases, and with three shifts a veritable small army was needed. All were GPU men, and the chief guards in particular were among the most trustworthy of the GPU top brass and thus obviously of rather high military rank.

Our life in this peculiar building and apartment actually was divided into two shifts. My wife and I worked during the day. I worked in my own office daily. The Lenin School was open from morning until evening, and I lectured there in the daytime. My wife, who at that time was attending a language seminary, also worked during the day. Kuusinen, who was Stalin's personal secretary,* naturally had to adapt his schedule to that of Stalin. All who were close to Stalin or dependent on him had to work at night; even if they didn't work they had to remain awake.

On the desk in Kuusinen's study were two telephones—there were even more in his office—one a regular city telephone and the other a hot line that we called *Verhushka*. Only the top bosses, members of the Politburo and Comintern secretaries had *Verhushka*. I was not entitled to one. The exchange was in the Kremlin, and whenever the phone rang one knew that a bigwig was on the line. There was no mistaking that ring, for it was quite distinctive.

---

* In addition to calling Kuusinen "Stalin's personal secretary," Tuominen called him "Stalin's trusted personal secretary," "Stalin's confidential secretary," "Stalin's ideological and theoretical secretary," "Stalin's adviser on ideological and international questions," "a specialist whom Stalin needed," who "wrote speeches for Stalin." Thus he was not a secretary in the usual sense of the word.

Kuusinen hardly ever answered the regular telephone. All kinds of people were apt to call; for example, Finns visiting Moscow tried to reach him that way since they dared not come to the building itself. But Kuusinen snapped his fingers at that telephone's ring. I don't know of many instances when he answered it. On the other hand, no matter where he was—in bed, having coffee, or at some other important task—whenever he heard *Verhushka's* ring he moved like greased lightning: there was always the possibility that Stalin himself was calling.

Hence Kuusinen worked nights and often went to bed at five or six in the morning or even later, so it was not unusual for him to awaken at two or three in the afternoon. Because of this the work at his secretariat, as at many others, was arranged so that only the clerks were on hand in the morning to take care of the routine business. All conferences invariably were scheduled for the evening or toward midnight.

In our apartment, work was thus performed in two shifts, and we met only in the evening, when our work ended and his began. We hardly ever shared a meal, since Kuusinen ate at the dining room reserved for the Comintern bosses that had been set up in the Kremlin hospital. As a member of the Comintern I, too, had the privilege of eating there but used it rarely. Usually I ate either at the regular Comintern dining room or at home, since my wife had to fix her own meals.

But coffee the three of us often drank together. When we arrived home in the evening and my wife put the coffee on, Kuusinen never had to be invited twice; he was always ready to join us. Coffee was, in fact, his main source of enjoyment. Of course, he always had a cigarette between his teeth, but that I would call rather a habit. Coffee he would sip throughout the night, and the pot always had to be hot.

The acquisition of coffee was among his major concerns, for only small amounts of its arrived in the Soviet Union and even that was of poor quality. Usually a three-months' supply arrived at a time, and then the news would travel by grapevine from one Finnish family to another: "A shipment of coffee has arrived!" and the store shelves would empty. Russians—even those who could afford it—generally did not buy coffee, since they are tea-drinkers, but there were many foreigners in Moscow on the lookout for coffee. Kuusinen obtained his primarily from Sweden through the good offices of friends and acquaintances, but some also came from America. Nevertheless, the coffee ran out all too often and then Kuusinen knew bad times. But the wise are not without resources: he had faithfully saved the old coffee grounds and always kept a large pile of them drying in the event of just such a trying period. God only knows how often they were brewed.

One thing often amused and sometimes annoyed us. The kitchen, which was no model either as to furnishings or equipment, did have gas. Kuusinen would put on the coffee pot and leave for his room to think his own thoughts or to answer *Verhushka's* ring. When he remembered the pot half an hour, an hour or even two hours later—perhaps reminded by the scorching smell—and ran to rescue it, the pot was empty, the water had evaporated, the grounds were burned, the bottom was ruined, and that was the end of that.

Atop the kitchen shelves Kuusinen had an impressive array of the sad remains of coffee pots: electric, aluminum, brass, copper, and enamel, in all probability well over a dozen. We contributed several coffee pots to the household but they, too, were soon burned. It so happened, however, that a large department store received a shipment of Finnish coffee pots under the trade treaty, and Kuusinen bought a supply of them, including replacements for ours. Happy times had arrived.

We had lived this quiet family life for quite a while when suddenly it was drenched with color. A young Finnish woman, who previously had lived in the Kuusinen household as a foster child, returned from Paris where she had been working under orders with the Red Aid and came to live in Kuusinen's apartment. This young, animated being brightened our three lives considerably, for she was full of Paris, Parisian fashions, and Parisian spirit—also in the political sense. She was extremely intelligent and an exceptionally gifted linguist, and during her contacts with many different kinds of people had acquired a splendid store of anecdotes.

She also was endowed with a God-given talent that deserves mention as a reflection of existing conditions: she could speak forcefully in six languages, Russian naturally being the most important. When stores received a shipment of fabric or other ladies' goods, my gentle wife had to queue up and be content with whatever she got. But that girl bypassed the lines with a crackle of sharp words, put the fear of God into the salespeople and somehow managed to reach the head of the line. When some matter had to be expedited—for example, obtaining a pass from some dilatory minor or even major bureaucrat—this young woman seized the telephone while we three gathered around to admire the virtuosity with which she handled the range of Russian epithets—and it is wide indeed. The pass was produced on the spot.

The young woman served as Kuusinen's secretary and as such remained in our household for almost a year. Basically she was not interested in that work, and her existence became even more unpleasant when the GPU focused its attention on her, called her in and threatened to take her into custody on the charge that she had conducted herself improperly while on her mission to Paris. A person could not, however, be arrested at the home of Kuusinen, a Comintern secretary, simply on the say-so of some minor police official, especially since Kuusinen took her under his wing and even gave the authorities to understand that the girl was close to him.

Such an existence became difficult, of course, and Kuusinen turned to me for help in getting the girl out of Moscow. We hit upon the idea that the party needed a special worker in Stockholm, where there actually was much to do, but we didn't depend on that alone to turn the trick. We devised an even more effective lure: she would go there especially to handle affairs pertaining to the Spanish Civil War. The war, which had erupted in Spain in 1936, enabled many people who perhaps never could have left the Soviet Union to obtain a visa and passport and travel funds with no delay and without investigation as to whether or not they were trustworthy, for they were departing on an important mission to a theater of war.

I suggested to Manuilski and Dimitrov that the girl be sent to Stockholm to arrange for the recruitment and maintenance of Swedes, Finns, and other Nordics traveling to Spain; she was well suited to it because of her linguistic abilities. That did it. We quickly obtained a travel permit for the girl, escorted her to the airport and thus were rid of her as she was of us.

Once again the three of us lived peacefully and pleasantly for a while. We all had our work and our activities and our moments together were pleasant, for Kuusinen was a well-informed man—I have forgotten to mention that his books filled two sizeable walls, and that he subscribed to Finnish newspapers and periodicals. Not even the smallest differences of opinion developed. My wife and I wondered what Hertta and Riikka had meant in saying that one could not get along with their father. True, we noticed that sometimes he would be crotchety with others, but apparently we had somehow achieved a favored status. Occasionally he would be less loquacious, somewhat downcast, in his own thoughts. When that happened we didn't inquire the reason but left him alone, until a few days later he would begin to speak again, becoming quite talkative and friendly.

For five years I was the man closest to Kuusinen, who, in turn, was Stalin's trusted personal secretary. When Kuusinen wrote to Stalin about more or less confidential matters, he invariably read the reports to my wife and me, since we polished them together. Kuusinen did not use a typewriter at all; my wife typed everything either in Russian or German. Both languages were used, but whatever went to Stalin was in Russian.

Incidentally, my wife always refused to join the Communist party, even when Kuusinen brought up the matter while the three of us were residing together. My wife declared flatly that she was not a communist. She had married Poika Tuominen solely because he was a pleasant man, but she had never accepted his beliefs. Kuusinen explained that, because I held such a high position here, it would help both of us if she would join. To this my wife replied that she regretted if her stand made his position awkward, but she would not accept communism. She had never prevented her husband from doing whatever he wished, she added; on the contrary, she had given him technical support as a typist and translator, but she did not approve of communism.

Kuusinen said—and it reflected his tolerance—that he understood. She was her father's daughter. He knew the man well: he was an old member of the Diet and an editor-in-chief, with the same revisionist views that she seemed to have. Despite that they had enjoyed an exceptionally amicable association.

There are in existence numerous Comintern resolutions and theses written by Kuusinen and polished and typed by my wife. She was an excellent stylist and knew Russian, German, English,

Swedish, and Finnish well, in addition to being a rapid typist and having a good knowledge of shorthand.

Our life as a threesome did not last long, for while in a Crimean sanatorium, Kuusinen had fixed his eye on a young woman doctor—or perhaps she was a candidate—named Marina. This girl-child was a typical Soviet product, wholly of the intelligentsia developed by the new rulers, and with her came a breath of Russian life that we did not know—and neither, it seemed, did Kuusinen.

Specialists were the big thing in Russia, and in medicine, too, specialization was carried to an extreme. Marina did research work on canine pituitary glands and was distressed when the dogs died in her hands before she could remove the pituitary gland, crush it and inject the extract into the same dog's hind leg. Naturally, I understand absolutely nothing about medical science, but I have great respect for brains—even a dog's brains. If research is done on such a precious organ—albeit at the behest of a professor—one would think that the researcher needed a sounder knowledge of nature's laws than that possessed by Marina. The flimsiness of her basic education manifested itself in many ways. Once when we were spending a weekend at Kuntsevo, my wife looked at the alders to see which buds had stamens, which pistils. Marina marveled at her activity, and when it was explained to her that trees also had males and females, her amusement knew no bounds. She considered such an assertion a good joke.

Otherwise she was an enchanting girl, and after their marriage according to Soviet law, Kuusinen had a good wife in her. Life in our kolkhoz proceeded pleasantly until Marina's mother arrived to visit her son-in-law. She was an Armenian who had lived in Tiflis as the wife of a wealthy merchant and apparently still dwelt in the thoughts and hopes of czarist days. She had no opinions, no interests. All she could do was to cook chicken, and that she did constantly. Actually, she would hardly have disturbed our household had it not been for the common toilet. She didn't know how to use it and was unwilling to sit even though the seat was of polished mahogany. No, that fat old granny clambered up to stand on the seat and made the whole room impossible. Marina argued with her in Armenian, Kuusinen reprimanded her more discreetly, and, in cleaning up the mess, my wife also admonished her, but the woman merely made a sweeping gesture of deep disgust and innocently explained in tones of conviction that as a clean person she simply couldn't think of soiling her hands at such menial chores. When she was urged to sit, she declared that she was too fine a lady to use the same seat as others.

Obviously, she could not remain a member of our commune for very long. Kuusinen vigorously began to work toward shipping her back to the Caucasus to her own environment and Marina, too, concluded that her mother really was out of place in our surroundings. When we returned from a vacation in the spring of 1937, the mother already had been sent on her way. Attempting to brew ourselves some homecoming coffee, we couldn't find our coffee pot anywhere. Kuusinen explained that a number of things, among them our coffee pot, had been given to the old woman. Its handle was insulated, and she couldn't stop marveling at and admiring the pot whose handle didn't get hot. We gladly granted her that wondrous utensil as a farewell gift.

Our neighbors belonged to the highest hierarchy in the Soviet Union. All the Soviet bosses who did not live in the Kremlin—there were only three or four, sometimes only two in addition to Stalin—lived in this building, or at least most of them. I shall mention only a few names. For example, one of the apartments on the floor below was occupied by Minister of Transportation Rykov, who had been premier prior to Molotov, until 1930, and who thus was one of the most notable and influential members of the government.

Above us lived the celebrated Radek; opposite us on the same floor was Lozovski, the secretary general of the Profintern, the Red International Trade Union, and who later became second foreign minister; a little lower lived Tomski, member of the Politburo and general manager of the Federation of Trade Unions; and in another stairway lived my old acquaintance, Bukharin.

Naturally we did not associate very much with these neighbors but we did meet them occasionally. We had more contact with Radek than with the others, since he rode the elevator frequently with his black poodle, whose name, as befitted both dog and Radek, was *Chort* (Devil). Radek was a lively man, so that we saw much more of him than of Rykov, Tomski, Lozovski, or the other personages who lived there.

We became involved with him in yet another way. One night, when water began dripping into our room through the ceiling, we awakened Kuusinen, called the gatekeeper and, since the water came from above, also called Radek, who confirmed that the water pipe in his bathroom was broken and pouring out a torrent. He cursed the building, the plumbers, and the entire household as we all watched from the stairway to see what would develop. There was plenty of room on the eleven floors for the water to gurgle along all possible routes, especially since the walls were full of rat holes. Soviet rats were an industrious and high-reaching race, and prompted Radek to deep sarcasm.

The building also had a special dining room not intended for the highest bosses but for the medium or slightly lower aristocrats. Sometimes when I didn't have time to go to my regular dining rooms I dropped in to the one in our building, and now and then I would meet Radek and Bukharin. They were often together and on those occasions took delight in poking fun especially at Kuusinen, who at one time had been a bosom friend of both but was no longer. Since they knew that I lived with him, they would ask whose noose Kuusinen was now greasing and make other taunting remarks. I defended Kuusinen's honor and reputation vehemently and pretended to be hurt that anyone should even hint at his helping to grease a noose for his friends.

It was Radek who, out of the fullness of his heart, originated and circulated anti-Stalinist jokes. Stalin summoned the perpetrator to rebuke him especially for circulating derisive jokes about him, Stalin, who, after all, was the beloved leader of 200 million Russians. To which Radek retorted, "That joke I did not originate."

My first years in that building passed quite pleasantly until the great purges began near the end of 1936, climaxing in the spring and summer of 1937 in unprecedented destruction. It no longer felt comfortable to ride those ten stories in the elevator; one could not erase the horror from one's mind with the appearance of the GPU seal. It was a large red seal, some four inches in diameter, and was placed on the door of an apartment whose occupants had been arrested. It began appearing on every floor from the bottom upward. One of them appeared below us, on Rykov's door. As we ascended to our floor, we could not take our eyes off that door. Soon almost every floor had those seals: on Tomski's door, Radek's door, and many others. It was a terrifying time. People spoke only in whispers and wondered for whom the bells of the Kremlin would toll next. Whose turn would it be tomorrow? In those days we lived with a blanket already rolled in a bundle, for everyone knew that when the time came for departure one could take at most a blanket.

The seal might remain on a door as long as three or four months, until the investigation of the apartment's tenants was completed, or, rather, until their fate was decided. I don't know of a single instance in which one of those arrested returned to his apartment; all simply disappeared. Their relatives were left to fend for themselves and to find shelter wherever they could, provided they had not all been arrested at the same time.

The apartment was given to a new boss, who took over the duties of his predecessor. Only then was the seal removed from the door, but there was not the slightest clue as to the identity of the newcomer, since no names appeared on the doors. This system naturally was instituted for security reasons: identification could not appear on the doors of such bosses for fear of assassins, even though the building and the stairways were so tightly guarded.

Inasmuch as life for us sociable people was getting a bit dull, my wife and I thought it would be nice to give a party to meet old friends and neighbors. We decided to make it a birthday party, in honor of Kuusinen's turning fifty-five in October 1936. We didn't mention our plans to the hero of the day, but made all the preparations and invited a group of his closest acquaintances and friends. Naturally we obtained special permission from the pass-dispenser, the chief guard, and assured him that all those who would come to see us on that day were trustworthy. Only the day before did we inform Kuusinen that he had to be at home on the morrow.

It was an especially merry get-together. I don't know whether Kuusinen suspected what lay ahead, but the rest of us were blissfully unaware of the future. Two months earlier there had been the "trial of the sixteen traitors" at which Zinoviev and Kamenev were liquidated, but we considered that the end of one phase of development and certainly not the starting gun for another. Gylling already had been dismissed from his post as prime minister of Soviet Karelia but was still free in Moscow. Naturally, we did not invite him because Kuusinen's guilty conscience impelled him to avoid the man.

The next year's horrors thus were behind the iron curtain of the future, and that lighthearted assemblage was able blithely to enjoy the crayfish that were plentiful at that time of year and that we had provided bountifully. Kuusinen's relatives were represented only by Riikka; Hertta was in a jail in Finland; his son Esa was in Karelia; and his brother-in-law Laaksovirta had been executed the previous year in connection with the Manner court process.* The guests were residents of the Lux and Soiuznaia hotels along with some Swedes. We wound up the evening by dancing exuberantly— so exuberantly that, during the twirls of a polka, one of the dancers fell and almost cracked open his skull, thanks to the loose boards in the parquet floor of Kuusinen's study.

Weekends we usually spent at Kuntsevo, some twelve miles west of Moscow, along the road to Minsk. We would leave sometimes Friday but usually Saturday evening and remain until Sunday evening in Kuusinen's favorite villa. As a member of the Comintern Presidium I could have had my own villa, but there was ample space in Kuusinen's house. Each had his own room and in addition there was a joint sitting room.

We lived the usual weekend life at Kuntsevo, were outdoors a lot and went hiking or skiing. Occasionally—but only rarely—other Comintern and Soviet bosses participated in our activities. They were not athletically inclined as we were but instead favored the billiard room and card table. Our closest neighbors were such notables as Comintern Secretary Manuilski; Wilhelm Pieck, subsequently president of East Germany; Professor Togliatti, leader of the Italian Communist party; French Communist leader Marty, who by wisely remaining silent lived on his earlier reputation; and Gottwald, leader of the Czechoslovak Communists, who subsequently lived and died as president.

There we got to know the Comintern's big leaders, secretaries, and Presidium members better than we did at work, which consisted merely of talks and conferences. Most of the foreigners always had their families along, so we became acquainted with their wives and children also, which was most unusual in Russia since the Russians usually did not take their wives along to any event.

Manuilski was the only one to appear frequently with his wife, but he had his own approach to things and could act quite independently. In the early 1930s he left his wife and horde of children, moved from *Dom Pravitel'stva* to live at the Lux, where he en-

* Kullervo Manner and his wife had been sentenced to death, but the sentences were commuted to ten years of hard labor.

gaged a luxury suite, and married a noblewoman of the czarist era. She was not especially beautiful or young but was otherwise quite charming. Naturally, the marriage was the subject of much gossip, particularly since the new wife was of unproletarian origin, but Manuilski battled fiercely on her behalf in the party purge.

The area of Kuntsevo, which had been preserved largely in a natural state, was surrounded by barbed wire and high wooden fences and closely guarded by dogs and GPU men. No unauthorized person could enter it from any side. We, however, were permitted to leave on hikes to other areas, but the guards made certain that no one ranged beyond the reach of their watchful eyes.

Protected by the guards, we enjoyed the advantages of the upper class there as we did in our own building. We had everything needed for bodily nourishment, whether in the restaurant or by having food brought to the villa; diversions ranged from billiard rooms and concert halls to sports equipment and firearms. Our own chauffeurs, who drove us there, waited for us while we remained there.

Kuusinen still had in him enough democratic leavening to invite a chauffeur to dine with us. However, he was reproached for it so strongly that not even he dared violate the laws of precedence a second time, and his chauffeurs, like the others, had to eat and spend their time in their own barracks. They had their own isolated area; in the classless society it was not fitting for a chauffeur to sit at the same table with gentlemen.

In this chapter I have commented on some of Kuusinen's women. There is still one who deserves mention, though the tale is not associated with *Dom Pravitel'stva* at the time my wife and I lived there. It is, however, a page from Kuusinen's earlier life that I also have tried to touch upon.

In the chapter "Dirty Linen in Petrograd" I wrote about Aino Sarola who in 1921 hiked in low shoes and silk stockings through the woods of Karelia from Finland to the USSR and was brought to Petrograd just as the Finnish Communist party was about to begin its party congress.

A year earlier, in the autumn of 1920 in Helsinki, Mrs. Sarola had toted a batch of handwritten pages to me: poems and aphorisms that she said had been written by Kuusinen who had left Finland a little earlier. They were in an open envelope, and she actually

urged me to read them, so that I might come to understand the kind
of man Kuusinen really was.

Naturally, I glanced at them—in fact, I read the approximately
three hundred pages thoroughly. They were almost entirely love
poems and aphorisms inspired by love.

In handing them to me, Mrs. Sarola had said, "Notice that they
were inspired by me and most of them were written to me."

I had to admit that the woman to whom these effusive poems in
the style of the "Song of Songs" had been written had reason to be
proud. I knew that Kuusinen had done some versifying but until
then I had believed the poems to be political "torpedo verses" in
which "harlots . . . and bitches smell," as he sings in his famous
poem, "Torpedo," which we diligently recited in those days. But in
these love poems a woman's odors and fragrances were entirely
different.

This kind of love could lead only to marriage, and after Aino
Sarola had arrived in the USSR, Kuusinen married her a little later.
As Aino Kuusinen she soon angered the women in the Comintern's
women's division with her lust for power, her intelligence (and
perhaps also her feminine charm) and caused unrest also in some
men. She even caused a serious break between Kuusinen and Sirola.

Sirola had been in Berlin under orders at the beginning of the
1930s and there had met Aino Kuusinen. Something slight had developed between them—I could swear that it was at most a fleeting
kiss—but Sirola's unhappy lot was a perpetual guilty conscience
and, back in Moscow, it impelled him to make a confession to
Kuusinen.

Kuusinen naturally became angry and roared, "Get out of here;
you're a complete fool! How dare you tell me such childish tales?"

It was a dreadful blow to Sirola, who had expected forgiveness
and hoped that he would be told, "Now don't worry; it was really
nothing."

When his wife created such havoc within the Comintern circle,
Kuusinen began sending her on missions outside Moscow. Several
times she even visited the United States and Canada where, as a
political whip and the Comintern's emissary, she involved herself
in all matters and managed to entangle the affairs of both the
Canadian and American Communist party quite thoroughly. Even
a quarter of a century later, Finnish-language newspapers in the

United States and Canada published barbed references to what Mrs. Kuusinen had accomplished during 1929–32.

Despite the fact that Aino was away on trips much of the time, life nevertheless reached a point at which Kuusinen finally deemed it necessary to obtain a legal divorce. When I arrived in Moscow, Aino no longer had any contact with Kuusinen. There was no real animosity between them, but they spoke of each other as little as possible. After the divorce, Aino's life entered a new phase. Having disorganized Comintern affairs quite enough, she was dismissed from all duties connected with the Comintern. I understood that she joined the Red Army's Fourth Section, its political and intelligence branch. During my years in Moscow, she was almost always traveling.

Once she invited Sirola and me to see her apartment. She lived lavishly with elegant travel souvenirs from all over the world. At that time she had just returned from a long journey to the Far East, having visited Japan, China and stopped off here and there along the way. Although she tried to be cautious and even mysterious, and we made few inquiries, the conversation revealed that she was accompanied on her trips by a retinue of a lady's maid or two, and occasionally a male servant. She passed for an English lady or an American dollar princess, and the setting had to be appropriate to the station. When we visited her, the room was overflowing with American and English trunks. Since she spoke English and German and, I believe, tolerable French, and as a linguist had learned a little Japanese as well, she had the qualifications to complete successfully the tasks entrusted to her. At least she traveled on such missions during 1932–38.

Much after my departure from the Soviet Union, a man called to say that he had met a woman who claimed to be Aino Kuusinen. At that time she had been in a camp for elderly released prisoners. She had at first been very cautious but later had opened up and related that she had received a twenty-year sentence in 1938, all because—she claimed—Otto Wille Kuusinen had wanted to be rid of her and have her sent as far from him as possible.

Kuusinen's involvement in Aino's sentencing seems odd to me. In 1937–38 it was natural that a person who had been in hot water as often as Aino Kuusinen should be purged. What is most remarkable is that she remained alive.

Here ends my own personal knowledge of Aino Kuusinen. However, in 1972 she published her memoirs in Finland; they have appeared in English as well. In them she relates that she was imprisoned in 1938 and sent to a prison camp in Vorkuta, from which she was released in 1946. In 1949 she was again arrested and released in 1955. She succeeded in getting out of the Soviet Union in 1965 and died in Italy some years later.

LIFE ON A COLLECTIVE FARM

KUUSINEN, who wanted to prepare me thoroughly for my work and above all to see that my knowledge of Russian improved, obtained a Comintern order for me to spend three months in the provinces in the summer of 1934.

Until then all I had known about rural life was what had been taught at the Lenin School and what the Soviet press told its own people and foreigners: how, after the collective farms had been set up in 1929–30, the great majority of peasants had joined them and how their lives had changed as though by magic. Everything was different, housing many times better, clothing improved and even the cultural life entirely different from what it had been prior to the kolkhoz era, much less the czarist times. As Stalin put it a little later: "Life has become better, comrades, life has become gayer."

I had visited a number of kolkhozes around Moscow with foreigners' excursions as well as with my school, and they were positively model establishments. The kolkhoz peasants lived in passably good rooms, one could find no fault with the tools, the sanitary conditions and social welfare as a whole were amazingly well organized. My visits left me with the impression that, while not everything in Russia was perhaps so well off, conditions nevertheless were bearable and assuredly much better than before.

My journey took me to the Teplo-Ogarevski district, situated on the border of the Moscow and Ukraine regions, approximately sixty-two miles from the city of Tula. In this district was the collective farm Sovety Lenina, or Lenin's Councils, the patron of which was the Comintern. Patronage meant that some urban establishment undertook to aid and service a kolkhoz by sending it labor for the duration of the harvest drive, giving it financial support, and so on. I had been scheduled to stay at the Sovety Lenina but when proper accommodations could not be provided I was sent to live at the politsection of the machine-tractor station.

After the creation of the collective farm system such stations had been established throughout the countryside. Depending on size, they serviced twenty to fifty kolkhozes; mine was responsible for about thirty. In accordance with the system it also had a political bureau headed by a politcommissar. Now he also had me to take care of.

The commissar was one Maslov, who previously had served in Moscow as party secretary of *Pravda's* personnel, in other words, in a responsible position. For some reason, perhaps because of his competence, he had been ordered to manage this vast district.

He was a sharp-witted, pleasant man who made a favorable first impression, but the same could not be said of the surroundings. The technical staff was large, yet I didn't see a single happy face; everyone seemed to be deeply depressed, and the mood was like that at a prison camp. The work clothes were wretched, sheer rags, the kind not seen in Moscow, though the clothing wasn't much there, either. The living quarters, however, exceeded the clothing in wretchedness. The machine-tractor station had been built only a few years earlier, but already it was gaping inside and out. Considered from the Nordic viewpoint, the entire method of construction was absolutely hopeless. No foundation had been excavated, so it was no wonder that the whole shebang had begun to develop cracks right after the first winter.

I lived in the building reserved for the station's officials. All the top brass save the politchief himself—the agronomists, mechanical engineers, and the architect who had planned and constructed the buildings—were lodged there. My roommate turned out to be that very architect, an unusually pleasant and friendly man whose knowledge of the world extended beyond Russia. Somehow he had fallen into disfavor with the government and gotten a five-year sentence—it wasn't quite clear to me for what, and he himself probably didn't know either. At any rate, he had been sentenced, but because the prisons were full he had been exiled here to build these houses, among others. He could move freely around the area but couldn't leave it without permission. In other words, he was a prisoner.

Our room was not among the worst in the building but from the Finnish viewpoint it seemed wholly uninhabitable, at least in winter, for the wind blew in through innumerable cracks around the windows and doors. Now, in late summer and fall, it didn't matter—after all, we got fresh air—but the ghastly swarm of parasites, bedbugs, fleas, mice, and rats, was quite another matter. Here on the steppes it seemed to be a way of life that mice and rats moved into human habitations particularly in the fall when the grain had been harvested from the fields. In these hovels they had room to move about under the floors and in the attic, and when no war was waged against them one can understand what a torment they became. But most of all I was amazed and still am, that the people were not bothered. Although the rats and mice made a racket, and the bedbugs were so thick that one had to wipe them off one's face at night, those people considered it a normal life.

During my years in prison I had become accustomed to seeing vermin, but this Russian countryside was something else again. In describing it to my friends, I have seen from their faces that the borderline of credibility has been exceeded. When I went to bed the first night, I was attacked by such an army of bedbugs and fleas that I gave up and fled to the yard. After gathering enough courage, I tried the bed again, but brute force is brute force, and I spent the rest of the night sitting under the stars.

The next day I cleaned the miserable bed and shook the bedding outside, leaving only a few hundred bedbugs instead of thousands. But what could be done about the fleas? My roommate, who had watched my activities with interest—though he himself didn't give a damn about the vermin—came to my aid.

"*Chernaia kavaleriia* (the black cavalry) is easy to repel," he said. "A flea is able to leap from sixteen to twenty inches. If you pull your bed to the middle of the floor and spread a band of oil from twenty-four to twenty-eight inches wide around it, you'll be left in peace."

I followed the instructions and they worked splendidly. The black cavalry truly was unable to cross that death zone, and my own army of bedbugs could not get reinforcements. Every night I carried a large bucket of kerosene from the supply room and applied it liberally, for the isolating band had to be renewed constantly. The racket made by the rodents could not be stilled, but so great is human adaptability that after a few nights I slept like a log.

One thing had caught my eye immediately. The cement base of the building was high and the floor thus well above the ground. The entry and long hallway, however, had no floor and one had to walk along a single loose plank resting on the floor joists. I remarked to the architect that this building wasn't even completed and already it was on the verge of collapse. He assured me that it was completed but said that the previous winter there had been a shortage of wood, and the residents had burned the floor boards. Nevertheless, no one took it upon himself to begin putting down a new floor. I am sure that that one plank remained a permanent fixture. Such things were characteristic of the Russians and approached outright destructiveness—not only carelessness but actual destructiveness.

Generally neither the kolkhozes nor the machine-tractor stations had toilets, but this was a model establishment and hence two years ago a privy had been built there. In my time it no longer served any purpose, for at first the privy had been used, then its floor and then the front of it, until by now the outhouse itself was completely inaccessible. I asked Maslov whether there was another privy or whether they intended to begin renovating the first one.

He smiled broadly. "Vot, Arvo Oskarovich, what more could a person want? Here in the countryside for centuries already we've been using an outhouse that begins at the Arctic and ends at the Black Sea. An airy and pleasant place!"

As I have already mentioned, over thirty collective farms were serviced by this machine-tractor station, which meant that it rented tractors, agricultural machinery, and all kinds of tools to those kolkhozes. The number of kolkhoz members, or households, ranged from 100 to 500. The largest membership denoted a huge household: 500 families, many with numerous children. Inasmuch as these families averaged a minimum of six persons, the larger kolkhozes consisted of about three thousand individuals. That was no small garden patch—in fact, the lands of such a kolkhoz were of a vastness previously unseen by Finnish eyes. No landmarks were visible. When the kolkhoz's tractors left to harvest the rye, they had to make perhaps a half-hour loop before returning to the starting point. Naturally the loop grew smaller each time, but the outside one was huge.

Because the task of this politsection's chief was to see to it that the kolkhozes fulfilled their quotas, he had to visit these collective farms daily. Generally the plan was to take one kolkhoz at a time, remaining there the entire day, holding meetings and inspecting the results of the labor with various groups. I traveled with him and had a chance to familiarize myself thoroughly with the structure of a kolkhoz, its residents, and their living conditions.

The most common construction style in this area—and my observations on journeys indicated that the same was true in the entire Moscow region all the way to the central Volga—consisted of thatch-roofed huts of clay with usually only one room. They might vary a little in size, but on the average they were perhaps twenty or twenty-two, sometimes as much as thirty-two feet in length and thirteen or sixteen feet wide. The interior was usually partitioned by a thin board wall that rarely reached the ceiling. One side served as the human habitation, with a large oven that took up half the floor space; the other side served as a barn and henhouse. It might contain a cow or a calf, which quite a few had at this time; some places had a pig and almost all had poultry.

Furnishings were virtually nonexistent. Few places had beds; the people appeared to sleep atop the oven. Some had a table and a makeshift bunk. Usually, however, the furnishings consisted of a tablelike sleeping surface and a crude bench. It seemed odd that only an occasional hut had a wooden floor. Some had a tile floor, with the tiles set apart and ordinary clay between them, but the most common type of floor was merely of earth and clay. If these hovels bore little resemblance to dwelling places during the dry season, they were dreadful during the protracted rainy season in the fall, when the region's exceptionally soft mud was carried by wet footwear onto the clay floor. Little children who were almost naked—only some were swathed in adults' rags, and few had even makeshift pants—sat and walked and crawled in that ooze, and it is easy to imagine how they looked.

Over the centuries, however, the people had become accustomed to such conditions. The country folk did not appear especially undernourished or thin, but seemed normally plump. Naturally one saw far more rickety, bowlegged, and potbellied children than

in Finland, but comparatively few when one considers that environment, life-style, and diet. One would have expected to see no other
types at all—that was the wonder of it. What singular power spared
the children sprung from such miserable barns and made them
strong and healthy people? Does this explain the fact that the Russian nation is able to withstand any kind of treatment whatsoever?

Most of the collective farms had their own elementary school,
and in the center of the district itself was a large secondary school,
ostensibly the equivalent of our intermediate school. The teachers'
incompetence and the inadequacy of education, however, were
amazing. The principal of this school was the wife of the politsection's assistant chief, a young woman who in quick order had passed
her college matriculation examinations, graduated from a teacher's
college and been ordered here to be a principal. She was a very energetic and pleasant woman whom I met often at the station and
whose home and school I visited many times.

Typically, in addition to her principal's post, she had to hold
down the German teacher's position, though she had absolutely no
idea of the language. When she had attended school, German had
scarcely been taught and when it had, the teachers had been incom-
petent. Textbooks had been sent to her, and now she inquired of
me how German diphthongs should be pronounced. My knowledge
was based only on self-study during my prison years, but somehow
I was able to set the German teacher of this large school at least
partly on the right track.

It was interesting to note that here, in this country school, political subjects—communism, party history, Leninism, and historical
materialism—took up the major part of the class hours. Furthermore, the instruction, which I was able to observe on many an occasion, followed such formulas and dictates that not even the most
gifted pupils could grasp its meaning. When fourteen to sixteen-
year-old boys and girls were taught Marx's labor theory of value—
the comprehension of which requires a sharp and alert mind even
in an adult, the whole system seemed to be, to put it mildly, on the
wrong track. Amazingly enough, the school's principal and teachers
felt the same way; the results did not justify the effort.

Compared to the other subjects, the level of instruction in mathematics was very high. So too, in certain respects, was that in physics
and chemistry, where the instructional materials were quite good,

but the humanities had definitely been relegated to the position of a stepchild.

No cultural life existed in this area within a radius of many miles. True, speeches and meetings were held in the kolkhoz offices, and the largest kolkhozes had available a sort of hall in which social evenings could have been held, but there was little interest in such events. The people had no desire to participate in voluntary celebrations; they did everything only under duress; attended meetings under duress, came to listen to discourses under duress, but if non-attendance was not punished, they stayed away.

Not even such a rarity as a motion picture attracted more than a few. Only in the center of the district, where there were numerous bureau clerks and also the best film theaters, did the showings draw an audience, but not kolkhoz people. They were completely apathetic and benumbed. At times the Finnish national character may manifest itself in stoicism and melancholy, but melancholy to this extent one cannot come across anywhere in Finland.

In the heart of the district was a hospital that was crammed full of patients. It had not been built specifically as a hospital; it was just an old manor house taken over for that purpose. The building had perhaps been fixed up a little before being put to its new use, but the cleanliness and overall management certainly did not remind a Nordic of a hospital but, rather, of a barracks or logging camp. Everything, including the operating rooms and surgical instruments, was so primitive that such institutions most likely did not exist in Finland even in the earliest times, for we have at least strived for cleanliness.

Be that as it may, only a small fraction of the sick were admitted even to this hospital, for in visiting the kolkhozes and homes I met sufferers almost every day, and most of them were so gravely ill as to absolutely require hospitalization. Epidemics were quite common at that time, though I have been told that two scourges are endemic to Russia: dysentery and spotted fever. The latter, which is devastating, was prevalent in this area, too, but there was not room in the hospital for all the afflicted.

Never will I forget the drama that I watched unfold daily from my window. A feeble old woman, perhaps not in her dotage but unable to work, every morning dragged a young man out into the sunshine and sat there killing lice in his head and clothing. As I walked by I once inquired about their life. The man said that he had worked at a machine-tractor station until he had been stricken with galloping consumption.

"I went to a doctor and he released me from work and told me to eat good, nourishing food. But where could I get it? There's nothing but black bread and not too much even of that." The man's expression was heartrending as he added, "Who knows, I might have pulled through if I had gotten that 'nourishing food' right from the start."

He knew that he was doomed. He and his invalid mother had no money for food, and even if they had had some it would not have helped, since better food was not available; at most, with luck, a pound of butter could have been bought somewhere in the city. As the insidious bacilli gnawed at his lungs, hunger simultaneously wrought its own havoc on every cell of his body. Soon the day dawned when the old woman no longer had to drag her son outside: the mechanic, wasted to skin and bones, was carried out of the hovel feet first.

Life is cruel when it wants to be, but it still does not have to be grotesque. When I looked at that young man gasping for air, and the feeble mother beside him killing vermin, I saw in my mind's eye Stalin's declaration that proclaimed in large letters both in Moscow and here on the kolkhoz walls:

MAN IS OUR MOST PRECIOUS ASSET; HE MUST BE GUARDED
LIKE A TREASURE.

It was grotesque.

JOINING VOLUNTARILY
UNDER DURESS

WE HAD BEEN TAUGHT in the Lenin School, and the same had been preached at all the Comintern's informational gatherings as well as in the press, that joining a collective farm was voluntary; no one was forced to do so. During the early period of setting up the kolkhozes an error admittedly had occurred in that a few polit-commissars had used strong-arm methods and threats, but as soon as Stalin had heard about it he had given the strict order that such threats and force had to be discontinued. The entire kolkhoz system, in other words, was based on voluntarism.

Even in Moscow I had not taken that claim literally, though I had not suspected the truth by far. Here at this observation spot to which I had been assigned, it did not take me very long to discover that less than half the kolkhoz peasants had joined voluntarily. Only a small part of the very poorest, whose plot of land was tiny and who had no possessions, such as a cow or horse, joined voluntarily, but not the regular peasants. In talking with them I soon found out who had joined voluntarily, and who had not, for amazingly enough, despite the scope of the GPU terror in industrial areas by 1934 and the caution with which people spoke in Moscow and other cities, here in the countryside the peasant spoke quite fearlessly.

My first impression, which remained lasting, was that everyone was a counterrevolutionary, and that the whole countryside was in full revolt against Moscow and Stalin. Here there were none of those paeans to the great Stalin that one heard in the cities. If the people occasionally were forced to give some credit to the Soviet government, the more coarsely they cursed the extortion attempts applied to them. Although five years had elapsed since the establishment of the collective farms, and strong pressure had been applied the whole time, still all of 18 percent of these peasants remained private traders. In a few districts over 90 percent had joined kolkhozes, in others less than 80 percent, but here 82 percent were collectivized, the remainder were not. Now, in 1934, a new attack on private peasants had been launched. I was able to witness how these 18 percent were forced to join a kolkhoz voluntarily.

The methods were many. The first was taxation, so high that it was impossible to meet—double and even triple the ability to pay. These people assuredly were not kulaks, wealthy farmers, for they had already been liquidated. These were so poor that, out of the scores of households that we visited, only one had a horse and three had a cow—in other words, we succeeded in appropriating only three cows and tried to make off with one horse.

The people barely managed to eke out enough grain from their land to enable their families to survive. The soil was tilled with a primitive wooden plow, the crop was harvested with a sickle and threshed atop rugs in front of the hut; not even the most primitive threshing machine was available. It was estimated that, if a plot yielded ten hectoliters of rye, the tax would be set at twenty hectoliters, and a sharp eye was kept on the place so that, when the rye had been cut and a little of it dried hastily in front of the hut and perhaps a peck threshed, it could immediately be distrained before the people had time to eat it.

If an individual peasant managed to make one payment of, say, ten hectoliters, he was immediately assessed a surtax of twenty hectoliters that was picked up the following day. Mostly, however, it was clear even before we started our rounds that such and such a man would be imprisoned without further ado, and threatening behavior provided a good reason for imprisoning others. And when the men had been exiled to a camp, the wives and children joined the kolkhoz. So simply was the voluntary joining accomplished.

I have been in the soup many times, but rarely in anything more hideous. We got going, seven or eight armed tax collectors, and curses and tears followed our footsteps. The men threatened and swore—Russians really know how to swear—the women wept and prayed, the children bawled. But in vain—everything that was there was taken, not even a piece of bread was left. Those hovels didn't have many hiding places; whatever was hidden was usually among the rags on the oven. And even so, though we went to scores of places, we didn't get a whole sack of grain from anyone; mostly only from ten to twenty kilograms and some pieces of bread.

We continued in that manner day after day. Now and again we stopped off at houses that had already been robbed, to see whether any grain had appeared. Often it had, for the peasants had concealed their hoard someplace farther. Repeatedly the following exchange took place:

"When are these robberies going to end?"

"Why don't you join a kolkhoz?"

"We know how to die even in this misery. It's no better in kolkhozes. There you're robbed blind, too, and the children die of hunger."

Occasionally somewhat tense situations arose. A certain yard could be reached only by a passage between two hovels, and there stood an old fellow with an axe in his hand.

"Whoever tries to pass knows he'll get the axe!"

Naturally a terrific fuss ensued in the Russian manner. The man blustered and brandished his axe, our men swore and waved their weapons. On the steppe, some 300 yards away, we saw a half-grown boy galloping away on a horse. The old fellow glanced back and said, "I didn't mean anything except to let the boy get away with the horse."

This was the only incident that might be said to have contained a modicum of humor.

I shall remember forever a scene that was enacted in the district office where we carried our booty. A certain woman had been absent from her home when we had gone there to clean it out, and she arrived at the office to plead that a little be returned to her, at least enough to feed the children that day. She was wretchedly clothed, as were all the people in that area; clinging to her ragged skirt were two children, one about two, the other about five years of age, and under the skirt a third obviously awaited its arrival into this magnificence.

She wept and pleaded until someone snapped, "Why don't you join the kolkhoz?"

The woman fainted and fell, her skirt slipped up and the older child tried unsuccessfully to pull it over her mother's thighs. The politchief, the district chairman, and the militiamen paid no attention to her. As a foreigner I could not intervene in the matter. I only thought: "Man is our most precious asset."

What was it like in a kolkhoz? Why were individual peasants even at this late date, unwilling to exchange their own miserable lots for a place on one?

Briefly, a kolkhoz is a cooperative whose every member works as hard as he can; when the year's collective result has been totaled, the amount of the wages for each workday can be calculated. Conditions determine which branch of agriculture is pursued; at the place to which I had been assigned virtually all the kolkhozes grew rye; very little wheat was cultivated. Vegetables were grown only for one's own needs; wages were paid exclusively in grain. I took detailed notes on the procedure since I happened to be there during harvest time, and the grain had already been reaped when I left the latter part of September.

The daily wages varied from four to nine kilograms of grain; the average was six kilograms, which were for one's own use. The highest paid family could be considered the one with five working members: a man, his wife, and three sufficiently big children, each putting in an average of 200 workdays a year. Nothing was done in the winter, and 200 workdays meant that during the busiest summer period two norms sometimes had to be done within twenty-four hours. The best kolkhoz families did 5 × 200 workdays or 1,000 workdays a year. If a day's wages are calculated as averaging six kilograms, this family earned 6,000 kilograms of grain a year, plus whatever it raised for its own use on the tiny plot outside its hut.

Such a maximum category family is quite large, with as many minors as adults, or a total of nine or ten persons. About 350 kilograms of grain per year are to be calculated for each member's subsistence, which is a lot by Finnish standards but normal for Russians. This family thus received 3,500 kilograms of cereal grain for its own use, and 2,500 kilograms remained for selling. If it could have sold that amount, as promised in the kolkhoz constitution, it would have taken the grain to the free market where the price was two rubles per kilogram and earned 5,000 rubles, or 1,000 rubles per worker as an annual wage—in other words, a passable income.

However, year after year, when the grain had been harvested, the state directed that, in addition to the grain that the kolkhozes had paid to the state as taxes for the use of the machinery, the surplus grain also had to be relinquished to the state. Usually the decree was prettily phrased: certain areas had had a poor harvest; to alleviate the situation, those areas with a better harvest had to sell the grain to the state at the price stipulated by the state.

All the grain was in the same hands here, and hence the precise amount of the surplus was known. Simple calculation indicated that the kolkhoz "Lenin's Soviets" could sell the state 20,000 kilograms of grain at fifteen kopeks per kilogram. And so it was that the Ivanov family, which could have gotten 5,000 rubles on the free market, had to sell its grain to the state and received only 375 rubles, or 75 rubles per person for a year's labor.

I heard similar accounts from many kolkhozes, but this particular case concerned the Comintern's own "Sovety Lenina." The chairman of this kolkhoz could only observe that the results would have been quite good, but when the state takes it all, one is left with empty hands. What can be bought for seventy-five rubles is not worth mentioning. Clothes and footwear are as expensive in the country as in the city. For seventy-five rubles you couldn't buy even a pair of boots.

One should not assume, however, that the sale of that surplus grain was accomplished painlessly. From the Finnish viewpoint the yield was not high, only 800 to 900 kilograms to a hectare, but for Russia it was so good that the kolkhozniks began calculating what all they could buy for themselves with the money from the surplus grain—this time, at least, the state would not steal everything.

They did not suspect the fun that Stalin had in store for them, and even Maslov was horrified when he received the figures. Because the state had not received enough grain through regular taxation to take care of the industrial areas, Stalin ordered the kolkhozes in surplus production areas to sell the state all the grain not required for the minimum needs of the kolkhoz members. The politruk in each area was given control figures indicating how many tons he must buy from his area.

"Impossible!" cried Maslov. "One can't get 8,000 tons from this area unless one steals the seed and everything!"

But an order is an order. Maslov hastily made out a list specifying how much each of his approximately thirty kolkhozes was to "sell" to the state.

I had a chance to follow the "purchase" procedure as an observer. In addition to Maslov, the purchasing brigade consisted of two militiamen, one GPU official, a representative of the district committee, and myself. In other words six men, five of whom had *Mausers* dangling from their belts.

The procedure was to call a meeting of the collective farmers for a certain day, then our brigade would arrive to negotiate a deal. Maslov read a Politburo decree declaring that 8,000 tons were to be obtained from this area of the Teplo-Ogarevski district and then said that this particular collective farm would have to sell such and such an amount. A howl of protest arose at every farm. With one voice the people explained that nothing would be left to them on which to live.

"Hasn't Comrade Stalin promised that we can sell the surplus at the marketplace. We can get two rubles for one kilo there, while the state pays us only fifteen kopeks. How can we buy salt, sugar, and tea if the grain we intended to sell is stolen from us at fifteen kopeks?"

One man held forth in the whining tone often adopted by Russian peasants in lamenting their fate. "Alone I support a large family. The children are all small. Industrious I was, working 300 days for the kolkhoz. For that I got 1,500 kilos of grain. Five members in my family; they need 1,300 kilos. I would have sold the difference at two rubles a kilo. For that I would have gotten 400 and bought clothes for the children. Now I'll get thirty rubles. What can I buy for that?"

The muttering continued for an hour or two, but then the militiamen and the GPU official became stern: that is counterrevolutionary prattle, and Comrade Stalin has ordered that all counterrevolutionaries and enemies of the people be arrested and punished severely. Unless this kolkhoz sells the required amount it must be liquidated as counterrevolutionary.

After such a pronouncement Maslov would demand, *"Kto za, kto protiv*—Who for, who against?" In some instances enough hands were raised "for" already the first time to carry the motion. Frequently, however, the first vote had a negative result. A new "meeting" with harsher threats by the militiamen, the GPU official, and the politruk would bring the desired majority on the second or third vote.

In that manner we successfully bought a total of several hundred tons of grain from many collective farms, and each day the district newspaper would report how the members of that or that kolkhoz "with great enthusiasm unanimously decided to sell the state even more grain than had been requested."

Then one day we came to a collective farm called the Red October. It was medium-sized, consisting of about 200 households and was among the best in the region. The farmers had assembled in full force. Maslov repeated his old exhortation, announced that the Red October would have to sell 200 tons, and finally demanded, "Who for, who against?"

All were opposed. There was not a single affirmative vote. In previous cases the eventual compliance might have been attributable to the fact that the chairmen of the kolkhozes were Communists who had conditioned the people prior to our arrival. The Red October had not a single party member and only a few who belonged to the youth league. The chairman, a youngish man who was a former farm hand, opened the discussion.

"We had a good harvest because we worked hard and the reaping also went well. But we cannot sell the grain. We need footwear and clothing to see us through the winter."

Then he read excerpts from the "Stalinist collective farmers' constitution" that promises that surplus grain may be sold on the open market at the going price. This promise by Father Stalin—whom the chairman swore he loved above all—no one could break, not even Father Stalin himself. He argued that the collective farmers were without clothing and footwear, without salt, tea, and sugar. The money from the grain was to be used for these supplies, but if the state stole the grain at fifteen kopeks per kilogram they could get nothing.

"You may shoot us," he said, "but the Red October will not sell any grain!"

Many other kolkhozniks, both men and women, echoed the vow. The situation had become tense, but Maslov, the militiamen, and the GPU official seemed unconcerned. Now and then they would thunder a threat, vowing for their part that the kolkhozniks would sell. Again a vote was taken, but the result was slim: only one sickly man, a candidate for party membership, voted yes; all the others were opposed.

The meeting adjourned, but a few minutes later a new meeting was called, and the politruk made the same demand with the same conditions. This continued throughout the night, and the result was always the same: one for, all the others opposed. Only when dawn broke did the travesty end, but not before Maslov again had vowed that the farmers would, too, sell once all methods were tried.

On the return trip I was curious to hear what secret weapon the politruk intended to use against the apparently invincible Red October.

He just smiled confidently and remarked, "You'll see tomorrow night."

We rested that day and in the evening returned to the Red
October. Our party was joined by a truck from the machine-tractor
station, two militiamen, and an additional GPU official. This time
we traveled with three automobiles and nine men, not including
the three chauffeurs.

The collective farmers once again were assembled in strength.
When they noticed that the number of armed buyers had increased
and saw the truck, they assumed that the grain would be confiscated.
The tension increased. Electricity was in the air. Even before the
meeting began I heard many groups growl, "If they try to take it
forcibly, we'll fight!"

Maslov opened the meeting and without further ado announced
that, according to information obtained by local officials, the chairman of the Red October and two other kolkhozniks (who earlier
had most vehemently protested the sale) were guilty of grain specu-
lation, selling rye in the marketplace at a profit. It was thus his sad
duty to arrest them, since Soviet criminal law severely punishes
those guilty of profiteering: a minimum of two years in prison and
exile to distant regions.

Having said this, he signaled the militiamen who immediately
led the accused to the truck outside. In the same breath he continued, "Now we'll take a vote on who is for, who against."

A tremendous roar arose. Everybody shouted. No one asked for
or was given the floor. Threats were heard on every side. Others
screamed that they would write to Comrades Stalin and Kalinin,
who would not countenance this. Relatives of the arrested men
pleaded for mercy.

When Maslov had managed to quell the noise, he asked for a
show of hands and, to my amazement, I saw six joining yesterday's
one. The great majority, however, still was opposed.

Even though by now I was accustomed to one thing and another,
I was stunned and at the same time curious to know how Maslov
would react to the Red October's failure to surrender to his secret
weapon. But he merely announced as calmly as though nothing
had happened that a new meeting would begin.

Again he pulled a paper from his pocket, announced that the
local officials also had learned of the involvement in grain specula-
tion of collective farmers Kulikov and Stepanov as well as many

other members of this kolkhoz whose names he would not yet reveal, and said that it was therefore his duty to have them arrested. At that Kulikov and Stepanov were taken into custody and led out to an automobile.

Again there was shouting and clamoring, followed by voting. This time, in addition to the six earlier "ayes" there were perhaps a score more. After that Maslov put the matter to a vote two more times and arrested five kolkhozniks, but majority support for the grain sale was not reached that night.

Our group returned to the machine-tractor station well after midnight in a somewhat gloomy mood despite our booty of ten prisoners, who were taken to the district jail and from there would be sent to forced labor beyond the Urals or to some northern regions.

The struggle at the Red October had aroused the keen interest of other collective farms nearby. I heard that all the kolkhozniks in the area sided with the Red October and sent encouraging messages urging no surrender. But the row had developed into a question of authority and honor to the politruk and the GPU. Maslov was in touch with Moscow throughout the following day and received new instructions.

I humbly offered my own opinion that such tactics were horrifying. Since the arrested persons were not guilty of the crimes with which they were charged, wouldn't the entire region rise in revolt? And what would Stalin and the other leaders in Moscow say to such terrorizing, for naturally the collective farmers would lodge a complaint? Wouldn't it be simpler just to take the militiamen and seize the grain from the kolkhoz storehouse rather than go through the farce of voting, which was tantamount to stealing?

Maslov smiled genially and explained, "You don't realize yet how these kolkhozniks have to be handled. Do you really think that I'm doing this at my own risk? My orders come from the highest quarters in Moscow. I've also been ordered not to resort to confiscation, but to force the kolkhozniks by all legal means to vote in favor of selling. In that way, you see, they're selling the grain 'voluntarily,' which is entirely different from confiscation."

To his official explanation, however, Maslov did add the admission that such terrorism and mock voting were indeed horrible but what could he do? He was under the strictest orders to obtain a certain number of tons from this area, and if he failed he would be liquidated.

On the third evening we prepared for the final crushing of the Red October. Purchasing agents were increased, and two trucks were taken along. Crowds of curious people from other collective farms congregated in front of the office. The militiamen and the GPU official drove them away before the "meeting" began.

When the purchasing brigade entered the assembly room a voice was heard to say, "Now those pigs intend to arrest everybody on the kolkhoz, because they came with two trucks."

From the very beginning of the meeting it was apparent that the Red October was on the verge of defeat. But tenaciously it resisted. A vote was taken. No result. Again several kolkhozniks were arrested. Another meeting. Another vote. New arrests. Seldom have I experienced so nightmarish an atmosphere.

The night darkened. Kerosene had not been seen in this area in years and there was not enough to light a lamp, though the machine-tractor station had some. The meeting continued in the darkness, a darkness that breathed hatred and stubborn defiance. Only a candle was lighted when Maslov ordered the detention of more men. Vote followed vote, the battle continued, and more than ten men had been arrested.

Finally, after midnight, an old man said, "This won't get any better. They'll just come again tomorrow and the day after, until no one is left."

Maslov immediately ordered another show of hands, and this time he got a slight majority, just enough to suffice. While the minutes of the meeting were being recorded, the bitter lament of the old man was etched in my memory: "You could at least have brought along enough kerosene so that we could see to sign this robbery resolution!"

If I thought that by now I had some understanding of Russian ways I was badly mistaken, for then followed the most astonishing scene of all. When the robbery resolution had been signed, the leader of the theft asked whether anyone had an accordion so that there could be dancing. And behold! An accordion was produced, the unarrested kolkhozniks formed a circle, one began to play the accordion, others clapped their hands in rhythm, and in the center of the circle some kolkhozniks and the politruk and the GPU men danced the hopak.

On the previous evening I had assumed from the uproar and threats that not many of the "purchasers" would leave the place alive, but while watching the dancing I realized that my judgment was based on Finnish criteria. In fact, on the homeward trip I told Maslov that if such "purchases" were to be attempted among Finnish peasants, knives and clubs would be wielded so furiously that not a single "purchaser" would escape alive.

He replied that the Russian people had grown accustomed to such ways over the centuries. Admittedly a few collective farm chairmen had been shot in the back after dark, and some tractormen had been killed, but such outbursts of bitterness passed and life continued as before.

When I returned to Moscow and told the other Finns what kolkhoz conditions had become and what brutal and inhumane robbery methods were resorted to, no one could believe it. Kuusinen was flabbergasted; he could not have imagined that matters had taken such a turn. And I greatly fear that for idealistic Sirola my revelations meant another nail in his coffin.

Actually, it was not a wonder that we Finnish leaders were unfamiliar with the situation. Others seem not to have been aware of it either, for in his major speech in the spring of 1956, Khrushchev declared the following:

Stalin knew the countryside and agriculture only from motion pictures, and these films had altered and glossed over the condition in agriculture.

Many motion pictures portrayed kolkhoz life as if the tables groaned under the weight of turkeys and geese. Obviously Stalin believed that this actually was the case.

Vladimir Iljich Lenin viewed life differently; he was always close to the people. . . .

Stalin dissociated himself from the people and never went anywhere. This lasted for decades. He last stopped off at a rural village in January 1928 during a visit to Siberia in connection with grain deliveries. How then could he have been familiar with rural conditions?

When one discussed these matters with some knowledgeable Russian, he had a simple explanation and defense:

The capital goods that we need for creating heavy industry do not drop down from heaven; they must be obtained through the wealth that is most accessible to us, the peasants' labor and property. Prosperity cannot be achieved without an emphasis on heavy industry, and when it is achieved the peasants may sell their grain freely, but not before.

A good answer, though it doesn't explain why it is necessary to act so ruthlessly. But be that as it may, the main thing is that the Soviet rule had not succeeded, at least by then, in elevating the rural population from its czarist status.

When all is said and done, however, the oddest thing was that the semiweekly provincial newspaper described how the peasants, in revolutionary fervor, sold their grain to Stalin dirt cheap, and then those papers were distributed to the victims of the robbery.

A European—at least a Finn—is not able to comprehend that.

THE REFORMATION OF THIEVES

ACCORDING TO THE Marxist-Leninist-Stalinist theory, stealing is one of the social phenomena that should disappear along with capitalism. But at least in the early years of Soviet power, and presumably even today, there has not been the slightest indication that robberies, embezzlements, and similar occurrences have decreased, much less ended.

On the contrary, stealing was an amazingly flourishing way of life in the Soviet Union still in the 1930s, and because we Finns did not dare discuss politics especially when the Stalin cult was at its worst—the risk of getting onto a wrong path, a so-called *uklon* or deviation, was great—the chief topic of conversation was always theft: what had been stolen from each of us since our last meeting.

Perhaps one factor in the increase in stealing was the communist ethic that Stalin taught painstakingly during the latter part of his life, the main element of which was: all that you do for the good of the Soviet Union, for the good of communism, is morally right, whether the deeds be pilfering, stealing, murder, or whatever.

A famous example of this was the circular drafted by the administration of the Finnish Communist party in Petrograd as early as 1922, one section of which read as follows:

THE DEFENSE OF SOVIET RUSSIA

The needy must still be assisted in every way. Factory workers must be persuaded to make tools for their Russian comrades. For example, they can steal a carpenter's knife, a piece of wood for a hammer, or a piece of iron needed to make a compass or other tool, and make it when the employer is not watching. In this way the aid in kind to the Russian comrades will not be burdensome to the workers, since it will be paid for by the capitalist whose raw materials have been taken.

This baseness of communist morality is one of the major points that has been successfully concealed from the multitude to this very day. That theft directive of 1922 has long since been forgotten, but the Finnish Communist party and the Communist parties of all countries still organize similar schemes on a continuing basis. The only difference is that these crimes are perpetrated much more subtly and on a much broader scale.

At any rate, the Revolution had not put an end to stealing in the Soviet Union but rather had increased it, though it had almost completely done away with any articles worth stealing.

There was not a person from whom something had not been stolen, not even such notables as Gylling and Rovio, who traveled in special cars. Once Rovio, though he was in an international car with an armed guard at either end, was robbed of all his clothing. Only his pajamas remained when he awakened at the Moscow station, and as of our last meeting he still was unable to explain, as were the Chekists, who the thief was and how the theft had been accomplished.

Sirola, who was the professorial type, regularly was relieved of his watch and wallet. Usually the pickpocketing occurred in crowded street cars; since one hand had to hold on to a strap or bar, the breast pocket remained unprotected, and in that way he was robbed of something almost every month. The Scandinavians had made it their prime responsibility to keep him supplied with watches. Every time some delegation arrived from Sweden, Norway, or Denmark, it invariably had a watch for Sirola. Despite that, he was without a watch for the greater part of those years that I associated with him. Naturally, the thieves' haul was not limited to the watch; frequently he lost his money and papers as well.

Tales were told, each more amazing than the last, and I, too, once experienced the heights to which the thieves had developed their technique. Having completed the course at the Lenin School in 1934 and undergone the sanatorium cure in the Caucasus, I received travel orders through Kuusinen to undertake a study trip, as described above, to learn the language and familiarize myself with the countryside at a place named Teplo-Ogarevski, that was situated on the border of the Ukraine and Moscow regions. Since the trip was scheduled to last three or four months, a considerable amount of paraphernalia had to be taken along. And so I had a large suitcase full of things, mainly clothing, and my wife saw me off at the Moscow station.

This time I did not travel in the first class of the international car, to which I would not have been entitled anyway, since I was not yet a member of the Comintern Presidium. Because of the many warnings to be wary of thieves, I told my wife that I would take my suitcase into the semidark car and place it on the table before the open window.

"Hold on to the suitcase and I'll come outside to talk for a while."

My wife clutched the handle of the suitcase until I got outside. We stood there talking, and I in turn held on to the bag for the entire ten minutes until the train's departure time.

As we were talking a man came over and asked, "Could you change fifty rubles? I sold my suitcase over there and have to get some change."

He was a suspicious looking man, well dressed—in fact, for a Russian he was very well dressed. I replied that I was unable to make change.

"Thank you just the same," he said. "Thank you very much. Are you Estonians?"

"We're not Estonians, we're Russians," I replied.

"Oh," said the man, laughed and went his way.

A few minutes later he waved from the car platform and said, "Everything is all right. I was able to take care of the matter."

Well, it didn't interest us particularly. We merely wondered why on earth we should be concerned with whether he sold his suitcase or not. Then the bells rang and the train whistled. My wife held on to the suitcase until I got on board. The train began to pull out, I said goodbye to my wife and started to lift my suitcase onto the rack.

Suddenly a man cried out, "Hey, where are you putting my bag?"

I replied that the suitcase was mine.

"No, it isn't," the man insisted. "It's mine. I just bought it."

The entire section of the car attested to the fact that the man had bought it and paid twenty rubles for it. I asserted that it most certainly was my suitcase, no matter from whom he had bought it; that I had put the bag there and my wife had held on to it until I had gotten into the car.

A terrific hullabaloo arose. Everyone agreed that I was a swindler and that once the man had bought the suitcase it was his. The uproar became so noisy that someone went to fetch the train's inspector, a Chekist. I was at a disadvantage in that I spoke Russian feebly—it was only my second year in the country, and I was just on my way to the provinces to gain a practical knowledge of Russian. About all I could do was to grip the handle of my suitcase.

The Chekist arrived. "What's going on?"

Everyone explained that this man bought a suitcase and that the man who sold it came over to consult with this person and later, after selling it, reported that everything was all right, so the only possible answer is that this one is a master swindler and the seller was his agent. For my part I tried to explain to the Chekist that the matter could be decided by the contents of the suitcase. Did the purchaser know what it contained? He said that he didn't, but believed it to be empty.

"It is not empty," I said. "It is full of things. And do you know what it contains?"

He did not.

"Well, I do know, because it's my suitcase. It contains, among other things, a leather suit which costs at least a thousand rubles. In other words, you have bought a suitcase containing a thousand-ruble leather suit as well as other things. How can you explain that?"

He couldn't, but what of it? What was bought was bought.

"Have you the key?" asked the Chekist.

"I have." I opened the suitcase and there was the leather suit that I had brought from Sweden as well as many other things. A single glance told one that, by Soviet estimates, there was at least two thousand rubles' worth of goods: European clothes and a special suit, in addition to the leather suit and all kinds of other things.

The Chekist resolved the problem. "If this man were a swindler, why would he let his agent sell all this for twenty rubles? You keep your suitcase, and you consider the twenty rubles as your loss."

I am convinced that my papers decided the case: the Comintern travel orders and Kuusinen's usual letter of recommendation.

All that night my travel companions told tales of thievery, very interesting ones though I didn't understand all the nuances. Now and then they returned to my case, wondering why the man had come to me before and after the sale. I tried to explain that he came to change money, but since my knowledge of the language was so-so, my listeners were probably left with the impression that I was, after all, a rather shady figure.

Many such tales could be told, but let this occurrence involving Tyyne Tokoi, Oskari Tokoi's daughter, suffice as a further example. She was traveling to the Caucasus from Leningrad in the same type of upholstered car as I was during my adventure; her job did not entitle her to the finer cars, but neither was it fitting for her to travel among the lower class. Sleeping cars were few and so that two-and-a-half day journey had to be made in a day coach. Because she, like everyone else, had been warned about thieves, she placed her suitcase on the opposite rack in order to keep an eye on it. She glanced at it frequently and arrived safely in Kislovodsk. When she took the suitcase down from the luggage rack it was peculiarly light. The people on the other side had slit the bottom of the bag with a knife and removed its contents.

After everyone, both high and low, had been thus victimized, it is not surprising that a letter published in *Izvestiia* in 1935 attracted unusual attention.

The letter was addressed to the public prosecutor—the supreme enforcer of the law—Vyshinsky, who subsequently achieved fame as foreign minister and the Soviet Union's representative at the United Nations. The writer was a preparatory schoolteacher who was not qualified inasmuch as he had obtained the position with stolen papers. He had intended to remain on the job only until a new robbery caper came along, but then had become interested in the work and realized that it was his true calling. Gradually he comprehended that such a thing as stealing was not necessary in this society, particularly since some of his close relatives were Stakhanovites and had won medals and fame. (The Stakhanovite movement, aimed at speeding up work, had been launched a few months earlier.) Moreover, when he saw his teaching colleagues making good progress with honest work, he was all the more anxious to settle accounts with his old life.

To top it all, it was also mentally imperative, because as a geography teacher he was constantly confronted by places in which he had committed his crimes: in Tjumen he had robbed, in Tobolski stolen, in Samara done some other trick, in Saratov embezzled. When one had lived for decades by embezzling, stealing, and robbing there was hardly a place on the map of Russia that did not evoke unpleasant memories. Now he wanted to report to the public prosecutor that he was ready to make amends for his crimes if this could be done, not in prison, but by pursuing his teaching career. But he would not sign his name because he first wanted to know whether such an atonement was feasible.

To that published letter the public prosecutor had appended a brief note asking the writer to report to the public prosecutor's office on such and such a day at such and such a time; adding, "We can only say that there are hopes of resolving your case in the manner that you wish."

After the appointed day, *Izvestiia* and especially *Vecherniaia Moskva,* an evening paper dealing with just such lighter matters, published a long account that related that on the specified day twenty or thirty persons had appeared at Vyshinsky's office, all carrying a copy of that *Izvestiia* with the teacher's letter and the public prosecutor's invitation. All asked to speak to the public prosecutor, and the guard asked them to be seated. They sat down along the walls of the waiting room, but one man began going from one person to the next, whispering in his ear.

It turned out that the whisperer warned them, "Don't go; there's a snake in the grass. They're trying to trick you into a trap. When you confess your crime, naturally you'll be arrested."

The situation was so tempting that no one left because of his warning, nor did he himself. Later it became known that the whisperer was none other than the entire Soviet Union's king of thieves, known in the thieves' world as Count Kostya.

When Vyshinsky finally came to his office and saw the crowd, he announced that he could not receive them since it would take at least a day. He asked them all to come that evening to *Izvestiia's* conference room, where the matter would be thrashed out.

And so it happened that on that day hundreds of people turned up at the *Izvestiia* conference room. During the afternoon the original thirty persons had spread the word throughout the thieves' world that there was a chance to make amends for their crimes. The newspapers described vividly the unique gathering and its nervousness when seven o'clock struck and Vyshinsky failed to appear. The people began shifting around and throwing furious glances at the thirty "intermediaries" as though to say: you're probably agents of the public prosecutor and have tricked us here into a net!

These men went quickly to call Vyshinsky. "Why don't you come; is something rotten going on?"

Vyshinsky reported that he was detained by other meetings but would assuredly arrive; there was no trickery involved.

He finally showed up some twenty minutes late and was surprised to see the large gathering. Stepping to the dais, he said that he would explain the situation before anyone began making confessions. On the basis of the teacher's letter he could say that minor crimes, embezzlements, robberies, petty thefts, and so on could be expiated without concentration or prison camps, depending on the circumstances in which they had been committed and whether the repentance and change of heart were sincere. But for political crimes and murders there was no hope of mercy.

We well understand, he said, that under the previously prevailing conditions stealing was almost a necessity and compulsion for Russian citizens. In the shift to Soviet power, it was handed down as an unfortunate heritage, but as the teacher's letter makes clear, now a Soviet person can live by honest work; Stalin has arranged matters so well that everyone can get along without stealing.

The newspapers reported further that, as Vyshinsky made his speech, three men in a corner held their own little meeting and when Vyshinsky had concluded, one of them—he turned out to be the king of Moscow's thieves—took the floor. He said that they had just drafted a declaration that they wished to read to the gathering.

Vyshinsky gave his permission. A chairman was even designated, and the meeting proceeded along official lines. This thieves' declaration was a remarkable document that subsequently was made public and to which reference was made in many contexts. In it the thieves explained, much as Vyshinsky had, how circumstances had forced them onto a path of crime, but now that Stalin had smoothed the way to a new life no one needed to steal or embezzle any longer. They appealed to all the thieves throughout the Soviet Union to stop stealing and to report to their local authorities so that an end could be put to this despicable evil, and they could all become worthy sons of the fatherland.

This was published in the daily papers as a major story, and then began a unique drama. Day after day *Izvestiia,* the aforementioned *Vecherniaia Moskva* and sometimes *Pravda* published the most imaginative crime novels, the rogues' autobiographies. Some had begun at the age of ten, others at fifteen, still others already during the czarist era or the early days of Soviet power; they had now given themselves up and confessed repentence. There was no end to these detailed accounts.

Among the most interesting life stories was that of Count Kostya, who had propagandized at the first gathering. His specialty was the Far Eastern express trains on which foreigners traveled; previously they had been used by the NEP (New Economic Policy) officials and then by other businessmen. As an assistant he had Sonja, a beautiful young Russian skilled in foreign languages, with whom he selected his victim when the train left Moscow or Vladivostok. Well dressed, they themselves traveled first class; Sonja made friends with the victim in the dining car and dropped some drug into his drink or coffee. After retiring to his compartment, the man would fall into a deep sleep; sometimes the drugging had resulted in the last sleep. And Count Kostya emptied the compartment of securities, money and valuables but did leave his victim's clothes which was unusual, since Soviet thieves made a clean sweep of a good haul. Count Kostya was a gentleman thief.

The account did not reveal how he had managed to engage in this activity year after year undetected by the Chekists and inspectors on the trains—did he perhaps have some connection with them, was he actually their hireling? It also remained unclear how he had been able to travel in that manner, because it was very difficult for anyone but high officials or foreigners to obtain sleeping accommodations and first-class compartments on Russian trains. At any rate, it was the life story of a true gentleman thief, for he was not charged with outright murders or treason.

Count Kostya's confessions were topped off with an impressive climax: he, miserable sinner that he was, did not trust himself; he could not assure the great Stalin that his life in the future would be blameless unless he were allowed to join an expedition working on the Arctic Ocean for at least two years under circumstances that provided no opportunities for practicing his old profession.

The authorities immediately promised him that penitential job, but before leaving he had to help arrange the affairs of his unfortunate colleagues. He was made the chief organizer in obtaining jobs for the thieves. The Federation of Trade Unions had been mobilized to assist the authorities; its subsections in various parts of the country smoothed the way for the reformed as the confessions arrived. At the same time orders were given that fellow workers must in no way shun these beginners of a new life even if they should know something about their dark past. On the contrary, they must be treated with consideration and respect like other fellow workers; in other words, they were under the special patronage of both the Federation of Trade Unions and the authorities.

Day after day, week after week, reports told of the spreading of this popular movement from distant Siberia, Turkestan, and the Caucasus all the way to Archangel and Murmansk, with all the thieves hastening to report. The accounts were, as previously observed, incredibly imaginative.

An example of our friend Count Kostya's reformation was this little tale: A foreign woman left two suitcases standing in the waiting room of the Kiev station in Moscow while she went to the other side of the building to buy tickets. Count Kostya happened to be there, dispatching three of those famous thieves to their jobs. One of them, the leader of a Moscow thieves' gang, noticed the suitcases. His eyes began to gleam and instinctively his feet began sidling toward those foreign leather suitcases. Count Kostya immediately noticed the other's intentions and clapped a heavy hand on his shoulder.

"See here, Comrade Mihailov, we have promised Comrade Stalin that we will never again steal anything. Remember, devil take it, that you don't lay a finger on those bags and that you'll never again stray onto this path."

To which the others replied, "Quite right, but imagine leaving one's bags like that! It's downright torment."

Count Kostya ordered them to remain where they were, then went to the woman waiting at a ticket window and clicked his heels.

"Madame," he said, "one must never leave one's suitcases like that here; they may be stolen. They are safe now because I have seen to it that no one could steal them, and I'll continue to do so but just the same, never leave your bags like that."

Thus it was these most famous thieves, Count Kostya and the worst rogues in the Moscow area, who saved this foreigner's suitcases. The newspapers called it a symbolic act: in this manner the evil of stealing would be weeded out of the entire Soviet state.

And so, according to newspaper accounts, tens—perhaps hundreds—of thousands of criminals had been placed in decent jobs, and now it was expected that at least the major part of this repugnant remnant of a capitalist society would be eradicated. Not only was it a question of thefts but of embezzlements and robberies; even murders might be expiated if they had been committed under highly extenuating circumstances.

All this made for vastly exciting and engrossing reading, and for three months we lived with this movement, Kuusinen, my wife and I, until one day it unexpectedly ended. In our own circle we wondered greatly why the newspapers no longer said a single word about those reformed rogues.

I brought up the subject with a big shot in the Federation of Trade Unions whom I knew. "Why don't the papers write about the thieves any more?" I asked. "Have you run out of thieves?"

A disgusted look came over his face. "If only people wouldn't talk about them! If only the whole affair could somehow be buried."

"How so?"

"Well, those of us in the trade unions as well as the Soviet officials, beginning with the Chekists and Comrade Stalin himself, started off in good faith believing that the evil of stealing truly could be eradicated. We placed the scoundrels in jobs by the thousands and tens of thousands, and it's true that a lot of them did report for work. We also assume that for the most part the reporting was sincere; they actually thought that they could reform.

"We placed them in jobs, but from almost the first day there were reports that stealing had begun with a vengeance. They stole their fellow workers' clothes, they stole whatever property was available—at first on the job, then later they began breaking in and stealing in the vicinity. Since the workers, as you know, live in barracks for the most part, a terrible commotion arose. They stole the workshops clean of tools and sold them until the decent workers set up a clamor, refusing to do another lick of work until the thieves were removed.

"Nothing would do but that we had to begin removing from one end while new ones were brought in at the other, and most of these are by now in prisons and concentration camps. The only benefit derived from this experiment was that in this way we managed to catch a considerable number of them for our prisons and concentration camps, even though that was not the objective. Comrade Vyshinsky's and Comrade Stalin's intentions were absolutely sincere, for they believed that in this way stealing could be diminished considerably."

"But what about the crux of the matter?" I asked. "Is stealing after all something other than the product of circumstances and environment?"

This high-ranking trade boss could say only that they still could not relinquish the theory that stealing could be totally abolished as soon as social conditions were so improved that people actually could get along without embezzlement, theft, and other crimes.

"Apparently our conditions are still so inadequate—the workers' housing, clothing, wages, everything—that stealing pays," he observed. "Stealing obviously offers a better livelihood than honest labor. Only in that way can we explain the outcome of this great experiment."

The drama thus had ended, and my wife and I had forgotten the entire matter until 1941, when the Finns had retaken Viipuri, and we saw an item in the newspaper about a prisoner of war, a Soviet official who had held an important post in Viipuri. He related how Viipuri, which had been captured by the Russians during the Winter War, had been evacuated and cleaned out in the fall of

1940 and early 1941, and everything even slightly valuable taken to the Soviet Union.

He mentioned that the evacuation had been set up and directed by Count Kostya, who had achieved great fame in the 1930s by arranging jobs for thieves. I have not been able to determine whether Count Kostya actually spent the two years on that expedition, and whether he had become a true Soviet citizen, but judging by the news item the Stalinist officials were able to put his old professional skills to good use in the evacuation of Viipuri. To what degree he functioned for his own benefit we cannot of course know, but perhaps he actually had reformed sufficiently to evacuate Viipuri entirely for the state's account. Who knows, Count Kostya might have been the only man to undergo reformation and a change of heart.

THE COMMUNIST INTERNATIONAL SEEN FROM WITHIN

MANY WHO ARE superficially familiar with Soviet developments and know that the Comintern was abolished during World War II, may surmise that as an apparatus it has only historical significance. I maintain that only after the war has the Comintern's influence become fully apparent. I shall return to this argument later.

Before the Comintern was founded in 1919, largely at Lenin's initiative, there had been two international organizations of the workers' movement: the First International, created by Marx and Engels, and, after its dissolution, the Second International, which went badly to ruin during World War I. In addition, there had been an international organization of trade unionists known as the Amsterdam International.

When the Third International was founded in Moscow, it was given the name Com(munist) Intern(ational), and its intention was not to accept as members just any workers' parties. Lenin planned it to be the vanguard of an international organization of revolutionary workers—in other words, only those parties and workers that endorsed armed revolution and the dictatorship of the proletariat as the only right road. For that reason, at the Second Congress of this International (1920), he dictated a program of twenty-one points to be imposed on each party that joined it. Only those parties that endorsed the twenty-one requirements would be permitted to join. The most important clauses were the endorsement of armed revolution, the forcible overthrow of the old capitalist or bourgeois social system, and the endorsement of the dictatorship of the proletariat. There was thus no recognition of any parliamentary path or form in the transition from capitalism to communism. This was the basic principle on which that organization was founded.

I have already related how we Finns, as well as some other delegations to the Comintern's Third Congress, doubted whether this International could create a true bond among Communist parties because it was situated in Moscow and enjoyed the hospitality of the Russian state—in other words, it was maintained by the Russian state. Under these circumstances we suspected that inevitably it would be used to further Russia's foreign policy and that sooner or later it would become—if indeed it was not that already at its formation—a special organ of the Russian foreign ministry. And that is precisely what it became.

In short, this International's structure was such that all the parties that endorsed those twenty-one theses acquired membership. If some national party was guilty of the slightest infraction it was reprimanded and finally expelled. Norway's Communist party, for example, endorsed the theses and joined the Comintern but a few years later found itself unable to fulfill the requirements and resigned voluntarily. According to the rules the same country could not be represented by two parties. In many backward countries, where neither communism nor any organized workers' movement had yet obtained a foothold, Moscow—in other words, the Comintern—helped found at least a nominal or formal Communist party.

Thus the Comintern's membership in the 1930s, when it was at peak strength, included the Communist party of almost every country in the world, even to Asia and Africa, to say nothing of Europe. Some of the Communist parties, for instance those of Scandinavia, France, Holland, and Belgium, functioned legally and openly, but a significant number operated illegally. The leadership of almost all these illegal parties—especially the largest, such as the Polish, Finnish, Yugoslav, Bulgarian, Romanian, Hungarian, among others—functioned in Moscow close to the Comintern and were funded by the Comintern. Even those parties that could operate freely in their own countries had a representative or a delegation at the Comintern, much as the Catholic churches of every country are accredited to the Vatican.

The structure of the Comintern thus consisted of Communist parties, and the Congress was its highest decision-making organ; it selected the Executive Committee, whose membership ranged from thirty to forty-six, and this committee in turn selected the Presidium, which had fifteen to twenty members and ten to twelve alternates. The Congress convened now and then, by 1935 only seven times, but in the interims so-called mini-congresses, called Comintern plenums, had been held. They were expanded meetings of the Executive Committee.

The actual leadership lay in the Presidium, many of whose members lived and worked in Moscow, as well as in the Comintern Secretariat. In the beginning the Secretariat was not very large but later it swelled until, after the 1935 Congress, there were all of ten secretaries, seven permanent and three alternate. The work procedure consisted of giving each secretary his own huge machinery that functioned throughout the year, day and night; the Presidium convened at short intervals, sometimes weekly, sometimes biweekly, as affairs demanded; the Executive Committee met only once or twice a year; the Congress once every three years.

The affairs dealt with by the Secretariat concerned almost the full range of political and economic matters. Each secretary had his own geographical area. The map of the world was divided so that each secretary had several countries; some areas were larger, others were smaller, depending on how important they were considered. Kuusinen, for example, had all Asia. Earlier he had been responsible for Western Europe, and at another time for America. Now China, Japan, India—in short, the whole of Asia, belonged to him. The secretaries, in other words, were responsible for the Communist parties of the countries in their areas. It was the duty of the parties to report to the secretaries on developments in their countries and on party activities. Often the secretaries, at their own initiative, would demand reports and explanations.

Thus, the whole world's events were centered in the Comintern apparatus, which was located in an imposing building beside the Kremlin wall, at the end of Comintern Street. In addition, it had many other buildings around the city in which the Secretariat's subsections functioned. From here attempts were made to control world developments, especially as they concerned the workers' movement; here revolutions were planned; here, in 1935, were initiated the so-called popular fronts that were launched in France with much fanfare and that were to have swept the whole world.

The Comintern was truly the staff or the headquarters of world revolution, and amazing things were accomplished both during its existence and, even more amazing, after the Comintern was formally abolished. I have often noted, for example, that the land mines that were set in the 1920s and 1930s in Asia and Africa began exploding swiftly and violently after World War II—all in large part the result of the Comintern's earlier work.

At the same time the Comintern was training fomenters of revolutions, professional revolutionaries, on a vast scale. The system was not limited to each party's responsibility for training its own cadres of revolutionaries, but such cadres were trained also in schools planned and maintained by the Comintern.

In another connection I have mentioned, among others, the University of National Minorities of the West, the Lenin School, and the Karelian schools. For the peoples of the Far East there was a University of the East; there were advanced military schools where military experts were trained for the various countries; there were also purely technical schools that taught only the techniques of revolution: street fighting and sabotage techniques and everything else relating to that field. Near Moscow there was also a special radio school, where the most trustworthy young party members from many countries had been sent under orders to learn radio techniques.

As a member of the Comintern Presidium I had the opportunity to observe this school's activities for a few days. The school's very existence was kept so secret that not many even among the Presidium members knew about it. Of the Finnish party leadership, Kuusinen was the only one aware of it, and he arranged with Manuilski and Dimitrov for me to spend some time at the school settling a conflict that had arisen between some Finns and members of other nationalities who were there under orders.

It was a large structure surrounded by a high barbed-wire fence, and in it were the most modern facilities then available for short-wave as well as medium- and long-wave broadcasting. The emphasis, however, was on short-wave activities. Those who were ordered to the school were preferably persons with a technical education or at least some basic technical training. There they received such thorough instruction in radio techniques that they—and their number included a few women—were able to build a radio transmitter and receiver from comparatively crude materials even under primitive conditions. And naturally they were all trained to become code experts.

There was hardly a spot on the globe with which the school did not maintain contact. Radio operators in one section were in constant touch with every continent, the various countries and the illegal radio operators of various parties. In that way the news was received in a flash from every country, and the Comintern obtained it from there. This contact was maintained by scores of people, but naturally those who attended the school at any one time were much more numerous. They had been strictly admonished not to reveal the existence of the school after leaving it no matter in what circumstances they found themselves. The school was thus the Comintern's nerve center through which the top Comintern leaders, the think tank, knew what was happening in every corner of the world. Understandably, the school's existence has been hushed up, and hardly a word has leaked out about it.

It is obvious that such a vast network of schools costs huge sums of money. The radio school alone and its broadcasting and receiving facilities required fantastic sums. Costly, too, were such institutions as the Lenin School where about a thousand boarding pupils studied throughout the year and on whose staff were hundreds of teachers and other personnel. Moreover, there were many other seats of learning in the Soviet Union to be financed, along with the schools that were maintained beyond the borders, in other words in those countries where the Communist party could legally or semilegally run communist cadre schools.

It is difficult to say how many thousands of fomenters of world revolution, professional revolutionary cadre workers, were turned out by these schools each year. The number might vary with the years but it must have been several thousand, since the Lenin School alone, with its usual two-year course, graduated some five hundred a year.

I have mentioned earlier that the Congress was the Comintern's most important decision-making organ. I participated in two major congresses, the Third Congress in 1921—considered the most noteworthy of that decade—and the Seventh Congress in 1935, at which I was elected to the Executive Committee and the Presidium and at which I made a speech published in *Pravda*. In addition, I participated in two Comintern plenums, which were expanded meetings of the Executive Committee, as well as in numerous meetings of the Executive Committee and the Presidium. I thus had more than fingertip contact with the work and methods of this organization.

In a short chapter it is difficult to describe the results that were achieved, but undeniably it is largely due to the Comintern's work that the Communist-controlled world today is as vast as it is. Functioning as the Soviet Union's foreign affairs bureau, the Comintern—whose name in a later phase was the Cominform—has expanded the influence of the Soviet Union greatly, particularly in Asia but also on all the other continents. The cadre training that I have described briefly apparently has paid high interest on the sums invested in it, huge though they must have been. In addition, each country's Communist party has had to be subsidized by the Comintern. I don't know of a single one that could have financed its own activities, not to mention one like the Finnish Communist party, which during its entire existence has depended wholly on Comintern funding. The Swedish Communist party likewise has never been self-sustaining. On the contrary it has been a vexation to the Comintern precisely because of its expensiveness. Although it has been able to operate legally, it has never been able to pay more than a fraction of its expenses. Large Communist parties, such as those of Germany, France, and Italy, naturally have required even larger outlays. Nevertheless, there has been no saving or pinching; they have been looked upon as profitable fifth columns, and the fantastic sums thrown their way have been viewed as being well worth it in the final or even continuing struggle.

Previously I have described in detail the Third Congress of 1921. In contrast to that, a few close-ups of the Seventh Congress of 1935 may be in order. This Congress was the largest in the number of participants and historic in that it was the final one. True, the Comintern formally functioned until 1943, but after 1935 no further congresses were held. From my viewpoint, what was most interesting during the entire proceeding was drawing comparisons with the Third Congress.

The locale of the Seventh Congress was not the Kremlin but the All-Union building where innumerable other congresses, large and small, have been held. Naturally the setting, here as in the Kremlin, was festive in every way, and the opening ceremony especially had a great deal of decorative glitter. The major difference, however—and it was downright depressing—was the fact that this congress was completely unified; no differences of opinion appeared, not the slightest discordant note. It was the embodiment of the definition: one flock and one shepherd, all bleat with one voice.

The Congress of 1921, with Lenin presiding, was a lively affair, with debates, arguments, and flaming speeches, pro and con. Various proposals were made and voted on; people gathered in small groups to talk and to argue—in short, freedom of speech still prevailed in the communist system, and that freedom dared to be used. Now anything like that was out of the question. There were no groups; rather, even the smallest gatherings and group conversations were avoided inasmuch as there was reason to suspect that someone kept an eye on them and might easily wonder what discord those three men were sowing. It was best to seat oneself immediately, in the places assigned to each country's delegation.

In 1921 most of the speeches were not prepared, and many were extemporaneous, inspired by the moment. Now everyone read his monotonous piece, always the same eulogy to Stalin and Stalin's wisdom. A record was achieved by Dimitrov, whose speech lasted several hours; in printed form, with its concluding statement, it ran to nearly 200 pages even though it was considerably abridged. It was directed against fascism, for at the Leipzig trial he had been crowned the leader in the fight against fascism, and as such had become the Comintern's secretary general. He enjoyed the fullest measure of Stalin's confidence and Stalin thrust him day by day into a more prominent position, with the result that the other Comintern secretaries—even such men as Manuilski, Kuusinen, and Togliatti—found themselves overshadowed by him.

Other notables also struggled heroically. Every speaker had tried to slip into his speech, as often as possible, the name of Stalin—the great Stalin, the wise Stalin—because it was a foregone conclusion that every mention of Stalin would evoke applause. The speakers would otherwise surely have remained without acclaim had it not been that the mention of Stalin's name in any connection, in any language, invariably was a signal to clap. Thus, many speeches were interrupted scores of times, sometimes even two or three times within five minutes, and often the enthusiastic audience would rise to pound its palms for the great Stalin, who also received special hurrahs at the conclusion of every speech.

When the speeches had ended, revolutionary songs were sung. Popular at that time were the Italian "Bandiera Rossa," the German "Red Wedding," and the French "Carmagnole," which echoed frequently.

All the speeches had been tuned in advance to the same key: the line that Stalin had dictated before the congress. Naturally, every speech was not checked in advance, but the line had been spelled out, and no one would have dreamed of deviating from it. Not a single vote had to be taken, since the results were clear beforehand. Only a candidate for suicide would have demanded a vote.

We had agreed earlier that I would speak on behalf of the Finnish Communist party. As a Comintern secretary, Kuusinen spoke on the role of international communist youth, inasmuch as one of his responsibilities was to supervise the activities of the Communist Youth International. My speech was on the role and tasks of the Finnish Communist party, and it, too, was carefully planned and weighed, examined time and again and gone over with Kuusinen. Many corrections were made, to make sure that not the slightest deviation from the line remained. Naturally this speech, too, had to include the standard hymns of praise to Stalin, and I have no reason to pride myself on having departed in any way from the worshipful tone that characterized the Congress. True, my speech did not contain Stalinisms as profusely as did those of the big leaders—particularly the Russians and those from the southern countries—

but of necessity it had to conclude with one, with a few others tossed in earlier.

The Congress proceeded in that manner and, as I said, despite all the hurrahing and bustling and conspicuous enthusiasm, it had a depressing effect on one who had attended earlier international congresses and seen people freely express their thoughts and dare to throw away the scabbard in their defense.

Immediately after the Congress, the newly elected Executive Committee, whose number one man was, of course, Stalin, held its first meeting. This Executive Committee then appointed a Presidium, of which I was elected an alternate member. From the very beginning, however, I served as a regular member since some regular members did not live in Moscow, and I substituted for them. Thus I found myself in an important position in this communist hierarchy, inasmuch as a member of the Comintern Presidium in most instances could be ranked with a member of the Russian Communist party's Politburo because they enjoyed approximately the same privileges. I attained a position from which I could observe developments in a far different way than could people with an insignificant position, or none at all, in that hierarchy, in other words, the regular Soviet citizens.

A few years later that Seventh Congress assumed the characteristics of a thriller in the eyes of us Finns and many others as well, when the Yagoda trial was staged in 1937. In the trial it was revealed that at precisely this congress a young man named Olberg, as I recall, who sat with the German delegation, ostensibly had been paid and ordered to shoot Stalin. Stalin had attended the opening of the congress, some joint sessions, and the closing events. Olberg confessed to the charge and explained how, during the entire congress, he had toyed nervously with the pistol in his pocket and waited for the opportunity to bang away.

By a coincidence, the German delegation had been right in front of us and Olberg, as we could ascertain, had sat in his row directly ahead of me. I am positive that if he had shown the slightest signs of nervousness, such as fumbling in his pocket, we would have noticed them. Furthermore, our seats were so far from Stalin's that probably not even a crack marksman could have been certain of a hit.

The whole affair involving Olberg thus appeared to be staged, and if one asks how such confessions were obtained from Olberg and all the other accused, Party Secretary Khrushchev gave a valid explanation in his speech at the 1956 Party Congress, at which he declared that confessions were obtained by Stalin's method: "Beat him, beat him, beat him until you get a confession! If you don't get a confession, you'll lose your own head."

To repeat, politically this congress followed Stalin's previously charted lines absolutely. With his staff he had concluded that capitalism at that time was in its death throes. The crisis of 1929–32 had been the beginning of the end: capitalism might temporarily make a slight recovery but it was a question of a few years at most, certainly not of decades. This was a major thread of their analysis of the capitalist world. Another dominant thread was the achievement of a popular front for the final overthrow of capitalism. In its death throes, capitalism had clutched at its final straw, fascism and nazism; to crush them, a popular front was needed and when that had been achieved the road to world revolution would finally be open.

The popular front thus was a major theme. Many speakers preached it, and after the Congress considerable results were attained along that line especially in France, where a popular front government under socialist leader Leon Blum was established. How incorrect that diagnosis of the capitalist world and its conflicts was, by and large, could be seen in Moscow's belief that the fundamental clash in the imperialist camp was between England and America, and that that affected all the conflicts in world politics.

It is obvious already from this how little the Comintern's great experts comprehended world politics and conflicts between great powers. To think that, in the year of grace, 1935, one could seriously believe that the fundamental clash in the imperialist camp was between England and America, that it would lead to an explosion and through that to the expected and hoped-for world war! In bitter disappointment even the Comintern leaders have had to concede that no serious rift has developed between England and America; on the contrary, in a tight spot they have marched as one. It was on such working hypotheses that the Comintern based its policies and planned its activities with an eye to the expected world war.

I have already mentioned Dimitrov's lengthy speech in which he dealt specifically with the struggle against fascism. Throughout the speech he severely condemned every citizens' group and every state and government that would aid Germany's Nazis or Italy's Fascists in one way or another. According to Dimitrov, all such parties or groups or states were enemies of peace and supporters of nazism and fascism must be dealt with accordingly: denounced and thoroughly crushed. That was the theme of his long speech.

When war was at hand in 1939, who was the man who first hastened to support nazism? Naturally it was Stalin, who, by signing a pact with Hitler, enabled him to start the world war. And the same Dimitrov, who in his long speech had denounced all parties, statesmen, and states giving aid to the Nazis, as the secretary general of the Comintern, had to give his blessing to Hitler's attack on Poland and then to support the telegrams sent by Molotov to Hitler when the latter had conquered Denmark, Norway, Holland, and Belgium and attacked France in full force. Then Molotov, in the name of the Soviet government, congratulated Hitler after every such victory, and the Comintern leadership always explained that Hitler actually fought for progress, since the world's reactionaries were represented by Hitler's enemies, England and France in particular and, of course, America as well. In such a peculiar light were the great speeches and resolutions of the Comintern's last Congress placed only four years later.

I have chosen an excerpt from the resolution adopted at that Congress as an apt reflection of the situation:

If some weak state is attacked by one or more imperialist great powers seeking to destroy its national independence and national unity or to bring about its division as, historically, in the case of Poland, the struggle of such a country's national bourgeoisie to repel the attack may assume the nature of a war of independence in which the country's working class and Communists cannot help but join. The duty of Communists in such a country—while waging irreconcilable battle on behalf of the security of workers' and peasants' and national minorities' economic and political positions—is to become at the same time frontline fighters for national independence and to wage the war for independence to the end without allowing their "own" bourgeoisie to reach a settlement with the attacking nations at the expense of their own country's interests.

I have chosen this excerpt especially to indicate in what a grotesque light the Comintern's resolutions were placed when Hitler, with Stalin's approval, attacked Poland on September 1, 1939. Immediately the Comintern, speaking through Dimitrov and Manuilski, denounced every Pole who resisted that attack by an imperialist great power. Nor did that suffice. When, seventeen days later, Stalin's own army attacked Poland and stabbed the already bleeding country in the back, all workers fighting for national independence were similarly labeled traitors. In other words, those who defended Poland's independence and freedom against Hitler were traitors, and naturally those who attempted to defend it against the Soviet Union's attack were doubly traitors.

These several examples indicate how lacking in independence the Comintern actually was, how it was merely a special organ of the Soviet Union's foreign ministry or, more precisely, how its leaders were Stalin's ideological hatchet men, forced to reverse themselves and to dishonor their own decisions and political lines.

It was thus natural that, while the world war was raging most furiously, the Comintern should commit harakiri—or rather, be hidden from view. Even now Stalin did not relinquish this instrument freely but sold it to the West at a high price. During the early years of the war he allowed the leaders of his allies to complain time and again that the alliance between West and East, Moscow and Washington, the Soviet Union and the Western powers, was greatly disturbed by the existence of such an organization as the Comintern. Without it the West's assistance would be much more effective. Hence Stalin saw fit to announce ceremoniously before the Teheran Conference that the Comintern had ceased functioning. For that he demanded a high price at both the Teheran and Yalta Conferences. He sold the Comintern to Roosevelt in particular for a pretty penny: the aid given to the Soviet Union by America during the war rose to 11 billion dollars, a sum that even today is said to be unrepaid.

That was how the Comintern was sold at that particular time, until after the war, in 1947, it again began to function publicly. Naturally it had operated all the while but now it popped up as the Cominform until that, too, was discontinued in 1956 a few hours before Soviet leaders Khrushchev and Bulganin landed in London on their famous visit to England. The hiding out continues.

The Comintern's role thus was primarily one of setting land mines for future wars and revolutions. This was accomplished by calling qualified people from everywhere to Moscow, to the Lenin School, and also to the Comintern's various divisions. These men and women in the 1920s and 1930s set the snares and mines that began to explode during the post-World War II period. So purposeful were the attempts to destroy the so-called imperialist world.

As one of those who helped to set the mines, it is interesting to follow the explosions as they have taken place in such areas as Asia and Africa. True, there emerged some leaders who had been educated at the Sorbonne, Oxford, and other Western universities, but there were many more Moscow-trained revolutionaries, and they crop up even today in some of Portugal's former colonies. These land mines are still exploding though the Comintern no longer exists.

THE MEMORANDUM OF
THE WILD ROSE

ONE DAY in late winter 1937 Dimitrov's secretary at the Comintern phoned me in my office, asking me to come over for a talk with Comrade Secretary General. I went and, as I had been summoned, was admitted at once into the presence of the exalted gentleman. I noticed immediately that something very special was afoot, for Dimitrov did not waste time on courtesies, just tapped on a wad of papers on the table and said:

"Take a look at this!"

"Well," I asked in my poor Russian, "what's in it?"

"Read it first and we'll talk afterwards. Read quickly! All I'll say right now is that I would never have believed that the leadership of any party could be so degenerate and so thoroughly immoral as the leadership of the Finnish party seems to be. My order is that you as the party secretary investigate the accuracy of this document within a fortnight and then present a memorandum to the Secretariat of the Comintern. For this is a uniquely outrageous document."

With these directives he pushed the wad to me. It contained nearly a score of typewritten sheets.

In our group there was a young man named Ahti Liedes who had attended some of the lectures in the Lenin School. His party name was Villy Roos, which sounded in Finnish very much like Villiruusu (the wild rose), and that's what he was called. This Villiruusu was the one who had written the document accusing the Finnish Communist party leadership of immorality.

He began by relating that he had become an assistant to some underground workers in Finland and told how these workers had behaved with impropriety. He was then ordered to Stockholm where he was received by Antti Hyvönen and Yrjö Enne. The former, along with Inkeri Lehtinen, took care of the party business in Stockholm, and Enne had technical duties in the same town. These fellows took him under their wing and the first lesson in party work was a visit to the Kungsgatan—King's Street—to hunt for girls. With childish naïveté he described how it was done. When he came to Moscow he noticed that there, too, most communist leaders lived in the same manner.

He began with Kuusinen. According to what he had heard, the private life of even Kuusinen was very questionable.

Liedes continued by telling unpleasant stories about Hertta Kuusinen and Toivo Antikainen who were then imprisoned in Finland, and about Tuure Lehén, who was working on a revolution in Spain. Further, he accused several lesser leaders of malfeasance and charged Inkeri Lehtinen with behavior unbecoming to a party leader. But the crowning touch was the vivid report on Antti Hyvönen. Antti had made known what a great ladies' man he was, how many times he had been married, and he had especially bragged about how many women of different races he had had. The account was really spicy and colorful but not particularly dignifying for one who belonged to the party leadership.

Liedes's papers compromised the entire upper echelon of the party rather completely, with the exception of Jukka Lehtosaari, Hannes Mäkinen, and myself. For that reason everyone looked at us: inasmuch as we were not accused, did we have any role in the disclosures? However much one searched, one could not find anything on Mäkinen and Lehtosaari, and I had been sitting for many years in prisons where such transgressions are not very easy to undertake.

Before I began questioning the writer of the memorandum, I showed it to Kuusinen who had not been given even an inkling of it by Dimitrov. Kuusinen glanced over the first few pages, lighted a cigarette, paced the floor many times, and finally said:

"Listen, that boy must be an agent provocateur. I've talked with him a couple of times, and he's not so stupid that he'd state such things out of sheer addleheadedness. There just might be a dash of truth in it insofar as I and the others are concerned, but the whole tale is so provocative and so naïve that it can't be real naïveté."

And then Kuusinen turned against me.

"You're the one who got him here! You're responsible for the whole mess."

It was true that I had cooperated in getting Liedes to Russia, for he had assisted in my flight from Finland to Sweden. As a result, he came under police surveillance in Finland. But I was not prepared to assume the responsibility for the behavior of other party leaders. On the other hand, I understood Kuusinen's nervousness very well: lesser accusations had toppled powerful men.

After this conversation I had Villiruusu summoned to my office and showed him the document. After we had studied it, he admitted that it corresponded to what he had dictated.

"How could you stoop to this?" I demanded. "Why did you do it?"

He told me the following story:

After several weeks in Moscow he had gotten into difficulties because of some unknown woman. He had told his supervisor about this essentially harmless and insignificant escapade, and the man immediately demanded to know if Finns are in the habit of entering into relationships with unknown women. The interrogator, who was the assistant secretary of the Youth International, played the great moralist and ordered the young man to tell all he knew about the leadership of the Finnish Communist party. And so he did.

Villiruusu assured me that the story was true. Part of it was from his own experience, part he had heard from others, but he assured me that he had not exaggerated one bit.

"And," he added, "how could I refuse to tell when the party membership and the oath of a Youth League member specifically obligate one to report to the supervisor even the smallest slip, whatever it may be, that one knows to have been made by other party members or by oneself? I've told everything under the obligation of my party oath and if I'm accused, I don't understand of what."

At least one thing became clear while I questioned Villiruusu. He had heard about Kuusinen's "immoral acts" from Armas Äikiä, a Finnish Communist and minor poet. Even as I had read the account, I had thought, really, now, imagination is galloping ahead too recklessly. Äikiä had evened out an old score with a critic of his poetry. It was obvious that Kuusinen had underestimated the man's poetic imagination.

Then I began to question others. Inkeri Lehtinen admitted to some small misdeeds, but they were insignificant. One could actually not charge her with anything listed in the document. Her only lapse was that, while being married under Soviet law, she had married another man who already had a wife. In other words, Inkeri Lehtinen had a husband, Toivo Lehto, known as Martti Nilsson, who taught in the Lenin School. But while working for the party in Stockholm she began a new married life with Antti Hyvönen, and they had a baby on the way when this hearing took place.

I questioned everybody I could get hold of. But most were either in prisons or abroad.

I was obliged to ask Kuusinen, too, about one thing and another relating to the matter. He explained that if it was considered a crime that he had been forced by circumstances to change wives often, there was nothing he could do about it. But he certainly didn't think that it could be considered a really immoral way of life.

Then I came to the protagonist of the tale, Antti Hyvönen. He said at once that he wanted to write the rejoinder himself. Antti is a quick-witted fellow with an incisive pen. He turned out a lively reply, and this was added to the others.

Hyvönen explained that, for the most part, Villiruusu's account was true. The document did contain a number of exaggerations—naturally he had been bragging about the women of many races—but there were no obvious and outright lies. He would not even begin explaining them, because it all seemed so childish to him.

I only wish to point out, he wrote, that Secretary General of the Comintern Dimitrov, when accused at the Leipzig trial by Hermann Göring and others of all kinds of outrageous crimes, including the one that he, Dimitrov, had been arrested in a Berlin hotel room with two streetwalkers, never denied the accusation but said: "I am a healthy man and no homosexual." At that time there were sensational homosexual affairs among the Nazis.

After I had completed the long document and had it translated, I toted it over to Dimitrov. He saw at once that there was a lot to read in it and said that it would take some time to go over it. He would get back to me later.

"It would be nice, though, if you took the trouble to glance at a few passages," I said and produced Antti Hyvönen's rejoinder.

He read it and leaped up. "What the hell is this!"

"The big ones show the way and the little ones follow," I said. "This is how Hyvönen will clear himself in this affair."

Dimitrov was a very temperamental fellow.

"They have their gall to compare me with these sordid little affairs."

But after raging a while he conceded: "It seems that Hyvönen is not a stupid man."

The case was transferred to the Comintern Secretariat, which categorically ordered that Antti Hyvönen and a number of smaller officials be deprived of their party cards. Thus Hyvönen, who was on the Central Committee of the Finnish Communist party and a member of the Russian Communist party, was kicked out from the latter organization, and when I was getting ready to leave Russia, there was an order that he be dismissed from the Finnish Communist party as well.

This affair had a sequel. When the Winter War started, and Inkeri Lehtinen became a member of the Terijoki government of Kuusinen, Antti Hyvönen was left out. Had he not been ousted from the party, he would have been one of the most important members of that government on the basis of his achievements and ability. Insolence—or was it immorality?—was the reason that he did not reach the heights that he should have.

One may ask why the charges had no more serious consequences for Antti Hyvönen and Inkeri Lehtinen, especially after both also were accused, together with Yrjö Enne, of having twice lost party funds in Stockholm, without being able to give any acceptable explanation.

The explanation is that both began desperately to accuse some of their closest friends. Together they accused Inkeri Lehtinen's real husband Toivo Lehto, alias Martti Nilsson, of many things that caused the GPU to arrest him. They made similar charges against a number of the teachers at the Lenin School. Trotskyism was one of the charges.

As it did so many times during Stalin's rule, it happened once again that those whom common sense deemed guilty—in this case, Antti Hyvönen, and to a certain degree also Inkeri Lehtinen—cleared themselves. But many persons who were totally innocent of wrongdoing through these denunciations lost their freedom and perhaps their lives as well.

When one ponders Liedes's memorandum afterwards, one must conclude that the young man was conscientious but inexcusably naïve. I have described it quite superficially, without mentioning drunkenness and other forms of hooliganism, as Dimitrov called it, adding, "Even if only 20 percent of this document is true, the leadership of the Finnish party is totally decadent and immoral."

I am not sure if Dimitrov was quite the right man to cast the first stone.

It is to be hoped that the document is in the archives of the Comintern, to be used in the writing of the much awaited real history of the Finnish Communist party. It would provide additional color to the often dry text of history.

STALIN CLOSE UP

I CAN'T REMEMBER precisely when it was that I first met Stalin face to face. In 1921 he was so overshadowed by the more famous that if I did happen to bump into him somewhere I have completely forgotten it. When I visited Russia in the summer of 1927 he had already reached the summit of the Soviet hierarchy, though he did not achieve his final victory over Trotsky until that fall. As the secretary general of the Communist party he was thus a powerful man. Under the guidance of Rovio I dropped in at his secretariat and was introduced, but no particular impression has remained of that meeting. At that time I knew no Russian whatsoever, and Finland was not as interesting to the Soviet rulers—or at least to Stalin—as it had been six years earlier. Stalin did not catechize me as Lenin had in his time.

In 1933 he had already disposed of his competitors to all intents and purposes; their final liquidation was merely a technicality. After I had completed the Lenin School and progressed far enough in my language studies to enable me to get along in Russian, Kuusinen considered me ready for activity in the "inner circle," and then I met Stalin frequently. He was a member of the Comintern's Presidium but rarely attended its meetings. Instead, he often took part in special conferences and was always there at events commemorating the revolution as well as in the funerals of party bosses, at which the members of the Politburo and the Presidium formed an honor guard.

He was "Comrade Stalin" and I was "Comrade Tuominen" at these meetings until he felt that the time was ripe to drop the use of titles. Actually, it would be more accurate to speak of an intermediate stage, for Russian social custom includes that endearing patronymic stage unknown in Europe: the father's name used instead of the surname in addressing a person. The formal mode of address—"you" instead of "thou"—is still retained, but one is halfway to familiarity. This intermediate stage facilitates the fraternization of equals but at the same time builds a bridge between those of different classes, inasmuch as in certain circumstances even the very lowly can use the patronymic in addressing the highborn. I would say that it has been created to moderate at least somewhat the class contrasts that have always been great in Russia—and still are.

When revolutionary festivities were held in Moscow's Bolshoi Theater, the members of the Politburo and the Comintern's Presidium always sat on a dais on the stage facing the audience. During intermissions this group of twenty to twenty-five members was served refreshments in one of the lounges. There we relaxed and unbent the festive expressions worn on the dais, and it was during one such pause—on November 6, 1935, if I remember correctly—that I engaged in conversation with Stalin for the first time.

I happened to mention that I was from Tampere, and Stalin immediately became interested. He had many reasons for this interest. The most important was that Tampere was a significant factor in the spinning of the legend about his past. There, at the December 1905 conference of Bolsheviks, Lenin and Stalin met for the first time—a historic event not omitted from even the shortest history of the Soviet Union's Communist party. At first it was merely stated, and even as a simple declaration of fact it cast a certain radiance about Stalin's temples. But then Iaroslavski, Stalin's court historian, amplified the tale year after year on appropriate anniversaries until Lenin wound up virtually playing second fiddle at that meeting.

But there is no doubt that Tampere would have remained in Stalin's memory otherwise, too. It represented his first trip abroad, his first personal contact with the Western world. The cleanliness of the city in itself had left an indelible impression. He had also been affected and amused by the way in which the Tampere labor leaders and active resisters of czarism had held their meeting in secret from the czar's secret police and gendarmes: the police officials, hotel owners, and doormen were all in the plot together. The revolutionaries from Russia rarely had a passport—at least not a genuine one—but matters had been arranged in Tampere so that, on arriving at a hotel, they merely announced in Finnish, "The passport has been left with the police chief." This password sufficed, and no one made any excessive inquiries; that had been the understanding with the hotel owner.

Stalin tried to pry loose from his memory the sentence that he had learned with great difficulty thirty years earlier but was unable any longer to twist his tongue into the strange words. It was amusing to watch him laughingly botch Finnish—amusing in itself but especially because it is amusing to hear a powerful man laugh. Kuusinen made a series of tacks in the vicinity of our table, hoping to be allowed to join in the laughter, which he was.

The memories of Tampere probably cast a certain radiance around my pate, too, for Stalin asked, "What is your father's given name, Comrade Tuominen?"

"Oskari."

"In other words, you are Arvo Oskarovich. I am Iosif Vissarionovich."

After this fraternization he never, even in passing, forgot to inquire what the news was from Tampere.

There was, in that pleasant moment of small talk, something fundamental to Stalin. During my years in Moscow I never stopped marveling at the contrast between the man and the colossal likenesses that had been made of him. That medium-sized, slightly pockmarked Caucasian with a mustache was as far removed as could be from the stereotype of a dictator. The sweeping gestures of Hitler and Mussolini were lacking completely in him; he did not gesture even when making speeches, no matter how impassioned the words. Was he then a simple, homespun man of the people?

If we reply affirmatively and more precisely define "simplicity" as honesty and modesty, how can we explain the propaganda created "father of peoples" and "engineer of souls," in whose name were sworn the holiest vows, without whom the Russian people's lives would not have been worth living, who knew everything and was capable of everything, who was as great a thinker and theoretician as he was a practical man in all fields. Stalin even taught dancers how to dance—a leading ballerina told an interviewer in all seriousness that she could thank Stalin for her skill—ski jumpers to jump, skaters to skate, filers to file, authors to write, and so on.

All this can be explained by saying that propaganda is propaganda, and that the nature of the propaganda depends on the cultural level of its target. It would not even have occurred to Hitler's and Mussolini's propaganda agents to pile it on so thickly. It may be said that the centuries-old veneration of saints lives on in the people's blood, for the "enlightenment" practiced by the Bolsheviks cannot have penetrated very deep. Orthodox Russians did not understand the language of the church services, Old Church Slavonic, and today's Soviet people, though they have learned to read and write, do not understand the gist of dialectical materialism any better. With this kind of teaching Marx remains a hazy thunderer beyond the clouds.

In his speeches and writings Stalin always withdrew into the background, speaking only of communism, the Soviet power, and the party and stressing that he was merely a representative of the idea and the organization, nothing more. But at the same time the propaganda was proclaiming his superhuman abilities.

In his famous speech of 1956, Khrushchev related how the Stalin myth was created. Stalin appointed a committee to write his biography. The committee did its best and lauded Stalin with all possible superlatives. This did not satisfy Stalin, however, and he added the following point, among others, to his biography: "Despite the fact that Stalin fulfilled his task as the leader of the people and the party with consummate skill and enjoyed the unreserved support of the Soviet people, Stalin never allowed the slightest vanity, conceit, or tinge of self-praise to impair his work."

Someday, perhaps, memoirs will appear and documents pop up to give us some idea of what Stalin himself, deep inside, thought of that deification campaign. True, it has been claimed that he believed himself able to understand the most diverse matters better than the experts: natural science, linguistics, art. But did he smile into his mustache as he read the outpourings of his propaganda chiefs? That we do not know. Perhaps some future psychopathologists may be able to determine on the basis of all the available evidence that he was insane in some recesses of his psyche, primarily suffering from megalomania, perhaps also paranoia. In those days it would not have occurred to anyone to call him insane, so shrewdly had he managed his game.

Lenin, as is known, enjoyed intellectual duels and seemed to be in top form whenever he had to face overwhelming odds alone. All this happened openly, at party organizations or in the newspapers. Stalin did not attempt to debate, nor could he have held his own with the sages of the old guard. He did present arguments in his major speeches and articles, but no one was ever given the floor after him. Nevertheless, the prevailing impression that he was an autocrat in all the initial stages of deliberation, a tyrant who dictated his decisions from on high to be executed by the party organizations and the government, was untrue. On the contrary, he was quite democratic and cooperative in certain matters, particularly when important questions were being resolved.

Such cases came first to the Politburo for consideration. After preliminary discussions, data were assembled, and the drafting of the motion was assigned to some member of the Politburo or expert.

At this preparatory stage Stalin often refused to state his own viewpoint lest it have a disturbing effect. Only after the matter had been thrashed out, deliberated and approved by Stalin did it become a law that one did not question.

The procedure in itself was good, but in practice it had little merit since divergent views were not offered for consideration. Instead, everyone assigned to the task attempted to ferret out the dictator's views in order to draft his proposal accordingly.

I had the opportunity to observe Stalin's method of working very closely during the many years I lived as Kuusinen's neighbor. Kuusinen was his advisor on ideological and international questions and often was obliged to undertake special tasks. I remember poor Kuusinen's face many a time when he returned from a session with Stalin in the Kremlin, and I thanked my stars that I was not in his shoes. Frequently he didn't have the faintest idea of Stalin's views even though he was quite good at sniffing out the various currents. He could only sweat and agonize and rack his brains trying to line up his sights. When he finally believed himself to be on the right track, the first and even the second draft were liable to be rejected wholly or in part. But while discussing these drafts, Kuusinen began to get the drift of the matter—or perhaps the dictator himself did, who knows. All in all, I believe that Kuusinen got through his assignments commendably.

I mentioned that Stalin did not subject me to the same kind of catechism about Finnish affairs that Lenin did in his time. However, one should not assume that he did not follow even minor developments with amazing closeness considering that he had enough to do in running Russia.

A typical example was the case of Toivo Antikainen in 1935. Antikainen was a Red officer who had been apprehended in Finland and charged with having a Finnish volunteer put to death in East Karelia in 1922.

Then a ten-man group was sent from the Soviet Union to the Helsinki municipal court to testify in Antikainen's defense. The secret police managed to persuade one of them, kolkhoznik Matvejev, to defect and to retract his testimony that was favorable to Antikainen.

I was at a meeting in the Kremlin with Kuusinen when Stalin noticed us and came over with a broad smile.

"I've just received a telegram from Helsinki," he said. "Matvejev has re-defected, fled the Finnish police and sought asylum in the

Soviet Legation. He won't do any more defecting, for he is being brought back here."

"Then the press in Finland and all the Western countries will write that Matvejev has been liquidated immediately upon his return," we replied, amazed that Stalin wasted his interest on such a comparatively trivial incident.

Stalin stared at us thoughtfully for a moment and conceded, "That's what they'll surely do." Then he turned to one of his aides who stood nearby. "Get hold of Yagoda; I want to talk to him."

A moment later that still all-powerful GPU chief arrived.

"Genrikh Grigorjevich," said Stalin to him, "you will be personally responsible that not a hair on the head of defector Matvejev is hurt when he returns here. Rather, you will arrange such a life for him that he can be shown to foreign newsmen even after a year or two."

As I have observed, Stalin could be a convivial companion in intimate, friendly circles. He enjoyed telling piquant stories and apparently made himself the butt of humor, though a closer look would reveal that not he but someone else was the laughingstock.

This was one such instance. The Politburo had decided that there was reason to install some trustworthy person in the Academy of Science to keep an eye on the activities of those erudite men. Iaroslavski was deemed suitable, for he had distinguished himself as the leader of the "godless" in the fight against the church's influence and had always been Stalin's dutiful assistant. And so the academy was ordered to elect him to membership.

The academy was headed by the world-famous physiologist Pavlov, who had received a Nobel Prize in 1904. He was devoutly orthodox and always piously crossed himself before images of saints. The bolshevik elite nevertheless respected him so greatly that it did not laugh at him but at the burly sailor who, on seeing Pavlov cross himself before an icon in a church wall, tapped him on the shoulder and said pityingly, "Spiritual unenlightenment, you poor old fellow, spiritual unenlightenment!"

To the orthodox Pavlov, the godless Iaroslavski was what a red cape is to a bull, and when he heard the order he roared, "Devil take it, I'll never do that! The Roman emperor Caligula, when he wanted to humiliate the senate by designating his horse a senator, at least had the sense to do it himself and didn't force the senators to disgrace themselves. Now we are expected to designate Stalin's ass a member of the academy. I don't want to be a party to that mockery. Let Stalin do it himself!"

And with that Pavlov threw his gavel heatedly onto the table.

The Politburo member who was to arrange the matter naturally became greatly worried. How could he explain it to Stalin and what would happen to Pavlov? But evasion didn't help. He had to make his report.

Stalin stared at him in amazement for a moment, then burst into a guffaw, laughing so hard that his whole body shook.

Finally recovering himself he said, "Make sure that Pavlov gets everything he needs in his laboratory. He is a truly great scientist."

Stalin enjoyed telling this anecdote to his closest assistants, and naturally the entire inner circle joined in his laughter—except, of course, Iaroslavski, who received balsam for his wounds later: he was designated a member of the academy when Pavlov no longer headed it.

The old physiologist was probably the last to express his opinion of Stalin's actions so courageously. If there were others, they were given short shrift. Soon Stalin was the only one who dared jest about "superman Stalin," insofar as that jesting was genuine.

In all ages clever leaders of the people—whether they have been emperors, kings, dictators, or whatever—have realized the propaganda value of anecdotes about themselves and have circulated them. The following tale told about Stalin is among the best, first because it's a fairly good story in itself; second, because it indicates how things can be straightened out when the boss himself goes into action to rectify the misdeeds of his good-for-nothing assistants; and third, it completely conceals its aim.

Once Stalin arrived at a Politburo meeting with a pile of books under his arm. When all the business of the day had been concluded, he turned to the commissar of education, Bubnov, and asked, "Have you any idea what is being taught in Soviet schools?"

Bubnov became uneasy but in a convincing voice tried to explain that education was in a fine state.

Stalin was not satisfied with the answer, declaring, "I don't have much time to devote to my children's schooling, but one day my son Vasili, who is in the third grade in elementary school, came to me and said proudly, 'Listen, father, I have learned Marx's labor theory of value and his doctrine of surplus value.' How interesting, I thought and asked, 'Well, what is it that you know about Marx?' And then the boy actually reeled off several pages on the theory of value and surplus value. I asked him where he had learned it and he said from a schoolbook. The class had been told to memorize it.

"I was shocked," continued Stalin, "and asked the boy to fetch the book. And sure enough, there it was and a lot more like it. Think of that, comrades, and especially you, Bubnov! Children in the second and third grades of elementary school are required to recite the theory of surplus value by heart, just like parrots, without understanding a word. Even in our party leadership we've had several comrades who have not understood Marx despite their great erudition. One of them, Bukharin, is even asserted to be the party's best theoretician."

Stalin loved such sideswipes.

"I thought that it would be best to glance at Vasili's and Svetlana's other schoolbooks, and I was really horrified. The textbooks on party history and Russian history, for example, are altogether inferior. I questioned Svetlana about Catherine the Great. She answered that Catherine was a 'product of society.' Wonderful! The history textbooks must be rewritten."

This tale was told in Russia with many variations—the propaganda saw to that. It made the point that, if matters had gone awry, the fault was not Stalin's (just as during the czarist era the fault was not the czar's but that of his wretched advisors). It also caused many of the dictator's critics to think well of him.

By this time Stalin had achieved complete power, but it was not yet reflected in the schoolbooks or the teaching. For that reason the books hitherto used, especially the histories of Russia and the Communist party, had to be burned and new ones written. The dictator used little Vasili and Svetlana merely as instruments in his pursuit of that goal.

The upshot of this apparently innocuous conversation in the Politburo was that a considerable part of the schoolbooks was ordered to be burned. Months passed before they were replaced by new ones written in the Stalinist spirit and according to his dictates. The history of the party had to be rewritten three times. Only the third attempt was satisfactory since Stalin himself dictated it. Russian history underwent the same kind of metamorphosis. Lenin's spirit, according to which such strong czars as Ivan the Terrible and Peter the Great had been tyrants and oppressors of the people, had to be abolished, and they had to be made great czars loved and idolized by the people.

With this seemingly minor episode a mighty avalanche was set in motion on the doctrinal front, meaning that Lenin's era ended and Stalin's era began. Piles of burning books have at times served as signal lights before, in changing from one era to another.

The celebration of Christmas was among the things still banned in the Soviet Union when I arrived there. But old customs are not rooted out by orders and decrees, and the peasants in the countryside continued to celebrate Christmas as well as Easter, though naturally as secretly as possible.

Long ago, when the Christian church was unable to get the people to abandon their pagan rituals, it endowed the ceremonies with Christian significance and thus saved the situation. Perhaps the Soviet government theorized in a similar vein, or perhaps it sensed that the people were becoming weary of their drab lives, the incessant goading, work speed-ups, and Stakhanovism—or perhaps both these factors together prompted an article by Ukrainian Party Secretary Postyshev in *Pravda* late in 1935, in which he proposed that the celebration of Christmas with its trees and gifts be initiated in the Soviet Union, since it was only natural that the Soviet children and Soviet people needed some source of enjoyment. A few years later the initiator of the idea, Postyshev, was liquidated, though I don't believe it was because of his suggestion to celebrate Christmas.

We Finns, who are a stubborn people not given to relinquishing our customs regardless of the ideology or political system under which we live, or whether we are bourgeois, Social Democrats, or Communists, had celebrated Christmas in large or small groups and in our own way even in the Soviet Union despite the ban.

Some time after the publication of the article, a decree actually was issued in the name of the party and the government: this year, 1935, the Soviet people, too, will celebrate Christmas. Let it be celebrated as a New Year festival, on which the Soviet people will gather around a tree to rejoice in their free and happy lives.

Preparations for Christmas were entered into enthusiastically and vigorously. Because everything in a planned society occurs according to plan, vast quantities of Christmas trees, for example, were brought into Moscow with the inevitable result. Although Moscow is a big city with a large population, at least half the trees were superfluous, since there was not room in the crowded communal apartments for as many trees as there were families. But we who had more spacious quarters enjoyed two trees and compensated for the years when we had none.

Thus Christmas came also to Moscow and was celebrated wholeheartedly after a hiatus of twenty years. Even Stalin in his own exalted person joined in the revelry. He arranged an elaborate Christmas party in the Kremlin, in a suite especially reserved for such occasions. The invited guests were a small group of the elite, members of the Politburo, and the Comintern's Presidium, and thus I, too, was included.

The festive suite was decked with Christmas trees, the largest in a hall containing a lavishly set banquet table. Stalin seated himself at the head of it, and the rest of us took our places in the order determined by that moment's prestige-exchange quotation. Tensely we waited to see what would happen next. Careful preparations had been made in the Politburo and the Comintern's Presidium for long, thorough speeches extolling the virtues of the great Stalin who then was approaching the zenith of his power. We considered it only natural that these festivities had been arranged for the glorification of Stalin. Four or five Politburo men had speeches tucked away in their pockets, while in the Comintern's Presidium we had agreed that Dimitrov and Manuilski would express our most heartfelt sentiments.

As soon as we were seated, Stalin, to our surprise, clinked his glass for silence, rose and spoke ceremoniously in this manner:

"Comrades! I want to propose a toast to our patriarch, life and sun, liberator of nations, architect of socialism, omniscient genius (he rattled off all the appellations applied to him in those days) and great leader of peoples, Iosif Vissarionovich Stalin, and I hope that this is the first and last speech made to that genius this evening."

Our initial shock dissolved into small bursts of slightly uncertain laughter, after which we all relaxed and enjoyed ourselves, except perhaps for those whose secretaries had sweated over the speeches. Spirits. soared freely without any unpleasant interruptions, stories were told, we ate a lot, drank a lot, peace prevailed, and good will was felt by all.

More recently, Stalin's closest aides have related incredible tales about his insatiable demands for adulation and how he sometimes went to preposterous lengths in expressing his power. Secretary General Khrushchev, in his revealing speech of 1956, cited as one example the occasion when Stalin ordered him, Khrushchev, to perform a solo dance, and nothing would do but that he must dance, undoubtedly to the great amusement of the spectators.

I cannot comment on this example one way or the other. Possibly the dictator felt that his servant needed a little slap and took care of it himself rather than leaving the task to the GPU. Be that as it may, I attended many affairs at the Kremlin, even rowdy ones, but I never noticed any signs of vainglory in Stalin, not even when he was under the influence of alcohol; he merely became more garrulous than usual, his voice grew slightly louder, and he laughed more readily.

On the other hand, some of the other leaders, for instance Zhdanov, would get drunk easily. He was an unusually amiable and animated man when sober, but after a few glasses of vodka his contentious and sarcastic self would appear, and after a little more vodka he would fall under the table and be carried out.

Despite such occurrences, one must not think that Stalin staged drinking orgies in the manner of Peter the Great. Actually, parties were held rather infrequently, inasmuch as the major Soviet leaders were beavers for work, with Stalin a good example.

It is true, however, that even as Stalin was thus mocking himself (which he could afford to do in a closed circle), the propaganda chief of the party, Stetskii, gave strict orders to every single level of the Soviet hierarchy that every public speech, no matter how brief, must give Stalin his due both at the beginning and at the end. When Gylling was apprehended he was charged, among other things, with having neglected to extol Stalin either at the beginning or the end of a speech.

On that Christmas, too, all holiday speeches, no matter what their length, had to glorify the great Stalin. Only in the Kremlin's cozy little company was an exception permitted.

In 1937 the famous novelist Lion Feuchtwanger visited the Soviet Union and also dropped in to see Stalin. The following is his own account of the conversation.

After salutations had been exchanged, he asked whether Stalin was not disgusted with the phenomenal Stalin-worship that was practiced throughout the Soviet Union. Stalin's portraits were everywhere, and his praises were sung, but the height of everything was seeing, amidst the great old art at the Tretiakov Gallery, some propaganda painter's version of Stalin staring out from almost every wall.

Stalin was absolutely flabbergasted and asked whether it was really true even in the Tretiakov.

"Yes. You can send your men to take a look."

"That's strange," said Stalin. "That's downright sabotage."

And he jotted down something on the paper before him, obviously a notation ordering the removal of his portraits from that gallery. Incidentally, it was said of him later that he used to sketch wolves as he talked with people; that I don't know, but it is true that whenever he talked with me he would draw or write something on a piece of paper.

Feuchtwanger related that Stalin declared himself to be as disgusted as any foreigner with the ubiquitous pictures and their worship. But there was an explanation for them: over the centuries the Russian people had become accustomed to thinking concretely. Such things as the Soviet state, the Communist party, and everything pertaining to it were an abstraction to the ordinary peasant and worker, a purely abstruse concept, whereas Comrade Stalin was concrete, a tangible fact.

In the old days, Stalin continued, the Russian people had God and the czar. Both were concrete in that even the most wretched hovel had a picture of the Holy Virgin and a picture of the czar in a corner and, if the means permitted, a candle burning before them, at least on holidays. When God and the czar were removed from the corner the people had to have something as a replacement, and so one must bear with the fact that Stalin's picture was put there and that a candle is lighted before it if the means permit. They know that such a person exists, have heard his voice over the radio, perhaps a few have even seen him with their own eyes and can attest to his existence. Thus, idolatry is a necessity from the standpoint of governing and the socialist building of Soviet power, and for such a great cause personal antipathy must be overcome.

As we can see, this explanation seems quite logical and natural and makes one doubt whether he actually believed in his semi-divinity as his closest colleagues and friends subsequently claimed. In his aforementioned speech Khrushchev asserted that Stalin's egotism went so far that he added adjectives—omniscient, unerring, and so on—to all descriptions of himself, even though the scribe in his own opinion already had used them ad nauseam. Well, it is true that Khrushchev and the present Soviet leaders knew Stalin better than I; naturally I am unqualified to refute their contentions.

Kuusinen, as Stalin's confidential secretary, often mentioned some of Stalin's little traits. He frequently had occasion to visit Stalin, mostly on official business but sometimes for a small party or even tête-à-tête. However, I never heard him recount such senseless tales as were subsequently told. On the contrary, Stalin, according to Kuusinen, was pleasant company and could regale his guests with all kinds of anecdotes, even anti-Soviet ones if not many listeners were present. One can only conjecture where he had heard them—probably from his wife, Nadezhda Alliluyeva, who died under mysterious circumstances in 1932. According to some sources she was murdered by Stalin, according to others she committed suicide. She was an intelligent woman who moved in many circles. Of course, Stalin also could have heard those jokes in his own small Georgian circle; his old pals Jenukidze and Ordzhonikidze didn't stand much on ceremony. At any rate, Stalin related them with great relish in intimate company and laughed at them heartily.

One of Kuusinen's tales I remember especially. He had spent a late summer in the same sanatoriums at Sochi where I first experienced upper-class life and had been invited by Stalin to visit the little castle that I have mentioned earlier.

It was certainly a place in which a person could enjoy himself, said Kuusinen, once he forgot the high and well-guarded walls that surrounded it. At first they had discussed the serious matters that had prompted Stalin to summon him, but then they had begun to eat, drink, and joke. Although Kuusinen was not one to shy away from a drink, and for a small man held up splendidly, he said that Stalin had drunk much more than he.

They had been quite plastered when Stalin suddenly got the idea of going shooting at his rifle range. Kuusinen said that, even though drunkenness makes one courageous, he nevertheless had enough sense to be horrified: to think of going shooting in their tipsy condition. What if there should be an accident? No one would care if Stalin shot him while intoxicated; there might not even be a news brief in the papers. But if he should happen to shoot Stalin? He tried to discourage it, but Stalin just laughed. They were going shooting and that was that. And they did. Stalin shot exceptionally well; Kuusinen lost every round in the match. I can attest to the fact that Kuusinen, at least when sober, was an excellent shot; we used to practice together at Kuntsevo on weekends.

"Did you lose deliberately?" I asked Kuusinen. "Would you have dared best a dictator if you had been able to?"

"Well, in that condition I wasn't greatly concerned with which of us won. All I could think of was to make sure that the gun wasn't pointed in the wrong direction. And I wasn't the only terrified one; Stalin's guards were even more frightened and tried to see to it that the weapon was aimed correctly."

But Stalin fended them off. "They misunderstand their job completely. No need of guards when friends are engaged in shooting."

Many such close-ups of Stalin could be offered, but these may suffice to indicate what life was like in his immediate circle and to rectify somewhat the impression given by his closest friends after his death. The other chapters in this book prove that he actually was a tyrant. The era known as Stalinism was sufficiently tyrannical and brutal not to be nullified by the human aspects depicted here. But let there be moderation even in vilification.

STALIN THE JUGGLER

POLITICAL CIRCLES throughout the world have wondered how, in less than two decades, one small political group could create so boundless a personal dictatorship as that which Stalin had achieved already by the mid-1930s. Dictatorship itself is an ancient concept that world history knows in various forms and kinds, knows as no less unscrupulous than Stalin's.

But there is one essential difference. For example, the dictatorship of Rome's most rabid autocrats was "bourgeois." In other words, it did not perceptibly disturb the subjects' habitual way of life; at most it struck fear in some segment of society. But Stalin's dictatorship was revolutionary; it clawed deeply into the life of every single citizen, forcing everyone continuously to do things that do not please a person. When that essential difference is taken into consideration, I don't believe that the equivalent of Stalin can be found even on the fringes of world history—not even in darkest Africa.

What I said about the Roman emperors applies also to the bloody Zulu chiefs Dingaan and Panda. Only the most heroic hunters, those who might have become a threat to the chief, had reason to be fearful. In the Soviet Union in Stalin's time there was not a single person who did not live in fear and uncertainty.

Other dictators of modern times, such as Hitler, cannot be considered in this context despite their fanatical racism and lust for gas chamber murders. Their dictatorships could not become total since they were restricted first by long-established life-styles that they hardly were able to change at all, and second, by the financiers. But Stalin's power, once and for all (naturally within the bounds of human, or should one say inhuman, life) was limitless.

Khrushchev stated it outright in his big speech:

The power concentrated in the hands of one single person, Stalin, led to serious consequences during the great patriotic war.

Because he had unlimited power, he indulged in great arbitrariness and stifled another person morally and physically. A situation was created wherein it was not possible to express one's own will.

In this matter we may consider Khrushchev a competent witness: if even the dictator's intimates, who otherwise were mighty men, could do nothing with him, his power was truly unlimited.

True, a superficial observer might have reached other conclusions, and even the foreign correspondents of Western newspapers could be misled into taking at face value the parliamentary and cooperative act that Stalin staged for them.

Stalin seized the power deftly after Lenin's death. Lenin had left a political testament in which he had foreseen difficulties following his passing. He had especially warned about Stalin, whom he called brutal and unsuited to teamwork. "Under no circumstances give him power," he warned.

Trotsky read Lenin's testament on all appropriate and inappropriate occasions, stressing that on no condition would Lenin have wanted to leave power to Stalin. Trotsky's primary purpose was to point out that he, as Lenin's close colleague and friend would perhaps be the best and most qualified person to carry on Lenin's work.

At these meetings, which were held continuously following Lenin's death, Stalin admitted that Lenin was quite right. He really was coarse and brutal and had at times behaved with impropriety. But at the same time he emphasized that Lenin surely had not sought to discriminate specifically against him in the testament. Lenin had simply wanted to underscore that the Soviet Union must be ruled with the aid of the party. In other words, the Communist party of the Soviet Union was the organ through which the power obtained in the revolution should be wielded.

In these circumstances Stalin began increasingly to strengthen the party as the months went by, since he had the post of party secretary. He initiated a sweeping drive for members, concentrating primarily on students and young people in general. During those years—from the end of 1924 through 1926—a considerable number of members was recruited. At the time of Lenin's death the membership still was comparatively small.

While Trotsky was just making speeches and conducting propaganda against Stalin, Stalin, in addition to recruiting members, skillfully formed a triumvirate with Zinoviev and Kamenev. Both, likewise, were power-hungry and would willingly have been Lenin's successors. These three considered Trotsky in particular to be their most dangerous enemy.

These moves by Stalin succeeded so well that at the 1927 Party Congress Trotsky lost. A large majority supported Stalin's motion that Trotsky had hurt the party and party work, as well as Leninism. Thus Stalin succeeded in having Trotsky ousted from the party and subsequently banished from the Soviet Union.

Now began a period when Stalin step by step strengthened the party while still maintaining the triumvirate. Its other two members, Zinoviev and Kamenev, also held prominent positions.

Then suddenly, quite unexpectedly, Kirov's murder occurred in Leningrad in 1934. Kirov at that time was Stalin's most serious competitor. In his famous speech Khrushchev implied that this murder of Kirov had been organized by Stalin, who had persuaded the chief of the GPU, Yagoda, to join in the intrigue.

After Stalin had become the sovereign dictator around 1932–33, he began to use a great deal of his personal power as well. In 1936 he had the other members of the triumvirate, Zinoviev and Kamenev, arrested and shot and so became the fully sovereign autocrat. In 1938 he liquidated Yagoda.

Stalin's structure of government was as follows: closest to him was the Politburo, the principal organ, a group of twelve to thirteen men chosen from the party's Central Committee. Then came the Central Committee of the Communist party and after that the party Congress. This was the setup on the party side. On the administrative side, at the apex was the Soviet government, followed by the soviets, or councils, at various levels, from the village councils to the Supreme Soviet. All these organizations had been planned as power-wielding, governing organs, but Stalin, by breaking all the laws of organizational democracy, made them the executive organs of his personal power at least in all major matters. Only in minor matters might they have decision-making power as well.

According to Lenin's schema—which Stalin, too, pledged to uphold in his vow at Lenin's grave—the Communist party was the Soviet system's highest power-wielding organ. But upon attaining full authority, Stalin disregarded even the party almost completely. Although party regulations provided for the convening of a party congress biennially, he prolonged the interval between the Eighteenth and Nineteenth Party Congresses, for example, to thirteen years. Nor did he need even the party's Central Committee, which is the supreme power-wielding organ in the intervals between party congresses. Khrushchev declared, "The Central Committee was convened hardly ever. Suffice it to say that, during all the years of the patriotic war, not a single session of the Central Committee was held."

It is hardly likely that the members of the Central Committee, any more than the delegates to the party congresses, had any special desire to convene or to be elected to these organs, inasmuch as being on them made one vulnerable to Stalin's hatred and revenge.

For example, according to Secretary General Khrushchev's frequently cited testimony, of the 139 Central Committee members elected at the Seventeenth Congress, 98 or 70 percent were arrested and shot in 1937–38. Of the 1,966 delegates to the same congress, 1,108 or well over one-half were arrested and shot. According to Khrushchev, all these people were good Communists.

Stalin made all the other organs of government as meaningless as the party. Such institutions as the Supreme Soviet with its two chambers, the Council of the Union and the Council of Nationalities, were merely stage settings. They convened twice a year at most to listen to a reading of the budget, a fanciful series of figures that no one could control and whose utilization could not be ascertained. They had no legislative purpose; their task was merely to applaud when Stalin's aides spoke.

Stalin's autocracy was genuine, and hence he could assume a different attitude than Hitler and Mussolini. These men emphasized themselves, flaunted their power, whereas Stalin did not speak of himself but of the party and the government and the Soviet people. Had I not been aware of the limitlessness of his power, I would have been greatly misled in seeing him at meetings. He never sought to dictate but always said, "Why speak of me? Speak of the matter at hand."

Only rarely did he lapse from his style and forget his role. One such period of forgetfulness occurred in 1945, when a Finnish delegation in Moscow broached the subject of extending the payment period of war reparations. Stalin inquired how the Finns felt about extending it from six to eight years. Splendid, they said. "Good, let's extend it then," said Stalin.

According to Soviet law, the power of decision in such matters rests with the government and the Soviet Parliament. But they were not needed, not even the Politburo.

"May we announce it publicly?" asked the Finns.

"You may. The matter is settled," replied Stalin.

Whatever may have prompted it then, such a lapse in style did not occur often with Stalin. Outward modesty was his masquerade costume. But those who had occasion to follow the deliberation of the most important matters have attested to his complete independence. During the wartime conferences—so affirmed the United States Secretary of State Byrnes, among others—Stalin made his decisions personally, without consulting anybody. Molotov, for example, had no possibility of negotiating on his own; he had to call Stalin at every turn for instructions.

But Stalin's independence was not tinged with smugness. He had a large group of good advisers, and he listened to them. I personally had occasion to observe that he had great respect for technical experts, among others. But these technical experts, on the other hand, respected the alacrity with which Stalin liquidated those who had offended him. They, too, could scent his wishes, as all the political advisors did regularly. An engineer relying on the inflexible logic of his figures might somehow keep his head above water, but when one shifted from clear, numerically expressed mathematics to, shall I say, the dusky mathematics of emotions, one immediately resorted to scenting. An architect might forget Stalin as he calculated volume and strength, but in planning a building's exterior he tried to recall what profound thoughts the dictator had expressed some time or other about architecture.

Matters went even more awry when the more popular arts were involved. True, Stalin did not commit the error of posing as a great aesthetician, as Hitler did, but, naturally, he had opinions as every person has—the only difference is that his opinions were those of a dictator, the opinions of perhaps the most feared dictator in world history. When he made the mistake of expressing them publicly, they ipso facto became laws.

One well-known tale concerns the Polish author Wanda Wasilewska, whose work "The Land" had received unfavorable reviews. Stalin announced publicly that he liked it, and in that moment the critics disappeared from the scene. Wanda Wasilewska became a fixed star in the Soviet literary firmament, and even the author's husband, one Korneitshuk, whom the Soviet aristocracy considered a complete fool—with or without reason, I do not know—acquired prominence.

Another example is provided by the film industry. In 1935 the Soviet film industry released a motion picture that was like all the other Soviet films before it, a tale strongly flavored with propaganda. The film—titled "Chapaev"—portrayed the civil war times, with its hero a peasant type who led a small band of horsemen and performed heroic deeds. It did not attract any particular attention—in fact, it was considered to have some negative aspects.

Stalin had a small motion picture theater in the Kremlin where "Chapaev" happened to be shown. For some reason the film pleased the master of the house, and he gave it the highest rating. After that a great number of extra prints were made, it was shown throughout the whole country, the leading man received the highest honors and the directors, the Vasiljev brothers, became greater than all the other film directors. "Chapaev" served as a model for similar films that virtually inundated the land.

I shall leave for consideration in other contexts how demeaning an effect such words from a dictator have on a country's intellectual life, as well as the fact that all science had to adapt itself to the Marxist-Leninist-Stalinist doctrines. Suffice it to affirm that science ceased to be the touchstone of truth and art the reflector of truth. I shall return to the areas in which Stalin considered himself to be an undisputed expert.

These fields were domestic and foreign policy, the national economy, and, later, the science and art of military operations. The other experts thus found themselves in hot water, among them the top political advisor, Kuusinen, who showed considerable skill in sniffing out Comrade Stalin's opinions. Another long-time advisor was the economist, Professor Varga, but he was not as fortunate as Kuusinen.

Varga's task was to cast the capitalist world's progressive horoscope for two, three, and five years. He worked feverishly with the assistance of the best experts but, at least during the years in which I was able to observe his activities, he had many failures that were frequently discussed in the Comintern's Presidium. Kuusinen considered him a bungler, but Stalin thought otherwise. Varga was his personal friend and as such maintained his position until his master's death.

When he attained power and began to have an influence on international politics, Stalin expressed the opinion that the capitalist world was in a perpetual slump and would soon find itself in a visible depression. Varga had to establish the truth of this thesis. The poor professor and his assistants got gray hairs trying to prove that America and the entire capitalist world were in a depression. When the economic slump finally did begin in 1929, Stalin exulted, "Didn't I tell you!"—though he had made the same assertion many times before in vain. With Varga's aid he then proved it to be a permanent condition. According to earlier (Marxist and Leninist) theories, a depression occurs approximately once every decade, but because it suited Stalin's policy to have the capitalist world's depression permanent, it was proven to be that.

While Stalin lived, rumors were repeatedly spread about the dissension sometimes between him and the military leaders, at other times between him and Molotov or him and Zhdanov. All such talk was ridiculous. The last overt differences of opinion in the Politburo, the party, and the government occurred in 1927–29, and there they ended. Of course there was any amount of dissent, but the dissent of those in concentration camps was not taken into consideration, and the dissent of others could manifest itself only as a conspiracy, not as overt opposition.

With these sketches I probably have substantiated Stalin's total autocracy in perhaps even unnecessary detail.

On what was it based? How could a man wield power unprecedented in world history? Until Stalin's death, Communists claimed that it was based on Stalin's personal genius: he could represent in an extraordinary way precisely what the people wanted, and it was with these traits that he achieved his greatness. This was believed much more readily by foreign Communists and the utopian intelligentsia than by Russians who knew the truth.

Stalin undeniably was a highly gifted and above all a highly energetic man, and the writer of world history must give him full credit for the diligence and personal contribution that he made to his great edifice and, primarily, admire his wisdom in creating the amazing system with which he was able to realize and maintain his autocracy.

I would say that Stalin's autocracy was not based on personal greatness but, rather, was founded on three institutions that he was able to utilize in a unique way. First of all, he formed as an adjunct to the party a powerful Control Committee that actually was a police organization functioning within the party. It had the authority to have people arrested, prosecuted and sentenced. By its orders thousands of people were imprisoned and shot.

Second, with the assistance of Yagoda, he greatly strengthened the standing of the GPU. No longer an ordinary secret police, it became an army of internal security. Incorporated under its jurisdiction were the border guards and militia, over a million men.

The third focus of power was, of course, the Red Army.

This system created by Stalin was an especially clever and cunning invention. All the ammunition depots were under the administration of the GPU. The Red Army had the weapons, which it used in training, and for this training it received a small amount of ammunition, but it had no ammunition depots. In other words, the GPU had the ammunition which in itself was not dangerous, and the Red Army had the cannons, tanks, and other weapons that, likewise, in themselves were not dangerous without ammunition. Thus only together did these two elements form a huge armed might. Individually, each was powerless.

With these three focuses of power Stalin played as a juggler in a circus plays with three balls, two always against one. The party and the GPU formed a common front when the Red Army was beaten down. The GPU, on the other hand, was beaten down with the aid of the party and the army. This was precisely the skillful manipulation of power that Khrushchev and the others did not mention for some reason.

Then came the formation of that terrifying espionage system in which every citizen, especially every citizen in a prominent position, but also workers and kolkhozniks, suspected one another. No one knew who spied on whom. Actually, everybody was spying on everybody else. For example, in my office every offcial was linked to the GPU espionage network. Everyone was obliged to report what happened in my office and around me, to report at least once a month.

Foreigners have found it even more difficult to understand certain puzzling events in the Soviet Union because they have had no knowledge of these organizations and their activities. Oddly enough, professedly knowledgeable experts have remained silent about them or have confused one with another. All evil has been charged to the institution whose name has been in turn the Cheka, the OGPU, the GPU, the NKVD, the MVD, and the KGB, otherwise known as the state or secret police. That institution is considered abroad to be the organ of terror through which Stalin ruled. In a way that is true, but only in a way.

Of the three institutions the state disciplinary organ, the GPU, was numerically the largest, with several million salaried employees. The party's Control Committee likewise was huge, but it did not have as large a salaried staff, relying instead on voluntary party work. The army's political section and secret police were comparable to the counterespionage of all countries but had been developed on a much broader scale. Its activity extended not only to the army but beyond it as well, and it, too, utilized the services of a vast mass of humans.

Some unwritten law had decreed a competition among these three institutions, the results of which Stalin unscrupulously turned to his own advantage. Each spied on the others, trying to do its job better than they. In this respect there was no peaceful coexistence; on the contrary, competition and gory conflict were at their zenith. Stalin seemed to believe in that competition: it made for better and more thorough work. Perhaps Stalin felt that it was precisely that much vaunted socialist competition. Those competitors continuously struck at one another and trod on one another's toes. All three in their own way supported the autocrat's position and kept an eye on one another.

The bolshevik leaders may be the only politicians and statesmen who have read history in order to learn something and actually have learned something. After the revolution Lenin said, "There's no fear of Bonapartes appearing here; we'll clip the wings of such young eagles in time." This sentence may help to explain certain peculiar events during the civil wars. In building his autocracy Stalin had read that it could not be done without a powerful bodyguard. But he had also read that in Rome the Praetorian Guard had seized power, named emperors and murdered them at will.

Stalin's Praetorian Guard originally was the GPU, which had evolved from the modest Cheka. At any moment it might decide on a coup d'état, and even the greatest dictator has but one life that can be taken. Against such a contingency Stalin thus held two aces: the party's Control Committee and the army's Fourth Section. If either of them should become a threat, he still held two aces. Interorganizational competition, envy, and pride made alliance impossible save at Stalin's command. During the years 1936–38 tremendous upheavals and power shifts took place in the Soviet Union, and their rumble carried throughout the world. The world, however, was not permitted to look behind the scenes and did not comprehend that they were effected by Stalin to preserve and strengthen his authority.

By 1936 the GPU had grown ominously powerful. Its chief, Yagoda, began to play his own political game—or at least he kept to himself matters that Stalin should have known. Suddenly this powerful man was shifted to an insignificant position, and subsequently arrested and liquidated. The party's Control Committee and the army's Fourth Section had struck together, arrested the GPU's top leaders and thousands of prominent persons as well. All were seen no more.

It seemed as though the entire organization were about to disappear, but it soon grew strong again when the chief of the party's Control Committee, Yezhov, took over the reins. And before many months had passed, the army and its Fourth Section in turn were vanquished. Tukhachevsky, one of the Soviet Union's five marshals at that time, had shaped up the army and become very popular. General Gamarnik, chief of the Red Army's political branch, had developed the army's Fourth Section into a powerful organization. There was reason to fear that they could not resist using such a splendid vehicle against the dictator.

But the dictator struck first. The GPU and the party's Control Committee joined forces and cut down the army. Tukhachevsky and his staff were arrested and shot; Gamarnik committed suicide as he was being arrested; Kiev's commandant Yakir, chief of the western military district Uborevitsh, director of the Moscow Military Academy, Kork, cavalry commander Primakov, and a great many other generals were liquidated along with their families. Two other marshals, Blücher and Yegorov, met the same fate after they, as members of the military tribunal, had first pronounced the death sentence on the others on Stalin's orders. Of the Red Army's 80,000 officers above the rank of lieutenant, 30,000 were liquidated.

However, the GPU had grown too strong from this victory and the giant purges of these years allowed it to rage freely and to send many millions of the country's inhabitants to concentration camps. The job was done by the army's Fourth Section with support from the party's Control Committee. Yezhov was arrested with his staff and destroyed. I don't know whether Yezhov posed any real threat, but it's always best to be sure, and, besides, with this blow Stalin killed a second and probably even a third fly.

What statesman has not read Machiavelli? And so Stalin undoubtedly was familiar with Cesare Borgia who, after allowing his hirelings to rampage like wild beasts, had them killed as evidence of his own innocence and righteousness. Yezhov's liquidation made him the scapegoat, and millions of people imagined that their innocence was revealed now that Yezhov had gotten his just deserts. Even so experienced and knowledgeable a man as Kustaa Rovio believed that. It was, however, a vain expectation. The third benefit was that the liquidation of Yezhov and his staff silenced many dangerous witnesses.

MY SIX PERSONAL SPIES

THE GPU is known primarily as the most unscrupulous and brutal political police in world history. Its deeds are discussed with horror, but only seldom are its organization and true structure exposed; still less frequently are its methods of operation described.

As I mentioned previously, millions of persons were on its payroll. Its well-trained special army alone had over a million men and included all branches, from poison gas units to air force. These mercenaries had been chosen from the politically most reliable material in the Red Army. The GPU had in each city, large and small, its own huge houses, sources of terror for everybody. Every Moscovite knows Ljubjanka, everybody in Leningrad Gorokhovaia, everyone in Petrozavodsk the White House, and so on. The GPU had its own prisons and execution sites. In every foreign embassy there was a GPU man. Its tentacles reached everywhere.

All this was generally known, but its surveillance and spying system was less well known. It was this system that made it unique in world history, and it partially explains Stalin's omnipotence.

When Polish-born Dzerzhinsky founded the Cheka at the time the Soviet rule was established, it was not much different from the state police of the czars after which it was patterned, except that it was more despotic because it was not in any way subject to the criticism of public opinion. But only the Stalinist reorganization in the mid-1930s made it a terroristic organization that reached everywhere.

I will take a practical example from my office to explain the system.

As a party secretary I had six male assistants, all members of the Communist party. In addition, there were a few female secretaries in the bureau. Not all of them belonged to the party.

One day my assistant, A (I am using letters to avoid causing them any harm, should they still be alive) got a private and secret invitation to Ljubjanka to see Zaitsev, an Ingermanlander, who was the chief of the Finnish section there. Zaitsev asked him to be seated and then began talking to him in a friendly and confidential tone:

"You know that the Soviet Union continues to be surrounded by capitalist countries, and you can also assume that they keep on sending spies and saboteurs here. You will understand that we are forced to increase our vigilance to the best of our ability. As the guardians of democracy we should be aware of even the slightest expressions of opinion in every establishment, for they may provide us with valuable hints.

"We have made inquiries and have found out that you are a reliable, observant, and intelligent person and for that reason we have decided to ask you to report now and then, once or twice a month, systematically, on everything that happens in your bureau, what you discuss during coffee breaks, as well as outside working hours.

"This is a special courtesy to you and an important mission of confidence. Because of your trustworthiness, you are the only person in your bureau whom we are contacting. Of course, it goes without saying that you will not breathe a word of this to anyone. It could cause you trouble."

Zaitsev spoke in a gentle manner but cold shivers ran down A's back.

"Am I supposed to report on Comrade Tuominen as well?" he asked.

"On everyone and especially on him."

"But he has a high position in the party. According to a party resolution, I as a party member am accountable expressly to him for everything. How could I not tell him of this visit? If I don't, I will be committing an offense against the party, and as an old party member I cannot allow myself to be guilty of that."

"You're a little childish, Comrade A," Zaitsev said. "We don't distrust your superior in the least. We know that he is an old party member and that he is looked upon with favor in the highest quarter. We also trust him. We have no suspicions about anyone in your bureau and no unfavorable information about any of your colleagues. This is primarily no more than an additional security measure. We must know everything. Everything, I say. Comrade Kuusinen also visits your bureau from time to time. You will report what he says and everything you hear others saying about him. You will not be committing offense against the party though you follow our orders but—I repeat this—if you tattle to anyone, you will find yourself in great difficulties."

The interview had ended.

The very next morning Comrade A, who was a good friend of mine, came to me and told the whole story as I have related it. He was very nervous.

"What shall I do? I am ready to go straight to Zaitsev to tell him that I have told you."

"Now don't," I said. "Let's wait and see. At least don't tell anyone else."

A few days went by and my subordinate B came to see me privately. He told me a tale that was almost verbatim the one A had told me. He, too, had argued with Zaitsev that it was impossible for him to spy on his superior, but he had received a very sharp answer.

Several weeks later a third subordinate—let's call him C—came to me in distress with the same story. Although the three others did not come, I knew now that all six had been recruited to spy on one another and me.

I told Kuusinen of the system that functioned behind our backs, but he only snorted, "It's the same story throughout the Comintern!"

But I noticed that he became very nervous on hearing that he, too, was spied upon. There are things to which a person apparently does not grow accustomed.

A, B, and C reported from time to time and, probably to ease their conscience, told me what they had reported. And they could truthfully report everything, for nothing anti-Soviet took place in our bureau.

Nothing special happened, and everyone calmed down little by little. But one noticed clearly that the atmosphere in the bureau changed. One could no longer hear spontaneous jesting, everyone was on his guard, and political conversation consisted of mere phrases about the great Stalin and the mighty Soviet Union.

A few months passed. One morning Comrade B came to my room, very nervous, and told me that the previous evening he had paid his usual call on the GPU.

After he had given his report, Zaitsev asked, "Where were you last Thursday evening?"

B thought back and answered, "We spent the evening at Comrade C's. There were five of us, all from our bureau."

"Well, what did you talk about?"

"Just the usual coffee chat, I suppose. At least nobody said anything unsuitable."

"But didn't you discuss a *Pravda* article on Finland? And didn't Comrade A say something about it?"

B was very surprised.

"I think Comrade A said it was well written."

"What else? Didn't Comrade A express other views as well?"

"Well, I think he said that the writer does not know the situation in Finland very well. But he didn't mean anything belittling by it. Comrade A is a faithful Stalinist. It didn't occur to me that the statement could contain anything questionable, and therefore I didn't report it."

"You must remember things like this better. You discussed a delicate matter, a statement of the main organ of the Communist party, which in addition concerns your own country. I have noticed before, Comrade B, that your memory is a little weak. You don't seem to be quite honest with us. Although this matter is minor, I find it my duty to warn you."

B looked at me like a beaten dog.

"We were five men there, all from this office. There can be no listening devices in the walls. Therefore, someone else must have made a report also."

The poor man seemed to suffer the torments of hell.

I could only say, "You should have realized that you are not the only contact man to the GPU."

B noticed that I knew something, said nothing, and withdrew, his head bowed.

It did not take long before A and C arrived, equally terrified, to tell the same story. They understood, these three as well as the other three who told me nothing, that they were all spying on one another. All joy died out in the office, for everyone felt the fingers of the GPU at his throat. Besides, I had reason to believe that the GPU had recruited the women in the office for the same task, for their behavior, too, became strained and tense.

My staff members were honest people who tried to give such general and broad reports that they would not do harm to anyone. I draw this conclusion from the fact that nobody was arrested "prematurely"; when they went, they went in the general streams of the purge.

A spy system like this is even more terrifying because an immoral individual can cause extraordinary damage. He need not even invent anything. He merely reports that someone has laughed at an inopportune moment; that is enough to destroy a life.

Long before this system came to the Comintern and to the circle of Finns and other foreigners, it had been tried and found good in Russian institutions. I could follow closely the work of other offices and a number of important factories, and I could see that they used the same system. For example, in the factory that was led by the famous Finnish Communist Heikki Kaljunen and that employed about one thousand workers, the system was applied considerably earlier than by us. I know this because among its workers were former prison mates of mine, and when I talked with them, they all concluded with these words: "I know that others have visited the GPU also, and it seems that my days are numbered."

I remember especially Aleksi Hirvelä, a steadfast Communist, who for over a decade had led the work of the Communist party secret police in Finland, and who now got a curt "severance payment" from the GPU.

In ordinary places of work the system was not extended to every person, only to those who in some way were in representative positions, such as work supervisors and the abler party members. If a

factory had 1,400 workers, 150 to 200 of them could be obligated
to report to the GPU. Office staffs were often burdened with these
duties because their positions were more representative. In Karelia
and the Leningrad area the situation was the same. The Russians
seemed to do this job much better than the Finns who were unable
to turn informer, nor were they able to fabricate lies or to misunderstand innocent talk. Thus they fell victim to the system and
disappeared without a trace.

In discussing the Comintern schools I mentioned the international military school in Leningrad. Estonians, Latvians, Lithuanians, and Karelians had studied there, but the Finns had always
been most numerous. But during the years 1935–36 there were only
twelve Finns, and it was then that the GPU organized a characteristic provocation.

All twelve had been recruited into the GPU system, but the reports they wrote told nothing; from week to week they were a big
blank. The GPU then gave one of the men the order to attempt an
escape to Finland, taking two of his comrades along. Supposedly,
there was reason to believe that they were anti-Soviet. "Get maps
and supplies and escape together."

He then recruited the two other men, and the three made plans
to flee together. When everything was done as instructed, the GPU
arrested all three and ascertained that they had maps and ample
other evidence. A little later the whole course was arrested. All
were court-martialed for counterrevolutionary activity and three
for attempted escape.

Of course, the one who planned the escape was innocent. The
other two said that, since they had been ordered by the GPU to
keep an eye on the others, when they saw that one was planning an
escape, they promised to participate in order to uncover the whole
plan. They already had reported what was going on. In other words,
they never kept anything secret and had no intention of escaping.

The whole group was sentenced to three to four years of hard
labor.

I was able to follow the case quite far. Since the men were members of the Finnish Communist party it was my duty to look after
their interests or to find out what kind of rabble had come into the
country. The court record contained nothing more than that they
were unreliable counterrevolutionaries. The true story came out

in the letters they sent from the prison camps to Kuusinen and my-self, and it was supported by the school's politcommissar, Antti Pylsy, who was married to Tyyne Tokoi, daughter of Oskari Tokoi. Pylsy knew the system, had had the chance to follow its activities from the beginning and was aware that the escape affair was a provocation. He also had received an order to report if he saw something suspicious. He told the true story but to no avail. A little later he, too, was arrested and soon disappeared.

Most of the Finns were sent to different areas, some to Siberia, others to Turkestan and still others along the Volga. Their letters showed that all were desperate. They were twenty-four to twenty-five years of age, and six months in the concentration camp had already broken them down completely. I never heard of them again, just as I hardly ever heard about other Finns who had been arrested.

Let me mention a few additional examples of the kind of havoc the system wrought among the Finns.

In the middle of the 1930s I traveled in Karelia a number of times to raise the spirits there. I visited several workplaces explaining the situation according to the policy line: you're badly off now, there is a shortage of bread, clothing, and just about anything but these are only growing pains, for this industrial giant grows so frightfully fast that the clothing does not suffice; some part is always bare.

The men were ordered to the meeting, and I made a rousing speech, someone else made another speech, and then I asked them to take the floor and to discuss the issues. But though I tried in every way to stir up enthusiasm in these men who were all Finns, many former members of the Finnish Communist party, old labor union men, I was not able to get any reaction. These hundreds of men were so thoroughly apathetic and depressed I seemed to be talking to an utterly hostile mass. They did not laugh at my jokes, and yet in Finland, and in Russia as well, I was accustomed to being applauded for the quips during my speeches. Although I desperately tried to warm them up, they said absolutely nothing, and that was the end of the meeting.

One of the gloomiest occasions I attended was at the forest camp of Vilkka, in Karelia. Hannes Juvonen, who later became the director of the Lenin Museum in Tampere, Finland, was then in charge of the camp. He had ordered his men, numbering about

200, to the meeting at which Rovio and I spoke. We tried to get a discussion going, but the only reaction was a hostile glare from 200 pairs of eyes and a gloomy silence.

One of the men was an old acquaintance of mine, and I lamented to him how terrible it was.

He answered, "When you begin to describe conditions and demand that we discuss them, you have no idea how things are here. If you say what you think, it means deportation. If you praise them, it means a beating in the shack afterwards. There is no other possibility than to keep your yap shut."

The situation was the same in Syväri, where a power station was being built.

One could see how far the terror of the GPU had driven these Finns, and yet it went even further: it destroyed them. They were moved to where they were not dangerous to the Soviet rule, to the steppes of Siberia.

Most tragic was when some of those who had been sent to the labor camps began to feel themselves some kind of criminals, unable to adjust to the Soviet system and to the demands of the GPU. Thus, in addition to everything else in the prison camp, they were burdened by self-reproach. This was the most shocking aspect of the fate of these people doomed to destruction. After he had been sent in this manner to a concentration camp an orthodox Communist did not feel honest: he had the feeling of having committed a crime for which he deserved punishment. He was being ground between two millstones: as an honest man he could not destroy his best comrades and childhood friends; but neither could be betray the communist idea, of which the Soviet rule and the GPU were the concrete representatives. The majority did not want to betray either, but because one of them had to be betrayed, often they tried to go along with the GPU as long as possible.

In other words, the system was ghastly. If someone tried to apply it in Finland or anywhere else in Western Europe where the pattern of thinking differs from that in Russia, it would have created still greater conflicts and still greater human destruction than in Russia. Only the Russians could have submitted and adjusted to it.

These few examples reveal the GPU's method of operation. The system was similar in the control organ of the party. In the Fourth Section of the army it was considerably different because most of the staff was salaried. But there, too, the same system of investigating and spying reached everywhere. Nobody was spared, not even Stalin: there was a dossier on him, too. And who knows if a strange hand ultimately did not have a chance to pluck the three-stringed instrument of power that Stalin had for many years played so masterfully.

I can mention an interesting example of the competition among the three organizations. It took place in the summer of 1937 while my wife and I were taking the cure in Zheleznovodsk, in the Caucasus.

Hella Wuolijoki, Finnish Communist and playwright, had visited Moscow during the first half of June. Officially she was on a business trip, but actually she was doing something else. She had met Gylling, who was then working in the Varga Research Institute of World Economy, and afterwards, Kuusinen, to whom she, in her own lively style, had released torrents of information about her own affairs and given him as a souvenir of her visit a copy of her play, "The Women of Niskavuori." When we returned from the Caucasus, Kuusinen told me of the visit and of Hella's chat.

A few weeks after the visit, a large number of persons again were arrested in Karelia in the so-called "July purge," as a result of which Gylling and Rovio also were arrested in Moscow. Gylling was a member of the Central Committee of the Finnish Communist party, and I as the party secretary had to find out why he was arrested. The party leadership was badly compromised.

Besides, the arrest of such men as Gylling and Rovio, who are close to one and whom one knows to be innocent, seems many times more harrowing than if thousands of unknown persons are arrested. Emotional values depend greatly on the proximity of those doomed, how close to them one has been. Too, the fact that the victims of the terror were mostly Russians and other nationalities made the terror somewhat easier to bear, just as the death of a neighbor hurts less than the passing of a family member.

Hence I asked to see the head of the GPU, Yezhov. Yezhov likewise was a member of the Comintern's Presidium and therefore an old acquaintance. Also present were the head of the Finnish section, Zaitsev, and his assistant Evreinov.

I demanded to know forthwith why Gylling, Rovio, and a number of other well-known Finns had been arrested.

Small, warped Yezhov looked very serious.

"It is an unpleasant affair," he said, "unpleasant to the Finnish party and especially for you. The investigations are only now beginning but the evidence seems to weigh very heavily against them. Hella Wuolijoki has visited Gylling, and we have every reason to suspect—and not only suspect, we have proof—that she is in the service of the British Secret Service. Besides, she told Gylling that she is in the service of the Fourth Section. I don't know if it is true but we know for sure that the Secret Service business is."

"But you can telephone the Fourth Section and ask if it is true," I suggested.

"We wouldn't think of asking them. But if it is true we will prove that the Fourth Section employs the same person as the Secret Service."

Evreinov joined in the conversation and said that Hella had also visited Kuusinen.

"We don't know what she said there but you could find out."

"No. I absolutely refuse to ask Kuusinen anything."

"It would be very important to know what they talked about and what Kuusinen ordered Hella to do, for it's known that he uses the woman for special tasks."

I shook my head.

Evreinov continued, "Kuusinen's position is very precarious, and since you live with Kuusinen and even work in the same organization, it's also precarious for you."

"Naturally I realize that it's a dangerous affair, but I didn't even meet Hella here and haven't met her in ten years. Incidentally, I cannot take her seriously."

"But you could ask Kuusinen anyway."

I knew that if one gave this devil a little finger even temporarily, he would irretrievably take the whole hand and the whole man.

"I cannot start spying on Kuusinen, and you have no right to impose such tasks on a member of the Comintern's Presidium."

Evreinov tried to persuade me; he wanted to know, among other things, how close the relationship between Hella and Kuusinen was. Then he began to tell long tales about Kuusinen's private life, for Evreinov had been working under Kuusinen in the Comintern and knew his weaknesses and strong points.

"His position is very weak," Evreinov asserted. "He can be arrested at any moment." The main charge was that he had attested to the reliability of hundreds of Communists who had been arrested during recent months. Second, he had compromising foreign connections and, third, other suspicious women also visited him and not even his relatives were reliable, Evreinov insisted.

The conclusion was that Kuusinen's position was shaky. Since he could provide no protection, it would be wise of me to help in his liquidation.

Throughout the conversation the top man Yezhov remained seated and confirmed his assistant's statements by nodding his head.

When I returned to *Dom Pravitel'stva* from this almost three-hour information session, my spirits were far from high. I told Kuusinen immediately part of what had been discussed at the GPU. I didn't care to mention the matter of the women nor the weakness of his position in precisely the words used at the GPU. But I mentioned the charges against Gylling, Hella's role in the mess, and the suggestion that I should find out what had occurred between him and Hella.

Kuusinen became unexpectedly nervous, rose and began pacing the floor. He sucked vehemently on one cigarette after another, cursed Hella, and finally asked me to go and meet Yezhov that very evening to report what Hella had said. In the end there was not much to tell, only Hella's typical tales about her book and boasts of its success. The only relevant story—provided it was relevant—was Hella's statement that she had come to Moscow at the invitation of the Fourth Section. Kuusinen had tried to pretend not to hear that information but Hella had repeated it. He had not breathed a word to her of any confidential matters of the Soviet government, Comintern, or the Finnish Communist party.

"Go and tell them this," he pleaded.

"Under no circumstances will I go. You know Yezhov better than I. Go yourself. But do you believe that Hella is in the employ of the Secret Service?"

"It doesn't pay to believe anything. At least she didn't say anything to me about it, but it's not impossible with such a character. Listen, why don't you go, it's so difficult for me to go and talk on my own behalf."

"They are older acquaintances of yours. Even Evreinov was there."

When Kuusinen heard that he became even more reluctant to go—probably because he had given Evreinov a bad time as a supervisor. Instead, despite the lateness of the hour, he asked for an audience with Manuilski who was the contact man between Stalin and the Presidium of the Comintern.

Once Kuusinen was there, they had also called in Dimitrov and then phoned Stalin directly, telling him that Yezhov was threatening to liquidate even Kuusinen.

After a few hours—by then it was the small hours—Kuusinen returned home and came straight to our bedroom. We noticed at once that he was much calmer. The cigarette that at his departure had barely clung to his lips, was now much steadier. He explained in great detail what had happened and twice repeated how Stalin had replied to Manuilski's call: "Tell Otto Vilgemovich that Yezhov will do nothing to him. He should just go back home to bed."

Although he thus had received the word of the great Stalin, he nevertheless spent many sleepless nights cleaning out his files and books so that nothing compromising could be found in case there would be a search after all.

And so it was that even in *Dom Pravitsel'stva* as everywhere else fear was the dominant factor in life, fear and again fear. Nobody, not even Stalin's personal secretary O. W. Kuusinen, could ever be entirely sure that he would arise in the morning from the same place where he had laid his head the night before; one could be taken to another place during the night.

After the war it was grotesque to think that, following the signing of the Atlantic Charter, which promised "freedom from fear" to all nations, the terror system spread to numerous countries which previously had not known fear, at least not in such a terrible form.

Once having felt the pressure of this fear, it seems impossible that people can stand it year after year without rebelling. But at that very instant one comprehends that under such circumstances there are no possibilities for rebellion. Even to rebel one needs at least a little freedom of movement.

It remained a fleeting dream of individuals of which they did not dare even whisper. Stalin's dictatorship was truly total, unlimited.

Oskari Tuominen, Arvo
Tuominen's father, at the
age of 70.

Elina Tuominen, Arvo
Tuominen's mother, at the
age of 60.

Arvo Tuominen began his life in this cabin, in Finland. On either side of a small kitchen were two rooms: one in which the family lived and where the seventeen children were born; the other was the carpenter shop of Tuominen's father.

Tuominen as secretary of the Tampere Revolutionary Committee, 1917–18. "One can see," he wrote under this picture, "that I considered that task very important."

Tuominen in his mid-twenties.

Lenin and his stark
shadow.

Photo courtesy of the
National Archives.

Old Bolshevik Nikolai Bukharin.

Karl Radek, sarcastic
Bolshevik, who made
jokes about Stalin.

Old Bolshevik Leon
Trotsky, who lost to
Stalin.

**Photo courtesy of the
National Archives.**

Otto Kuusinen in
the 1920s.

Aino Kuusinen, the second
of Kuusinen's many wives,
followed him to the Soviet
Union through the forests of
Karelia—in silk stockings
and high heels.

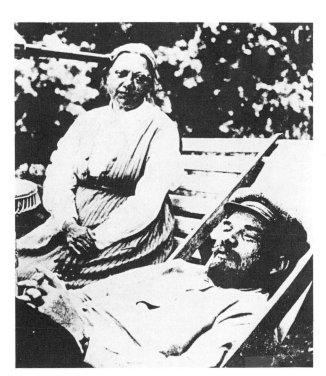

Sick Lenin and his wife in 1923.

Tuominen's road led to *Dom Pravitel'stva* in Moscow, the large government building within earshot of the bells of the Kremlin, across the Moscow River. In this building almost all the top Soviet brass lived. (This picture was taken through the kitchen window of the Kuusinen-Tuominen apartment.)

Kuusinen's daughter Hertta in Helsinki, after the hard years in Moscow.

Yrjö Sirola, a sensitive
Communist.

Edvard Gylling, idealist and practical man whose life came to a tragic end.

Kustaa Rovio, friend of Lenin.

Heikki Kaljunen, boastful and cruel Red general.

Comintern secretaries in 1935. *Standing from left:* Kuusinen, Gottwald, Pieck, Manuilski; *seated:* Dimitrov, Togliatti, Florin, and Wang Ming.

Children bring flowers to Stalin and durable old Bolshevik Molotov.

Photo courtesy of the National Archives.

Marshal Tukhachevsky during his days of glory. Was liquidated.

Bela Kun, speaking to the Hungarian masses. He was later liquidated.

Zinoviev, one of the original revolutionary leaders, and Tomsky (with hat), President of the Trade Unions. Both were liquidated.

Photo courtesy of the National Archives.

Yagoda, who as chief of
GPU did Stalin's dirty
work and was then
executed.

Molotov signing the 1939 agreement that formed the Terijoki government of Kuusinen. *Standing from left:* Zhdanov, Marshal Voroshilov,
Stalin, and Kuusinen. Had Tuominen returned from Stockholm, he
would have been standing in the place of Kuusinen.

This villa was the seat of Kuusinen's government in Terijoki.

Finland's Minister of Interior Yrjö Leino, who was more Finnish than Communist.

Lyyli and Arvo Tuominen in their home in Tampere, Finland.
Photo by Ensio Kauppila.

Arvo Tuominen at home, in 1976.
Photo by Piltti Heiskanen.

Arvo Tuominen at 85, two years before his death.
Photo by Juha Tujunen.

THE STALIN CONSTITUTION

THE CONSTITUTION of the Soviet Union, the so-called Stalin Constitution, was adopted in 1936.

This constitution has been one of the most utilized means of propaganda directed abroad. Strangely enough, it has also been used in the Soviet internal propaganda, especially in the beginning. To the Western way of thinking, it is impossible to understand how a people can be told as truth that which it knows and feels in its own skin to be false. Yet this happens.

After a number of years the Stalin Constitution was used in domestic propaganda only during the elections. But in propaganda directed abroad the Soviet radio and press still continue to use the constitution as an example of marvelous achievements of the Soviet Union on its road toward social justice. It claims to be the most democratic constitution in the world, both in letter and spirit superior to even the most democratic constitutions.

But this is not the most important difference. The most important difference, according to the propaganda, is that every article and requirement in the Soviet constitution is being adhered to in practice while the capitalist countries do not carry out their constitutional guarantees. These rights apply only to the privileged classes. The law there is not the same for all and the majority of the constitutional articles in the capitalist countries are only on paper.

This is the standard claim of the Soviet propaganda, and the communist press in the various countries repeats it often. The matter is worth examining.

When you look at Stalin's Constitution clause by clause, you can see at once that even on paper it is not a miraculous achievement. If you compare it to the constitution of Finland or any other democratic country you will find only small differences even in the most democratic passages. There are in the Soviet constitution very good and useful—even exemplary—provisions that can compete with the provisions of the constitution of any democratic country. With slight differences, the same things are in the Finnish constitution, among others.

It is not my aim to describe the contents of the Stalin Constitution; enough has been written about it. I will only present a few comments on how it was carried out during the Stalin era. For this purpose I will at first list a number of the most important provisions:

Universal, secret, and equal suffrage;
freedom of speech, press, assembly, and of forming associations;
freedom of religion;
censorship of the telephone, telegraph, and mail is forbidden;
all Soviet citizens have the right to rest, the right to use rest homes, sanatoria, and other places of recuperation;
free schooling for all, without regard to the social position or race of the parents of the children;
work for all—unemployment is an unknown concept in the Soviet Union;
social security;
the Soviet Union is a combination of many different nationalities, built on the idea of voluntariness; every nation can secede whenever it so wants by a simple majority.

On paper, each of these provisions is excellent and completely in the democratic spirit. But let's examine how they are applied in practice.

The provision for *free elections* is made meaningless by the fact that only one party is permitted. All other parties are forbidden. The Soviet election system is defective also for the reason that great numbers of citizens are without voting rights because they are in concentration camps. While Stalin lived, these numbered at any given time from 10 to 15 million.

Even if we overlook these two factors, which already make the system fairly meaningless, there are other considerations which still further reduce its importance.

According to the constitution, not only the Communist party but also all other functioning organizations, such as labor unions, youth and cultural organizations, and so on, are permitted to nominate candidates for soviet, parliamentary, district, and village council elections. But what is the practice?

I know the practice very well, for I followed the matter closely and served as a sort of election functionary. The naming of candidates happened as follows: the Central Committee in Moscow nominated the majority of the candidates for the Supreme Soviet, several hundred persons who were considered necessary because of their achievements or for various political reasons. They were assigned to various districts already in Moscow. Important leaders in Moscow, along with an outstanding engineer or aviator, were assigned as candidates even to the remotest areas of the country. Often a district got a candidate totally unknown to its population, one that had never even been heard of by the people. Nevertheless, he was the one they ostensibly chose to represent them in the Supreme Soviet.

Thus Papanin, a man who had flown to the North Pole, was ordered to be elected as a representative of the Karelian Republic in the Council of Nationalities. He was not Karelian and had never even visited Karelia. The people of the Uhtua, Kiestinki, and Aunus counties had no interest in electing him as their representative. To them it made no difference if he had been to the North Pole or not, but their views were not asked. Moscow had made its decision, and so Papanin represented Uhtua, Kiestinki, and Aunus in the Council of Nationalities in Moscow for a long time, beginning in 1939. How well he knew the needs and wishes of the people he represented is another story.

Naturally, not all members of the Supreme Soviet were nominated by the Central Committee of the party. A number of them were assigned by district committees, but the lower echelons of the party had practically no say in the choice of candidates.

So the procedure is that the district committee of the party in Karelia gets an order: select such and such candidates, select a Papanin whose flight to the North Pole is worth remembering. The district committee in turn sends the order to Uhtua, Kiestinki, and Aunus. At the same time scores, even hundreds of Communist party organs propose the same candidate in various trade union, youth, and cultural organizations' meetings. He is nominated unanimously in every meeting though nobody knows anything about him except that he has visited the North Pole and must be elected.

The same method is used for the nomination of all the other candidates in Karelia, some of them Karelians, leaders in the Karelian government but part of them Papanins.

After the candidates have been thus named and have been voted in in every meeting, they have been actually unanimously suggested as the representatives of the Stalinist list from that particular election district. There are no competing candidates and none must be proposed. Thus each person who has been set up as a candidate has simultaneously been elected.

For three months people have marched many miles to agitate for Papanin, though everybody knows already that he will be elected because there are no other candidates.

But the play must be performed to the end. The election day arrives. Everybody has to vote. Large factories come to a halt while the workers march to the polling places behind a brass band. It is a demonstration: every worker wants to cast his or her vote for Comrade Stalin. They are singing and marching, but one can ask, if the marching is joyous. The great majority of the factory workers and of those other people whom I could observe probably did not understand what it was all about.

But it meant a few hours free from the daily routine. It did not benefit them, but neither did it harm them to take this walk, since it had to be done anyway, and they did get some fresh air. They did not understand the election procedure as it is understood in a democratic country. That may be fortunate, for it is easier to participate in the play when one does not understand how foreign this hustle and bustle is to truly democratic elections.

From a practical viewpoint, it should make no difference if the casting of the ballot takes place secretly behind a curtain—as it does—or in the presence of all, for one can vote only for Papanin's list. The only other possibility is to tear the ballot and not vote at all or write in some other name behind the curtain. But that would be futile and even dangerous.

Usually the results of the election are dazzling, so dazzling that once, in the Stalin district of Moscow, participation was 100 percent. When one considers that there were 200,000 voters in the Stalin district, one has to speak of a miracle, for everywhere else in the world in such a crowd someone always—even on election day—is dying, someone else is giving birth, still another one is ill. The Nazis were considerable miracle workers, but their vote was limited to 90–95 percent.

This playing with figures, which was evident also in the five-year plan and the budget during Stalin's time, provoked laughter in the rest of the world and even in the thinking segment of the Soviet people, but it is perhaps not quite so silly as a straightforward Westerner might think. The prankster's role is advantageous in that one never knows when he is serious. Therefore other countries must always be on their toes.

For a simple kolkhoznik whose arithmetic is weak, those figures are a sort of semimystical diversion. He, too, likes to play with figures, and so it happened that voter participation even exceeded 100 percent in many areas—results that the local election board offered with a serious face. But in Moscow they knew that it was not advisable to present results that topped 100 percent.

In fact, the polling places drew more than one would assume of those people that were on a free footing and thus able to vote. This was made possible by a unique system in connection with which one cannot speak of free elections but of election terror. Every person in the Soviet Union had a passport and a work book. During the electioneering, which lasted for months, every worker, as well as housewives who did not hold a job, was given a categorical order to go and vote. It was a civic duty. If someone tried to shirk it, his passport served as a control document that indicated, through appropriate notation, whether or not he had exercised his right to vote. If there was no such notation in the passport, it was absolutely impossible to obtain ration cards, an apartment, medical care, or any other benefits life in the Soviet Union may offer. How could a citizen who does not vote demand any rights?

This was the system used to produce those institutions that the foreign press called the Soviet Parliament. It convened in Moscow twice, sometimes three times a year, for two or three days. During these meetings leaders of the Soviet regime, often Prime Minister Molotov, or the minister of finance, or an engineer from the heavy industry gave tremendously long situation reports, and the listeners applauded, often without understanding anything of the content. But every time the name of Comrade Stalin was mentioned, they applauded. Particularly the great wisdom of Stalin had to be praised, in every speech. This jollity continued throughout those two or three days. All resolutions were passed unanimously and in an atmosphere of great enthusiasm.

To my knowledge, two proposals were never presented simultaneously for a vote in the Supreme Soviet or the Soviet Parliament.

As the system otherwise imitated Western parliaments, one might have assumed that a counterproposal would have been introduced pro forma. But Stalin did not find that necessary.

Mussolini's great council and Hitler's parliament were a farce compared to democratic parliaments. They, nevertheless, had more democratic features than did the Soviet Parliament in Stalin's time.

This was the situation at the highest level and the lower levels acted roughly in the same manner. In this field, too, the hierarchy has many levels: there are regional soviets, the supreme soviets of the various republics, district soviets, and village soviets. All their elections are conducted similarly, and the people have no other choice than to vote for one specific name.

The most important part of the Soviet constitution on universal, secret, and equal suffrage is like this. It is amazing to see articles in the foreign press that persist on writing about free, universal, equal, and secret elections in the Soviet Union.

Freedom of speech, press, assembly, and of forming associations.
Those who wrote the constitution were great humorists. After stating that no party other than the communist one is permitted, in the next paragraph they promised free assembly, association, speech, and press for everyone.

But this is only the beginning. The constitutions of capitalist countries, too, grant freedom of speech and press, but every Soviet citizen may even print newspapers and books; furthermore, he is given free paper for that purpose and the use of a printing press by the government. "These rights of the citizen are secured by giving the working men and women as well as their organizations free paper and the free use of a state printing press," the 125th clause of the constitution states. This clause is often cited in lauding the Soviet constitution. In what other country does the state let a party or a private citizen use its paper and its printing press?

But the whole world knows that in the Soviet Union no other newspapers are allowed than those of the Communist party and even they are under a strict and narrow censorship. Thus talk of freedom of speech and press concerns only the Communist party. Censorship and standardization extend to the smallest details of literature and to music and the graphic arts. Strange as it sounds, even music can be capitalistic and unsuitable for the Soviet Union.

True, the newspapers contain political articles that are critical of the commissars, but those always come from above and mean the end of life for that commissar or official. Few Soviet citizens are so simpleminded that they would offer *Pravda* or *Izvestiia* criticism of the system and the leadership. Criticism comes as an avalanche and always at the hint of a high leader, though ordinary people may have been mobilized as signatories.

Freedom of religion.
The paragraphs concerning freedom of religion are equally strange. In the beginning there was an attempt to destroy the church completely in the Soviet Union. Churches were changed to movie theaters and restaurants, or they were torn down and the building material was used for other buildings. In the cities only 10 or 15 percent of the churches remained, considerably more in the countryside.

Then, during the years 1941–42, when the Soviet Union was hard pressed, and Stalin had to mobilize all possible reserves—the reserves of the Red Army and the Communist party were enough only for a few months to check the German attack—it was announced with grandiose gestures that the complete freedom of religion promised in the constitution would be reinstated. The church was granted all kinds of benefits, most of them conspicuous ones, and it was advertised especially abroad that Stalin had given the orthodox church full freedom to operate.

But the whole orthodox church was used to serve bolshevik propaganda. If someone attempted to dedicate himself to religion, his official duties were terminated very quickly. In every speech and every writing of the Moscow patriarch one could see clearly that he had no special position among the other politruks. He was forced to sing Stalin's praises in each speech, just as the politruk on each collective farm had to do.

Now the Soviet Union began sending delegates abroad to religious congresses. In one Baptist convention the Soviet representative gave a lecture that lasted over an hour and was similar to the lectures Soviet trade union, sports organization, or Communist party representatives might deliver in an international congress.

The lecture described the heroic struggle of the Soviet Union against the German attack, the importance of the victory achieved by Stalin's troops, under Stalin's personal leadership, and how the Soviet people are preparing to crush Western imperialism and free the whole world. In it there was not a single word about church matters, not a word about the life of Baptists in the Soviet Union. When the speaker was asked why he did not speak of Baptists at that international Baptist congress, he said he had delivered the speech that had been given to him. An eloquent commentary on the freedom of religion in the Soviet Union.

Censorship of the telephone, telegraph, and mail is forbidden.
An event illustrating this paragraph took place in 1937, after the constitution had been in effect for one year. Kuusinen was spending his summer vacation in the Crimea. From there he sent me several letters in which he asked me to take care of a number of urgent matters. It takes mail two days to reach Moscow from the Crimea, but these letters needed two weeks or even more. A censor had put his rubber stamp on each of them. A couple of the letters had not yet arrived when Kuusinen himself returned and asked me if I had taken care of the matters described in those letters.

"I never received such letters," I answered. "But don't worry, they will come. Nothing gets lost in Russia."

And I couldn't help adding: "It's funny that postal censorship ended a long time ago but letters still lay at the censor's for a long time, the longer because we write in Finnish. Yet the sender is such a high boss like yourself, and the receiver is another high boss, myself. And they even slap a rubber stamp on the envelope. That is bad business especially since we're trumpeting that the new constitution differs from the constitution of Finland precisely in that every paragraph of the Soviet constitution is being followed to the letter and is not merely on paper as in the bourgeois countries.

Kuusinen snatched one of the letters, glanced at the envelope and fumed:

"Why do they have to put a rubber stamp on it?"

Although he had lived for nineteen years in the Soviet Union and had tried to adjust to the Russian mentality, there still remained in him such a sense of propriety instilled at the Jyväskylä

Lyceum and the Helsinki University that the rubber stamp hurt him greatly. He no longer was hurt by the violation of the constitution, but he was angered by the stupidity and insolence.

A few days later I took the letters and went to Manuilski, then the influential secretary of Comintern. I asked:

"Do you know that censorship is still in effect?"

"Yes. What about it?"

"Well, the constitution forbids it. And we have declared in scores of articles and pamphlets that Soviet laws are being observed to the letter and not violated as they are in the capitalist countries. This has been emphasized especially in propaganda directed toward Finland. Now we can be called liars."

I showed the letters but Manuilski didn't even glance at them, just burst into laughter, spread his arms, and said:

"I knew that you Finns are simpleminded but I didn't think you are that simpleminded! How can you take this matter so seriously?"

He laughed heartily and added these significant words:

"*Vot bumaaga bumaaga i praktika praktika.*" Precisely: a document is a document and practice is practice. He had not the inhibitions that Kuusinen had. Agreements, laws, and signatures were understood in this manner. I thought it shocking, but Manuilski thought it amusing.

Manuilski's maxim casts light on many things. After the Winter War against Finland the Russians demanded the nickel mines at Kolosjoki, in Petsamo. When Finns explained that the mines are owned by a Canadian company, the Russians had a simple solution: "change the law."

All Soviet citizens have the right to rest, the right to use
rest homes, sanatoriums, and other places of recuperation.
Here I refer to the chapter in which I write about my own experiences in sanatoriums.

Free schooling for all, without regard to the social position
or race of the parents of the children.
In the early years of the Soviet Union there were attempts to carry out this law. But now only the children of the Soviet aristocracy and of the highest officers can have a higher university education.

Ordinary folks cannot get their children into the universities, nor do they have a chance since tuitions were raised so high that a worker's wages do not send a child to the university. In this respect Stalin achieved the level of the most backward capitalist countries.

Work for all.

This is the only provision in the Soviet constitution that one can say was fulfilled during the Stalin era. Because the whole population did forced labor, there was no unemployment. One could not change one's place of work, nor could a young person choose his occupation. A young worker was directed to the field where manpower was needed most, not to the field of his inclination. And when one got into a certain occupation, one had to stay in it. It was hopeless to try to change. Once in a while exceptions were made, and much ado was made about these cases, but these were very rare.

When there is a need for 10,000 to 100,000 workers in some project, the required labor force is commanded to go there. This group might do forestry work one year, mining the next, and build a railroad the year after. This way the workers have a chance to do different kinds of work but always by orders from above.

Work for all has been used much in propaganda, but it has become most grotesque from the point of view of the working people. Stalin made it into a forced labor law.

Social security.

Under this heading there are such things as old age insurance, sickness insurance, aid to mothers, accident insurance, and so on. Some of these were carried out already before the Stalin Constitution and the results were excellent, for example, in aid to mothers. A working mother was granted maternity leave two months before and three months after giving birth, with full wages.

Strangely enough, the direction in the Soviet Union was retrogressive. Mothers began to write to Stalin that they did not need so much vacation. As a result, their position began to be weaker even with regard to vacations—and one cannot even mention other benefits—than for example in Finland.

The workday in the Soviet Union was ceremoniously shortened to seven hours and the work week to five days. But after the war the Soviet people themselves arranged great demonstrations and sent Comrade Stalin petitions and appeals demanding that the workweek be lengthened to six days and the workday to eight hours in order to speed up the building of socialism. Of course, Stalin could not ignore the voice of the people, and the worktime in the Soviet Union became equal to that of the capitalist countries or even longer.

In the early years of the Soviet rule much propaganda was made among the women over the freedom to undergo an abortion. This privilege lasted until 1936 when the Soviet women got the idea of rising in a massive movement against it. They sent tens of thousands of letters to Comrade Stalin, demanding an end to the freedom. So Stalin very reluctantly agreed and had a law passed that forbade abortion. Every doctor or any other person performing an abortion was from then on penalized much more severely than in any other country.

Earlier, a Soviet citizen could obtain a divorce more easily than in other countries. All he or she had to do was to send a postal card telling the spouse that she or he can leave.

Nowadays one can still get a divorce easily, provided one has money. There is a progressively increasing tax on divorces. An ordinary official or worker is unable to pay for a third divorce. Divorces beyond that are only for the upper classes.

The right of individual nations to secede from the Soviet Union.
This subject does not need much comment, either. For example, it is generally known how Stalin smothered in blood the dreams of independence of his own country, Georgia, and how Lenin was furious over his Great Russian methods. Should someone in the Karelo-Finnish Republic refer to the constitution and suggest that the republic secede from the Soviet Union, he would not have time to add a period to the end of his suggestions before the GPU (or whatever that organ would then be called) would give him a slug on the forehead.

But I need say nothing about Stalin's nationality policy when I can speak with a more eloquent tongue, that of Khrushchev:

"Comrades, let us consider a few facts. With good reason the Soviet Union has been considered a model of a state which includes many nationalities. We have in practice secured the equality and friendship of all nationalities in our great fatherland.

"The more terrible are the deeds that Stalin initiated and that are in flagrant violation of the Leninist principles of the Soviet nationalities policy. I refer to the forced removal from their home lands of whole nations with all their Communists and Komsomols (young Communists). No military necessities dictated this activity."

In summary, one can say that Stalin's Constitution during his rule was merely a piece of paper. As a man and a liberal it pleases me to think that differences between the nations are only ostensible, and that we all are the same wretched, struggling race which, at least in some things, thinks and feels in the same manner. The idea that the law guides and obligates us all—or at least all proper collective bodies—seems to be self-evident.

But apparently this is an area where there is a deep rift between the East and the West, or to change the biblical phrase to a modern one, an "Iron Curtain." To the east of the curtain the idea that a law obligates someone is completely unknown. The only thing that obligates is a command, an order, a degree. One can read once in a while in a Western newspaper that a certain measure violates the constitution of the Soviet Union. Should one show such an article to a simple muzhik (a peasant) or a factory worker, it would get just as good a laugh as I got from Manuilski: a document is a document.

Actually one can consider strange only the fact that soon *after* the Stalin Constitution became law, there began in the Soviet Union a most senseless and unbounded curtailment of the rights of the citizenry: as if the constitution were a memorandum ensuring that no villainy would be overlooked; as if the arrest of a Soviet citizen and the search of his home would be forbidden so that, with greater certainty, it would be remembered to arrest millions upon millions merely at the command of a GPU offcial.

It becomes clear that the life of an ordinary Soviet citizen was worth nothing when we hear what Khrushchev said about the fate of the representatives to the Seventeenth Party Congress and the leaders in the Central Committee: over one-half of them were arrested and shot.

THE MANY CLASSES OF A "CLASSLESS SOCIETY"

WHEN ONE has had the occasion to follow the development of the Soviet Union at as close a range as I, one finds oneself thinking again and again: if Lenin had lived.

Lenin did not live even to the age of fifty-four. From a medical viewpoint he still had fifteen years left. When he died, the Soviet Union was becoming stabilized. Its borders were peaceful and NEP—the partial restoration of capitalism—had set the wheels turning and brought goods to market. True, NEP signified a stinging backlash for Lenin the theoretician, but in the bolshevik ideology there were matters of importance other than the purely economic system. Should we consider Lenin fortunate for having been spared seeing the collapse of his other dreams as well?

Of one thing we can be certain: because Lenin was Western oriented in spirit, he would at least have attempted to brake the process of social stratification prevailing during the era of his Eastern-oriented successor.

One of the most important points in the Bolsheviks' program was the creation of a classless society. Long before their assumption of power they proclaimed that they would create a state without exploiters or exploited, an entirely new kind of society in which no one would live off another's labors but each would earn his own livelihood; where everyone, regardless of his position, had the same possibilities in life: equally good housing, equal opportunities for achieving a higher education, and equal opportunities to use such social institutions as welfare, recreational, and convalescent facilities.

If there should be some difference between people during the early phase, the difference would be that the working people—in other words, the actual manual laborers—would be the upper class, while the other former classes would be in an inferior category, at least during the period of transition. The goal was a workers' state in which the workers were the dominant class until such a time as all classes were eliminated.

This idea is realized in Stalin's Constitution. Its author presented it at the Eighth Convention of the Soviets in November 1936 as follows, according to "The History of the Communist party of the Soviet Union":

By 1936 the economy of the Soviet Union had changed completely. . ·. . The exploitation of one person by another had been abolished forever. The socialist communal ownership of the means of production had become established as the steadfast foundation of a new socialist system in all areas of the national economy. Depressions, misery, unemployment, and poverty had disappeared forever from this new socialist society. . . .

The working class has ceased to be the exploited class, deprived of the means of production, which it was under capitalism. . . . It has changed into an exploitation-free working class that has destroyed the capitalist economic system and assumed socialist ownership of the means of production, a working class hitherto unknown in the history of mankind.

Equally great changes have taken place in the status of the Soviet Union's peasantry. . . . An entirely new peasantry has taken shape in the Soviet Union; no longer are there landed proprietors or kulaks, merchants or usurers who could exploit the peasantry. . . . Such a peasantry also has been unknown in the history of mankind.

The intelligentsia of the Soviet Union likewise has changed . . . It is a new type of intelligentsia, serving the people and free of all exploitation. Such an intelligentsia the history of mankind has never known before.

In that way class distinctions between workers in the Soviet Union are wearing away and the old class sequestration is disappearing.

These deep changes in life in the Soviet Union, these decisive successes of socialism in the Soviet Union, have manifested themselves in the new Constitution of the Soviet Union.

Such was the situation already in 1936 according to Stalin's theoretical oration. But how was it in actual practice and everyday life?

During the years 1918–21, the period of War Communism in which the whole country lived in virtual chaos, class distinctions were the least pronounced. Then one could hardly speak of an orderly society, but from 1921 on, with the stabilization of the bolshevik rule, new social classes began to form at a rapid pace, though the Revolution of 1917 supposedly had abolished them for all time. True, the old privileged classes were done away with, by and large;

a few million members fled abroad and those who remained in their homeland were annihilated. Just as quickly, however, new privileged classes arose and developed.

It is generally believed that the privileged class as a whole consists of the Communist party. This is a misapprehension, for even the members of the Communist party are not nearly all equal. This party has people from all classes of society, and most of the party members are virtual pariahs without rights. A Communist party membership card does not bestow any rights on a simple working woman, but it does obligate her to attend a colossal number of meetings at night. Class distinctions are not drawn rectilineally; the party, along with the army and the GPU, which were the foundations of Stalin's power, must be considered separately and categorized according to the Russian class system. I would say that the various degrees of the privileged classes are determined by the social status of their members in relation to other people, in other words, by how much authority—or, to use capitalistic terminology—how large a flock of the exploited each person has.

In capitalist countries, particularly in the civilized countries of Western Europe, three classes generally are recognized: in Eastern countries the division of classes is much more complicated. The Soviet Union in its system is much closer to the Eastern countries, for example, to India's caste system, than to the Western countries. It is impossible to say how many different degrees and ranks could be distinguished in the Soviet Union's class hierarchy, but the student of Soviet affairs has no difficulty in enumerating ten on the basis of their various rights and obligations. Someone might be able to condense them into fewer, but another might list even more. The classification has been determined by the bolshevistic needs. I shall mention only a few class groupings here, starting at the top.

The first or highest caste is comprised of the few individuals around the dictator, members of the Politburo, only a few members of the central government. Perhaps some especially prominent party boss even outside Moscow might belong to that highest caste, whose power downward is limitless. A member of this caste enjoys all the many privileges that the huge Soviet land can offer. Only the dictator himself can limit their use of power.

The second privileged class is much larger in number. One could include in this the major factories' directors, whether or not they are Communist party members, the most prominent GPU chiefs, and, in general, the group of the highest party bosses. These people likewise exercise almost limitless power, but above them neverthe-less is that first class that strictly sees to it that this class does not step above its estate and not much beneath it, either; that, too, has its limits.

Moving downward, the power diminishes. The third class in the social order might include leading engineers, the industrial plants' top technical leadership, the highest trade union bosses, and (if we disregard the Red Army, considering it a separate caste) the civil defense officers who do not actually belong to the army but are re-sponsible for the civil defense of the nation. These officers occupy a comparatively high social position and are quite numerous. The third caste might also include some representatives of the cultural scene, such as noted authors, a few leading journalists, and so on, but they are individual cases.

Considerably lower in rank are the groups comprising hundreds of thousands, perhaps millions, of intellectuals. For example, uni-versity instructors and leading figures in the cultural field do not belong to the upper class but rather are only in fifth or sixth place.

In this manner one could divide these classes easily into ten be-fore reaching the actual working class, the laboring people. In other countries they are considered one class but in Russia they are divided into six or seven ranks. The leading working class has all the privileges but still nothing comparable to the special privi-leges of the three highest classes. A worker, no matter what he does, cannot even get a whiff of the advantages enjoyed by those of the highest caste, but within his own group he may belong to the upper class.

Skilled workers are classified according to the importance of each trade during each particular phase of socialist construction. During the five-year period of heavy industry, the highest groups consisted of metal turners and filers, and, of these, the Stakhanovites were particularly important. As their importance decreased so, too, did their value, and the lowest of all were the common laborers and helpers. The difference in wages was considerable, and all the social advantages were in relation to the position in society. A working woman of the lowest caste, a street sweeper or a worker in light industry, had no rights. She earned her meager bread and tea and never had any hope of going to a rest home or sanatorium. She had the right to do heavy work and collapse under its burden; her position was the same as that of an Indian or Chinese coolie.

Probably nowhere, save for the Eastern countries, would it be possible for the range of classes to be publicly displayed so blatantly as in Russia. In a factory dining room, for instance, eating takes place on at least three, sometimes even more, different levels—I don't mean shifts or sittings but specific levels. The same kitchen prepares for the same dining room food served to the directorate, the subordinate directors, and the workers. This is the general custom, and when the factory comes to a halt at mealtime, each level goes behind its own curtain to eat the food prepared for its level. It seems insulting and degrading; one hardly dares go into the privileged section.

The Comintern dining room followed the same system and, since I had all the privileges of the second caste, at least, my place was with the first level, while my assistants ate at the second and third levels. I often tried to join them there, but it was not considered seemly. The reproachful glances in themselves said: your place is not here; go to your own caste! Master and slave could not fraternize, and amazingly enough the lower castes submitted to the system without grumbling. They considered it only natural because it had always been thus, but our kind of person had difficulty in becoming accustomed to it.

Innumerable times in large factories—such as the Stalin factories where I presented surveys on international politics—I found myself, because of my position, behind the same curtain with the directorate. The group was never very large, whereas the second and third groups, which ate separately, were sizeable, but I never noticed anyone considering this arrangement inappropriate. Everything happened quite naturally.

To give some idea of that class hierarchy and how it affected a Westerner—specifically, a worker—let me relate an event that proved to be one of the most ticklish and trying that I have ever experienced.

It happened during the first half of 1936, as I recall. Three Finnish Americans came to my office—the party secretary's office—as a delegation representing a group working in an army factory near Moscow and seeking relief from the unwonted oppression to which they were subjected. They were middle-aged men of the finest type of Finnish American, outspoken and apparently thoroughly upright working men. After presenting their case succinctly, they plunged directly into the question of class distinctions.

"Since you belong to one of those leading groups that ought to know what's really going on in this country, tell us straight: is this a classless society?"

"It's supposed to be," I replied. "Comrade Stalin has said so."

"Comrade Stalin may have said it but we're asking you. One Finnish man is asking another: is this a classless society?"

I hemmed and hawed a little and then said, "It can't be answered just like that. At least an effort is being made in that direction. Comrade Stalin has declared that socialism has been achieved and that we are now moving toward communism, which will be classless."

The men became a little irritated. "How dare you tell us that we don't know what we're talking about, we who have spent six, seven years in concentration and forced labor camps!"

"I don't really understand what you mean."

"We're just asking whether we, common laborers, are allowed to live in the same kind of quarters you have?"

"Well, I live in *Dom Pravitel'stva,* a government building which is reserved exclusively for leaders."

"Exactly! Not a single worker lives there except the gatemen and the slaves who serve you. You live in a government house, and we live in barracks so flimsy that the wind howls through them. As for food—is ours the same as yours?"

"Well, it isn't exactly the same."

"Are we allowed to buy from the same stores as you? That's not possible either, since there are different classes of stores. You have an A card and we have C cards. You buy from an A store that stocks everything, footwear and food—we've seen the window displays. Our C card lets us buy from a store that carries nothing but bread and sometimes tea and yet is three times more expensive than your store. How's that for difference in rank? And can we travel the same way you do? Your railroad tickets are always for either first class or international car—we travel by cattle car. Once in a long while we can get into a regular 'hard' car."

The situation certainly was not very pleasant. Every word the men spoke was the truth—I knew it as well as they. I no longer could muster up enough conviction to make the inspiring speech my position demanded, nor could I do what the politruks of our host country did under similar circumstances, bellow, "Shut up and get out of here, or—! Such talk is counterrevolutionary—watch yourselves!"

To indicate what he really thought, one of the men, a limp beanpole of a fellow, seated himself on my desk, lifted his feet up, too, and began expounding, "We came here from the States, the land of dollar devils, if you know what that is. You probably know—and the Americans themselves do, too—that only the almighty dollar matters there. But even with this dollar worship, conditions there were not what they are here. When we finished our work, whether in a coal mine or forest or wherever, when we had our dollars and wanted to live it up, we would travel to a big city by first class, sitting in a Pullman in our ragged work clothes, talking Finglish and smoking cheap cigarettes until the dollar princesses sitting near us fumed in anger but couldn't do anything about it because we had our tickets.

"What would happen if we tried the same thing in this country: bought a ticket and went into the international car, smoked a fag and sat among your ladies and gentlemen? In the States it's allowed but not here. If we tried to enter the same car, a GPU man would throw us out. Workers have to use another train or at least another car. That's what this is like, this classless society."

All I could do was to smile wanly and concede that everything was not as it should be but that perhaps it would yet straighten itself out.

"Never in this country," said the man. "It's in such a bad fix. Things have only gotten worse during these six, seven years. Workers ought to have some privileges, but they just keep sinking lower and lower while you bigwigs rise higher. You, too, drive a fancy car, travel international class on the train and eat in fine restaurants. You bet there's a difference between classes."

That was lecture enough for one time. When I returned home from work, I related the incident in detail to Kuusinen.

"Well, there's some truth in what those roughnecks said," he acknowledged.

He did not dare, however, to admit that they were entirely right.

Nor did it amuse him to joke about the progress made by Russia since the czarist era. At that time the railroads had had only three classes. Under the classless society they had reached seven. First was the international car, divided into A and B classes, the compartments in the former being large double salons. Perhaps only two or three passengers occupied that end of the car; the other had a few more. (In contrast, workers' cars carried 150 persons.) The third class, that also divided into A and B, was "soft" (in other words, with upholstered seats); the fifth class was semisoft, the sixth was "hard," and the seventh was the cattle car.

All that the Finnish Americans knew very well. They were among the "Last of the Mohicans" who dared express their thoughts and not only to me. They spoke straight from the shoulder to the GPU men as well, with the result that, after a while, they lost even that freedom that had been theirs in Moscow and once again wound up in some concentration camp.

Vexatious moments also occurred during my visits to Karelia and Leningrad and the Syväri power plant, where over a thousand Finns were still working. At the conclusion of my report or speech, some of them sought to talk to me privately, and once at Syväri my good old friend Kopra came over to chat.

We had spent many years together at the Tammisaari prison and after obtaining his freedom he had gone to eastern Karelia, where he had been moved from one camp to another, finally winding up in Syväri, half free, half prisoner; he had no right to leave the Syväri work site without permission. He was a group leader—in other words, not of the lowest caste but low nevertheless.

He smiled a bit feebly as he asked, "I suppose you still remember the days in Tammisaari?"

"Why not; one doesn't forget them in a hurry," I replied.

"Then you remember how we walked and talked about what it's like in Russia. Do you remember?"

My back began to perspire, but I tried to control my facial muscles and mumbled, "Of course."

"We knew that this was not yet a paradise but we said that it's a good country in which workers in particular are well off."

He paused as though to allow me to speak, but when I said nothing he continued, his voice rising a little.

"You seem to have found a paradise there in Moscow; that's a good suit you're wearing, and you look well fed. There are over a thousand of us here—take a look at me and at those others. No one here has had enough to eat except the camp commandant. We have no human rights, no cultural life; we sleep in barracks in three tiers like herrings in a barrel; women and children in the same place, there's no family life. I, too, have my family with me. Everyone seems to live like this. This is how it is with the Finns and how it is with the Russians. Now is this the way we projected it? Is this a classless society and socialist order?"

In talking with a close prison companion I had to say—as risky as it was—I simply had to say that there was something impossible about this development; it was the antithesis of what we had imagined and projected.

After such a conversation it didn't feel right to travel from Leningrad to Moscow on the "Red Arrow," continue from the station in one of Stalin's' cars, drive to the Comintern's first-class dining room to eat and then to the Comintern's apartment house to sleep.

I couldn't help thinking in the daytime and dreaming at night of the Tammisaari prison cell on the one hand, and on the other of the Syväri barracks and Karelian forests where those Finnish dreamers—the same kind I had been—today were doing socialist construction work without any of the privileges of a classless society. Those privileges, however, belonged only to the highest castes and in the first class were so boundless as to be impossible in any capitalist country. If it occurred to a member of that class to want some pretty girl, married or single, it was completely at his discretion.

It was the same with all other forms of luxury. Even during the severe depression years, when the rest of the people were dying of hunger—as they were in 1933–34—that highest caste had to indulge itself in all the pleasures that the country could provide. Probably not even the most dissolute czars could command as much of everything as did Stalin and his favorites. These advantages diminished by degrees, but even for the fourth-class aristocracy they were still so great that in the Western countries they would have made life worth living.

The sanatoriums, of which I have already written, are an excellent example of class distinction. Stalin's Constitution declares that every citizen is entitled to them. It sounds nice and is an excellent propaganda ploy, particularly when people have a habit of swallowing claims without checking even the facts that are available. A quick calculation will indicate that that right must of necessity remain merely on paper.

As many sanatoriums as there are in the Caucasus and the Crimea, they cannot in one year—assuming one month's stay to be the average—accommodate more than 300,000 persons. According to statistics, there were some 100 million adults in the Soviet Union in 1939. To enable the entire population to avail itself of a sanatorium would take—well, count for yourself how many hundreds of years.

Hence, only a few Soviet citizens at best have the possibility of warming their bones in the southern sun. In practice this possibility shrinks to nothing, because the sanatoriums are reserved for the privileged classes. I have already mentioned having stayed at them for five summers, and I always saw the same faces.

Among the many Russian patron saints, St. Byrokratius has played an important role through the ages, but only now has this new perfected caste system made the bureaucracy omnipotent. The seed of bureaucracy lurks within the Soviet system itself because it does not spur and encourage individual responsibility. That was realized at the very beginning of the bolshevik rule, and Lenin raised his voice against it. If he had lived, he might perhaps have been able to guide the development along healthier lines—Stalin developed it to such a degree that the Westerner who berates his own country's bureaucracy would find it healthy to visit the Soviet Union. Obtaining even the smallest affidavit through official channels entails endless running around. The Russian people are so accustomed to it, however, that in order to obtain a ticket to travel to another town, they faithfully queue up for days.

Occasionally even the inner circles tire of such a situation and make random attempts to rectify it, which the newspapers then report for the people's diversion.

This was one well-known example: the agricultural commissariat was so sluggish that nothing could get going. Stalin ordered his right-hand man Ordzhonikidze to look into it. Among his discoveries was a questionnaire containing 10,000 questions, thick as a metropolitan telephone directory. It asked the most amazing things. For example, simple collective farmers were asked the bacteria count of their soil. Ordzhonikidze had the perpetrators of the questionnaire shot and that ended the havoc for the time being.

It had enjoyed a rebirth, however, by the time I arrived for my kolkhoz training some three or four years later. The kolkhozes that I visited had two or even three men doing nothing but filling out forms, of which new ones arrived daily. I said to Maslov, the politruk, that maybe it was time once more to have a few dozen form-pushers shot, since it was downright scandalous, especially during harvest time, to tie up people filling out forms that asked how many workers had worked yesterday, how many hours they had worked, and how large an area they had harvested.

"I wouldn't mind if just a few kolkhozes were kept busy compiling such statistics," I said, "but when tens of thousands of kolkhozes do the same job! And if the forms had only a few questions, but when every week one has to list the kolkhoz furnishings, cattle, and everything else possible, what sense does that make?"

Maslov smiled dejectedly. "Where are you going to get things when everything is stolen? It's difficult enough to maintain control now, though only a week elapses."

What could one say to that? But if socialization throughout the world requires such machinery, its opponents are right; it won't do to utilize an impossible percentage of time and the work force in nonproductive work.

This is anything but Leninist communism, I thought. The Soviet Union is temporarily being governed by a madman. This condition cannot continue forever; Stalinism must collapse, allowing the return to Leninism. The adoption of this system shocked me deeply.

Nevertheless, I did not, for example, discuss with my wife the need to get away. Rather, we discussed the ways by which we might make our life more comfortable, so that it actually would begin to reflect socialism. We felt that we must still strive for something better. Once one has chosen a certain path and proclaimed one's intention of following it through thick and thin toward a better future, it is not easy to relinquish it. It was difficult to disengage oneself. I had been a communist leader for a long time. To leave the party now—a renegade, a turncoat. In other words, a traitor.

THE WITCH HUNTS OF THE 1930s

DURING my Moscow years the stage was already being set for the trials that amazed and, in part, horrified the whole world. Lesser cases, that were dealt with in "administrative order" and about which the Soviet papers did not carry even news briefs, occurred constantly since 1935, but I have discussed them in other contexts in this volume. Now I shall examine the public trials that justifiably have been compared with the witch trials of the late medieval and early modern times. These phenomena have surprisingly many points in common, but I shall limit myself to one aspect: the readiness of the accused to confess.

The chief defendants of the first big case, in 1936, were Zinoviev and Kamenev; of the second—the following year—Radek and certain high Soviet officials; and the leading character in the third, in 1938, was Bukharin. The first case I followed as an eyewitness; during the second I was traveling, and when Bukharin's fate was decided I had already left the Soviet Union.

Zinoviev and Kamenev were charged with Kirov's murder, a case on which Khrushchev's speech threw new light; presumably it was done by entirely different people, but I shall not touch upon that here.

The court was in session at the Trade Union's building. Seats had been reserved there for members of the Comintern Presidium, and I was naturally eager to take advantage of that privilege. The slew of impossible-sounding charges did not surprise me greatly; I was already accustomed to the fact that in Russia everything tended to be excessive. But I had learned from my own considerable experience that the first duty of a defendant is to deny the accusation, and I assumed that these hardened politicians would understand as much. But no. They willingly confessed to being guilty of all the crimes with which they were charged, and as though that did not suffice, they even endeavored to increase their burden of guilt.

I watched them closely to discover the reason. In my mind's eye I saw a scene from 1921: Zinoviev, the almighty director of the Comintern and the czar of Petrograd, an imposing man, a head taller than the other notables. This Zinoviev, who admitted to all those horrendous charges, no longer was the same man. He had grown thinner and his bearing sagged, but I could see no signs of ill treatment.

At home I discussed this odd fact many times with my wife and Kuusinen, as well as with Finnish and foreign friends. If they actually were guilty, how was it possible that men who had been in the soup so often would confess? In our opinion it was contrary to all common sense.

Taking that as the basis, the legitimacy of the charges became dubious. When at the same time we received information continually from our own front about charges against our Finnish comrades and their arrest and sentencing—persons with whom we were thoroughly familiar, along with their cases—we no longer had any doubt but that a tremendous falsification of documents and a softening up of the accused was under way.

But what was the method of softening? Although we were near the top of the power ladder it remained a secret to us. My own impression, and that of many others, was that physical torture alone—the "beat him, beat him, beat him" method said to be favored by Stalin—would not have worked on these people. The same method, the third degree, presumably had been used in other countries as well without corresponding results, these seemingly senseless group confessions. Nowadays no one still doubts that physical torture played an integral part in the interrogations, but at these great trials the explanation had to lie elsewhere, namely in mental torture, concerning which some information subsequently seeped out.

Society in Stalin's Russia was collective, and collective, too, was the communities' responsibility. Zinoviev, Kamenev, Radek, and associates were told that they had no hope of deliverance. It was immaterial whether facts were as they claimed or as the accusers claimed; their fate already had been decided on a higher level, and they would be shot no matter what they said. But one service they could do for their survivors. If they confessed to being guilty of everything with which they were charged, they would be assured of the safety of those near to them: their wives, children, fathers, mothers, and other relatives (who had been registered and whose names had been read at the hearing). If they cared at all for their families, they would naturally try to render this service.

If someone declared that he could not confess to such outrageous crimes regardless of his kinsmen's fate, members of the family were shot before his very eyes to demonstrate that this was no idle threat.

My personal opinion was then, and is still today, that these confessions were motivated primarily by the desire to protect relatives. Moreover, the very lack of publicity helped break down resistance. Even at such a tribunal as the Leipzig High Court in Nazi Germany, Dimitrov had an opportunity before the world's free press to express his innocence and to hurl accusations and vent his hatred of the judges. The chance to demonstrate his heroism for posterity, to show that he had the strength to fight for justice to the very end, in itself reinforced his endurance and resolve to reject all kinds of preposterous confessions.

But in the Soviet Union the accused were told, "You will have no opportunity to explain anything to the world; on the contrary, you will die like dogs, and we will tell the world that you have confessed to everything with which we have charged you. So, isn't it better to go to an open trial and confess what we demand? In that way you will save your relatives while leaving posterity at least a tolerable impression, since confessing to villainy and crimes that you have not committed is in its own way heroic. You will have no other opportunity to appear in public."

Even a strong man will be unnerved by such logic. The same procedures were used subsequently in the Rajk case in Hungary, the Slansky case in Czechoslovakia, the Kostov case in Bulgaria, and many others. Thus, the most horrifying of all interrogation methods has been the threat to destroy relatives. Yet in most cases the sacrifices of the accused were in vain: wives and children, fathers, mothers, and close relatives were imprisoned and sometimes even shot.

What was the attitude of the Russian people toward such trials? That interested us foreigners greatly. I tried to ascertain their views generally as well as by bringing up the subject with my Russian friends and coworkers, but I had to admit that these dramas did not appear to interest the Russians very much. Naturally, deep down they were gripped by fear, since the situation had begun already in 1936 and by 1937 had reached such dimensions that hardly a family had escaped the imprisonment of some member, and there were even fewer families untouched by the arrest and exile or the prosecution of close relatives or friends.

Descriptive of those times was an anecdote that was whispered from person to person: Five families live in a Moscow apartment. One night there's a knock on the outer door. Everyone awakens, but no one dares to open the door. The pounding grows louder. Finally the head of one household goes to the door, opens it a crack and the others hear low-voiced conversation. At last the man returns from the door with a look of relief and announces, "Don't worry, comrades, everything is all right; the building is just on fire."

The Russian people thus had to have a great deal of interest in these trials, but they were not concerned with the principles at stake: whether an unprecedented staging of false charges was under way, or whether the accused actually were guilty of some crime. Who was right, who was wrong—that problem they did not ponder, at least not publicly.

If one asked a direct question, "Do you believe that Zinoviev or Radek actually committed the heinous acts of which he is accused?" the reply was, "Of course. Soviet justice cannot find a person guilty without cause, much less sentence him to such severe punishment."

But one could sense that the response was not prompted by sincerity or conviction, but solely by security considerations.

I shall offer an example of how even those of higher standing, upper-class people, viewed these purges and sentences. In the early summer of 1937 my wife and I were spending a vacation at the Zheleznovodsk sanatorium in the Caucasus, and on a June day we went to the neighboring city of Piatigorsk. The Lermontov Museum, which we especially wanted to see, is located there. At the station we bought the previous day's *Pravda* and read it as we walked along, until on the back page we noticed a news brief reporting that Tukhachevsky, Eydeman, Kork—the list of names was long—had become guilty of treason. They had been imprisoned and, on the decision of the war tribunal, condemned and shot.

We stopped short there on the street, read the item again and again and found it shocking. When we had left Moscow, the elections for city council were under way, and pictures of these same men had been carried in the streets, the walls of the buildings were full of them, and *Pravda* had lauded them to the skies. "Imprisoned and shot." What would happen now? What did it mean?

Our trip to the Lermontov Museum was cut short. We turned around, returned to the station and took the first train back to our sanatorium in Zheleznovodsk. It happened to be teatime just as we arrived. In a great flurry, believing that *Pravda* had not yet arrived at the sanatorium, we hastened to the restaurant, to the table we shared with some high Soviet officials.

Several lieutenant generals and the prime minister of one of the Soviet republics were already seated.

Paper in hand I asked them, "Have you seen this? These high military figures have been arrested and shot. What does it mean?"

The men sipped their tea and were unconcerned. They merely grunted, as one grunts to a person who has babbled some trivial tale, or to children who rush to tell their parents that they have seen a dead fly.

When I didn't stop my palavering one of the generals remarked, "Yes, it was good that Comrade Stalin got there before Tukhachevsky did." And then he moved away to play chess.

I tried to talk about the matter with some other high officials but the result was the same. "It's good that it happened as it did."

My wife and I were completely bewildered. Back in our room we discussed the matter many times, as excited people do. What would these bigwigs have said if Tukhachevsky had gotten there first? We came to the conclusion that the answer would have been the same: "It's good that Comrade Tukhachevsky got there first; good that we're now rid of that devil Stalin."

And then the tea drinking and chess playing would have continued.

This tale indicates that not even the high officials, much less the ordinary Soviet people, were especially interested in the system or in those at the peak of the system. Everyone was interested only in himself and kept his weather eye open for how best to preserve his own wretched life—how to sense in advance who would beat whom to the draw, or *kto kogo,* as Lenin asked, meaning "who whom?" or "who shall prevail over whom?"

Such was the atmosphere in which that nation lived. It almost seemed to enjoy those dramas in its own way: there they are, shooting one another; it's all the same to us. They're all masters anyway, all oppressors, and it's the masters' conflict.

This was the attitude of the ordinary people. When Stalin had been declared as absolute a deity as a mortal can be, one would have expected that at least this Stalin myth would have been maintained during the present generation, perhaps even the next, but when it was destroyed with a horrendous crash, and the deity was made a devil, the Soviet people—insofar as was apparent on the outside— did not react in the slightest, neither for nor against. Georgia was the only place known to have small demonstrations resulting from the explosion of the Stalin myth, but even these were quite modest and probably occurred because Stalin was a Georgian and certain elements took pride in a native son.

But even pride could go only so far, for Stalin was inordinately cruel toward his own land, Georgia. When Lenin was alive it was Stalin who, together with Ordzhonikidze, sent punitive expeditions to Georgia and effected appalling scenes of terror. On his deathbed Lenin, worried about the future, sent the party's Central Committee a letter in which he sharply accused Stalin of misusing his power.

Previously, the method of staging those trials had been more or less conjectural, but after Khrushchev's famous speech nothing—or at least not much—was left to conjecture. I am appending an excerpt from that Khrushchev speech to indicate how, according to his argument, Stalin and his GPU (or NKVD) organized these trials.

Facts prove that many abuses occurred on Stalin's orders without considering any norms of party and Soviet law. Stalin was highly distrustful, morbidly suspicious; we knew this from working with him. He would look at a man and say, "Why are your eyes so shifty today?" or "Why are you squirming so today and not looking me in the eye?" The morbid suspicion aroused in him a general distrust of even eminent party workers whom he had known for years. Everywhere and in everything he saw "enemies," "double-dealers," and "spies."

Because he had unlimited power, he indulged in great arbitrariness and stifled a person mentally and physically. A situation was created wherein it was not possible to express one's own will.

When Stalin said that someone was to be arrested, it was necessary to accept on faith that he was an "enemy of the people." Meanwhile,

Beria's gang, which ran the state's security organs, outdid itself in proving the guilt of the arrested and the validity of the evidence that it had falsified. And what kind of evidence was offered? The confessions of the arrested, which the investigative judges accepted as "confessions."

And how was it possible that a person confessed to crimes that he had not committed? In only one way—by the use of physical coercion, torture, reducing him to a state of unconsciousness, depriving him of his judgment and divesting him of his human dignity. In this manner were the "confessions" obtained.

When the wave of mass arrests began to recede in 1939, and the leaders of local party organizations began to accuse the NKVD personnel of using physical coercion on the arrested, Stalin dispatched a coded telegram on January 20, 1939, to the provincial and district committee secretaries, to the central committees of the various republics' Communist parties, to the People's Commissars of Internal Affairs, and to the heads of the NKVD organizations. This telegram announced:

"The Central Committee of the All-Union Communist party (Bolsheviks) explains that the use of physical coercion in NKVD practice is permissible from 1937 on in accordance with the authorization of the Central Committee of the All-Union Communist party (Bolsheviks) . . ."

Thus Stalin, in the name of the Central Committee of the Communist party, had sanctioned the most brutal violation of socialist law, torture and violence that led, as we have seen, to the slandering and self-accusation of innocent people.

Not long ago—only several days before the present Congress—we summoned to the Central Committee Presidium for interrogation the investigative judge Rodos, who in his time investigated and interrogated Kossior, Chubar, and Kosarev. He is a vile person with the brains of a bird and morally quite degenerate. And it was this man who was deciding the fate of prominent party workers; he was also passing upon the political aspects of these cases, because having established their "crime," he forthwith produced material from which important political conclusions could be drawn.

The question arises as to whether a man with such an intellect could alone make the investigation in a manner to prove the guilt of people such as Kossior and others. No, he could not have done it without proper directives. At the Central Committee Presidium session he told us, "I was told that Kossior and Chubar were enemies of the people and for this reason I, as an investigative judge, had to make them confess that they were enemies." *(Indignation in the hall.)*

He could do this only through lengthy tortures that he carried out according to detailed instructions from Beria. We must say that, at the Central Committee Presidium session he cynically explained, "I thought that I was executing the orders of the party." In this manner Stalin's orders concerning the use of physical coercion against the arrested were carried out in practice. These and many other facts demonstrate that all party norms for the correct solution of problems were nullified and that everything depended on the arbitrariness of one man.

Naturally, that Stalinist terror affected me devastatingly, as it did my wife and many other Finns. The initial reaction, truly Finnish, had been that this was impossible to endure. Something had to be done. Many Finns did do something, notably the Finns from the United States who had become accustomed to saying what they pleased. Because of this they found it much harder to accept the dictatorship to which they were subjected upon arrival in Russia during the Stalinist period. In this respect they were a really special group of Finns.

I, too, reacted many times, particularly when it began to burn me personally and the Finnish Communist party led by me. Thus when Gylling and Rovio were arrested, I told Kuusinen that we simply had to do something. I demanded that we ask for an audience with Stalin.

Kuusinen pondered the matter for a long time, then said that I was absolutely right. But would it help matters? It would in no way stop the wave of terrorism.

"I certainly don't approve of the terror," he said, "but if we went there we would expose ourselves to danger. We would only harm ourselves but would not help the cause."

No doubt, he was right. The forthright Finnish character would have insisted on heroic suicide. Many a Finn did just that by reacting strongly. For example, a former minister in the Karelian government declared in court that all the documents presented there had been falsified. He was shot forthwith.

One must realize, as Kuusinen realized and I came to realize, just what absolute dictatorship is. There are many kinds of dictatorship but when the dictatorship is absolute, not even suicide has any meaning. It can accomplish nothing, it disappears like a stone dropped into a well. If one commits suicide for some belief or cause, there must be at least enough freedom of movement to allow news of it to reach the world. That possibility did not exist in Russia, because the cry carried nowhere.

COMMUNISM DEVOURS ITS CHILDREN

"THE USSR affords the right of asylum to foreign citizens persecuted for defending the interests of the working people, or for scientific activities, or for struggling for national liberation."

Thus the case is stated in Article 129 of the constitution of the Union of Soviet Socialist Republics.

But even without this constitutional article, Communists and revolutionary workers in general had the impression until the late 1930s that they would find refuge in the Soviet Union among kindred spirits and at least there would be free to engage in communist political activities. The last two decades of Stalin's rulership demonstrated, however, that it is precisely the Soviet Union that is the most dangerous and unhealthy place for Communists. I am sure that in no other country have as many Communists been purged—either numerically or as a percentage of the population— as in the Soviet Union. Exact figures will probably never be available on how many of those from countries bordering upon the Soviet Union, among others, are in concentration camps, how many have perished, and how many were simply shot.

Already in the years 1936–38 all the foreign Communists who had made their way to the Soviet Union had the feeling that they were completely at the mercy of the GPU. They had no assurance of tomorrow or whether they could ever leave the country. Many had come from what at that time were semidictatorships, such as Poland, Romania, Bulgaria, Yugoslavia, Estonia, Latvia and Lithuania, and in coming to the Soviet Union had burned all their bridges behind them. They had no haven in their own countries, and when they were hounded in Russia they were the most defenseless people in the world. Other Soviet citizens also lived in considerable fear but not nearly so great as did the foreign Communists who had come there in search of asylum. If ever there was an appropriate place for the inscription, "All hope abandon, ye who enter here," it would have been the gate through which Communists entered the Soviet Union.

During the years 1936–38 the Comintern had many hundreds of foreign Communists as regular employees and countless others in fringe activities. There one most keenly sensed the feeling of alarm. Life was a gamble from one day to the next: will I still be free tomorrow, or is it now my turn? At daily meetings we dealt with long lists of persons who had become suspect during recent days and been ousted from the party or, in many instances, already jailed. The most fantastic charges were leveled at these persons, and whether they hailed from a Balkan or a Baltic country or from Finland, the charges were quite similar.

Suspicion and persecution focused especially on the communist parties' highest leadership, the members of the central committees. A number of the Soviet Union's neighboring countries had the central committees of their communist parties in Moscow, close to the Comintern, and their top leaders resided in Russia. Only secondary party leaders and others engaged in practical party activities remained in their own countries because of the constant risk of imprisonment especially for the leaders. Because the Communist party was banned in all the Balkan and Baltic countries, as well as in Poland and Finland, their leaders could not function in their homelands but were in Moscow. During these years—especially 1937 and 1938—the central committees of all the border states' Communist parties were liquidated along with the majority of their members.

During these years of the great purges, the Comintern's Presidium was convened abruptly again and again to hear that this or that personage had been shown to be a traitor and an enemy of the people. We lived as though in a nightmare. Even many members of the Presidium had followed in the wake of Zinoviev, Kamenev, Tukhachevsky, Rykov, and others, and each remaining member gambled from day to day that he would not be the one for whom the bells of the Kremlin would toll next.

One such ominous Presidium meeting was convened in the spring of 1937. As soon as it had gotten under way, Georgi Dimitrov, who acted as chairman, announced laconically that the Bela Kun case would be considered and that Comintern Secretary Manuilski, who served as liaison between the Comintern and Stalin, would present the case.

Thereupon Manuilski began reading from a document and after several paragraphs he asked, "Does Citizen Bela Kun recognize this?"

Manuilski's use of the word "Citizen" appeared to galvanize Bela Kun like an electric shock. He became greatly agitated. The rest of us, save for Dimitrov and Manuilski, also were startled. When "Comrade" was changed to "Citizen," it was tantamount to a death warrant in this situation.

Pale and shaken, Bela Kun stammered, "I recognize it; it's a circular that I wrote for Communists working in Hungary."

"Good," said Manuilski and continued reading from the circular. One of the paragraphs criticized the Comintern's activity quite harshly and mentioned among other things that the Communist party of the Soviet Union was ineffectually represented in the Comintern.

Having read that part, Manuilski asked again, "Has Citizen Bela Kun written this also?"

"I have," replied Bela Kun falteringly, suspecting that something dreadful was about to befall him.

"Good," said Manuilski. "Citizen Bela Kun presumably also knows that the Communist party of the Soviet Union is represented in the Comintern by Comrade Stalin."

Bela Kun could no longer contain himself. Leaping to his feet he shouted, "This is a vile conspiracy! I wasn't referring to Comrade Stalin but to you, Manuilski, and to Moskvin, who are secretaries and poor Bolsheviks. I know that Stalin is a member of the Presidium as are Zhdanov and Yezhov, but they rarely attend the meetings. They are good Bolsheviks, the world's best, but you, Manuilski, are no Bolshevik at all. Already during the emigration Lenin called you a 'god seeker.' "

This attack brought a flush to Manuilski's cheeks. He, too, lost his composure; then, struggling for self-possession, he observed sarcastically, "So great a leader as Citizen Bela Kun considers himself to be would hardly waste ammunition on a small bird like me. But Comrade Stalin is a sufficiently large target even for him, and it is he to whom the circular alluded."

Manuilski, who was one of the Comintern's most caustic and venomous orators, developed his speech into a raging indictment in which he claimed that even in the past Bela Kun had been guilty of serious deviations. He went so far as to imply that, already during the Hungarian revolution, Bela Kun had had contacts with the Romanian secret police and had betrayed the revolution.

Bela Kun, who had tried many times to interrupt Manuilski by rising to his feet and flailing his arms, now made a last desperate effort to defend himself. He, too, was a brilliant orator, a true tribune type, and now in realizing that his days were numbered and that judgment had been passed, he roared like a mortally wounded lion.

"This is a horrible provocation, a conspiracy to have me murdered. But I swear that I didn't want to hurt Comrade Stalin. I want to explain everything personally to Comrade Stalin."

I and the other Presidium members who were not conversant with the case remained uncertain as to whether Bela Kun actually had intended to dim Stalin's glory as well. That, at any rate, is how the matter was interpreted. Attending the meeting, in addition to Dimitrov and Manuilski, were Presidium members Kuusinen, Togliatti, Pieck, Gottwald, Florin, Vang Ming, and I, and, by invitation, Professor Varga.

All of us, silent and appalled, had followed this great and powerful tribune's struggle for his life, and the sharp and virulent blows of his executioner. No one dared or could say anything either for or against. No votes were taken on these occasions, not this or any other time. At least in the Soviet Parliament votes are cast, though everybody is of one mind. But not even formal votes were taken at the Comintern meetings.

When the duel was over, Manuilski rang a bell, declared the discussion concluded, and announced that Citizen Bela Kun's case would be investigated by a three-man committee, and until this was done he would be suspended from all confidential activities of the Hungarian Communist party and the Comintern.

The session had ended. Bela Kun was allowed to leave, but as he stepped through the door, two GPU men seized him. Nothing was heard of Bela Kun after that, nor was his case again considered by the Comintern's Presidium. There was just a rumor that he had been shot.

A few days later almost all the other members of the Hungarian Communist party's Central Committee who were in Moscow met the same fate. To my knowledge only a few survived the purge, but all were arrested and exiled to unknown regions.

Only once after that dramatic scene in the Comintern's Presidium did Bela Kun's name pop up in Moscow. It happened in 1938 during the famous Bukharin trial. Public prosecutor Vyshinsky and his witnesses tried to hint that Bela Kun, together with Bukharin, had participated in some revolt staged by leftist social revolutionaries in Moscow, at which time the assassination of Stalin, among other things, had been planned. Evidently Bela Kun had already been shot by then, for otherwise he would have been brought to that session either as a witness or for sentencing.

Not until nineteen years later, in February 1956, was his name mentioned once again in a long article in *Pravda,* in which his compatriot, Professor Varga, proved that he had been one of Stalin's countless innocent victims. Bela Kun was "restored to his rank" as the term has it, but not even Varga could—or was permitted to—say when and where Bela Kun had been shot and what the formal charge had been in the pronouncement of the death sentence; whether it was merely the defamation of Stalin's character to which Manuilski had referred or whether something additional had been fabricated along the way.

Especially significant was the liquidation of the leadership of Poland's Communist party, which likewise occurred in 1937. The Polish Communist party had one of the largest memberships in the Comintern. Its leaders were old Communists, many of whom had been famous even before the founding of the Comintern, had worked underground during the czarist regime, and some—such as the noted Communist Walecki—even had been in Siberia with Trotsky and Lenin, where they had come to know the old bolshevik guard.

Despite his age and merit, however, Walecki was not the head of the Polish party; that position was held by Lenski, an estimable and well-known Communist who was highly regarded in Russia and the Comintern. The leadership also included Bronkowski, an Old Bolshevik, who was one of the Comintern's undersecretaries and had been in charge of the Baltic countries until 1935. Finland also was under his supervision which meant that, for a while, he was chief of the Finnish party as well. The fourth noted Pole was Krajewski.

All four thus were men of distinction: Lenski and Bronkowski as members of the Comintern's Executive Committee and Presidium; Walecki and Krajewski as members of the Comintern's Control Committee, the highest international tribunal in the communist hierarchy. In addition, Krajewski was chief of the Comintern's cadre division, a highly important post in that he had the power in his own sector either to confine or to liberate. There were sidium; Walecki and Krajewski as members of the Comintern's in Moscow as well as scores of subordinate officials.

In the late spring of 1937 the Comintern Presidium again was convened without warning, just as it had been in the Bela Kun case. We surmised that once again some villainy had been unearthed and prepared to listen to the standard charges. The fact that no Polish members of the Presidium were present surprised us, and a moment later we had reason to be even more surprised—surprised and shocked.

Dimitrov assumed the chairman's seat, we took our own places, and Manuilski began his speech in this manner:

"Comrades! I am about to tell you a tale so black and foul and incredible as to be unimaginable. In 1920, when our brave Red Army stood at the gates of Warsaw, a whole Polish regiment, 700 men, suddenly surrendered to it. The regiment was received with joy, since a large part proved to be Soviet sympathizers, with some Communists included, and it remained in its entirety in the Soviet Union. Many of its members joined the Red Army, some as officers, others as political commissars, and still others were given prominent positions in the Soviet machine. It was understandable that the transfer to our side under such circumstances aroused great confidence; the past of those 700 men was not investigated. We fell into the trap—just as the treacherous enemy had planned."

Manuilski, a skilled speaker, paused. The tale had swept us along, and breathlessly we waited for him to continue.

"Our enemies have laid many kinds of traps for us but never anything more cunning or dangerous. Who could have guessed that those 700 were specially chosen and trained spies—a whole army of spies able to gain a foothold in important places where for seventeen years they have done their dirty work undisturbed? And who was behind that dastardly trick? Naturally the Socialist rene-gade Pilsudski!''

Our amazement was almost total and became so when Manuilski announced that among the 700 were some members of the Polish Communist party's Central Committee, with Lenski and Bronkow-ski also involved in the espionage. Accordingly, there was no alter-native but to arrest the supreme command of the party, and that had already been done.

The procedure thus had been simplified. Whereas Bela Kun had been permitted to be present at his arraignment, the Poles were convicted without having been heard even though they were members of the Comintern leadership, two on the Presidium, two on the Control Committee. Dimitrov's solemn, synthesizing speech that concluded the brief session could only be considered a sentence since it established as self-evident that the GPU had acted correctly in imprisoning all the Polish leaders. It also revealed that all the 700—insofar as they had been found or were still alive—had been arrested.

Understandably, we were very thoughtful as we left the meeting. The imprisoned men were celebrities, sorely tried old revolution-aries. (Such puppet-Communists as Bierut, Cyrankiewitz, and other organizers of Poznan's bloodbath were totally unknown at that time, and not even such a leader as Gomulka could fit in the com-pany of these truly renowned Communists.) And we realized that, as those 700 were being hunted down, vast numbers of their rela-tives and friends—in general, all who had had anything to do with them—were caught in the same net. Most likely several thousand Polish Communists were annihilated in that leadership purge.

Lately the question of how much Togliatti knew about Stalin's crimes has been under discussion in Italy. Earlier in this chapter I mentioned his presence at the sentencing and imprisonment of Bela Kun. He was also present when the entire Polish communist leadership was sentenced. Generally, all the members who were in Moscow always attended the Comintern meetings. Neither Togli-atti nor anyone else registered a protest.

The Comintern's Presidium had expressed its deep revulsion of such treachery and impressed upon all us party leaders that we must keep a sharp eye and ear open lest similar cases occur within other parties.

Nevertheless, it did. Only a few months after the Polish affair, the matter of the Estonian party came up.

After Estonia achieved its independence, there were two great names, Kingisepp and Anvelt, in the country's communist circles. When the Estonian border guards shot Kingisepp at the Russian border in the early 1920s, Anvelt was left as the sole leader, and in the Estonian party he was a comparatively bigger man than Kuusinen, for example, was in the Finnish party. I knew him, as well as the entire leadership of the Estonian party, very well. I often had dealings with him, and he left the impression of a talented, pleasant, and just man.

Important tasks had been entrusted to him. In the Leningrad area he had held high Soviet posts; to my knowledge he had been a significant figure in the Leningrad GPU. From the beginning of the 1930s he had had leadership positions in the Comintern, and at this particular time he was chairman of the Comintern's Control Committee—in other words, he presided over the international tribunal. He could also be called the head of the Comintern's GPU, inasmuch as his task was to investigate all political sideslips within the Communist parties, infractions of party discipline, and cases of espionage. His power was great, for he could present charges against some party that would be ruinous to the leadership of the entire party. He knew a lot about the villainy of Stalin and his agents; thus, he was dangerous.

And so his liquidation was dealt with at a meeting of the Comintern's Presidium as a summary conviction. It was announced that he was involved in the activities of Soviet enemies and that he had done great damage in the positions that he had held for almost two decades. That was that. At the same time it was announced that the Central Committee of the Estonian Communist party was equally compromised. Anvelt's closest assistant, Allas, took care of the Estonian party's practical affairs in a small office next to that of the Finnish party. He was a quiet man afflicted with tuberculosis and was kept alive only through collapse therapy. He and three or four other Estonian leaders in Moscow were arrested along with Anvelt.

At the same time, and with as little ado, the leadership of the Lithuanian party was liquidated. One was a man well known on the Comintern rolls: Angaretis, a Lithuanian Jew who attracted attention everywhere with his handsome grey beard—with that perhaps more than with his brains. He, too, was a member of the Control Committee, Anvelt's assistant, and he was arrested along with the other members of his party's Central Committee, charged with involvement in espionage. All of them supposedly were tools of Lithuania's then semifascist dictator, Smetona.

The third Baltic country, Latvia, had no notable representative in the Comintern, and so its liquidation occurred almost unnoticed.

When Stalin in his 1939 pact with Hitler had reserved these countries for himself and then occupied them, I and many others who had followed the life of these countries' communist parties fairly closely expected that now the well-known leaders, who for twenty years had fought for the Soviet Union and communist ideals stubbornly and fearlessly, would be recognized. But no. When a communist government was formed in Estonia in the summer of 1940, not an Anvelt or a single real old Communist was in sight but rather bourgeois professors like Vares and such social democratic renegades as Andresen—all men whom Anvelt's Communist party had attacked as agents of President Päts. The same was true in Lithuania and Latvia. The leadership was assumed by some Social Democrat or preferably even some bourgeois, and it meant nothing that he had previously been denounced as a supporter of Lithuania's dictator Smetona or of Latvia's Ulmanis.

In Poland, likewise, one saw no Lenski, Bronkowski, or Walecki; instead, petit bourgeois or bourgeois names or unknown Communists emerged. An exception among the countries with communist leaders in the Soviet Union was Bulgaria, for at least Dimitrov and his hatchet man Kolarov saved their lives and after the coup even got high positions—only for a short while, true—until they died under questionable circumstances. A part of Yugoslavia's leadership also was liquidated, but some members were saved, among them Tito, who had managed to leave the Soviet Union in 1936 before Stalin's terror reached its peak.

In those days Tito was not yet a great leader. At the 1935 Congress he was not even accepted for membership in the Comintern's Executive Committee as Yugoslavia's representative. Under the name of Walter he did work as a Comintern functionary or, as we put it, "as an official for certain tasks." In addition to seeing him at the general functionaries' meetings I met him a number of times at Kuusinen's secretariat.

Once when I happened to mention that I had spent a lot of time in Finnish prisons, he remarked that he, too, had been in a Finnish prison, though only for a short time. He said that he had been in Petrograd in 1917 during the so-called July Revolution and had fled from there to Viipuri, where he had been apprehended. The Finnish authorities had questioned him but then released him. He did not criticize the Finnish interrogators; on the contrary, he called them objective and fair men. I jokingly suggested that we should inspect those interrogation records, which probably were in the Finnish state archives, to determine whether he had behaved as a good Communist should behave before a bourgeois class tribunal. Walter assured me that his behavior had been exemplary.

As insignificant an official as Tito was, the discerning Kuusinen already then foresaw a marshal's staff in his pocket. When he undertook to accomplish something, he carried it through.

One of the old Communists did rise to the top in Hungary: Rákosi, but he managed to escape Stalin's broadaxe only by not being in Russia at the time, but rather in Horthy's prisons. In the same way such little errand boys as Pessi and Aaltonen, Ryömä and Janhunen, were saved for Finland because they were not in the communist mecca but in the dungeons of Finland's "White terror."

In Rumania, so-called "Red Anna" Pauker was spared in the manner of Rákosi, but the leaders who were in Russia did not return to Rumania. This story was repeated from the Mediterranean to the Arctic, along the full length of the Soviet Union's western border. Trained and tried leaders, who had fulfilled many party tasks with distinction, languished—if they were still alive—in Russian prisons while new upstarts, petit-bourgeois and bourgeois, governed and govern these countries as the Soviet Union's hatchet men.

The question naturally arises as to what the GPU was aiming at in liquidating precisely that group that presumably would have been the most loyal when the Soviet Union's border was moved westward. We who observed the terror at close range asked that question, and it is asked by everyone considering this matter. Only one answer is rational; namely, that Stalin feared that these old leaders of the labor movement, many of whom had distinguished themselves in revolutionary activities long before the birth of the Comintern and the Soviet Union, would not have submitted to furthering his political aims. Already then he must have been planning possible collaboration with Hitler's Germany and because of it eliminated those obstacles, since such party leaders as Lenski and Bronkowski would never voluntarily have sanctioned the partition of Poland between Russia and Germany. Stalin feared that the old guard would not have understood his ideological maneuvers or consented to serve as vassals of his Great Russian imperialism. He obviously calculated that Hitler's policies inevitably would lead to war in the West during which time, as a reward for his neutrality, he could peacefully expand the Soviet Union's territory. It was thus necessary to liquidate before it was too late those men whose prestige might obstruct his ambitions. His objectives were better served by new faces. Needless to say, no one—least of all Stalin himself—really believed that those old tried-and-true Communists suddenly had become enemies of communism and betrayers of their cause. Not even at Comintern meetings was any attempt made to establish the credibility of the charges by introducing evidence. Even explanations were offered only in the cases of Lenski and the other Poles and of Bela Kun; the rest were disposed of in announcements.

The terrorism was not limited only to the border countries. Germany had its share, because the German Communists would have found it even more difficult than the others to accept fraternization with Hitler. A large part of the Central Committee of the German party was in Russia; the only members to be saved were Wilhelm Pieck and his assistant Ulbricht, whereas such a well-known man as Remmele, one of the Comintern's founders, and the even more eminent Heinz Neumann, disappeared without a trace. Such a notable as Heckert, a member of the Comintern's Executive Committee, died in Moscow under circumstances that justified the rumor and assumption that his death likewise was not natural, though he was given an honorable burial—or perhaps it was precisely because of this that he was given it. The years 1937 and 1938 in particular were one continuous hunting down of German Communists, since the GPU believed or pretended to believe that every German was a Hitler spy.

Earlier I related how, on my arrival in Moscow, Riikka Kuusinen was grief-stricken because her husband, the Bulgarian student Popov, was being tried in the High Court at Leipzig along with his compatriots, Dimitrov and Tanev, charged with arson in the Reichstag fire in Berlin. The case seemed hopeless, for the Nazis needed a few communist bodies to supplement their provocation, but as is known they had to be content with exchanging the Bulgarians for some Nazi spies imprisoned by the Bolsheviks.

Then the Soviet propaganda mill began turning. The three heroes who had escaped from the clutches of the Nazi terror to the free communist world were sent with their wives on a triumphal tour encompassing all Russia. It lasted three months. Speeches were made, hurrahs shouted, and accounts given of how they had extricated themselves from that Leipzig maelstrom with the powerful aid of the Soviet Union.

For Riikka this was a well-deserved period of happiness that lasted even after the triumphal tour. During 1935–36 the fame of the Bulgarian trio remained high, and wherever Dimitrov was mentioned so, too, were Popov and Tanev. However, already in 1936 whispers arose in the Comintern's inner circle to the effect that Dimitrov was not, after all, the strong man that he appeared to be; his legal battle, which had seemed so magnificent, had contained some weak spots—it was even whispered that there was something shady in the trade to which the Nazis had consented in relinquishing Dimitrov and his companions to Russia. Dimitrov supposedly had promised to render services in return.

I don't know where these rumors originated. Indirectly someone hinted that Popov and Tanev had had something to do with them, but to me at least Popov always extolled Dimitrov and considered him the ex officio leader of the Bulgarian party. Popov sometimes visited us with his wife and, in the spring of 1937, when Riikka spent a month with her sister Hertta's son Jurkka at the villa outside Moscow that was reserved for the use of Kuusinen's and my family, Popov, who by then had completed his engineering studies, dropped in often to see his wife.

Gradually the whispering campaign was deemed to have done its work, and it was time for action. The action did not focus on Dimitrov, however, since he was so visible as the Comintern's secretary general that his disappearance would have been noticed. Besides, it would have made a bad impression both at home and abroad if a champion of justice had been revealed to be a scoundrel and a viper. The blow missed his head but still struck unerringly.

One day near the end of 1937 Riikka arrived in tears at the *Dom Pravitel'stva*. Her husband had been arrested and taken away without any questions, any explanations. In her distress she came to the only person from whom help might be forthcoming, her father.

Riikka had sunk into a chair and watched her father as he paced the floor.

Finally Kuusinen halted. "Let's just see. Let's wait. Perhaps it'll clear up."

Riikka understood; her father would not intervene. He had not lifted a finger to help his own son Esa, or his best friend Gylling, or his brother-in-law Laaksovirta, Riikka's uncle.

"No! It will not clear up. He'll never come back."

Poor Riikka! All she wanted was to live her life, spreading joy around her and letting others live, too. She didn't understand and didn't care to understand anything about politics, but she did realize that all hope was gone. The time her husband had spent in the Gestapo's clutches had been appalling, but dismal though everything had seemed, a flicker of hope had remained. Consoling, too, had been the sympathy of all her friends and the whole world, the flood of protests from all over that had swamped Leipzig. Even if the Nazis had had their way, death there at the hands of the executioners would have been a beautiful and noble death, horrible of course but easier to bear with the whole world joining in her mourning.

Now the flame of hope had died out. A judicial murder was again in the making, but no protests were forthcoming; the whole world was mute and indifferent. Not even her closest friends, not even her own father, dared express words of sympathy. On the contrary, everyone made a point of shunning her, and she was expected to join her husband's accusers and censurers though she didn't even know of what crime her husband was accused. He whom the Nazis' noose would have made an unforgettable hero was now a wrecker who languished in some GPU dungeon, Siberian concentration camp, or unmarked grave.

In Popov's case the matter ended happily but only a long time later, after Stalin's death in 1953. He managed to survive imprisonment and served in Bulgaria's foreign ministry. Only a few were as fortunate.

In the Scandinavian countries the Communist parties were legal, and thus their members were spared, for the party leaders were not in Moscow. If they were, they were citizens of their own countries and, hence, not at the mercy of Soviet officials. But despite that certain events did take place, the outstanding one being the case of the Danish Communist party's Central Committee member Munk.

This minor nobleman of sorts had joined the Communist party and as the representative of the Danish Communist party had come to the Comintern. There every Communist party has an accredited representative (even though one might argue about his orthodoxy), a little like the Vatican, where the country rather than the church is represented. Munk was a Danish citizen and in Moscow only in a delegate's capacity, but one day the GPU arrested him, and thereafter his whereabouts were unknown. He had been discussed at a meeting of the Control Committee and semiofficially his arrest was attributed to his relationship with Axel Larsen, the official head of the Danish party. In the late 1920s and early 1930s, Larsen had harbored Trotskyite sentiments deemed highly suspicious by the Comintern. Munk was Larsen's closest associate and thus obviously became a surrogate sufferer for the Trotskyism of the leaders in Denmark.

If the Swedish Communist party leadership had been in Moscow it undoubtedly would have been liquidated, for the whole party was considered anything but communistic and trustworthy. Its representatives—Wretling, Kempe, Fritiof Lager—would surely have been exterminated much before Munk, the Bulgarians, and the Finns. The Swedish Communist party was, in fact, called the beer club in Comintern circles because its leaders were happier with a stein of beer than with the Comintern's theses and communist doctrines.

Besides, that party cost the Comintern (the Soviet Union) a great deal and accomplished virtually nothing. There was a saying in the Comintern that if the Swedish Communists someday made a revolution, it would presuppose a long dry spell, since they would not go out to fight in the rain. The saying originated with Kuusinen and was prompted by the fact that the Stockholm Communists once canceled their May Day parade and festivities because of cloudy weather.

If those liquidated foreign communist leaders left survivors—many had a wife and children—the GPU dealt with them as though they were Russians: the wife had to curse her husband, condemn him as the worst wrecker and Fascist ever to have walked the earth, and demand the harshest penalty, the firing squad, for him; otherwise the wife had no hope of remaining free. And so oppressive was the atmosphere that most of them voluntarily, or with only the slightest prodding, submitted to cursing their nearest and dearest and swearing never to have anything to do with the blackguard.

At least 20,000 Finns were sent to Russian concentration camps. An equivalent percentage of Communists from the other Soviet border countries perished, but I imagine that the destruction of Latvians and Lithuanians was even greater. The number of Polish victims must be reckoned in the hundreds of thousands. The history of mankind has had more than enough rulers who left a bloody trail. Genghis Khan's and Tamerlane's pyramids of skulls are startling; the Catholic Inquisition's pyres of heretics are horrifying; and the history of Finland is touched by the icy executions of the Danish king, Christian the Tyrant. But all these heinous crimes of history pale beside the liquidations carried out by Stalin; only Nazi atrocities with their gas chambers and other mass slaughters, can be compared to his inhumanities. Andrei Zakharov, member of the Soviet Academy of Sciences, has concluded that "no less than fifteen to twenty million Soviet citizens" were shot or otherwise destroyed in Stalin's prison camps.* Those whom Stalin liquidated were his friends, even his guests, who trusted him. Day by day Stalin's dictatorship became increasingly absolute. Finally no one dared say anything; there was not a single person in all Russia who could say that he would still be alive on the morrow or would return to his home. So absolute was that dictatorship from top to bottom.

* Andrej D. Sakharov, *"Wie ich mir die Zukunft vorstelle"* (Zurich: Diogenes Verlag, 1968), pp. 40–41.

FACADES

STALIN used many highly effective forms of propaganda, but the most effective may have been the invitation of foreign delegations and tourists to the Soviet Union, and their entertainment there. Almost since the beginning of Soviet rule it has proven to be quite an effectual and significant form of propaganda at which the Bolsheviks have shown unique skill.

Every country uses this form of publicity. Tourists and foreign delegations are shown whatever is positive and gives a good and favorable impression of the country; if possible, one that is even better than reality. To the best of my knowledge, however, in no other country has this been developed into a downright science and no other country has needed it as an absolutely essential form of propaganda to the extent that Stalin's Soviet Union did.

Countless hostile books have been written about the Soviet Union, but there have been at least as many, if not more, books favorable to the Bolsheviks, gilded accounts that have flowed from the pens of the tourists and observers who were invited to the Soviet Union and enjoyed its hospitality. Notable books have been published especially in the major countries, in Great Britain, the United States, Germany, and France, books that strive for objectivity and scholarly competence and that are used as source material by the press, propagandists, and schools of those countries. The Bolsheviks have noticed that if they spend a few thousand rubles on the provisioning of a delegation, it can return a hundredfold, even thousandfold, harvest in propaganda. The use of embassy attachés for obtaining the same result would be much more expensive and not nearly so effective.

This guiding of foreigners and the organizing of delegations has reached such a high level that rarely even a perceptive and experienced observer need be dishonest while lauding the achievements of the Soviet Union. He does not have to lie; he reports only what he sees. Circles hostile to the Soviet Union readily brand a journalist, for example, a liar for writing favorably about his several weeks' stay. I would say that in most cases he is not a liar—merely a describer of illusions.

I had my own experiences in 1927 when I spent two weeks in the Soviet Union with a large labor delegation. As a fully reliable Communist, a member of the Finnish Communist party and the head of it in Finland, I could have gone anywhere freely, not just with this delegation that was half communist and half social democrat.

Two weeks of sightseeing in Leningrad and Moscow made a positive impression on all seventy-five participants. All—especially the Social Democrats—said that what they had seen was much better than what they had imagined. My faith was greatly strengthened, for what we saw and heard was first-rate, and the few drawbacks could be easily explained and understood.

Then, when I lived in Russia, beginning in 1933, and could observe this tour activity closely and even organize the programs for Finnish, Swedish, and Norwegian delegations, the beautiful image of 1927 was smashed. The mere thoroughness with which these trips were organized gave the impression that there was no intention of showing actual conditions but rather false fronts, or stage settings, erected for this purpose. At once history came alive for I, too, had read about Prince Potemkin and the impressive artificial villages he had erected to deceive Catherine the Great on her inspection tour. Only now did I realize that the story could be true.

Let's take a few examples of how delegations were looked after. First of all, we must remember that no individual or delegation could travel to the Soviet Union just because of a desire to see the country. The majority had a direct invitation, but even those who had taken the initiative were permitted to enter only after long delays so that all necessary preparations could be made. This was the case at least during the Stalin period.

If the Soviet Union's standing in some country needs strengthening in a specific area, a delegation is invited to get acquainted with conditions in the Soviet Union. When the signal (of a specific need) is received, an official invitation is extended, and the selection of the persons takes place on the basis of a very carefully prepared and detailed plan. Nothing is left to chance. When a delegation was sent from Finland, such as the labor union group in 1927, I received detailed instructions from Moscow as to the type of persons to be included, and then each was approved by Moscow individually.

Later, when I observed this business from the Moscow end, I learned the other side of the matter. An invitation was extended not only by the central leadership of a party in Moscow but on the basis of negotiations with the pertinent Soviet bureau. As far as the delegations from Finland during the years 1934–37 are concerned, the Finnish Communist party Central Committee in Moscow partially decided who were invited, who were prevented from coming because of some objection, and in what instances a risk was worth taking because of the desire to strengthen the relations in that direction.

A number of specific factors determined the composition of a delegation. The major factor was that the delegation was invited for some important purpose. If some especially important moves in Soviet foreign policy were in the offing, an effort was made to get newspapermen into the country. They were then informed in a roundabout way about the upcoming event, so deviously and indirectly that only the most perspicacious among them could suspect that this was the whole purpose of the trip. The move itself might come up only half a year later. Sometimes the invitation was extended while a certain campaign was going on. In other words, the invitation invariably had a specific purpose. I don't know of a single instance when a delegation was invited just to see the country's social, cultural, or scientific achievements, as is the case with most other countries.

Many individuals, too, have been invited—scientists, artists, journalists, politicians, among others—and they have done even greater work propagandistically than unwieldy and expensive groups.

To return to some details: when a signal was received that there was a crack in the propaganda wall—the Soviet legation in Helsinki might inform Moscow that wide circles in Finland were saying certain unpleasant things about the Soviet Union—the question immediately arose, how can it be repaired? This message came through the Soviet foreign ministry to the Central Committee of the Finnish Communist party in Moscow, and at once we began to discuss how it should be managed and the weak spot strengthened. Often we could make a concrete suggestion: let's try to invite a certain person or such and such delegation. Through our direct initiative—and I as the party secretary had a big part in it—all the most important visitors and delegations from Finland were invited during those four or five years.

Thus it was our initiative that led to the invitation of a delegation of Finnish journalists. During their three weeks in the Soviet Union they were wined and dined royally, and after returning home, they almost without exception wrote beautiful and friendly articles, both the bourgeois and socialist newsmen. In 1935 and, as I recall, the following year as well, delegations of Finnish actors got acquainted with the Soviet theater. The propaganda effect of these visits is felt in Finland even today.

As I said, we planned to the smallest detail how each guest was to be handled, who was affected by vodka, who by finer drinks, who by a nonalcoholic political drink. Some received personal coaching from us. We presented the achievements of the Soviet Union in a very attractive light and gave them, at first carefully and then more boldly, tasks to be undertaken in Finland. The visit of Professor Väinö Lassila was one of the most successful from the standpoint of bolshevik propaganda. We noticed that he had developed surprisingly far in communist thinking and was willing to perform certain services for the Soviet Union. Kuusinen and I outlined his tasks in detail. He was to organize communist cells in his university and among the students. Moreover, he got an important task in the League of Human Rights.

While planning the programs, we always kept one thing in mind: everyone had to get the impression that he had freely selected what to see. We could not tell them that this and that had been arranged for this day. Instead, we had to ask what they wanted to see. Of course, the participants had various suggestions, perhaps ten to twenty from a group of sixty to seventy persons. The guide listened quite democratically and then said something like this: "We can fulfill all your requests, by and large. But obviously everyone cannot be sent individually to see a hospital, collective farm, or theater. We must form smaller groups, perhaps three. Those who want to visit factories, hospitals, children's homes, nurseries, and so on will form one group; another will consist of those who are interested in housing; and a third of those who want to see theaters, schools, etc."

This sounded so uncommonly democratic that nobody could demand anything better; everyone got approximately what he wanted. Thus the immediate impression was that we can choose freely what we want to see. Actually, everything had been worked out precisely in advance. Each group went to see the sights that had been selected and prepared for the purpose. These might include in Leningrad, the Putilov metal and Treugolnik rubber factories; in Moscow, the large Stalin automobile factory or the ballbearing factory that was dedicated to Kaganovich. The tourists were always taken to a section that had been especially prepared for them. The factory halls were splendid, the work could not have been rationalized better anywhere, and the dining and dressing rooms of the workers were exemplary.

In the whole large factory possibly only in this particular section did such conditions prevail, and very rarely did a visitor want to go through the entire huge factory, for one could spend two or three hours in this section alone, if one so desired. Those workers with whom the tourists came in contact had invariably been well rehearsed. Usually the director of the factory or an expressly selected specialist served as guide, and they had learned their lessons well. If someone wanted to talk with the workers, it was easily done. Immediately a worker was asked to step forward. But if a visitor wanted to be smart enough not to accept the worker suggested by the guide that, too, was fine for all the workers in that section were accustomed to visitors and could answer well. They gave a splendid picture of the wages, living conditions, social security, and other benefits. Every worker seemed to be so well informed that the visitors had to marvel at the high level of Soviet workers.

It was the same story on the collective farms and in the hospitals. Only model institutions were shown. In the children's homes there were marvelous youngsters who gave concerts at the age of three or four, and the guide explained that they were children of workers in this factory or district. However, all were child prodigies. I went along several times and arranged these concerts myself, yet it was impossible not to be enraptured by them. How much more so the innocent foreigners, many of whom got the impression that the entire Soviet Union was such a children's paradise. The aim had been achieved.

Someone always wanted to see prisons, and that, too, was arranged. There wasn't one decent prison building either in Moscow or nearby. They were all damp, dark, and wretched, but it was explained that the Soviet Union does not build prisons, all these are from the czarist period. But in those prisons that were shown, exceptional order and amazing self-government prevailed, and the prisoners were more content than free workers in the capitalist countries. Everything was so well arranged that one couldn't even have chased anyone away.

Bolshevo youth prison was a very special achievement and tourist attraction. Books have been published in almost all languages about this reform institution for young criminals that is located a good fifteen miles from Moscow. Delighted prison officials spent days there and then, after returning home, wrote enthusiastic books about how juvenile crime had been liquidated in the Soviet Union and how it should be liquidated in other countries as well.

This institution, which had no guards or anything reminiscent of a prison, was a large old mansion, fixed and remodeled enough to house 300 boys. It was explained to them that they had complete self-government. There were no guards or directors, only one man from the GPU who would keep an eye on them a little. There were many difficulties, many escapes and revolts but the results were splendid. When I visited it, it had functioned for twenty years. Hundreds of men had been released from there, and they had become the best of Soviet citizens; many had taken wives from collective farms and functioned as chairmen of these farms. The educational influence of Bolshevo was superior, and every tourist who usually spent the hours between two meals there, talking with anyone he wished, got the most positive impression. I have not met a single person who was unfavorably impressed.

But it occurred to only a few tourists to ask how many of these prisons there are, and if anyone did ask, he didn't get a satisfactory answer. I was asked that often, and I had to hedge badly because I should have admitted that there was only one of them in the Soviet Union and that all the concentration camps were bursting with young criminals. During those years I had occasion to verify personally how many young criminals there were whom they did not even try to send to Bolshevo. They were taken to a concentration camp, perhaps to the miserable youth prison of Kem where there were hundreds of boys of this age. Bolshevo was one of the most typical Potemkin villages, the propaganda effect of which was tremendous. What if its upkeep cost a few tens of millions? Propaganda returns were worth much more. But there should have been at least 500 of these institutions were the education of all young criminals to be on the same level.

Tourist attractions and fine experimental institutes were available in various fields of science as well so that it was possible to show everyone admirable achievements in his own field.

Let's take a longer look at how visitors to the Soviet Union were worked over psychologically. In the summer of 1935 a large tourist group arrived from Finland to visit the Soviet Union for ten days, spending half the time in Leningrad, the other half in Moscow. The group had been put through a tight sieve before it left Finland. In it were many persons from the labor movement, Social Democrats and Communists, whom I knew from way back. Unknown Finnish immigrant Communists who, if asked for their names, gave pseudonyms, were assigned as their guides and interpreters. Rooms for the visitors were reserved at the Hotel Europa in Leningrad. The day before their arrival I traveled there with Sirola and took a room at the hotel. When the hungry group arrived in the dining room, we were sitting and eating at a table where we could not be missed. They did not know Sirola by sight but it did not take long before someone noticed me.

"There's Poika Tuominen!"

Two men, both old acquaintances, came bustling over.

"What are you doing here?"

"What? My being here is not peculiar, but what are you yourselves doing here?"

I introduced Yrjö Sirola and said that we just happened to be visiting here, taking care of party affairs, and couldn't imagine that there would be Finns here. We asked eagerly when they had arrived and if there were any acquaintances in the group. The conversation ran on very pleasantly, they fetched more acquaintances, and soon the whole seventy-five-man group knew that Poika Tuominen and Sirola were there.

They asked if we wouldn't have time to talk with them. We did not have time, we said; we had to leave the same day. But because they pleaded with us, we decided to stay because it was such a unique opportunity.

Then they began to request that we accompany them on their travels. We resisted: surely it would not be possible. But they went to ask the guides whether these Finns couldn't come along. The guides, who were our subordinates, pretended to inquire about the matter from someone higher up, then said that it would be possible. We were very grateful and spent the whole time in Leningrad with them, after which it was only natural that we continued to be with them in Moscow. We were the political instructors of the group.

Not a single one of even the social democratic functionaries realized that the whole thing was a comedy that had been planned from beginning to end. Of course, some Communists noticed the curiousness of the "chance meeting" since we had worked with them for two weeks arranging the details, but they knew enough to keep their mouths shut.

I performed similar random duties of a politruk when non-Communist Sylvi-Kyllikki Kilpi and Communist Mauri Ryömä visited Moscow. Ryömä was so advanced in communist activity that we dared plan things with him. The main work was in trying to cultivate the mind of Mrs. Kilpi. Ryömä sincerely believed that this sister-in-law of his should have been shot long ago. Straightforward and outspoken as he was, he asked Kuusinen and me if it couldn't be arranged to have something happen to Sylvi-Kyllikki here in Moscow. In Mauri's opinion, K. H. Viik was another incorrigible who belonged on the list of those to be liquidated.

Kuusinen and I smiled and assured him that trying to convert Sylvi-Kyllikki was far pleasanter work, and we spent much time enlightening her. She was totally anti-Soviet. Nothing pleased her; she saw only flaws, argued and berated everything. As she was garrulous, bold, and audacious enough to speak her mind even among strangers, we had our hands full with her.

Was it perhaps the result of successful organization that she later became a great friend of the Soviet Union? If so, it speaks for the effectiveness of the work.

The plans were so detailed that persons were even assigned to ferret out defects, since experience had shown that Finns, at least, do not ask indelicate questions. We picked dependable Communists who got the task of saying in certain places: "It's all well and good to show us this but things must be rotten underneath. The Social Democrats and the bourgeois claim that shortcomings are being concealed." Whenever someone made an observation like that, the whole group would usually say that one ought not to make such remarks.

In the labor union someone said: "Everything looks good but I believe that much of this is just eyewash."

Chairman Tomski, who had ordered the charge and prepared the answer, said, "Well, young man, when you have visitors in Finland is it your custom to show them first the dunghills and backyards and all the dirtiest places?"

"No, that's not our custom."

"Nor is it ours. We try to show the visitors something a little better. But if it would amuse you, it's all yours to see."

Everyone laughed and accepted the explanation. They were surprised that the questions did not offend the leaders, that they responded with a smile. Thus everything was arranged in advance down to the smallest detail.

The delegations that came in large numbers to the November 7 anniversary of the Revolution and the May Day celebration, had their own Potemkin villages. They were invited to observe the tremendous military parade, uniquely mighty and impressive. A million-and-a-half persons participated in it, marching as one tremendous sea of flags across Red Square. This had an overwhelming effect on everyone, and an intimidating and terrifying one on some. It was an incomparable display of mass and power and, with respect to the military parade, a singular presentation of technological achievements. There were hundreds of tanks of all sizes, from Klim Voroshilov* to the smallest. Simultaneously, huge numbers of airplanes completely darkened the sun, and this hellish thunder between the tall buildings had its own portentous effect. When one looked at the foreign ambassadors and military attachés, one could believe that they must think with dread of the great Soviet Union's might and strength and high technical level, not to mention the impression it must have made on the ordinary worker or scientist or author, hundreds of whom were invited from abroad for this event.

Of course, the parade was real: those were not tin soldiers marching but crack troops. But the framework of Moscow and its life was partly fake. Great cleaning operations had taken place along the

* Type of tank named after Marshal Klim Voroshilov.

main streets, and the houses along these streets were painted for almost every festivity. But such amazing water colors were used that they lasted only through that particular day and festival. Similarly, a showy, modern wall was built in front of some houses, especially in the vicinity of the Red Square. From the street one could see only the facade, but Muscovites knew it was just a sham, built for the benefit of foreigners. The Russians did not find it surprising or objectionable because such things were everywhere in the country.

One of the strangest cases during those five years we spent there involved the Lenin Library, a veritable colossus. Throughout that time it was half-completed, though, according to the five-year plan, it should have been finished in 1934. Yet the building was still under construction during the years 1937–38. When festivities were under way the scaffolding was taken down because, according to the decree, the building had been completed already in 1934. The facade was cleaned, and the statuary intended to grace the exterior was put in place for the duration of the festivities and then removed afterwards. Some of the statues, cast in plaster, were already broken, but the comedy was repeated again and again. Sometimes we estimated what huge amounts of funds and manpower were expended in dismantling and rebuilding the scaffolding. That work alone would have finished the building in short order.

The record achievement in this field—a combination of the Potemkin villages and the emperor's new clothing—was the Soviet Palace, which was to be the tallest building in the world, an eternal monument in the manner of the pyramids. A 260-foot tall statue of Lenin was to top it. Moscow was full of pictures of this place, descriptions of its coming magnificence, and information on the construction speed that would break all records. There was much ado about it all the time while we were in Moscow.

The construction began in 1931 and was scheduled to be completed in 1938. Tens of thousands of tons of steel were sunk into the foundations, but even these were not finished when we left the country in 1938. Then during the Great Patriotic War, 1941–45, the steel was needed for other purposes and was pulled up again. The whole project was buried after the death of Stalin.

The Bolsheviks were very skilled in making use of Western petit-bourgeois thinking and stupidity, traits that amused them highly. According to the Western view, one would be a complete scoundrel if, after having been a guest for a few days or weeks and having been wined and dined and treated well, one wrote something unfavorable about the host. On the contrary, it was one's duty to write something nice and favorable. Therefore many journalists, helped along by vodka, champagne, and caviar, week after week wrote almost nothing but laudatory reports, with a guilty conscience, to be sure, for they suspected that what they were writing was not quite true. And the hosts laughed.

I clipped and saved these articles; the collection did not amuse me. With the help of mere vodka and caviar even the most reactionary Finnish types wrote only favorable things. No threats or orders from the Red Army could have had the same result. This was even true with regard to some American, British, and French journalists.

Thus the Bolsheviks made use of that product of Western culture called decency and benefited greatly by it. But when Finland or Sweden or the United States invited a newsman from Russia, showed him their own achievements, and awaited results, they were negative. Once a delegation from the Russian labor union visited Sweden followed shortly by a Russian choir. Eagerly the Swedes waited to see what they would write. Would they acknowledge the good housing and the high standard of living? No, the Russians were vituperative. The workers in Sweden lived in miserable hovels, they declared, and the Swedish standard of living was altogether primitive.

The same has happened every time Ilja Ehrenburg [well-known Soviet journalist and author] has traveled in the United States: he enjoyed the country's hospitality and then, in all the world's communist papers, heaped abuse on conditions in America.

If the world, or at least the bourgeois and social democratic press, would like to put a stop to the Bolsheviks' propaganda that serves only their aims and damages other countries, it could demand genuine peaceful coexistence in that field. It could simply say we will give equal amounts of column inches for the description of the Soviet conditions in our press as the Soviet press gives for the description of our country and its conditions. We will be glad to reciprocate and will pay what we owe, both quantitatively and qualitatively.

KUUSINEN AND HIS ABILITY
TO SURVIVE

IT IS NOT my intention here to write a biography of Otto Wille Kuusinen, still less to analyze his political activity. My sole intent is to show how the Stalinist system used individuals for its own ends, forcing them into situations in which they could not defend even their closest friends and relatives whom they well knew to be innocent.

To get a better point of departure there is reason to examine briefly the activities of Kuusinen before he went to Russia. He was born in 1881 in Finland, the son of a poor tailor, and completed secondary school in Jyväskylä, in central Finland. According to his contemporaries he was considerably above the average as a student. After his matriculation examination he joined the conservative Old Finnish party, becoming active among the youth. He was full of patriotic zeal that he let gush forth in the form of highflown poetry.

He married during his university years and a total of five children were born: Hertta, Esa, and Riikka (whom we have already met on these pages) and, also, Heikki and Tani. When Kuusinen left the country in 1918, the children remained in Finland with their mother. A little later the three oldest moved to Russia. The two youngest boys were put through schools by their mother; they both took the master's degree in chemistry. They never experienced any difficulties because they were sons of O. W. Kuusinen. I asked them about that many times while they went to school. During the Winter War, when their father was the prime minister in Terijoki, they faithfully performed their jobs.

The year 1905, when Kuusinen took his master's degree, also brought a major turn in his life: the conservative became a Socialist. That year, during the general strike in Finland that was directed against Russia, he joined the Social Democratic party, along with many other academic citizens, as a so-called November Socialist.

He was soon discovered to possess a special talent for the cultivation and study of socialist theory. This was very rare in the party because the most prominent leaders were not theoreticians to any particular degree but, rather, practical party workers. Nor were there any others among the academicians who inclined toward theoretics. Such well-known persons as Manner, Sirola, and Gylling joined the party at the same time, but only Kuusinen had a theoretical bent and, hence, was given his own field to cultivate in the party: the analysis and teaching of Marxist theory. Even before the First World War he was considered a frontline party theorist.

But he did not achieve a leading position in the party; many of the other old party leaders were well above him. He was not inspiring as a speaker, nor were his writings enthralling, though often very sharp and caustic. During the civil war in Finland, in 1918, Kuusinen did not rise to prominence, though he was an activist and among the first to prepare for the revolution. Initially, Oskari Tokoi had been the primary leader, but after the adoption of the line of overt violent revolution that Tokoi opposed, Kullervo Manner became the top man. Kuusinen, of course, participated with all his might, but the best post he could get in the revolutionary government was that of minister of education. However, he was the strongest and most purposeful man in this insurrectionary government, though even he did not then aim at bolshevism and communist dictatorship. This is evident from the proposal for a constitution that he drafted, a document that was basically democratic and in many respects suitable even today for the constitution of the most democratic countries.

After the unsuccessful insurrection Kuusinen fled with the other revolutionary leaders to Russia. But from the beginning it was clear that he did not feel at home in those chaotic conditions, and thus he immediately began planning either a return to Finland or a move to another country. He did go to Finland, but Lenin soon enticed him back to Russia and made him a secretary of the Comintern. During the years 1921–30 he played a notable role in that post as an independent theoretician and helmsman in international politics. His studies were published in the communist press and as pamphlets, and he attained quite a high standing. He also enjoyed a considerable amount of independence and freedom of movement. One can say that Kuusinen then had more power than any other Finn ever has had.

Toward the end of the 1920s Stalin definitively stabilized his personal dictatorship. Then Kuusinen realized—or more likely, had already realized—that he had a choice to make: either to maintain his independence, which would have meant fleeing the country, or remain to serve the dictator and write what was ordered. Kuusinen chose the latter alternative. He put his own opinions into a box or burned them to be on the safe side. From then on, he obtained Stalin's approval of everything he did for the Comintern— every declaration and resolution—before he even set them down on paper.

Many saw this surrender of independent thinking as cowardice, but it was quite understandable considering the circumstances. Once having chosen this road, Kuusinen was forced to play a role that will not be judged highly by historians. For Stalin continually gave him tasks that must have been repugnant to him, though, in keeping with his style, he often carried them out splendidly.

Here are a few examples of how Stalin used Kuusinen. When the struggle for power between Trotsky and Stalin had reached the point where Stalin was a little ahead, Kuusinen was the first one to write a doctrinaire, defamatory article in which he showed that Trotsky had never been a real Marxist but had sought to betray the whole Russian Revolution. This was a first-rate present to Stalin, for he did not have then, nor would he have later, any other worker in this field the equal of Kuusinen. Thus it was the Trotsky affair in which Kuusinen earned his spurs in the service of Stalin.

Incidentally, this explains why Kuusinen was the only Finnish communist leader to survive. He was a specialist whom Stalin needed because there was not another one like him. Besides, Kuusinen was not ambitious for power. Neither Stalin nor Khrushchev had to fear that Kuusinen would try to overthrow him.

A little later, when a struggle developed between Stalin and Zinoviev, Kuusinen was the first to prove Zinoviev heretical. In the mid-1930s it was the turn of Bukharin, former president of the Comintern and himself a skilled theoretician who had participated in knocking down Trotsky and Zinoviev. When Bukharin came under heavy criticism, Kuusinen again was ordered to prepare a memorandum of indictment based on communist theory. Through dogmatic nitpicking he proved that Bukharin did not understand either Marx or Lenin. To err in this area was a crime against the Holy Ghost.

In spite of his prudence, Kuusinen at least once was close to finding himself in a very difficult situation. Sometime in 1931 or 1932, in a Comintern plenum, he had insulted Dimitrov who at that time was not very important, just the representative of Bulgaria in the Executive Committee of the Comintern. Kuusinen had guessed that the bells might soon toll for Dimitrov and hastened to be among the first to knock him down. Who could have foreseen that a strange chance would make Dimitrov a hero at one stroke, but that was what happened when the provocative burning of the Berlin Reichstag building made him a big hero in the Soviet Union. For a while he was the most important man there after Stalin; he was granted Russian citizenship and, after returning from Germany to Russia, rose to be the first man in the Comintern, its leader.

Kuusinen was now a secretary under Dimitrov, one of many, and in the worst predicament of his life. It could be assumed that Dimitrov would take revenge on him. As was his custom, Kuusinen therefore made himself very important, almost indispensable, to Dimitrov. The latter realized that his high office required him to be also a theoretician and that he could be one only with the help of Kuusinen. Therefore he, too, was ready to accept Kuusinen's services, to shine with the aid of his resolutions and speeches on theory.

Already in the Comintern congress of 1935 Dimitrov reaped much fame, mainly with speeches Kuusinen had written. Kuusinen knew the Stalin line and was a master formulator. He created his own style, peculiarly extreme hairsplitting, the so-called Comintern style. His services to Dimitrov were so great that, while thundering Kuusinen's words in a four- or five-hour speech, the temperamental Bulgarian readily forgot old insults.

Kuusinen got into a very difficult and embarrassing situation in his relations with his former colleague and friend, Kullervo Manner. Hanna Malm, who was married to Manner, had attacked Kuusinen abusively in the plenum of the Finnish Communist party's Executive Committee. It was clear that this could not continue forever. Either Manner or Kuusinen had to fall. Kuusinen was leading through his stronger position at the feet of Stalin. Of course, the majority in the Comintern was on his side. Manner's position grew steadily weaker, and finally in 1935 he, his wife, and their close friends were arrested. I cannot contend that Kuusinen played a direct role in Manner's arrest, but the GPU obtained a good basis for destroying Manner and his friends from the heightened quarrel between Manner and Kuusinen.

The number of the accused rose to about fifteen. Besides Manner, Eino Laaksovirta, a jurist and Kuusinen's brother-in-law (the brother of his first wife) who had come to Russia in 1918, was the key person. His wife, who had remained in Finland and worked there in a bank, had visited Russia two or three times to meet her husband, most recently in 1934. The GPU now charged that Mrs. Laaksovirta was in the service of the Finnish secret and military police and claimed that she had been seen in a Helsinki restaurant with a Finnish officer.

There was no other "evidence," but this report of a GPU man working in Helsinki was enough: obviously she was in the service of the Finnish secret police and, because she had met her husband, he too must be, and since he, Laaksovirta, was in the service of the Finnish secret police and was friendly with the Manner family, Manner must have been aware of it; thus the whole group had a direct connection to the Finnish secret police. All denied the charge.

Peculiar charges were brought against two other Finnish Communists as well, "Red Professor" Väinö Pukka and Esko Kivi, whose real name was Heikki Repo. Pukka had held on to his Finnish passport, renewing it in the Finnish legation. This was enough to prove that he must be in the service of the Finnish police. Heikki Repo was suspected of being an agent of the Finnish secret police.

Laaksovirta, Pukka, and Repo were shot. Manner and his wife also were sentenced to death, but through the efforts of Manuilski and other Comintern leaders the sentences were commuted to ten years at hard labor. The others, among them several well-known Finnish Communists, got sentences varying from three to ten years in prison.

That same year, 1935, the persecution of Finns began in Soviet Karelia, and all the leading Communists there, including Prime Minister Gylling and party secretary Rovio, had to face charges. Kuusinen did not dare utter a single word in their defense; on the contrary, he demanded that the Finnish Communist party condemn the Communists who had been active in Karelia. Several times he urged me to go to Petrozavodsk to deliver speeches in which I, as one of the party leaders, would condemn Gylling's and Rovio's activities and show that it was Finnish nationalism of which the party had disapproved and did disapprove. I squirmed out of the affair through various excuses and wound up not having to go to Karelia; nor did I make a single speech during that period.

By then Gylling himself was already in Moscow, attending meetings but not participating in any discussion that concerned himself. He never opposed the party leadership. Once the Finnish Communist party had to prepare a declaration. Hannes Mäkinen and I had drafted it, trying to take a sympathetic view of the activity of Gylling and Rovio, ignoring, for example, the part focusing on Finnish nationalism. Kuusinen began criticizing our text at a meeting and absolutely demanded the inclusion of the point on which the Russians' main charge was based, namely the dangerous nationality policy that Gylling and his men had advocated.

That was the only time that Gylling got angry. "You can put down whatever you want but it makes me wonder why Otto Wille should demand the inclusion of this point, inasmuch as the nationality policy that was pursued there was primarily Kuusinen's policy. Don't you remember that every time some important question came up, I always consulted with you, because I'm not a political expert but rather an economic and cultural specialist. It was your nationality policy that I followed and another one who championed it was Sirola. I find it a little hard to swallow that you are now ready to brand it as my nationality policy."

Kuusinen responded that it wasn't his policy, either, but that they had discussed it together and that of course local people had distorted the line that might have been flawed to begin with. But Kuusinen could not bring himself to admit his own part, though in a small group or privately he could not deny it either, just tried to get off the hook by naïvely explaining that minor officials had been guilty of falsification.

Gylling lived in exile in Moscow for two years, and Kuusinen always avoided him. In the beginning Gylling tried to maintain the old friendship but soon noticed that Kuusinen feared him because of his own position. Every time Gylling came to see me in the *Dom Pravitel'stva*, Kuusinen immediately hurried off somewhere.

When Gylling was arrested in 1937 it caused an altercation between Kuusinen and myself—one of the few we ever had during our work together. As a member of the Central Committee of the Finnish Communist party, Gylling belonged to the group for which I, according to Soviet practice, was responsible. After his arrest I at once suggested to Kuusinen that we go to Stalin and demand a full explanation of why members of the Finnish party's Central Committee were being imprisoned. Besides, there were not many Finns who had such a role in the construction of socialism in the Soviet Union. I considered a visit to Stalin absolutely indispensable, if only for our own safety's sake.

Kuusinen dodged and hedged: no, we won't go.

"Are you of the opinion that Gylling is a spy or a counterrevolutionary?" I asked.

"No. I'm sure that there is some mistake," Kuusinen answered. "It's unnecessary to go now because when Gylling's case has been examined, he'll surely be freed."

"Is that so?" I said. "I don't know of a single such instance. Why should Gylling be luckier? We can't sit here idly, with folded arms."

"One must trust the Soviet officials and the GPU."

"That's what you said before when Finns were imprisoned."

But Kuusinen did not go to speak on behalf of Gylling.

A little later there was a new phase in the affair. I noticed that Kuusinen became nervous, sucked at his cigarette, sauntered from room to room and finally said that the Comintern wanted us, in the name of the party, to write a declaration condemning the work of Gylling and other Finnish Communists. He thought that I should draft it. But I didn't want to and a long argument followed. I didn't do it, anyway, and one was published only after I had left the Soviet Union. Probably Kuusinen wrote it himself.

Kuusinen did not lift a finger to save his old friends though many of them sought his protection when their turn came to be arrested. They got no answer to their messages. Whether he could have helped was another matter, but he did not even try, not even when his own son, Esa, and Esa's wife were arrested in Karelia. After the Winter War Esa was freed on Stalin's orders, but his wife could not be found. Esa had contracted tuberculosis in the prison camp and soon died.

It was always the same story when these matters came up: Kuusinen withdrew into his shell, isolated himself more than ever, refused to see anyone, did not even read their letters but pushed them to me, saying nothing, neither for, nor against.

How much Kuusinen could have helped these people was, as I have already said, an entirely different story. In my view he could have done nothing, for Stalin's mills were grinding away at their own tempo. Possibly he could have wielded some influence when it was a question of some unimportant person, but he was unable to help a bigger man. So it is useless to consider the matter from that angle. When Kuusinen once had the chance to choose which path he would follow, he chose the profession which the sarcastic Radek called "noose greasing." A Swedish paper put it a little more delicately when it concluded its article on Kuusinen with these words: "Thus the independent viking grows old as the servile hired man of Stalin."

This was the picture I got of Kuusinen during my Moscow years when I lived in his apartment.

After familiarizing myself with the speech given by former Prime Minister and party secretary Nikita Khrushchev at the Twentieth Party Congress of the Soviet Communist party in 1956, and subsequently having read hundreds of attestations of Stalin's total autocracy, I am of the opinion that Stalin's arbitrariness was even more unscrupulous and terrible than I had experienced it in my somewhat sheltered situation. Only that six-hour speech and the evidence that it bared showed how hopeless and impossible it was even for individuals in the highest echelons to interfere with Stalin's actions.

From the beginning I have been of the opinion that Kuusinen was not a Stalinist. My wife and I were amused when Kuusinen, in keeping with the custom of that period, had to offer at the beginning and end of each speech the mandatory glorifying phrases to the "great Stalin," to the "life and sun," to the "creator of a happy and joyful life." I remember how he used to hack and cough in annoyance.

Once in the 1930's the well-known Finnish Communist Mauri Ryömä sent a request from Finland to the leadership of the Finnish Communist party in Moscow that another Finnish Communist living in Finland, Raoul Palmgren, be expelled from the party because he had disparaged Stalin. At a meeting Palmgren had asked: "What kind of a theoretician is Stalin? He hasn't discovered anything but the theory of the liquidation of kulaks." And Palmgren used such ironic statements as "the sun rises in the east and sets in the west, as the great Stalin has so aptly put it." Palmgren constantly cultivated such deviltries.

After Kuusinen had read the message he had a good laugh—though he was usually very cautious—and said, "He's quite a boy, this Palmgren, but let's not get involved in such quarrels. We'll just let the boys over there keep on writing." We got the impression that he enjoyed these deviltries of Palmgren from the bottom of his heart and appeared to have the same opinion of the great Stalin's theoretical abilities.

For nearly a quarter of a century Kuusinen was obliged to serve Stalin, though he did not agree with his policies. On the contrary, the despot was repulsive to him.

At the Twentieth Party Congress Kuusinen finally got a chance officially to disown all the work in which he, too, had participated and to prove Stalin the most heretical of all heretics. Surely those were the greatest moments of Kuusinen's life. When I took a close look at Khrushchev's speech and the resolutions of the congress, I saw clear evidence of Kuusinen's hand in them. I found it easy to detect what parts of the speech and the resolutions had been written by Otto Wille. I am sure that Kuusinen wrote those resolutions that discuss Leninist theory and analyze how Stalin deviated from Leninism and violated the basic principles of Lenin. I also can say with certainty that at least the theoretic-ideological part of the Khrushchev speech was written by Kuusinen.

In my mind's eye I saw Kuusinen rejuvenated in his later years after finally having a chance to fulfill himself in Khrushchev's speech and on some other occasions as well.

In 1939, when I refused to return to Moscow and to assume the leadership of the soon to be established Terijoki government and instead began working on Finland's behalf and against Russia, Kuusinen must have been deeply wounded. Nevertheless, he never to my knowledge knifed me or condemned me in writing. I know that he read my autobiographical works in which he is a central figure. I once asked Hertta whether her father had ever said anything about me, and Hertta replied that to her knowledge he never had. If the Communists had obtained even a sentence from him, they would have used it against me, so dangerous an enemy was I.

A few years after my resignation from the Communist party, Hertta and her husband at that time, Finland's communist Minister of the Interior Yrjö Leino, went to Kuusinen in Moscow and pleaded with him to do something to stifle Poika Tuominen, who was launching propaganda from Stockholm that was very damaging to the Communists.

"Tell us what to do with him. Should he be poisoned or shot?"

Kuusinen paced the floor for ten minutes, hands behind his back, and then observed, "Ahem—you seem to be having some difficulties in Finland with that Prime Minister Pekkala because he drinks so heavily."

Leino has related that when they left, Hertta actually quivered in anger and snapped, "That's the way Father is; he doesn't dare say anything about Poika."

I believe that during those ten minutes of pacing he recalled our two decades of cooperation, thinking somewhat along these lines:

"When I met Poika Tuominen for the first time, he was right in asserting that a revolution cannot be carried out in Finland. After his release from prison in 1926, Poika began leading the labor movement according to his own credo, which held that underground activity will not succeed in Finland because it doesn't suit the Finnish character, and immediately the movement began to gain ground. In that manner we won points in the Comintern and the Profintern, and this raised my own standing there also.

"Poika was right when we lived together in Moscow and began planning the idea of a people's front. We worked on it collectively, then I sold it to Stalin, and Dimitrov thereafter proclaimed it with the aid of a speech I had written incorporating many of Poika's ideas.

"And now most recently this Terijoki government, from which Poika was spared by means of his own peasant wits but into which I was forced and then tossed aside like a wet rag."

I believe that Kuusinen's thoughts traveled in this manner during those ten minutes. Yrjö Sirola once told me that "Kuusinen keeps you in his home like a prisoner because he is a theoretician to such a degree that he needs someone with horse sense to deal with concrete matters in a concrete way."

During those two decades I initiated many projects but, in particular, saw to the practical application of Kuusinen's theories in a way that expressed them most usefully. Now in this moment of decision in front of his daughter and son-in-law, he didn't declare that the villain must be shot. He didn't say anything, either good or bad, but talked of other things.

It may be said that Kuusinen's and my relationship was, in a way, a father-son relationship. But by no means was it one-sided, for the son also influenced the father. Whenever a question arose concerning the Comintern and the Finnish Communist party, Kuusinen sought my advice as though I had been some sage.

I do not feel that, during those twenty years, Kuusinen ever misused me in the sense of exploiting me. Between us was the father-son relationship of two political workers, but a relationship in which the father gave full recognition to the son.

FOUR COMMUNISTS IN PARADISE

THE COMINTERN-OWNED Hotel Lux in Moscow assuredly had no equal in the world. Throughout the existence of the Comintern a considerable part of its leadership lived there and, in addition, as much assistant personnel as could be accommodated in the five- or six-story building. Its tenants represented forty, possibly fifty, nationalities. Most of the famous international Communists stayed there, some for longer, some for shorter periods.

Literally the whole world was this group's field of activity and operations. It stretched from Finland over the landmass of Europe to the tip of South Africa, as well as in the New World, from Alaska to Cape Horn. Even some small Pacific islands, ignored in ordinary geography books, could be important targets of operations for the occupants of this hotel during some international intrigue.

Every conceivable villainy was devised and planned within these walls. Probably no building under the heavens could provide such shocking themes for suspense novels as did this one during a twenty-year period. There, over a cup of coffee or tea and often a glass of vodka, cognac, or champagne, the fates of entire nations were decided. Dozens of plans for insurrections, some successful, most of them unsuccessful, were made in the catacombs, lobbies, and rooms of this hotel. There a throw of the dice decided thousands of human lives; there terror and murder leagues were created and then liquidated when they had done their work. Scores and hundreds of well-known Communists—not to mention other persons—have lost their lives on the basis of decisions made in the Hotel Lux.

In the Comintern office building itself more official decisions were made, many of which did stand the light of day and followed, as much as possible, the outlines drawn by open congresses and conferences. They had largely an ideological and political character.

But in the small groups at the Hotel Lux, almost without exception, were made all those decisions that shunned daylight. If the walls of the Lux could speak they could tell of the most ideal love stories, of dramatic twists in the married lives of the couples culminating in the murders of spouses, of minor political arguments or an exchange of words that led to a bloody power struggle within the party, of cynical destruction of the opposing faction, using either the GPU or its own party terrorists. The walls could tell tales ranging from the most purehearted communist dreams to bloody revolutions and revolts and plans to destroy entire states.

Among these unusual and remarkable people were a goodly number of completely honest, idealistic, and sincere individuals, actual geniuses, internationally famous literary figures, and notable political leaders. Hundreds of simple rank-and-filers, communist workers, and hirelings who worked only for the pay also lived in the Lux, as well as adventurers without any idealistic convictions, and completely hardened criminals and scoundrels.

O. W. Kuusinen lived in the Hotel Lux for about ten years in a row, at least until the beginning of the 1930s; his daughter Hertta lived there from 1922 to 1934, at first with her father, then alone, and finally with another Finnish Communist, Tuure Lehén.

This chapter is about Hertta Kuusinen and Tuure Lehén, as well as about two other Finnish Communists, Heikki Kaljunen and Yrjö Sirola. It would be difficult to find four other persons who are more different from each other than these four.

Hertta Kuusinen had considerable talent and leadership traits, but as a woman she found it difficult to gain sufficient authority. Her position was based largely on the name and influence of her father.

She was born in Finland in 1904 and received a political education the likes of which only a few persons in the whole world could have gotten. She was only a small child when her political education began, while her father was still at home. He fled to Russia in 1918, and at his request she followed him there in 1922.

For a short while she studied in Russian schools and later, between jobs, occasionally attended political schools. Biographical sources indicate that she worked in a library, but that was not her primary work. Actually she worked in the conspiracy department of the Comintern.

Her education in this particular area was augmented splendidly by her first husband, Tuure Lehén, with whom she lived beginning in 1925. This son of a Finnish carpenter, despite poor circumstances, managed to complete high school and to study at the University of Helsinki. Undeniably he was very talented and, as I understand it, in his youth had grandiose, far-reaching plans for the future, as young men from modest circumstances often have. But in the revolutionary tumult of 1918, in which he participated, his dreams were considerably deflated. He wound up in Russia with other Red Guardists, and the sight of all that misery and poverty must have influenced his thinking and his entire future. Occasionally, as if in passing, he remarked that life had no purpose or meaning, that man will perish anyway: why strive for something special, it's enough to live from one day to another.

Thus he abandoned himself to the unbounded cynicism to which he was naturally disposed, and I must say that I have never met a less idealistic person. Upon closer acquaintance one saw that he took nothing seriously. His personal political attitude was that of a cynic who was totally disgusted with life and the world, who despised himself, those closest to him, ideas, and, in general, everybody and everything.

He performed all his tasks well, but in an intimate group where he dared speak his mind, he maliciously and caustically derided and detested bolshevism and his own daily work. Never before or since have I heard anyone speak of Stalin so maliciously, venomously, and insultingly. Few bourgeois or Social Democrats could analyze Stalin as well as Tuure Lehén who knew the dictator and the whole old guard of Bolsheviks well and who had closely observed the struggle for Lenin's legacy, a struggle in which Stalin had destroyed all his rivals. Already during the years 1933–36 Tuure Lehén said about Stalin everything Khrushchev said in 1956.

Tuure Lehén was one of the few Finnish exiles in Russia who had had a good education and military training. Besides, he had those skills and talents needed in training for higher positions, which resulted in his acceptance into the "Academy of the Generals" in Moscow in 1921. He and another student of the Helsinki University, Eyolf Georg Mattson, were the first Red "generals" who were schooled there. True, they were not yet generals—the rank of general did not even exist at that time—but they were high officers anyway, commanders.

After finishing the academy, Lehén was not sent to the Red Army, however. Kuusinen, who was then the almighty secretary general of the Comintern, took the young man on as a Comintern military expert. He had in the Comintern a chance to specialize in revolutionary terror and tactics. Of course, every country had such persons for its internal use, but at that time a man who was trained and schooled to prepare and execute revolts on a worldwide scale was rare.

Under the name "Alfred Langer" Tuure Lehén wrote several books and leaflets teaching the workers and farmers of the industrial countries or colonial peoples in great detail how to rise in revolt and establish a dictatorship of the proletariat. In the 1920s and 1930s he moved around a lot in Germany and many other Central and Western European countries teaching Communists that important skill. He also taught revolutionary terrorism and tactics in communist schools of Moscow and Leningrad.

Without exaggeration, Tuure Lehén could say that his students included Chinese coolies, African and American Negroes, Spanish grandees, English lords, and German barons. He taught the art of fomenting rebellions to many such unusual persons who traveled on the outskirts of communism. Of course, most of his students were average communist workers.

Tuure Lehén has participated in the actual planning and execution of many revolts in one country or another. Most of them have failed completely and at best a few attempts have had slight success in the beginning. But they have been a source of concern for many capitalist governments.

When the civil war broke out in Spain between the Republicans and Franco in 1936, Tuure Lehén was among the first to be sent there by the Comintern. His first task was to create within the Communist party of Spain a special secret police fashioned after the GPU. Another important undertaking was the planning of internal disturbances and revolts in the area held by Franco.

This assignment occurred at the time when the most thorough purges were taking place in the Soviet Union and, specifically, within the Comintern. It is probable that this assignment was Tuure Lehén's salvation, for, in spite of their merits and importance, many similar persons working on the fringes of the Comintern were arrested and exiled to a concentration camp. When he returned to Moscow the worst of the purge was over. Thus he was spared for new tasks, among them the job of the minister of interior in the short-lived Terijoki government that Stalin established in 1939. He returned to Finland after the Second World War. It is difficult to say what duties he might have discharged there but, of course, he was used primarily in those fields where he was a specialist.

In the 1930s in Moscow, another Communist, Finnish lawyer Asser Salo, was a good friend of Lehén's. These cronies were given to tippling almost every night until they became quite voluble. Tuure held forth on Stalin, the Comintern, his father-in-law Kuusinen, and the system of government in general in a manner so frightening and terrible that it chilled the blood. I checked carefully to see that nobody was listening behind the curtains and that there were no listening devices in the walls. I also raised loud and often angry objections to Tuure's words.

In the beginning I believed that this mode of expression was some kind of a test for the new man who had just arrived there, that the old hand who held a high position in the Comintern, was finding out this way how well the newcomer knew the Soviet system and how strong was his belief in it.

Asser Salo agreed only seldom with Lehén. Mostly he just listened and sometimes objected mildly. Hertta Kuusinen, who was present at these soirées, followed approximately the same procedure as Salo, often deprecating Tuure's language. But mostly she was quiet and sometimes supported my remonstrances.

I soon noticed that there was no trap and no tactic. The essence of Tuure Lehén's character manifested itself in a small gathering. As is often the case with cynics, his cynicism spurred him to emphasize and exaggerate the assumptions and allegations that he put forth about Stalinism. Usually he laughed at my zeal for, as a true cynic, he did not get angry but said:

"When you've been here as long as I, you'll begin to know what it is. In Finland and in the Finnish prisons there can only be an idealized concept of Stalinism but we who are leading Bolsheviks, are of a somewhat different opinion."

Once Lehén discoursed on Stalin worship, offering grotesque examples taken from within and without the Comintern. He held up his father-in-law Kuusinen as a model example of a faithful servant, parodying Kuusinen's speeches and writings that attributed almost anything to Stalin. His main purpose was to disparage Kuusinen because he wanted in that way to annoy and hurt Hertta. Lehén had put together a collection of extracts from Kuusinen's speeches and writings over the years—specifically, passages giving Stalin credit for things which he had not done.

I, of course, fervently sided with Kuusinen and claimed that the deification of Stalin was very repugnant to Stalin himself but expedient in ruling the ignorant proletariat.

Lehén refuted all these claims brilliantly, demonstrating that Stalin in his own exalted person and by personal orders through his secretary, determined the details of this cult. Lehén's position in the Comintern was high enough to enable him to get his hands on the memoranda that Stalin's secretary and propaganda chiefs sent to the various organs of the Communist party, memoranda that decreed precisely and minutely how every occasion, every meeting of a cell, labor union, or collective farm, was to begin and end in the name of the great Stalin.

"To say a prayer that we can be thankful to the great Stalin, the leader of nations, that we exist. Do you think that the propaganda chiefs would dare send those decrees without a direct order from Stalin?"

During the years 1933–34 an internal purge in the Communist

party was under way throughout all Russia. This ceremony of public confession of sins unnerved and terrified all members of the Communist party, from top to bottom. For many weeks and months it was a colossal nightmare for Hertta Kuusinen as well. She was deeply conscience-stricken, fearing that Tuure's anti-Stalinist attitude and extended anti-Soviet propaganda had become known outside the small circle and might pop up in the party purge.

During those days I met Hertta frequently. In discussing all kinds of matters, we also touched upon Hertta's personal affairs, and I became a confidant of sorts because of my very good relations with her father. The relationship between father and daughter was pleasant, but they did not confide in one another. Therefore Hertta did not tell her father things that would have concerned him as the leading figure in the Finnish Communist party, quite apart from the fact that as a father he should first and foremost have been his daughter's adviser. Hertta forbade even me to talk to her father about matters concerning her.

At the conclusion of one of our conversations, Hertta said that she would soon be drawn into the party purge, perhaps within the next few days, and asked whether she should then tell all and denounce Tuure as a slanderer of Stalin and the party. As a party member she knew it to be her duty, for otherwise the party purge would be a mere farce. What should she do? She appealed to me not only because I was her friend but also a member of the Central Committee and the party secretary and therefore, in a way, duty bound to help her in this quandary.

I became terribly alarmed, though the question did not surprise me. I had often wondered how they would survive the party purge and whether I, too, would be stood up against the wall because I had been present listening to Tuure's tales. I asked how long Tuure had had that vice and what Hertta thought a full confession would result in for Tuure and herself.

Hertta said that Tuure had always been the same but that lately his cynicism and contempt for Stalin and other leaders had increased. He was not part of a conspiracy; on the contrary, he had performed his duties well, and it was that dualism that made the matter so strange. She added that if she took that plunge, undoubtedly others also would be questioned, including me and the Salo family, and there was no doubt about Tuure's fate. As for herself, she knew that because she had kept the matter secret for so long, she could not save herself merely through self-criticism but would get into great difficulties, dragging her father and all her close friends with her. The situation was as perplexing as it possibly could be.

Hertta tried to extricate herself by asking me to arrange a trip for her before the party purge. She would have liked to be an honest Communist, but when one considered the consequences, one dared not think through to the end. If her faith were strengthened, she would destroy herself and Lehén so that righteousness would prevail at the party purge. Tuure would not be ousted from the party but would be arrested, and that he deserved for his incorrigibility and unsuitableness for communistic life.

Hertta was highly dramatic. This analysis of personal feelings by a person so keen and free of bias showed how thoroughly shaken she was. In those days she was completely exhausted and haggard; the matter bothered her a lot. I sympathized with her from the bottom of my heart, for I liked her and her open, straightforward character; I suggested initially that I speak with her father, after which we would return to the subject. But Hertta was horrified and declared that the matter must not be mentioned to her father at all.

I finally concluded that I would not speak of the matter to anybody. She was a member of the Finnish Communist party and so well trained that she must be able to use her own judgment, telling everything she considered necessary at the party purge. But I sincerely hoped that she would carefully weigh the consequences. Although I had the best interests of the Soviet Union at heart, I considered it completely senseless to create difficulties for herself, her father, and the rest of us as well.

When Hertta's purge day arrived, she presented her life story and some self-criticism but mentioned Tuure only in connection with the length of her marriage. She came through the purge easily. Nobody wanted to pose problems or ask questions.

Tuure's purge, which followed soon thereafter, proceeded similarly according to all the doctrines and rules. Practicing self-criticism in the manner of a well-trained Old Bolshevik, he said that he had erred by voting for Zinovievism but had repented it and since then had not taken even the smallest side step from the Stalinist line.

Both survived the purge brilliantly. But, as a conscientious Communist, Hertta was not happy.

"It's terrible," she said, "that a person doesn't dare say what he should. As a Communist what do you think?"

I reminded her that everything had gone well and that more than that could not have been done. If one presented even mild criticism, extremely far-reaching conclusions were drawn from it, and human lives were destroyed.

At that time I was still a fairly staunch Communist, but I had to admit that I detested the party purge undergone by these good friends of mine and dozens of others. Although I had already had time to see one thing and another in the Soviet Union, this was one of my first opportunities to observe closely just how farcical and comic the whole party life was. It illustrated Tuure Lehén's discourses on the pharisaism of everything and everybody. One could not help but think that perhaps all these people would turn out to be Tuure Lehéns if one really knew them. And yet all professed to be supporters of the doctrine and followers of the Stalin line.

Despite her international schooling at the Hotel Lux, Hertta possessed so much healthy and idealistic communism that she had difficulty in regaining her balance after the purge. Her conscience continued to bother her. She began to pester me as well as other members of the Finnish Communist party with requests to be sent to Finland. The main reason, she told me, was that she couldn't live here as an idler when she could do something in Finland. She was not afraid of prison but would go there like the others.

Then, as we continued our discussions, it became evident that she had to get away from Tuure and his whole antibolshevik circle. Besides, their marriage had not been an ideal one, even in the beginning. Tuure's character was so cynical that there could not have been an ideal marriage. Furthermore, Tuure was not the most faithful of husbands, and Hertta tried more and more to concentrate on taking care of her son Jurkka. But life in a small hotel room was so crowded and difficult that it was impossible to raise the boy properly. Thus he became hypersensitive and nervous and had to be put into a home for hypersensitive children. There he remained until he was about eleven, two years after Hertta had left for Finland in 1934. Only then did her sister Riikka take the boy into her care.

Toward the end it was difficult for Hertta to live with Tuure, but because of the miserable housing situation they had to share the same hotel room. They should have separated years before. Hertta looked for an apartment constantly. Although she could have moved in with her father, she categorically rejected the whole idea. Sometimes she lived for short periods with her friends. Whenever Riikka had something that passed for an apartment Hertta stayed with her, but Riikka lived here and there while her husband Popov was imprisoned in Germany.

The reason for the couple's final breakup was Tuure's relationship with the wife of his best friend, Asser Salo. By that time Salo already was so inured to the misery that he no longer reacted but was completely indifferent to his life and surroundings. All his dreams had been shattered even more devastatingly than those of Tuure and many others who had gone to Russia. He was a gifted young man who had graduated with honors and then taken a law degree. He had had a meteoric career as a politician, but when he got to the atmosphere of the Hotel Lux and especially to Tuure Lehén's circle his dreams collapsed completely and his life became a tragedy.

Hertta Kuusinen's character is further illustrated by the fact that she never displayed any bitterness toward Aino Salo. Often, when I visited Hertta, both Salos were there. Or we would all go to the Salos's. But this happened less frequently because they had children, and therefore Hertta's and Lehén's room was the place where we usually met.

The evenings passed pleasantly and we took every occasion to celebrate. In addition to political discussions we had other entertainment as well. Asser and Tuure were usually a little tight. Although Hertta did not drink at all, she appeared more vivacious and intoxicated than anyone there and usually wound up having to dance for us.

Her top number was a wild knife dance, in which she held two long bread knives between her teeth and lifted whatever ragged shirt she happened to be wearing. In those days she cared nothing about her clothing, and it seemed unbelievable when I saw her after the war in Finland, fashionably dressed at the opening of the parliament—whose member she had become—or in the president's palace, that she was the same person who in her Moscow days wore an old blouse and something resembling a skirt. Well, then the savage dance began, at first on the floor and then on the table, all the while in the Spanish or Caucasian manner. We others beat time and bellowed, and the Amazon raged.

Most of my Christmas memories are monotonous and unpleasant. The ten Christmases I have spent in prisons and over fifteen as an exile in alien countries, have hardly been conducive to creating a Christmas spirit. But even they have left some memories.

It was the week before Christmas 1934, and our household, too, had started to prepare for Christmas little by little—not so much with presents but, rather, by procuring Christmas food—when Otto Wille Kuusinen entered our room and announced that we had been invited to spend the Christmas with Heikki Kaljunen. Lyyli, my wife, could stop her preparations for Christmas.

I had met Kaljunen in passing a few times, and my impressions of him were very indefinite. I was quite familiar with the literature that the White sympathizers in Finland had published about this Red Guards' chieftain called the "Terror of Karelia." Although I knew how exaggerated and even groundless most horror stories of that time were, I had, nevertheless gained the impression that Heikki Kaljunen had to be abnormal in some way.

This picture was not much improved by the report that one of Kaljunen's former colleagues had recently given me. It ended with words: "He is not only a braggart and a great liar, but completely mad."

Going by this information, I wondered how we could spend Christmas with such a man. Would it not spoil the whole evening? And was it even safe to associate with such a person?

But Kuusinen strongly disagreed: we could associate with Kaljunen without endangering our reputation, for he was, after all, a party member and in an important position. Besides, Kuusinen had already accepted on our behalf. Somewhat roguishly he added that because there had been no time to get any Christmas presents, our coming to know Kaljunen was the present. There was surprise enough in that.

"And as for the holiday table, I guarantee that it will be incomparable. I have been there before." Thus it was all settled.

At the given hour on Christmas eve, a little excited, we three arrived at the festal house. Considering the housing situation in Moscow, the apartment was altogether splendid: two large rooms and a kitchen, all finely furnished. The host, tall and stately, conducted himself suavely and politely like a true man of the world.

But the real charmer was the hostess, Madame Edla. Rather short and plump, she was a lively and gay Karelian. Alongside her husband Edla had weathered many a gale and squall, and though she probably was already around forty, she had the bloom of a young woman. Her tasteful attire and social graces amazed us even more than her beauty. In the Moscow society of that day, Edla Kaljunen was one of the best dressed and most charming ladies.

When we seated ourselves at the festive board, Kuusinen remarked, "Didn't I tell you!" There on the table were all the traditional Finnish Christmas dishes, including rutabaga casserole, herring salad, and rice porridge—only the codfish was missing, a fact that Heikki and Edla greatly regretted. Caviar and other Russian delicacies completed the meal. Nor was there any shortage of good drinks.

Although we, too, had the opportunity to get extras for our table, we could not possibly have achieved anything like this Christmas banquet of the Kaljunens.

One might wonder how it was possible for someone of questionable repute like Kaljunen to arrange a feast like this in the midst of a wretched and starving Moscow. We got a full explanation during the meal and the subsequent long sitting. It turned out that Kaljunen was the director general of a large factory in Moscow. Sometime around 1924 he had gotten hold of an old rundown factory where he began making skis and furniture. In the beginning the labor force had been made up of skilled workers who had come from Finland in 1918. Year by year the factory had been expanded so that there were now well over a thousand workers, only a few of them Finns and Finnish Americans. The products, too, had changed. Now the factory fulfilled mostly Red Army needs.

But the directorship of the factory alone would not have guaranteed the position he held. Much more was needed for that. Besides having proved himself a first-class organizer, he also was an inventive genius. He held dozens of patents and derived a large income from them.

Some of the inventions were indeed Kaljunen's own, but most of them were derived from the many modern tools that Finnish American workers had brought with them to the Soviet Union and to the factory. Heikki had his engineers and draftsmen make exact drawings of them, other specialists prepared the models, and he took them to the patent office as his own inventions.

Still other inventions originated in the descriptions of new work methods by workers who had come from Finland or the United States. With the help of his engineers, Heikki then patented them in his own name. One of these made Heikki's name highly respected in the Red Army. Brought over by Finnish Americans, the invention was a method for cross gluing supporting beams and planks in mobile bridges for the army. The system resulted in a bridge that was light, yet stronger than the ones made of solid wood.

When Heikki got a product patented, his factory often was commissioned to manufacture it. These dozens of patents with their drawings and impressive patent documents we examined and admired on that never-to-be-forgotten Christmas eve.

Finally we got around to Heikki's war memories and only then did the real Kaljunen come alive. We heard the most astonishing accounts of battles between a Red unit led by Kaljunen and the White Guards. I asked him how much truth there was in the claims presented in some books on Kaljunen that, when questioning White prisoners, he began by putting the man against a wall and shooting a part in the hair and only then started the interrogation.

"Just lies spread by the butchers," he huffed. "However, I did give one character, the one who wrote *In the Clutches of Kaljunen,* a reminder of his mortality when he became insolent. I set him against a wall, ordering him to spread his arms and fingers, then emptied two clips from a Mauser at a distance of some thirty feet, hitting the wall around his body and head, in the manner of knife throwers in a circus. I did place a few bullets between the fingers and arrange a part in the hair, but I assure you that he didn't get a scratch. After this show the man was very docile and the interrogation went smoothly."

However, that which had taken place in 1918 in Finnish Karelia was child's play compared to the great adventure Kaljunen had experienced while leading the fight against the armies of the White admiral, Alexander Kolchak. Like many other former Finnish Red Guards, he too had gone in the summer of 1918 to Siberia, beyond Omsk. Then, when Admiral Kolchak conquered Omsk in the fall of that year, eastern Siberia was cut off from the rest of Russia.

But Kaljunen was not in such a situation for the first time. Authorized by Lenin and Trotsky, General Kaljunen organized a forced mobilization, quickly formed a strong army and attacked Kolchak's army from the rear. These battles General Kaljunen led mounted on a beautiful gray Orlov steed at the head of his army. His supernatural shooting skill had played a decisive part in the battles. When War Commissar Trotsky's Red Army, attacking from the west, slew a thousand men in a battle, Kaljunen, attacking from the opposite flank, slew ten thousand that same day. In other words, history repeated itself: Saul slew a thousand but David slew ten thousand.

Twice in these battles Kaljunen had been shot with a machine gun so that he resembled a sieve, but he just had not given up the ghost. When we doubting thomases could not help snickering, the general quickly took off his jacket and pulled off his shirt so that we could put our fingers into the bullet scars. Admittedly, they were all over his body in countless numbers. We understood this scar business better when Madame Edla told us a little later that while they were in Siberia, Heikki had had a vast number of boils that left big scars.

If the picture of Kaljunen were to be formed solely on the basis of that Christmas eve, it would remain a little vague. Therefore I must supplement it with some facts. Heikki Kaljunen, with his wonderful tales, was not only the Münchhausen* of these decades; he was also a man of action and his fingers were not all thumbs. When his war adventures came to an end in 1919, he made a brief-case embellished with Lenin's name, the Soviet arms with their hammer and sickle, and the text "Workers of the world, unite!" The briefcase was a display of real skill. Heikki obtained an audience with Lenin, handed over the briefcase, received many warm thanks and became recognized. During this and a later visit he met Lenin's wife Krupskaya and sister Ulyanova, who later on became Kaljunen's guardian angels.

* Champion liar in German literature.

After that he made similar briefcases for Trotsky, Zinoviev, and Kamenev and, if I remember correctly, a few years later for Stalin, after his rise to the front rank. These little presents and visits with these important men smoothed the path for him later on when he made a dash for the directorship of the factory. Heikki could make use of his acquaintance with the great men when he battled the lower echelon bureaucrats.

As brilliant as Heikki Kaljunen was as an organizer, inventor, and patent hunter, and despite his rise to the directorship of a large factory, he never rid himself of his Münchhausen stories. They were his weakness and caused him many difficulties. If there is one man who has caused much work for the Soviet secret police that man is Heikki Kaljunen. He was arrested several times, and it always took weeks and months for his guardian angels to get him free.

Once he claimed to have been the commander-in-chief of the Finnish Red Guards during the civil war in Finland. On another occasion he described everything he had learned during long study trips to America, France, and Germany. But since the biography Heikki had given to the party declared that he had not traveled outside of Finland and Russia, he was again arrested.

Those fantastic battles against Kolchak occasioned Heikki many a hearing and arrest. Spies around Kaljunen and in his factory continuously sent reports about this garrulous man to the Cheka headquarters. Inasmuch as the chiefs there changed frequently, and the new ones were not familiar with our hero, yet another arrest ensued. But his guardian angels, Lenin's wife and sister, stepped forward every time and saved him. They testified that Lenin, who saw through a man at a glance, had said that Comrade Kaljunen was a little peculiar, so one could not put much stock in his tales, but that he was an energetic, hardworking man, the type needed in building up the Soviet Union. He had to have a chance to work.

So Heikki always returned from these study trips to the GPU prisons to continue directing his factory, as if nothing had happened. But during the great purges at the turn of 1937, poor Heikki was taken for a more extended purge, and I have not heard of him since. By that time his guardian angels were weary, and their influence no longer was as great as it had been during the years immediately following Lenin's death.

As a person Yrjö Sirola was in many respects the exact opposite of Kaljunen. He was sympathetic and impressed one as a sincere, honest and reliable human being. He also was insecure and impractical.

The Communist party of Finland idolizes the late Sirola as a leader who is given much credit specifically as an educator and trainer of party functionaries. He is called "the father of the Finnish Communist party cadres." His name has gained additional fame because the propaganda school of the Finnish Communists—which, incidentally, is supported by the Finnish government—is called the Sirola Institute.

The Communists try to make Sirola an orthodox Bolshevik, who followed Stalin's slightest hint without any mental reservation and who trained and educated communist functionaries in the true Stalinist spirit. He is praised as a man who passed along Leninism and Stalinism to the younger generations unadulterated and undiluted. This is entirely different from the real Sirola who moved in broad spheres and held wide perspectives, virtually a universal man.

It has been demonstrated many times that the communist recording of history is distorted from beginning to end. In this instance it is more or less inadvertent, since most of the leaders who influenced the party work even more than Sirola during the early years of the Communist party have completely disappeared from the pages of communist history. Kullervo Manner is a good example of this. They cannot be mentioned, not even to be defamed. Thus all the work that scores, perhaps hundreds of persons have performed, must be credited to one or two persons. That is considerable falsification.

The Finnish Communist party history has been written in the same style as Stalin wrote the history of the Russian Communist party: there are only two leaders, Lenin and Stalin. Scores of Lenin's fellow workers from the party's early years have been eliminated. They have achieved nothing or, if their names are mentioned, they have done nothing but damage.

During the years 1933–36 I had the opportunity of working very closely with Sirola and was therefore in a better position than anyone else to observe the last years of his life. I had had good relations with Sirola ever since 1918, and during the last three years we became very close.

Sirola was never a party leader in the sense that Kuusinen was from the very beginning. He could be extremely uncertain in his political actions and totally dependent on persons near him, especially on Kuusinen who followed a clear, logical line that he developed step by step. Sirola, on the other hand, tried to test the line with all possible doubts and evidence. He was well suited for Kuusinen's usage, because his vast knowledge enabled him to offer many arguments in support of Kuusinen's points. At the same time he made himself appear unreliable, or at least impractical, in Kuusinen's eyes by reason of his inability to develop a logical line out of his material. Because of this Kuusinen would often interrupt Sirola peevishly even when he had the floor at meetings of the party Central Committee and say:

"We really don't need to get into such universe-encompassing propositions. What we need is a simple decision on a simple question, on which we will concentrate and not fantasize."

Sirola took such remarks as a personal insult and resented them, even as he praised Kuusinen's great leadership qualities at the meetings. When the two of us were alone, however, he often expressed his indignation at Kuusinen's insulting behavior.

Sirola was a kind of surrogate sufferer. His weakness was that he was never quite sure about anything, not even if any of his writings or speeches were right or if the persons he had taught had really received a true Marxist-Leninist-Stalinist schooling. This was reflected in his every move. If someone in Finland who had attended his school did not succeed, Sirola was immediately ready to take the blame, because presumably he had given him a wrong grip on life.

When there were schisms and quarrels in the Communist party of the United States—as there were constantly—Sirola was ready to assume the responsibility even for them, because previously he had been the director of a labor academy there and later, as a Comintern emissary, on several occasions had tried to straighten out the American Communists' affairs. Whenever such a sad message arrived, Sirola always said it was a result of his inability to provide the right guidance and advice.

During the years 1935–36, up to the moment he died, he struggled with the thought that all his work in Karelia had been utterly wrong and downright sabotage. When a wave of arrests hit Karelia in 1935, it was at first directed specifically at teachers and schools. Because Sirola had been the commissar of education there precisely during the phase when the educational foundations had been laid, he felt that the arrests of every teacher, inspector, or commissar was the result of his faulty indoctrination. Furthermore, because the standard charge was a false nationality policy, Finnish nationalism, each case was like a knife thrust in Sirola's heart. They were all victims of his false policy; he had given them the wrong point of departure!

Later, when Gylling and Rovio and the whole government of Karelia were removed from office and banished, Sirola's self-reproach grew hourly, and his state of mind finally resembled madness. Almost every morning he told us at the party bureau what a struggle he had undergone, hardly able to sleep for his battles with the thought that hundreds of persons were in GPU prisons as his victims.

Toward the end of 1935 he demanded to be allowed to go to Karelia to explain that everything was his fault and to try to rescue the innocent people from the clutches of the GPU. Only with great effort were we able to prevent his trip to Karelia. We knew that it was folly. He could have damaged the cause of those who were already arrested, and above all he would have destroyed himself. When the Karelia trip did not materialize, he began demanding that we should go to Stalin—I as party secretary, he as the main culprit—to explain the truth of the matter.

"I am the father of the false nationality policy, I laid down the line," he kept on repeating.

The truth that he did not dare or did not want to say was that the father of that policy was Kuusinen. Now and then the truth flashed out in private conversations, but as a surrogate sufferer he wanted to assume full responsibility in order to save Gylling, Rovio, and the other leaders. It became an obsession with him. He absolutely had to see Stalin. For a long time I rejected the idea point-blank but finally talked about it to Kuusinen.

"Impossible!" said Kuusinen. "It's just some of Yrjö's muddle-headedness. He's always been muddled about these matters—never understood politics and now understands even less."

Sirola continued this internal struggle for nearly half a year. It was shocking to follow. Almost every day this matter had to be deliberated in the office, and in the evening he often dropped in at my apartment, hoping for a chance to talk with Kuusinen. But Kuusinen avoided him, and actually Sirola could not really unburden his heart to anyone but me.

This inner struggle reached its climax one night, early in March 1936. Sirola phoned me between eleven and twelve, panic-stricken and nervous, asking me to come and see him at once.

I was already in bed and tried to resist. "What should I do there at this time of the night? Besides, the distance is long and it's difficult to get a car because the Comintern chauffeurs are asleep. Can't we take care of the matter tomorrow?"

"No, it'll be too late then!" he shouted agitatedly. "You must come at once!"

When I asked if he was sick, he replied that his condition was even worse than sickness. Of course, I went. When I arrived at his apartment I noticed at once that something unusual had happened. He was very pale and alarmed, really in the grip of terror. He was out of his mind, and I feared that he had become deranged. He sat down behind a desk and unburdened himself in a voice that rose almost to a falsetto in apprehension.

"Do you know that I am one of the biggest scoundrels that has ever walked the earth? I have deceived everybody—close friends and comrades, but most of all the Communist party, the Soviet Union, Lenin, Stalin. I have lied and pretended to everybody. My whole life's work has been dishonest from beginning to end."

From these opening sentences my mind's eye created a horrible picture of all that this man might have done. Spy? Saboteur? The introduction seemed to point to such shocking disclosures that I could not refrain from snapping: "But tell me, man alive, what you have done! Have you committed murder? Have you spied? Let's hear it!"

"No, my dear friend, what I have done is even worse. A murderer and a spy cause only temporary and local damage, but for nearly two decades I have eaten the bread of the Bolsheviks, been in their service, believed myself to be a Bolshevik, pretended to myself that I have performed honestly all the tasks entrusted to me—and yet I am not a Bolshevik . . ."

Now my worst fears were dispelled. This began to sound like the old, familiar Sirola once more—though shocking, nevertheless.

He continued his self-flagellation. "You see, I am not whole. Ever since I was a small boy, all my thinking, my whole intellectual self has been ruled by a terrible dualism that you can hardly understand . . ."

"What do you mean by that?"

"I have been split in two. In my youth I tried most sincerely to embrace socialism and now in my later years communism, as it is most honestly manifested in the communist doctrine. I have tried—and all the time my second self has whispered that this is not genuine, not as it should be, there is in it something transitory and false. Do you understand? No, you cannot understand such a thing. During the early years of the Soviet Union I already believed that I had rid myself of that dualism. The future was bright, all possibilities were open, one had only to build, but now . . . This present development has again strengthened my doubting self—it makes me believe that this is neither socialism nor communism.

"You see, my misery lies in the fact that all my life I have searched for the truth. From the moment when my brain was able to comprehend important associations, I have tried to discover what truth is. The more I have considered it, the more uncertain I have become and the more alluring seems the bourgeois view that there is no ultimate truth. Do you understand what that means? I myself have preached that the truth no longer need be sought. It has been found already: it is the Marxist-Leninist-Stalinist view of history and concept of the world. That is the criterion, the touchstone to which all life's phenomena are applied. Whoever still seeks the truth is a heretic and damages communism."

He was deadly pale and his face glistened with sweat. I began to speak but he hastened to continue:

"You have no idea how much I envy you! You've been able to accept the communist doctrine without any doubts, in all sincerity. It must be because of your proletarian background. You are not hampered by the burden of a bourgeois education. I, the product of a parsonage, must have gotten a wrong point of departure. My intellectual structure is fragmented, and I cannot become sound and whole. That is my curse and would that it were only mine!

Worse still, I have unwittingly transmitted that fracture to all my students. How can a person whose intellectual self is in tatters transmit a sound and whole idea of these important and great matters to others?"

I tried to smile. "Now that is utter nonsense!"

"Don't say that, don't say that! I could tell from the way you all looked at me. If you only knew how terribly insecure I felt when I rose to the dais to lecture. I felt that you—at least some of you—sensed that there preaches a false prophet. And I tried to make the lectures as extravagant and specious as possible, so that my great erudition would shine from them and that it would hide my inner raggedness. I was fully aware that most of the students couldn't follow, but I was more and more beset by the idea that I must deceive the wisest among you, create the impression that I mastered this entire field to its highest peaks. Thus I flaunted my knowledge and did a disservice to the cause I was supposed to teach."

He had spoken with head bowed but now he looked up and stared at me in a strangely timid manner.

"I realized that I couldn't deceive all of you. I kept an eye especially on you. I'm sure you saw through me and knew that I lied. I've always had the feeling that you despise me."

"Don't talk nonsense," I said. "On the contrary, you can believe that you're one of the few communist leaders whom I generally respect."

"It's kind of you to say so but it doesn't help. I am a criminal. My crime is greater than that of any spy. I have committed a crime against the Holy Ghost, deceived the party and the whole working class. I am breaking down under this pressure."

"Now see here," I tried to persuade him, "wouldn't it be best that you go to bed? You're tired and nervous. That's the reason for these self-accusations. They're all simply exaggeration."

"No, no! This horror is all too real. The first thing in the morning you must come with me to see Stalin . . ."

"That's impossible!"

"Or to Dimitrov in the Comintern. I must be able to make a full confession to them. I've now made it to you, my closest superior, but I must also make a confession to the leader of the Comintern or to Stalin. And while I'm confessing to being a swindler, I'll also demand that the Karelian question be examined anew as it concerns those who were arrested without cause, especially Gylling and those closest to him."

It was clear that Stalin's terror, the senseless destruction of human lives, had terrified Sirola to the core but, characteristically, he desperately tried to focus the guilt on himself, not on Stalin.

"Now it's your turn to listen," I said. "Whatever you imagine you've done, it's childish to talk of crime and villainy. You can be absolutely sure that every student of yours has received the communist doctrine from you as complete and whole as any doctrine ever can be transferred to another person. Insofar as I understand, it is not the aim of Lenin and Stalin to have the doctrine transferred literally. It is a living concept of the world that is applied to each country in accordance with its specific conditions, and it is precisely there that you have done great work: you have nationalized and localized it to our way of life so masterfully that nobody could have done it better. And as for your dualism and fragmentation, you can believe me: nobody has noticed it and even if he has, it has not meant anything except to yourself, of course, by gnawing at your nerves."

He listened eagerly, but the paleness did not disappear from his face or the agony from his eyes. I decided to use stronger medicine.

"Perhaps I'll disappoint you badly but despite all my proletarian origin I also—even though my ability to think has not been dimmed by excessive erudition and philosophizing—have not been able to accept this doctrine 100 percent. The more familiar I have become with it and especially now having seen it in practice—without your teachings—the greater my doubts about its veracity and justice have become."

"I am not saying that the communist idea is basically worthless, but here it is not what I imagined it to be. It is not the ultimate truth. One has the right to search for the truth and to expand its scope."

I noticed that he was becoming less tense.

"Let's agree not to speak any more about going to Stalin. Your confession would not give the right impression of yourself, and I am sure that, should Stalin care to listen to your story at all, he would believe that you have lost your mind."

"Perhaps you are right," he said quietly.

"But we could talk to Kuusinen."

Sirola became appalled. "Not to Kuusinen! He doesn't understand me. But something should be done. It's terrible to live under this burden."

"I realize that it is terrible, but thoughtless actions may result in even more terrible things. Just imagine what would happen if you—director of the Finnish Section in the Lenin School, member of the Control Committee of the Comintern and of the Central Committee of the Finnish Communist party—were to start making such confessions. The whole Finnish Communist party would become suspect. We could all be arrested. Already the head of the GPU in Petrozavodsk has declared publicly that 80 percent of the Finnish Communist party members are spies or other scoundrels. Your confession would let loose a herd of wild beasts. You understand that?"

"I do."

His voice was melancholy, but it was obvious that he was already over the worst. The most important thing was that he had had a chance to erupt, to confess. It did not take me long to persuade him to go to bed.

The next day we continued our conversation at the office. He felt better than he had for weeks. But a few days later the nightmare was upon him again, revealing itself in his talk. He was afraid of being arrested. Although he was ready to volunteer for prison, he was at the same time terrified by the thought that GPU men would come for him. I noticed it while talking with him, and it had been noticed more clearly by his wife, faithful friend, and helper, Milanova, who told me later that for a long time Sirola had lived in a state of fear and terror day and night, awaiting the arrival of the GPU men. It was the terror known to almost all persons in Russia who had even slightly important positions and especially to those who had had assignments in Karelia or among other minority peoples.

My night visit to Sirola took place in the early days of March. About ten days later I was told that he had become seriously ill and had been taken to the hospital at the Lenin School. I went there and learned that he had stepped onto the dais, begun his lecture on dialectical materialism and at that very moment had collapsed from a cerebral hemorrhage.

I could well imagine how, trembling internally, he had entered the lecture hall, sat down, looked at his audience, and seemed to see in the eyes of his students: you are a saboteur, you're trying to make us believe what you yourself do not believe. He must have felt such agony and terror in his heart that something burst in his brain.

I was sure that under easier circumstances he could have lived for a long time to come. After all, he was not old when he died and certainly not weak physically. He was agile and moved quickly. But not even the strongest could have survived for long his internal struggle with his own skepticism and the horror induced by terror. He died a "natural death"—one of the few notable Finnish Communists who did not die as a prisoner of the GPU—but actually even he perished under the pressure of GPU terror.

Of course, neither the Comintern leadership nor Stalin were told about Sirola's "deceit." The funeral was most impressive.

I have searched the eulogies and obituaries in vain for some mention of the testament of principles that Sirola wrote during the weeks before his death. Judging by the ceremonious introduction, it was to have been a lengthy study or a political statement. Perhaps he had intended to present his self-criticism and those terrible self-accusations, but his strength—or perhaps his courage—had failed him. Ultimately, the testament consisted only of a few handwritten pages.

Briefly, Sirola gave credit in it to Kuusinen as the founder and leader of the Finnish Communist party but noted that since he had more important international duties and was no longer young, the party leadership must be left to younger persons. He believed Poika Tuominen to have the best qualifications for the leadership of the Finnish Communist party and mentioned two other Finnish Communists in the Soviet Union as good men.

Perhaps the reason why the testament has never been published is because of these three names: the other two men died in GPU prisons. So far as I know, the testament has not been presented at the Sirola Institute in Finland, at least it cannot be seen there. They swear fealty to Sirola's name, but the documents he considered most important are kept secret and falsified. But Stalin did the same to Lenin's testament. It was published in Moscow only thirty-two years after the death of Lenin.

In the communist Sirola Institute in Finland, his life's work is explained in great detail, but an honest portrait of Sirola in the manner I have written here has never been published. When Sirola is presented as a rigid marionette or a mechanical man created in the Stalinist mold, his far-flung ideas, great erudition, and exceptional intellect are denied. He was something entirely different, in his way a Renaissance man, full of life, exuberant.

Justice is not done to his memory when almost every inaugural and commencement exercise in the communist school dedicated to him stresses the following motto: "One does not search for truth in this school. The truth has already been found. It is the Leninist-Stalinist social philosophy that is embodied in the Soviet Union, under the leadership of the great and brilliant Stalin. It is the task of this school to proclaim this truth."

Poor Sirola! A seeker after the truth cannot have a sorrier fate: at first a stereotyped "truth" and its cruel application crushes him, and then this same "truth" is bound to his memory so that he has no peace, even in his grave.

KARELIA'S AUTONOMY

CZARIST RUSSIA was generally called "the peoples' prison" inasmuch as it included scores of nationalities that had been forcibly incorporated into the empire. After seizing power, the Bolsheviks proclaimed that henceforth Russia no longer was a "peoples' prison"; now every nation was free and could decide for itself whether or not it wished to remain a part of huge Russia. It could determine its own internal and external affairs.

The self-determination of peoples had, in fact, been one of the most important cornerstones of the Bolsheviks' policy—a drastic and telling motto, particularly since a number of foreign nationalities were living under the subjugation of great powers in Europe as well as in Asia and Africa. Actually, all the major powers enslaved foreign peoples, some more, some less. Such a proclamation thus carried weight. With it the Bolsheviks, even before their acquisition of power, had gained considerable popularity, particularly among the constantly apprehensive minority peoples as well as the colonial peoples. Even members of the social classes to whom the Bolsheviks' social revolutionary policy with its dictatorship of the proletariat was anathema willingly approved of their nationality policy.

And it must be confessed that, after gaining power and for a short time thereafter, the Bolsheviks at least attempted to implement that policy. This was apparent especially in regard to Finland, for after the overthrow of the empire in the summer of 1917, the Bolsheviks were the only party to support Finland's becoming independent, should Finland desire it. They took the same stand toward Russia's other subject nations as well: Poland, Estonia, Latvia, Lithuania, and so on. To what degree this was genuine implementation of the policy is hard to say. Such tolerance may have been dictated by necessity, since at that time Russia had little possibility of forcibly preventing these countries from severing their ties with Russia.*

That tolerance did not last long, for as early as 1922, Stalin harshly subjugated Georgia, his own birthplace, which had declared its independence. Lenin, who was ill then and unable to participate fully in activities, expressed his opinion in notes sent to the Politburo: "The right of foreign nationalities to secede from the Soviet Union, a right guaranteed by the constitution, has become a piece of paper that is unable to protect Russia's non-Russians from these true Russian men, these Great Russian chauvinists who, like the typical Russian bureaucrats, are by nature cowardly and cruel."

Here again, as in so many other instances, the question remains to haunt one: what would have been the fate of the Soviet Union and the entire world if Lenin had been allowed to live longer? It is a futile question, however, because it cannot be answered. We must stick to the facts and examine what that fine sounding section of the Soviet constitution proved to be in practice. Soviet Karelia provides a graphic example. It is closest to the Finns and is one of the corners of Russia on which we have fully documented and verifiable data.

In 1920 Edvard Gylling traveled to Russia at Lenin's invitation to organize East Karelian affairs. Impartial history will undoubtedly

---

* Soon after the Bolshevik Revolution in Russia the three Baltic states proclaimed their independence. Nevertheless, the Red Army invaded each country.

give Gylling the credit he is due as a social scientist, particularly as one of the men responsible for the abolition of the greatest blunder in Finland's social structure, the crofter system. I shall not go into that earlier activity of his; suffice it to mention that he was the finance minister of the People's Commission, the "insurrectionary government," in Finland, refused to flee to Russia with his colleagues when it collapsed and hid out until he could flee to Sweden, whence he left for Moscow in the spring of 1920.

Lenin had the habit of jotting down brief memorandums on each day's most important events. For the day on which Gylling visited him to discuss the founding of the Karelian commune, there is this notation: "Today I met a university man who made an especially favorable impression. He would make a good prime minister for any country whatsoever."

Researchers have commented on those memorandums of Lenin, written articles and entire books about them. If Gylling had not fallen victim to Stalin's terror, that notation might well have inspired a small library. Now people try to forget it insofar as is possible.

Later, Gylling told me in great detail about these formative phases of his republic. It was a pity that he didn't have time to write down those recollections—though on the other hand one can be sure that they would never have seen the light of day. He considered his first meeting with Lenin to be one of the pleasantest memories of his life.

As was his wont, Lenin had gone straight to the heart of the matter: it was proposed to make Karelia an autonomous state, an area in which the Karelian people themselves could determine their fate within the framework of the Russian Socialist Republic. Since the Karelians, to his knowledge, had no one qualified and sufficiently trained to take over the formation of the state, couldn't the Finnish émigrés, of whom there were many in Russia, move to Karelia to assist the Karelians? The chief organizer would be Gylling who, according to the experts, was a skilled economist. In other words, Lenin offered Gylling the task of founding the state with the proviso that, once the formative phase was concluded, Gylling would stay on as head of the Karelian government.

Gylling had pondered the matter even before his departure from Stockholm and he, for his part, had his own explicit requirements.

He had three basic stands. The borders of the autonomous area must be drawn so that the population was predominantly Karelo-Finnish; if the Russians were in the majority it could not be a Karelian or Karelo-Finnish area. The people's own language must be the official language. The autonomous area had to be allowed to enjoy to a large degree the products of its own natural resources.

Lenin deemed these clauses to be perfectly proper, and so the men shook hands on the agreement.

Gylling then formed a revolutionary committee that convened the Pan-Karelian Convention on July 1, 1920. At this convention resolutions were adopted concerning the founding of the Karelian Commune, its structure and function, and telegrams of greeting were sent to Lenin, Kalinin, Trotsky, and Zinoviev, but not to Stalin. Stalin never forgave that, and the Soviet-Karelian leaders and the entire people paid dearly for the omission. Thus, from its very founding, the Karelian Commune became an eyesore to Stalin.

The founding of the Karelian Commune was greatly speeded by the fact that the question of East Karelia was of major concern in Finland at that time. It was important for the Soviet government to be able to tell the Finns at the upcoming Tartu (Dorpat) Peace Conference that the question of East Karelia already had been re-solved in accordance with the Karelians' wishes. Regardless of these measures, however, the question proved to be a tough nut to crack. The matter was finally settled when the Soviet delegation solemnly affirmed East Karelia's autonomy at the treaty signing ceremony on October 14. The affirmation contained three salient points:

1. Autonomy is granted specifically to the Karelian population of East Karelia.

2. The vernacular is to be the language of government, legislation, and public education.

3. The population of East Karelia has the right to organize its economic life in accordance with its own local needs.

These three points in the peace treaty that pertain to East Karelia should be borne in mind as we follow the fortunes of this corner of the world.

The border of the Karelian Commune, founded in 1920, roughly followed the Murmansk railroad from the White Sea to Lake Onega. According to the 1920 census, the population of this area was 145,753 persons, broken down as follows: Karelians 89,051 or 60.8 percent, Russians 54,742 or 37.4 percent, and others 1,960 or 1.8 percent.

During its early period this autonomous area thus was populated mainly by Karelians and was in the spirit of the Peace of Tartu in that the ethnic population, according to the population ratio, had a chance to make its voice heard and hence influence the administration of the area.

The population ratio that was consistent with the spirit and letter of the Peace of Tartu did not last long in Soviet Karelia, however. Russification of the autonomous area began almost immediately after the founding of the commune. The changing of the commune into the Karelian Autonomous Socialist Republic in 1923 had a cataclysmic effect on the population ratio.

Annexed to this new republic were almost all the areas included in East Karelia under czarist apportionment, as well as the large district of Puudozh, east of Lake Onega. The expansion added approximately sixty-five thousand new inhabitants, mainly Russians. At the same time the immigration of Russians continued at such a pace that in 1925 the population ratio in Soviet Karelia was: Karelians, Finns, and Veps, 111,861 or 41.7 percent; Russians, 152,104 or 56.7 percent; and others, 4,351 or 1.6 percent, in all 268,316 persons.

I shall have more to say about this development later. Now it is time to return to Gylling.

Of course East Karelia also had its own veteran revolutionaries who felt that they had a right to be rewarded for their efforts and get a taste of power. With the battle cry, "Karelia for the Karelians!" they immediately took a stand against Gylling, the newcomer. A dispute flared up in framing the new state's constitution when the question of the official language arose. The Karelians demanded the Karelian language. Gylling tried to familiarize himself with it quickly and came to the conclusion that it was simply a Finnish dialect; thus, the primary language of the Karelian Commune would be Finnish, the secondary one would be Russian.

The opponents fumed, "Oh, so you want the language of White Finland here in Karelia where there are hardly any Finns at all!"

Gylling immediately traveled to Moscow to present his views to

Lenin. After a comparatively brief deliberation, Lenin endorsed Gylling's stand, actually becoming enthusiastic about it. If the Karelian dialect were to become the official language, everything would have to be virtually started from scratch, whereas Finnish, which already had a flourishing literature, would be a ready foundation on which to build. He therefore ordered that Finnish be the primary language of the new state, a fact which Gylling's local opponents never forgot or forgave.

In conferring with Lenin as well as with the Soviet government's economic leaders, Gylling made explicit the relations between the Karelian Commune and its host state, the Russian Soviet Federated Socialist Republic. The original charter declared that the Karelian people could retain for their own benefit all the revenue from the natural resources within the Karelian Commune after reimbursing the host state or Federated Republic for its outlay in developing these resources. Karelia did, in fact, begin to prosper comparatively quickly—to my knowledge, faster than any other autonomous area in the Soviet Union. Sawmills rose at a rapid pace, and lumber was shipped abroad, primarily to England. Karelia got a modest share of foreign currency with which it purchased machinery and erected new industrial plants. If it had been allowed to retain for its own use even a reasonable share of the foreign currency it earned over a period of years, it could soon have developed into a prosperous state, thanks to its forests.

In other respects, too, development progressed promisingly. Schools were established in accordance with the population ratio, though the dearth of teachers was a great drawback. Karelia had no old cadre of teachers, no real intelligentsia as did Russia, where it still existed though a considerable number either had been annihilated or had fled the country. The few intellectuals in Karelia had fled to Finland during uprisings of 1919–21, hence there were hardly any teachers at all. Ordinary working men and women, who had a passable knowledge of reading if not always of writing, were assigned to schools, almost without preparation. Meanwhile two or three academies were turning out new teachers as fast as they could. The material was not of the highest quality; it had to be selected from the Red Guards who had fled there from Finland in 1918 and who had not been spoiled by too much learning. At any rate, a network of schools was established throughout Karelia within a few years, and in this respect, too, Karelia was among the best functioning, autonomous areas in the Soviet Union.

I have already mentioned visiting Gylling in Karelia after my first trip to the Caucasus. Although I knew him quite well before, I was able only now to observe him closely as both a person and an administrator. I do not hesitate to say that as each he approached the ideal, if indeed did not achieve it.

As the prime minister of the Karelian Autonomous Socialist Republic he could have had a government palace or at least a luxurious residence built for himself, but he settled into an apartment with two rooms and a kitchen. There was no police guard or militiaman at his doorstep, not even a janitor or a servant girl, though he had a fairly large family. All the citizens could come freely to speak to their prime minister at his small private quarters as well as at his office. And the citizens knew how to take advantage of that privilege.

This new ruler presented such a complete contrast in his mode of life to the bureaucratic satrap types who had governed East Karelia in czarist times that the Karelians at first had difficulty in believing him to be the head man of the state. Soon, however, they learned to accept the fact, and Gylling had many amusing and touching tales to tell of his meetings with his "subjects" during those early days. It was by no means unusual for some old woman from Aunus, who had come to the prime minister's office, to drop subserviently to her knees and crawl to him humbly to present her petition. And her amazement knew no bounds when the prime minister yanked the poor creature to her feet, sat her down in a chair beside him and explained amiably that it was neither necessary nor fitting to humble oneself before another. They would just sit there and chat as old friends do in her native village.

If Gylling had many pleasant memories of his realm's primitive inhabitants who found it hard to accustom themselves to this new lifestyle, the people had as many anecdotes and true tales about their very own czar, Eduard Aleksandrovich, as Gylling was familiarly addressed in the provinces. Thousands of persons from even the farthest outlying villages had shaken his hand and chatted with him companionably.

Gylling traveled a great deal, not only in population centers but above all in out of the way villages. I went with him on some of these inspection tours as he crossed and recrossed central and southern Soviet Karelia. He was never accompanied by a large party, much less by a security policeman or bodyguard. Mostly he traveled just with his chauffeur.

Usually he did not announce his coming in advance, but in some miraculous way the news spread even to distant country villages that Gylling was coming that way and would surely stop off to see them. And even though he himself did not know, as they left one village, exactly what side roads might be traveled, there was already a sizeable crowd awaiting him at the next village.

Once when our car stopped in the school yard at Vitele, scores of people soon clustered around, all wanting to shake the hand of the head of state and exchange a few words with him. Many of the older men and women already knew him and did not hesitate to show their familiarity. And to an amazing degree Gylling remembered the names of those Ivan Matvejeviches and Tatjana Petrovnojs and chatted with them in the Karelian dialect, which he spoke like a native.

When we spent the night at the school, people came even from faraway places, and the prime minister's reception lasted until midnight. Some had business to discuss, others said that they had heard of Eduard Aleksandrovich's arrival in the village and just wanted to say hello and wish him well. The cottage was full of people and conversation flowed easily. Many had such private business that they didn't want to discuss it in front of everyone, and so they withdrew with the prime minister to the teachers' room where it was thrashed out.

One beautiful late summer day we arrived at Rajakontu, a place that is near the shore of Lake Ladoga right on Finland's former border.* We stopped the car at the center of the village, and in a moment fifty or sixty persons had gathered around us. Mr. Prime Minister seated himself on a pile of logs beside the road, lit his pipe, and the customary reception got under way. The news that Eduard Aleksandrovich had arrived swept quickly over the countryside, and everyone who was able to put one foot in front of the other, men and women, oldsters and children, gathered around the pile

* This refers to the Finnish-Soviet border that existed until 1939 when the Soviet Union attacked Finland and took the southeastern part of the country.

of logs where the locality's problems, both big and small, were being resolved. The occasion at times was reminiscent of an old-time town meeting, with scores of people talking at once; at other times it quieted down to become a unique reception for a head of state, with one supplicant after another softly reciting his own personal troubles while the others withdrew slightly. Everything happened naturally without rush or fuss.

Lest the wrong impression be conveyed, let me state that such receptions atop log piles or in yards were not primarily the result of Karelia's primitive conditions. Even then Soviet Karelians knew how to, and did when required, arrange official, formal receptions and inspection tours for government leaders in high style, and many officials and government leaders did require it. But Eduard Aleksandrovich definitely had his own style that suited just him but not many others. And it was precisely that lifestyle, that open and unaffected attitude that made him as democratic and beloved as he was.

At these receptions I served as a sort of prime minister's secretary, at Gylling's request writing down people's complaints and wishes so that he might deal with them upon his return to Petrozavodsk. In this secretary's role I could see near at hand what an admirably close and trusting relationship the people really had with their prime minister. Advice was sought from him on the most delicate family matters, from a spouse's infidelity to the rearing of a disobedient child. Complaints dared be made to him about the highest local officials, the chairmen of the district, and village councils and the GPU chiefs. Such complaints could be made only to a person who was trusted implicitly not to make the complainants subject to the village bigwigs' revenge or to other unpleasantness.

Gylling knew how to handle all the people's problems with the utmost sympathy and tact. He tried to help and console each person, and his consolation was more than just pretty phrases, it was also deeds. Often he heard complaints and wishes that he had to reject outright or to postpone. As sympathetic and good-natured as Gylling was, he nevertheless did not make the mistake of promising something that he could not fulfill, or that was somehow in conflict with the views or line of the Soviet government or the Communist party. But he could give even a negative answer in such a way that the complainant was left with the impression that he was an absolutely honest and just person who would surely help if it were possible.

Gylling was a peculiar bird in the Stalinist Soviet world of that day. In the midst of an ever-tightening dictatorship and a concomitantly growing bureaucracy, he showed how freely an exceptional person could act even under those conditions, and how far democratic methods could be applied. But he was already doomed to destruction.

An account of the Karelian Republic would be incomplete unless some mention were made of Kustaa Rovio, the secretary general of the party in Karelia. His name is associated with the republic during its last five years as closely as that of Gylling, and his fate was equally tragic. Moreover, as a person he was in Gylling's class, an honest, high-principled man completely lacking in ostentation and arrogance.

Kustaa Rovio deserves mention if only because the typical communist historiography overlooks him completely, though he was one of the few Finns who can be said to have had a close relationship with Lenin. I have already mentioned how effortlessly, through his intercession, we got to talk to Lenin.

Originally Rovio was a metalworker. In his younger days he worked for a long time in the metal workshops of Petrograd. He learned Russian and joined the Bolsheviks early. When he returned to Finland early in 1917, his knowledge of Russian and his other attributes led to his being named chief of the Helsinki militia—in other words, the police chief—following the March revolution.

In July of that year Lenin had to flee Petrograd, at first to the Karelian Isthmus and then to Helsinki. Naturally he was lodged in the safest possible places, among them the residence of the militia chief. When that became dangerous, he was placed with a family named Blomqvist, where Rovio kept him supplied with provisions for body and soul. In these hiding places Lenin feverishly made preparations for the Bolshevik Revolution that was instituted on November 7. During this period the lodger and the host became such good friends that the close relationship lasted throughout their lives.

Lenin was one of those persons who never forget their friends and benefactors. After he had assumed power he would often invite Rovio over for a talk, and when they were finished he would take out a toy from his desk drawer for Rovio's little boy, Eero. It is astonishing to think that the man who had an enormous burden to bear during those chaotic times would remember some Finnish friend of his and even go to the trouble of buying toys for his child.

Lenin's collected works include one of his statements about Kustaa Rovio. In a letter sent to an Old Bolshevik, he commended Rovio highly as an exceptional person and in every way a dependable revolutionary. Lenin added a bit humorously, however, that he was somewhat slow and perhaps even a little lazy, and needed occasional prodding.

When this statement was published in the early 1930s, Rovio had already functioned for some time as the secretary general of the Soviet Karelian Communist party. In traveling with him through that region during the years 1933–35, I noticed in what high regard Rovio was held by even the Russian workers and Soviet officials. The mere fact that he had been a personal acquaintance and good friend of the great Lenin set him apart as a kind of superman. At every meeting questions would be asked about Lenin, and Rovio would be pressed to explain why Lenin had called him slow and lazy. Rovio admitted freely that he was a bit sluggish by nature and surmised that the charge of laziness resulted from the fact that he had not always succeeded in filling Lenin's requests to the letter.

Lenin always followed the newspapers closely, especially so while living at Rovio's home, when the situation in Russia changed from hour to hour, and he asked Rovio to obtain all the Petrograd papers as soon as they arrived at the Helsinki station. A few times Rovio was so busy discharging his official duties that he did not have time to attend to the matter immediately, and the papers, for which there was a great demand in Helsinki, were sold out. Lenin was a little annoyed, but it did not affect their relationship, as the aforementioned statement indicates.

Kustaa Rovio assuredly was not an exceptional person and dependable revolutionary only in Lenin's book. I believe that everyone who had anything to do with him would give the same evaluation. Between the years 1918–1937 he held many important positions of trust in the Soviet Union and always earned the admiration of his colleagues and subordinates. As the secretary general of the party organization in Soviet Karelia he, along with Gylling, was the state's most powerful and influential man. But on the many journeys that I made with him I observed that he did not use his power bureaucratically but exactly as Gylling did: every worker and collective farmer came to him as to an old friend to complain about his problems and to seek help against the bureaucratic district and village officials who oppressed and terrorized them.

Always they appealed to him, "You, who were the friend of Vladimir Iljich know well that he would not have condoned the oppression practiced by our village officials."

Rovio did know it and did his best until the tidal wave of tyranny swept him away, too.

THE TRAGEDY OF KARELIA

THE GOOD TIMES did not last long. As soon as Lenin's hand had fallen from the rudder of Soviet power in January 1924, many obstacles began to appear in the way of Gylling's constructive work. The higher echelons invented one extortionary trick after another. Stalin had not yet fully secured his dictatorship, but the influence of his economic, language, and nationality policies began to be felt immediately after Lenin's death, particularly in Karelia.

The immigration of Russians continued—and it must be remembered that in the Soviet Union even in those days, much less later, one did not move except on government orders. Gylling and his aides saw what the russification policy would lead to and courageously opposed it, even publicly. The following excerpt from the April 11, 1929 editorial in *Punainen Karjala* (Red Karelia), the official voice of the Soviet Karelian party organs and the government, clarifies the situation bluntly:

Later, the former districts of Poventsa and Puutos also were annexed to the autonomous area along with numerous villages and counties on the shore of the White Sea and in the south, bringing in 8,500 Veps, among others. Through this annexation and the immigration, which has added over 4,000 inhabitants yearly (mainly Russians), the nationality ratio of our republic's population has changed so that, according to the latest census (1926), instead of a Karelo-Finnish population of 61.4 percent, there is now only 38.3 percent, with Russians composing 57.1 percent and others 1.4 percent. It is obvious that this great change in the population ratio cannot help but be reflected unfavorably in practical matters . . . Hence, difficulties in strengthening and further developing the Karelians' autonomy have only increased. Consequently, there is reason to consider shifting certain areas temporarily annexed to the autonomous area back to the Soviet Union's other districts.

Gylling was thus an unusual ruler in that he was opposed to territorial gain for his state. The struggle was hopeless, however. Stalin, the "representative of Great Russian nationalism," pursued his policies and by 1932 the Karelo-Finnish population had dropped to 33 percent.

As a natural result of the annexation of Russian-speaking areas and the influx of Russians, what had been planned as a Karelo-Finnish state changed fundamentally into a predominantly Russian state, and the language of the majority became its dominant language. Thus the most important premise of this national area, the nationality clause, had been disturbed if not destroyed.

The third important point, the economic clause, was gradually made meaningless. Even initially the agreement between the Karelian Commune and the Russian Soviet Republic could not be said to have favored the former, since it left for the autonomous government's own use only 25 percent of the Karelian-manufactured exports that it could trade for goods from abroad, though the original agreement in principle specified that all the natural resources within the area belonged to the Karelian people. But even this amount, in the hands of men with initiative and organizational skills, would have guaranteed a prosperous future. Year after year it was reduced, however, as Karelia became the object of systematic exploitation. Already by 1930 Russia—in other words, the Moscow government—was using all the foreign currency obtained for the timber exported from Karelian areas.

As compensation Karelia received grain from other Soviet areas—insofar as it did receive it—and occasionally machinery as well, old tractors and trucks that only retarded its logging operations and industry. The tempo of the early years slackened steadily and by the beginning of the 1930s Karelia was sinking to the level of the other Soviet republics.

At the same time the russification of the school system and the entire cultural life got under way. In its early stage that, too, was tentative but the grip tightened until it became unscrupulous, violent chauvinism.

Gylling's immediate superior in Leningrad since 1927 had been Zinoviev. He was replaced by Kirov, whom the older generation of Soviet Karelians—if any still remain—remembers warmly. True, he carried out Moscow's policy of steady economic and national repression, but he was an unfanatical, reasonable man: he did not identify himself with his official duties as does the typical satrap. Furthermore, he was personally irreproachable and probably the last upright man among the power wielders in Stalin's era. Presumably this rectitude did not please Stalin, and so Kirov had to depart the land of the living. He was murdered in December 1934 under circumstances that indicated that Stalin had something to do with the event.

In his famous speech Khrushchev commented on Kirov's murder as follows:

It is worth noting that to this day there are many inexplicable and mysterious aspects of the circumstances surrounding Kirov's murder that require the most careful examination. There is reason to suspect that Kirov's murderer, Nikolajev, was aided by one of the persons responsible for safeguarding Kirov.

Following Kirov's murder, the highest officials of the Leningrad NKVD received very light sentences, but in 1937 they were shot. We may assume that they were shot to conceal the trail of Kirov's murderers. (*Agitation in the hall.*)

The aforementioned older generation of Soviet Karelians remembers Kirov as a man who was ready to spend the night in any old shack if a bear hunt was in the offing and considered him an unusually sensible man. Once Russian "architects" in Soviet Karelia put before Kirov charges of sabotage against the Finns for building complicated ovens with winding flues instead of flues leading directly to the roof in the Russian manner. Kirov immediately comprehended the explanation that it didn't pay to heat the outdoors and told the Russians to make an example of the Finns' ovens.

Kirov's murder was a landmark in Soviet Karelian history. He was replaced by Zhdanov, a man with many predecessors in the annals of unscrupulous Great Russianism. Kirov moderated Stalin's orders; Zhdanov intensified them. He was thus the right man to carry out Stalin's policy of destroying national states.

The attack against national states was launched on a broad front in 1935. *Pravda* and *Izvestiia* published long articles alleging that nationalism was rife and demanding that an end be put to it. A great campaign got under way in Karelia, and the Karelians were accused of Finnish nationalism. Zhdanov sent his henchmen Tshutov and Irglis to carry out the purge.

It was difficult to attack the leadership of the republic from an ideological viewpoint. The editor-in-chief of *Punainen Karjala* (Red Karelia) was Otto Vilmi, former editor of the Finnish paper *Työmies* (Worker), an experienced orthodox Communist who vigilantly kept his paper free of sideslips and deviations from the party line. The younger editors, among whom were Kalle Vento and Gylling's son-in-law Toivo Rantala, for the most part were products of the University of National Minorities of the West and, hence, well versed in the Marxist-Leninist-Stalinist doctrinal structure. The director of the state publishing house, *Kirja* (Book), Teemu Törmälä, and the assistant director, Simo Susi, who had been awarded the Order of the Red Flag, had adhered strictly to the correct lines. Lauri Letonmäki, the editor of the political works, checked with both German and Russian sources to make certain that nothing heretical slipped into the books.

When the ideological approach proved fruitless, something else was devised. A summer festival involving almost all Karelia had been arranged at the Kontupohja factory area for June 24, which happened to be a day off in the five-day workweek then prevailing. In the Karelian and Russian manner all kinds of decorations were used, mostly red but other colors as well. The festival was a great success; people by the thousands arrived from various parts of the land and spirits were high.

A few weeks later Gylling and Rovio received a harshly worded report from the GPU headquarters in Moscow stating that long-dormant nationalism had manifested itself in an unprecedentedly flagrant form in Karelia. Finnish nationalists, it stated, had deliberately staged a summer festival on Finland's Flag Day, June 24, when celebrations were taking place beyond the border in White Finland. Nor did that suffice. Blue-white flags had been flying, and, to top it all, Rovio, the head man of the party organization in Karelia, had been a speaker at the festival, but not even he had noticed anything improper in this fascist blasphemy.

This naturally came as a shocking charge to the Karelian Communist party, which immediately undertook a thorough investigation. The organizers of the festival, and at least ten reputable Communists who had participated in it, declared that they had seen no blue-white flags either small or large but only the commonly used pennants; not a word had been mentioned about Finland's Flag Day anywhere in the program. What had been said about Finland was sharply critical. Furthermore, the organizers swore that they had not even been aware of Finland's Flag Day, which was news to them. They had simply remembered that it was cutomary to celebrate an old national festival, Midsummer's Day, near the end of June.

When these explanations were forwarded to Moscow, the rejoinder was that no other evidence of treachery in Karelia was needed than such a denial of obvious facts; Russian and Karelian witnesses had seen blue-white flags at the festival with their own eyes.

The results were soon apparent. Suddenly, without warning, Rovio was ousted from his post as party secretary that summer of 1935 and exiled from Karelia. He was allowed to live in the Moscow area and was even given a nominal job temporarily. Succeeding him as party secretary was the aforementioned Latvian-born Irglis, second secretary of the party in the Leningrad area. Gylling's turn came in November. He was exiled to Moscow, which he was not permitted to leave, and was given a poorly paid job at the Institute of World Economy, which was headed by Stalin's expert on economic policies, Professor Varga. Gylling was replaced by the Tver-Karelian, Busujev.

The consequences were immediately felt everywhere. Envy and rancor erupted in the lower echelons. Russian teachers mistreated Finnish pupils and snapped, "Now go and whine about this to your Gylling." Petty bureaucrats did whatever was in their power to do. The misfortune of Nikolski, secretary of the Petrozavodsk city council, was that he had been born the son of an Aunus pastor. This lamentable fact prompted him to grovel before his superiors and to use every opportunity to indicate that this one and that one were enemies of the people. These he hastened to deprive of their party membership card. One such victim was Lauri Letonmäki, minister of justice in Finland's 1918 revolutionary government.

This action by no means signified imprisonment, and Letonmäki's valiant wife consoled her husband with the prediction, "Your party card will yet be contested in the Central Committee and perhaps even at the party Congress!"

But Letonmäki felt that he had been "disarmed" and collapsed utterly. A year earlier he had watched from his window the funeral procession of an officer who had committed suicide and had muttered, "A Marxist-Leninist Bolshevik would never do that."

"Do what?" his wife had asked.

"Commit suicide," Letonmäki had replied. And now, after being stripped of his membership card, Letonmäki killed himself. His Marxist-Leninist world had caved in.

Numerous arrests were made, but many of those imprisoned were released because the charges proved to be flimsy. Then new grounds for arrest were contrived.

In 1931 O. W. Kuusinen had thought that something should be done to enlighten the Finnish Communists living primarily in Karelia and the Leningrad area, the majority of whom did not know Russian though they were members of the Soviet Union's Communist party. Because their unfamiliarity with the language prevented these Finns from participating in Russian-language party activities, they remained unenlightened and ignorant of developments.

For this reason Kuusinen thought that these individuals might be gathered into special Finnish groups for which lectures would be held, educational activities conducted, and where rubles could be collected for the Finnish Communist party. He broached the idea to Gylling and together they went to see the prime minister at that time, Molotov. Molotov replied that he would have to discuss the matter with Stalin since it concerned the party and asked them to return the following day. Gylling went the next day, when Molotov announced that Stalin approved the plan and considered it a good one.

It was formalized with a written resolution, and on the basis of it the Finnish Communist party empowered Otto Vilmi, who was one of the party's founders and a long-time member of its Central Committee, to begin founding working groups in various localities cooperatively with the Karelian Communist party organization. These so-called Finnish support groups functioned energetically and were highly commended for their work by both the Karelian government and the Soviet authorities.

In the first half of 1936 Vilmi was arrested. He had sat in a GPU prison for six months without confessing to the charge that he was a nationalist, when a certain high GPU chief explained that the best proof of guilt was precisely his refusal to confess, since Lenin and Stalin had said that one was not a true Bolshevik unless one was self-critical and practiced self-criticism.

Vilmi replied that he understood that, and that all the old former Social Democrats who had left Finland had Finnish nationalism and social democratic leavening as a kind of subconscious heritage that could never be wholly shaken off, because it clung like the biblical original sin. About that matter he was certainly ready to be self-critical.

"I'm glad that you're finally confessing," said the chief and had the record drawn up.

Although Vilmi had lived in the Soviet Union since 1918, his knowledge of Russian was not worth mentioning. He demanded to know what had been entered in the record but was not told. A few weeks later the college of the GPU held a trial that was conducted in Russian. Vilmi demanded to have an interpreter or an assistant but the request was denied. Instead, the record, which ran to some twenty pages, was read. In it Vilmi purportedly related a horrible history of crime. According to the record he—following instructions from Gylling and Rovio as well as those from Finland—had founded a support network throughout Karelia, the purpose of which was to fan Finnish nationalism. Vilmi realized that something terrible was afoot, denied having said anything like that and again demanded an interpreter in order to find out what was in the record. But his request was refused. Instead, three GPU men attested to his having said everything entered in the record.

On that occasion Vilmi received only six years, since his "confession" did a great service to the GPU: the entire Karelian government had been compromised, for Gylling and Rovio were part of the same criminal conspiracy. The "confession," particularly after it had been affirmed in the high court, became a general bill of indictment on the basis of which almost all the Finns could be arrested as members of covert, illegal nationalist groups directed from Finland.

From his forced labor camp on the central Volga, Vilmi managed to send Kuusinen a letter that the latter, as was his custom, thrust to me without reading. In his letter Vilmi described his hearing and sentence. I mentioned it to Gylling who, resigned to his fate, was living with his wife in an attic room of an old run-down hotel in wretched circumstances. He was shocked. In Vilmi's case he saw a precedent according to which he and all the other Finns who had functioned in Karelia had been "proven" to be enemies of the people; he saw in it his own death sentence. Hence he summoned up his courage and decided to go to Molotov to explain the actual state of affairs. He was sure that Molotov, who remembered the founding of the support groups, would negate the schemes of the GPU men as well as the court's prejudgment.

Access to Molotov for a leader fallen from the hierarchy was not easy, however, despite their long acquaintance and the fact that they had met scores of times as prime ministers. Nevertheless, after many appeals and invocations of their old friendship, Gylling finally succeeded in obtaining an audience with him.

According to Gylling, Molotov behaved with cold formality from the start. After hearing about the GPU's unique plan for annihilating Finns and Gylling's invocation of their conversation of 1931, Molotov became irritated and said that he did not remember such a conversation at all. When Gylling pointed out that the archives of the Soviet Karelian district committee contained the document signed by Molotov himself as well as by Stalin that authorized the Karelian district committee and the Central Committee of the Finnish Communist party jointly to form among Finns the very support groups now being charged by the GPU with being covert and fascistic, Molotov became even more exasperated and declared flatly that such a conversation could not have taken place and that such a document could not exist.

"Neither I nor Comrade Stalin could have agreed to such a plan. And I don't have any more time now to argue about it."

With that the audience had concluded. Upon his return Gylling was completely shattered. He said that he would never have believed Molotov capable of repudiating a promise and a signature—least of all to him, an old friend and colleague. He could have understood Molotov's declaring that the Finnish groups had become something other than what he and Stalin had envisaged and hence the reason they had to be liquidated, but it was impossible to believe that the man would unequivocally deny any knowledge of the agreement. In whom could one trust, if not in Stalin's and Molotov's word and signature?

All of us Finns were shocked to the very core by the GPU's unprecedented provocation. Everyone who had belonged to such a support group counted the hours and the moments until the bells would toll for him. Most of them did not have to wait very many weeks. If the premonitions of Gylling and the rest of us had been ominous, reality was to prove even more horrifying.

Party secretary Irglis had done his best to weed out nationalism in Karelia. Arrests occurred throughout 1936, and the activity was stepped up in the spring of 1937 after Zhdanov had held a closed meeting of party activists at which he had attacked the Finns. Every issue of *Punainen Karjala* began denouncing leading personalities at various establishments. The Finns lived in subconscious trepidation until, in the early hours of July 25, evil was let loose. At that time Irglis himself was arrested as a spy, for during his tenure Finnish nationalism had only grown stronger in Karelia. That same night Gylling and his wife, as well as Rovio, were arrested in Moscow. In Karelia almost all the members of the district committee and the Karelian government were arrested regardless of whether they were Finns, Karelians, or Russians.

Not a single even slightly known Finn or Karelian remained in the government or the party leadership. All the posts were manned by Russians. The party secretaryship was assumed by the infamous Kuprianov, who raged in his inaugural address, "I won't sleep peacefully a single night until the last Finn has been banished from Petrozavodsk."

Thus began the "great hate," as the Finns called the succeeding period.

Public trials in the Moscow style, at which the accused confessed to being wreckers, spies, and dirty dogs, were not staged with the Finns. One such attempt sufficed to show the authorities that it was not easy to bend Finns to such a mockery of justice.

The GPU had prepared a confession for attribution to Urho Usenius, finance minister of the Karelian government, a confession wherein Usenius related the various subversive activities in which he had engaged while in his positions of trust, all with Gylling's cooperation. During the first half of 1937 the Leningrad GPU tribunal convened to conduct legal proceedings, and the occasion was public in that the Finnish communist leaders still at large were summoned to attend it, and the newspapers were assigned the task of reporting how a member of the Karelian government confessed to having done his subversive deeds. Usenius was then brought before the audience of perhaps a score of us, and the chairman of the court read the record that the GPU men had set down during the six-month detention of the accused and in which he was said to have admitted to certain activities. In other words, approximately the same kind of record as Vilmi's.

Usenius, who understood Russian well, listened to the reading calmly and then remarked, "That whole tale, from beginning to end, is nothing but lies and utter nonsense and a fabrication by the GPU. I haven't said anything like that."

The trial ended then and there, and we listeners were herded out. Usenius was sentenced to eight years, a sentence that was increased at subsequent sessions—though that of course was immaterial since the upshot was always the same.

Hundreds of pages could be related about the fate of even rather well-known Finns who became victims of the Stalinist great hate. All kinds of pretexts served as evidence for indictment. Communist members of the Finnish Parliament, who in the early 1930s had been forcibly taken to the Soviet border by the Lapua movement's violent wing and from there sent across the border, were liquidated one after the other. Because the state police had participated in the removal of some of them, they were held to be agents of the police. It was virtually impossible to do anything without having the GPU see villainy and sabotage in it. As examples of the pretexts used to indict and sentence these former members of Parliament, I shall cite a few cases of scores.

Former Finnish Parliament member Kyhälä, who had had a farm in Finland, had been given a state-owned farm, or sovkhoz, to manage. Because everything in the Soviet Union happens according to plan, the order had come to do the sowing at such and such a time. Since the region was still in the grip of winter, Kyhälä reported that the sowing could not be done until the frost was out of the ground. To be on the safe side, he asked Gylling about it and was told to disregard the order and to use his common sense. Then the Russians displaced Kyhälä and sent in a politruk who started the sowing at the designated time. About seventy-five acres were planted with seed, and the result was total ruin.

Kyhälä was then charged with subversive sowing. He testified that he had resisted it, but the GPU replied, "We know that you resisted it, but you should have prevented it." Kyhälä declared that he had appealed to Gylling but was told that he should have appealed to the Kremlin and to Stalin. He was stripped of his membership card, ousted from the party, arrested and exiled as a subversive.

Another former member of the Finnish Parliament, J. Perälä, was arrested for allegedly having been a kulak in Finland because he had owned six or seven cows and two horses and had engaged in horse trading. His relatives appealed to me and to the Central Committee of the Finnish Communist party. We reported to the GPU that in Finland a two-horse farm was not a kulak estate and that Perälä had not been a horse trader but merely had occasionally traded one horse for another; to no avail. He was a kulak and was exiled. Perälä's wife and smaller children were among the few families who, to my knowledge, succeeded in getting back to Finland.

The Hiilisuo case also is an example of GPU logic. Hiilisuo, or Soviet Farm Number 2, was a model farm under the special patronage of Gylling and was known even outside Karelia. One of its prides was its herd of 100 head of cattle. A certain old Finnish-born bachelor after toiling for forty years in American mines and accumulating a tidy sum, had gone with others to the Soviet Union. It was he who had purchased the herd in Finland with his own money and was now acting as stableman and manure shoveler. By some mistake the cattle were given arsenic instead of dicalcium phosphate in their feed, and every last head died. All the top men at the farm were arrested—in the final liquidation the cattle purchaser and manure shoveler as well. If he managed to remain alive in some exile camp he had a chance to ponder the forty years that he had sweated in mines and the reward that they had brought him.

Because of my position and the appeals made to me I had occasion to follow many other cases, of which these are typical:

Erkki Viitanen, well known in the Finnish city of Oulu as a party and co-op man and also a skilled machinist, moved to Russia in 1935 and served as tender of a power plant in Petrozavodsk. This plant was incredibly wretched; Petrozavodsk had been dark for weeks at a time. Viitanen managed to get it into a passable condition, however, and was given citations for this.

During the period of the great hate the generator once again broke down, and though the problem was not serious, Viitanen was arrested and charged with having destroyed it on orders from Finland. His wife came to Moscow to see me and appeal for help. We gave the Moscow and Leningrad GPU all possible guarantees for the man but were told that they had quite enough guarantees of Viitanen's guilt: only some guard's flash of genius had prevented the complete destruction of the power plant. The problem was so minor that it was repaired within a few hours, but Viitanen had been labeled a subversive, and he was exiled along with his wife.

Among the most noted of the Comintern's flying agents was Niilo Virtanen, who had served as party worker in Norway, Sweden, Denmark, Germany, and the United States. He spoke several languages very well and was familiar with the Comintern operations; hence he was sent to Germany after Hitler's coup and functioned successfully there for half a year until he was seized and sentenced to a year in prison.

After his release he, as a Finn by birth, was sent to Finland, where police took him into custody. Virtanen announced that he was a citizen of the Soviet Union, the Soviet officials confirmed it and demanded his extradition. He was sent to Moscow in the midst of the great purges. The GPU began charging Virtanen with being an agent of the Finnish police. The basis for this suspicion was the fact that he had gotten out of Finland alive. He had been Kuusinen's adjutant in Germany as well as the Scandinavian countries, and we protested that he simply could not be a stooge of the police. At his hearings Virtanen had happened to mention that he had been visited in Finland by an old university pal, social democratic editor Kalle Manninen. The conclusion was obvious: Virtanen was a most dangerous spy. He got five or six years and was not seen again.

I heard about the Tsheljabinsk case already in Russia, but not until the winter of 1941–42 in Finland did I meet the sole survivors, two women, and from them I received eyewitness corroboration.

Tsheljabinsk, in the southeastern part of the Urals, had a large tractor factory employing many Finnish Americans and people from Finland. One day in the summer of 1937, the Finns were told that all adults had to convene in a certain assembly hall. Although they suspected something unpleasant, they could not guess what awaited them. Even if someone had guessed, he could not have remained away. When all had assembled—some three hundred persons—GPU men surrounded the building and arrested everyone. The two women, who had United States passports, managed after many months to contact the American consulate and were able to leave the country. They had inquired about their husbands through both Finnish and United States officials but had heard nothing, any more than they had heard about their children, of whom one woman had two, the other one. Of the three hundred persons only these two women remained. All the families were scattered to the winds. Similar tales could be told by the score, and they would be but a fraction of the tragedies suffered by Finns.

Earlier I have alluded to the fact that, in gradually changing the Soviet Karelian population into one that was predominantly Russian, attempts were also made at linguistic russification. When Gylling was in power these efforts met with little success; in fact, one could say that the Finnish language was being fostered with greater care than before. Heino Rautio, who had been an elementary school teacher in Finland, and who served as director of linguistics at the publishing house, Book, during the years 1930–35, published a volume, *On Behalf of Pure Finnish*, in 1934. After Gylling's fall he was soon arrested and the book confiscated. He tried to vindicate himself by asserting that he had written the work at the urging and inspiration of O. W. Kuusinen, but in vain. Rautio was done for.

During the Irglis era the Finnish language was subjected to another kind of purification. For example, the Finnish name of the Soviet Union—*Neuvostoliitto*—was considered downright treasonable; the name *Sovettiliitto* had to be used. Naturally, all other Soviet terminologies likewise had to be restored to the correct line. But the deathblow came in the spring of 1937, when the first great wave of arrests was carried out. Finnish was declared conclusively to be a counterrevolutionary language of bourgeois nationalists that could not be used anywhere. All the Finnish-language newspapers—of which there were more than ten at the beginning of 1937—were suppressed; the printing presses were changed into Russian, as were the schools; not a word of Finnish could be spoken on the radio; theaters were closed and actors arrested; most of the schoolbooks were burned and the teachers naturally were arrested. The Book publishing house was closed and most of its stock destroyed.

The GPU published a list of banned books daily, and people disposed of their own accordingly. All of Marxism's hallowed books had to be destroyed, in particular *Das Kapital,* because it had a short foreword by Gylling and because the translator, named Kangas, had falsified it. All the works on whose editorial boards Bukharin or one of his kindred spirits had sat were absolutely banned, as were Finnish literary works—the sole exception being, if I remember correctly, the Finnish national epic, *Kalevala.* Works of pure science, of which there was a dearth in Russia, were spared.

Thus Stalin drew a thick black line over Lenin's resolution pertaining to the Finnish language. At the same time he drew the last line through the East Karelia clause in the Peace of Tartu and betrayed the entire nationalism policy of the Bolshevik party.

One of the great psychological puzzles is why people without any sense of shame suddenly become very qualmish about some trifle. People by the thousands were tortured, annihilated, and crammed into concentration camps without so much as a dog's bark of disapproval. Some Finnish and Scandinavian papers published a few articles, but the so-called great civilized nations feigned ignorance. Nothing prevented Stalin's rampaging exactly as he wished, and yet he chose to explain his conduct regarding a comparatively minor matter: Karelia certainly was not about to be russified despite the stifling of the Finnish language. No, now the Karelian people would have their own language, free of bourgeois nationalistic Finnish.

The University of Leningrad had on its staff a certain Professor Bubrikh, said to be some kind of philologist. Stalin gave him the shock assignment of creating a Karelian language within six months. With Stakhanovite zeal Bubrikh completed his task ahead of the target date by throwing together a language—surely the most extraordinary achievement since the days of Babel. In it 40 percent were words of Russian derivation in the Aunus dialect, the remainder were pure Russian. All the words had Russian suffixes, and the language was written in Russian characters. It was used in the publication of certain textbooks and a few issues of *Punainen Karjala* but even those with a command of Russian had difficulty in making sense of it.

After this language had been officially adopted in 1937, I brought up the subject in talking confidentially with a Karelian-born teacher, remarking that now they had their own language.

He glanced around, then said in a lowered voice, "Well, yes, a language of our own we have but hardly anything do I understand."

At that time no one dared speak Finnish in public. The Karelian language was Finnish; hence it, too, was banned. One had to speak either Russian or Bubrikh, and since no one knew the latter, people automatically slid into Russian. Thus schools could function only in Russian, books were published only in Russian, and theaters and radio operated only in Russian. In this way the russification of a purportedly independent autonomous republic became reality.

The destruction was complete. Stalin had annihilated the Karelian army already at an early stage. Karelia, you see, had its own national army whose supreme commander was the Finnish-born General Mattsson. He was banished from Karelia shortly before the downfall of Gylling and Rovio. In 1936 the Aunus battalion was assailed on the basis of its Finnish support groups. The Red commanders had their own support groups within the army, and the GPU asserted that they were in direct contact with the Academic Karelia Society in Finland and the Finnish general staff, and that they openly received the magazine *Hakkapeliitta,* published by the Home Guard of Finland. Evidence of this was the fact that several copies of *Hakkapeliitta,* to which the officers had lawfully subscribed from Finland, had been found in the support groups. According to GPU charges, they had also planned to adopt their own Red Karelia emblem, a likeness of a bear similar to the emblem of the Isänmaallinen Kansanliike (Patriotic People's movement), a right-wing party in Finland. They had their own flag and own coat of arms just like those of the Lapua movement, its predecessor.*

These officers, who were faithful Communists if anyone was, were labeled agents in the pay of the Finnish general staff. They were arrested, a large part of them were shot, and the rest were sentenced to long imprisonment or exile. Only those Finnish Red commanders—a score or so—who earlier had transferred to Russian units, saved their lives and freedom. When the Aunus battalion thus had been disposed of, Mattson himself was attacked. He was arrested in Moscow and charged with being the father of all the plans, flags, and coats of arms. He had attempted to instill in the Karelian brigade not only the spirit of Finnish nationalism but outright Prussianism, and the Karelian brigade was, in fact, a 100 percent Prussian unit.

The fate of Karelian authors forms its own sad chapter, which is personified by Jalmari Virtanen, proclaimed the Karelian national author. He was an Old Bolshevik favored by Gorky, though he was by no means a shining light. He had been stripped of his membership card at the same time as Letonmäki, but Irglis had rehabilitated him, saying, "One must exalt as well as beat down." He was celebrated, and a special author's residence was built for him. In 1937 he was arrested and proclaimed a subversive, and his works were destroyed.

In following this senseless frenzy one can no longer feel amazement at the purging of a large Karelian village that left only a

* The Lapua movement began in 1930 as a grass roots anticommunist movement but developed into a right-wing political party with strong totalitarian tendencies.

sixty-year old man and a sixteen-year old youth, or at the desecration of the grave of the long-deceased president, Santeri Nuorteva, but one can be astonished that someone can comprehend this senselessness. There actually was such a person in Russia.

Iida Alajääski was known as a gutsy communist woman, and when her family was imprisoned in Kasan, she traveled to Moscow in an attempt to see Stalin but failed. Kuusinen also barricaded himself carefully behind his bulwark, but Iida did manage to meet Dimitrov and to unburden herself by declaring that the Soviet GPU was more ruthless than the German Gestapo.

"How dare you say things like that in the Soviet Union about the Soviet government!" roared Dimitrov and had Iida thrown out.

She then met the Finnish communist, Mauritz Rosenberg, and lamented the fate of her family and other Finns to him.

But Mauritz said consolingly, "Within each of us is a residue of capitalism sufficient to justify ten years in prison."

Kuusinen once observed that Mauritz Rosenberg would never understand Marxism, but that he knew Stalinism inside and out.

The rest of us will not understand it during one lifetime. When I think of the Terijoki government, into which also the half-dead Rosenberg was forced to drag himself, when I think of its virtual total incompetence, I am filled with horror. Offhand I could enumerate enough names for four or five competent governments that could have been formed of Finns in the Soviet Union in 1935 and even in 1937. But no longer in 1939, so thoroughly had Stalin purged the Finnish Communists in the late 1930s.

Distance enables a person to look calmly at many things, even the most senseless. But can one think calmly about an intelligentsia that was almost completely annihilated—that group of some twenty thousand Finns who formed the mental and industrial backbone of the Karelian Republic and who, for the most part, were destroyed? Or about the Karelian Republic itself that, despite sworn promises, was mutilated and transformed into a Russian state, or the numerous small republics on the fringes of Russia that experienced the same fate? The Ukraine was spared only because—so said Khrushchev in his speech about Stalin's despotism—there was no place in which so large a population could have been accommodated.

DEPARTURE AND RECKONING

Undoubtedly a number of questions have arisen in the mind of the reader who has borne with me all the way to these final pages. I would assume that two of them quite naturally are the following, to which I shall attempt to reply here.

In the first place:

When one thinks of Stalin's empire as it has been described in the foregoing chapters, with conditions wherein life was not any more secure for a leader than for a rank-and-filer, how was it possible that you survived?

The second natural question is:

Inasmuch as your reports make clear that at least some persons sought to save themselves by accusing their comrades, what part did you have in the annihilation of your comrades?

TO THE FIRST question one could reply that, even in the worst upheaval, annihilation is rarely total—some people are lucky. Insofar as I am concerned, however, one doesn't have to resort to that theory. I can account for my survival quite plausibly.

For one thing, I arrived in the Soviet Union much later than the other leaders of the Finnish Communist party. I didn't arrive until 1933, whereas the others had come in 1918 or the 1920s, had held important positions in Karelia as well as the Leningrad area and had accumulated a backlog of transgressions—whether they were justified or unjustified is immaterial. Furthermore, I wasn't involved at all in tasks for the Soviet Union but worked exclusively for the Finnish Communist party, and even there I wasn't deeply involved in the internal factional disputes of those days. My record of transgressions thus was not like that of many others.

Second, upon arriving in the Soviet Union I had, shall I say, a large working capital at my disposal, since I had sat in Finnish prisons for almost ten years in the Soviet cause. I had fought for the Bolsheviks and specifically for the Soviet Union in every possible and impossible situation when it was still weak and in real difficulties. This factor naturally tipped the scales in my favor. My list of credits was hence considerably longer than those of many others whose halo had not been very bright to begin with and had only dimmed through the years. And so when I arrived in the Soviet Union I was lauded and rewarded in many ways.

Another important element contributing to the stability of my position was, of course, the fact that I shared Kuusinen's apartment. I was, and still am, certain that he reported favorably of me at all levels and guaranteed my trustworthiness. Even though the stability of his own position was, as we have seen, highly dubious in the eyes of the GPU at various times, he nevertheless enjoyed the full confidence of dictator Stalin, which was the decisive factor. And his word carried great weight, if and when he chose to give it on behalf of his friends.

A third factor, and perhaps the determining one, was that the worst blows at the Central Committee of the Finnish Communist party came in 1938, when I had already left the Soviet Union for Sweden. Naturally there was and is a considerable dossier on me, too, in the GPU archives containing perhaps a sizeable list of transgressions but, as far as I can see, the aforementioned circumstances were responsible for the fact that I was spared the fate of many of my comrades.

Then the second question: did I contribute, and in what way, to the destruction of my Finnish comrades?

I can assure you that I did not sign a single statement accusing my comrades. On the contrary, I signed scores of statements in defense of persons whom I knew and with whose activities I was familiar. I suspect that these attestations rarely helped, for the situation was such that the GPU functioned according to its own standards and its own definitions. As the party secretary I was able to arrange matters so that I did not have to sign letters or statements that were distasteful to me. According to the prevailing system, the responsibility for such statements had been shifted to a special person, in cases involving Finns to Tuure Lehén, who served in the Comintern's cadre section in precisely that capacity. A second person—Hannes Mäkinen, who was a member of the Central Committee and the Finnish Communist party's representative in the Comintern—also had to sign all papers going to the Comintern's cadre section. I saw Mäkinen's statements, at least some of them, and I can say that he put no pressure on his comrades. By his very nature he was a man who did not readily undertake anything contrary to his convictions.

Of course I can be accused, and justly so, of not courageously defending those of my comrades who found themselves in the danger zone. Even under those conditions it naturally would have been possible to go before the public and risk one's whole life by proclaiming one's unwillingness to participate in such a game and unequivocally dissociating oneself from it. True, I was and am to this day fully convinced that such a declaration would have been to no avail. It would have been nothing less than heroic suicide, for a proclamation like that would have been a man's last.

As it is, I cannot boast of having been a courageous man or in any way having differed from the others. I was exactly like the others in positions of leadership, almost without exception. An anecdote told about Secretary General Khrushchev's famous speech at the party Congress of 1956 applies to me perfectly.

When he had enumerated Stalin's horrible crimes and acts of despotism, a note was sent to him by one of the participants asking, "What were you doing, Comrade Khrushchev, while Stalin was committing those crimes?"

Khrushchev read the note aloud and then asked, "Will the comrade who wrote this note please rise?"

No one among the more than fifteen hundred delegates stood up.

Khrushchev stared at the audience and said, "We did exactly what the comrade who wrote this note is doing."

Yes, under those circumstances it was extremely difficult to act the hero. To enact such a role one needs a certain amount of freedom, at least enough to be able to tell some person or some audience, "I do not approve of this."

Thus one must have the opportunity to commit that heroic suicide. Had I been in Moscow when I was offered the post of prime minister in the Terijoki government in the fall of 1939, the chances are that I would have had no possibility of rejecting the task. I probably would have accepted it, since rejection would have meant my disappearance silently, anonymously. However, at the time I happened to be in Stockholm, where I had the freedom to decline the offer. By citing this example I have simply wanted to say that the ordinary person (saints and great ethical supermen are something else again!) needs at least some freedom in order to appear a hero.

When conditions in 1937 became more strained month by month, and party activity focusing on Finland grew increasingly difficult—in other words, when the Iron Curtain began to be quite impenetrable and the restriction of personal freedom seemed imminent, I suggested to Kuusinen that, from the standpoint of successful party work, as party secretary, I should be transferred to Stockholm inasmuch as the work could no longer be carried on from Moscow.

Besides, Antti Hyvönen and Inkeri Lehtinen, who had done party work in Stockholm, had been recalled to Moscow, and the technical assistant, Yrjö Enne, had been compromised so badly that the Comintern had ordered him to be relieved of all party tasks. Carelessly—hardly deliberately, as the GPU asserted—he had left the cipher keys as well as numerous addresses in a place where they had fallen into the hands of the police and resulted in many arrests. This trio left behind a considerable mess in Stockholm. Twice it had "lost" party funds—first 14,000, then 2,500 crowns. In addition, Hyvönen had sent another Finn, Jarno Pennanen, to Paris at the party's expense on matters about which the party had no knowledge or benefit but for which it had to foot huge bills, for Jarno just couldn't bear to tear himself away from Paris. The Comintern Secretariat rigorously demanded an accounting, and Moskvin refused to give the party a single crown or dollar until the mischief done by Hyvönen, Enne, and Inkeri had been straightened out.

For this reason, too, the moment was propitious for me to suggest that I travel to Stockholm myself. Kuusinen immediately warmed to the idea and together we went to explain our plans to Dimitrov and Manuilski. At the same time I obtained an exit permit for my wife as well. We had journeyed in step for such a long stretch that neither of us wished to part from the other. Besides, even from the standpoint of party work, I needed a dependable and capable assistant in my upcoming mission. Admittedly, behind it was the thought that under no condition would I leave her behind as a hostage.

Everything was arranged easily. Even the decision about my wife's departure was made immediately. She was not able to travel with me, however, but left to follow another route. After my wife's arrival, we reported together to the Swedish police in the spring of 1938.

The police officials naturally were amazed that we had returned there. They said frankly that they suspected me of being a representative of the Comintern's Executive Committee, and added that if this was not so, then I must give public notice that I had had a falling out with Moscow and had fled from there.

I announced curtly that I had not had a falling out with Moscow, nor had I fled, and neither had I come as an emissary; I simply wanted to await better times when I could return to Finland, my regular sphere of activity. The police naturally laughed at such an explanation and said that it was hardly likely that I would be given a residency permit.

I immediately went to see my old acquaintance, Sigfrid Hansson—Prime Minister Per Albin Hansson's brother—who at that time headed the Social Welfare Administration. It was this office which made the final decision regarding foreigners' residency permits, and Hansson granted us ours without further ado.

With a smile he added, "My only hope is that you don't become involved in Swedish politics, complicate the government's and my position or harm Sweden's interests. Otherwise you're completely free to live and move about like the country's own citizens, so long as you don't cause us any inconvenience."

I assured him that in no way would I become involved in Swedish affairs, and that promise I kept. I discharged many different duties, primarily relating to Finland. I retained my official positions as secretary general of the Finnish Communist party and member of the Comintern Presidium's Executive Committee, maintained contact with the communist leaders in Finland and carried out the secretary general's functions within the bounds of existing possibilities.

Naturally the reader will now ask, "Why didn't a man who witnessed all that has been described in the foregoing wrench himself free immediately upon reaching freedom and proclaim to the whole world what conditions really prevailed in Stalin's empire?"

It is very easy to slide into communism. Once I jotted down twenty-three—idealistic as well as practical—attractions of communism. But it is much more difficult to renounce it, and especially so for a person who has achieved a prominent position.

And it is difficult, especially for the Finnish character, to concede that one has erred. A Finn is persistent, not quick to complain, not quick to seek forgiveness. One must endure; one must not indicate that possibly one has made a mistake. In that "once having taken this path" there is a certain stubbornness. Although frost destroys one's grain, one makes do by adding bast from a tree to flour and presses onward to the end. Our poet Runeberg saw this as an expression of true Finnish grit. Someone else would have abandoned his fields after three years of a killing frost and moved on to better lands. Paavo of Saarijärvi could not do this.*

A number of Finnish Communists in Russia would have had opportunities to flee. Likewise, a number of those Finnish Americans still alive were ashamed to return to America because they knew that they would be ridiculed. Of two evils they chose the worse. A Finnish man must not waver.

When one has, as I have, devoted the best years of his life to working and suffering for a cause, one is reluctant to admit to himself that everything has been merely a delusion and wasted effort. It is characteristic of human nature to interpret one's deeds logically, and so I tried to convince myself that it was all Stalin's fault that communism had gone astray—how different the situation would have been had Lenin been the leader!

Furthermore, it is not easy to endure one's comrades' charges of betrayal. Another restraining factor is the realization that a renegade—especially one in a position of leadership—may jeopardize his life. For that reason most of those who renounce communism do so as unobtrusively as possible by withdrawing from activities and retreating to the background. It is the easiest way and less hazardous than public, open resistance. So I, too, lived from month to month, no longer steadfastly believing in communism but as though expecting better times. Perhaps something would happen; Stalin might be overthrown or die, and the situation could improve.

The months passed in this wishful thinking until the bombshell

---

* The hero of the poem by the same name, by Finland's national poet Johan Ludvig Runeberg.

of August 1939: the Hitler-Stalin pact. It was, so to speak, the final drop into my cup of expectations. To the very end I had kept alive the hope that, though Stalin had betrayed the cause in many ways, he could not or dared not betray the cause of peace. Now that hope, too, vanished with Hitler's attack and Stalin's stab in Poland's back.

At the same time it became clear that the Comintern and the communist parties—which meant the Finnish Communist party as well—had been harnessed not only to further the Soviet Union's imperialistic aims but even to sanctify Nazi Germany's attacks. The Comintern's leaders justified Hitler's attack on Poland and later the occupation of Denmark, Norway, Holland, Belgium, Luxemburg, and France. Stalin and Dimitrov ordered that the Finnish Communist party could no longer further Finland's cause but had to support that of Hitler and Stalin, which did not agree with the best interests of the Finnish workers.

In other words, the Comintern ordered the communist parties of all countries to hail the Hitler-Stalin pact and immediately after its conclusion actually forbade the workers of Poland, Czechoslovakia, Denmark, Norway, Holland, Belgium and many other countries to fight Nazi Germany, demanding that they submit to the Nazis' yoke without resisting.

As a family heritage I have very high moral standards in the sense that there exist certain moral laws, not literally laid down in the Bible or the New Testament but nevertheless shaped by Western culture. The ethics of communism are actually Jesuit ethics—the end justifies the means—and I for one could not accept that even in my most rabid period of communism.

Subsequently my critics have declared that even when holding the highest posts—such as in the Comintern Presidium and as the secretary of the Finnish Communist party—I was not a true Communist inasmuch as I did not approve of the communist ethic. They were absolutely correct. I was not one. I kept crashing into this Jesuit moral concept. In my opinion, the end does not justify the means. The means by which working people are bound must consist of certain laws as specified in party decisions, and, furthermore, one's conscience dictates what is right and what is wrong. This has played a notable part in my entire developmental process and, later, in my moment of truth during the formation of the Terijoki government, when just this end-justifies-the-means morality had to be resolved, this voice of the conscience spoke up strongly. I would not be used for such a purpose. I could no longer be a part of this game.

After discussing the matter many times with my wife, who gave her enthusiastic support, I decided that it would be best to withdraw quietly to the sidelines, to enjoy the repose of the prudent. I was already making preparations for this when a sudden decision had me irrevocably against the wall.

On November 13, 1939, the Comintern ordered me to Moscow to accept the post of the prime minister in the government to be formed in Terijoki. I replied in the negative and received a new command, this time from Stalin himself. There was no longer the possibility of retiring to the sidelines. The decision had to be made, yes or no, for I realized that the command I had received signified an imminent attack on Finland.

During that period I waged an intense battle with myself. My days and nights were spent in mental reckoning, wrestling between right and wrong, and its result was the realization that my place was at the front with those Finnish men and women who were defending their fatherland against an aggressor.

My thoughts returned to the long prison years when my comrades and I, in the solitude of a prison cell, dreamed of the time when the working people would be in power in Finland. We dreamed of the moment when we could proclaim that our sacrifices and sufferings had not been in vain. We dreamed of a new state, a new society that would be in accordance with our ideals and ideas.

During the trying days of that November, those years and their dreams surged forth time and again. Was that envisioned moment now at hand? Could Finland's working people, by taking advantage of Europe's chaos, seize power and gradually clear the way to socialism? If that were so shouldn't I, who had dedicated his whole life to that cause, be part of it?

I pondered these questions and always got the same clear, unequivocal answer: if it really were even slightly a matter of improving the Finnish workers' conditions and lives, naturally I should be a part of it.

Always on reaching this point I was beset by doubts whether that really was the issue. Did any signs indicate it? Didn't all the preliminaries indicate that what was involved was a deed contrary to our ideas and beliefs? Didn't the German-Soviet pact form an appalling background to the issue? Weren't those preliminaries suspiciously reminiscent of Austria's, Czechoslovakia's and Poland's replies? I saw myself in the guise of some wretched, quaking, and eternally despised Hácha* standing before Stalin and Molotov and asking that the Red Army come to liberate the Finnish people. Or I saw myself as a "governor" such as Hitler's vassals Forster, Henlein, and Seyss-Inquart.† And I was horrified.

As the struggle continued, the devil whispered in my ear, "But just think of the position you would have. Wouldn't it be grand—you with such status! Imagine being able to square accounts with all your opponents. You shouldn't pity Finland's powers that be. Didn't they keep you imprisoned for almost a decade and in exile for over seven years? Surely you can't claim that your fatherland has dealt gently with you. Perhaps the people will some day forget this terrible beginning and perhaps Finnish men will yet have the chance to determine Finland's fate. Besides, the march of events can no longer be changed—it has been decided by such men as Hitler and Stalin. You would only destroy yourself in battling such forces."

Thoughts like these tumbled through my mind. But to every such temptation it responded clearly, "It would be wrong; it would be criminal. It would mean betraying one's beliefs for a few paltry personal advantages. It would mean betraying the Finnish nation and its cause. It would mean betraying the tenets of socialism."

And after all this I saw clearly, as the outcome of that coming bloody war of extermination, not a free democracy, not a glorious and happy life, but the memory of those hundreds of my closest comrades who as forced laborers, exhausted human wrecks, were digging canals on Russia's endless steppes. In my thoughts they seemed to symbolize the coming fate of the Finnish people.

The longer I agonized, the clearer it became that this was not a question of the Finnish working people's liberation but of a dreadful crime in which I could not participate. We had explained to large groups of workers that what distinguished the Soviet Union from imperialist countries was the very fact that it did not make

* Emil Hácha, "head of state" in German occupied Czechoslovakia.
† Albert Forster in Danzig, Konrad Henlein in the German-speaking areas of Czechoslovakia, Arthur Seyss-Inquart in Austria.

secret agreements or military treaties behind the backs of its people or the world's working class; its diplomacy was open, and it would never attack another state. Its policy was the policy of peace, which condemned war as a monstrous crime. How could we now participate in this criminal activity, how could we look workers in the eye without feeling like villains, since we had taught them the opposite.

I would rather spend another decade in prison or live the rest of life in exile than submit to becoming a tool in such a game.

No, it could not be a question of liberating the Finnish people. Clearly this war was not the Finnish workers' struggle for freedom from the slavery of exloiters. It was not being waged by the Finnish working people against their own country's capitalists, but by a foreign power's army against the Finnish people, above all, against the workers.

What were the attacker's justifications? Stalin asserted that Finland started the war with the shots at Mainila.* Whether they were or were not fired is immaterial. They were not the reason for the war but an excuse for it. War had been decided on at the latest already on November 13, when I was first summoned to Moscow.

As the second reason for the war, Stalin announced officially that Finland was a hotbed, inimical and perilous to the Soviet Union and that the Finnish government did not accede to the Soviet government's demands concerning the security of Leningrad. Personally, I hoped that the Finnish government would have acceded to the Soviet demands in the fall of 1939. My understanding is that it would have been compelled to accede to them if Stalin had followed a more peaceful policy—his proclaimed policy of peace—and had had the patience to wait even those months during which he senselessly annihilated both his own and Finnish people. Stalin chose war before all the peaceful means of solution had been exhausted, which gives one the right to assume that he actually sought war rather than the peaceful acceptance of his demands. He wanted to show the world the powerful Red Army that would march into Helsinki inside a few days.

I concluded that the Finnish-Soviet war was not a justified communist war but purely an imperialist attack. Depressing.

---

* Immediately before the Red Army attacked Finland, on November 30, 1939, the Soviet Union accused the Finns of having shelled the Soviet border village Mainila.

On November 23 I sent another negative reply to Moscow, indicating that the tasks that were being offered to me were too demanding, and that I would not travel.

About the same time as I refused to join the Terijoki government the situation grew more critical and came to a head on November 30, 1939, when the Soviet Union launched an attack on Finland. Thus began the Winter War.

On the first day of December the Finnish people and the whole world were astonished by a bulletin read over the Moscow radio: "On the basis of an agreement between various leftist parties and mutinous Finnish soldiers, a new Finnish government has been organized in Terijoki: the People's Government of the Finnish Democratic Republic, under the leadership of Otto Wille Kuusinen."

Terijoki was a Finnish county seat, six miles from the Soviet border and twenty-five miles from Leningrad.

What were those "various leftist parties"? At that time Finland had two leftist parties, the Social Democratic and the Communist, and neither was involved in that undertaking. Whence came those "organizers" and whom did they represent? They were contrived shadows, as were the "mutinous soldiers."

Two armies were engaged in battle, but also opposing each other were the apprentice and his master. The master, Otto Wille Kuusinen, became the prime minister in the Terijoki government. He tried to get me for that post by all possible means; the office of president had originally been reserved for him. After my refusal he had to form a government around his own name, since all the others in the Terijoki government were so unknown that the majority of the Finnish people were not even aware of their existence. They were resorted to primarily because, of the seven members of the Finnish Communist party's Central Committee who had been chosen in the Soviet Union, only Kuusinen himself was still free.

I have calculated that many quite competent governments could have been formed for Finland from the Finnish Communists in the Soviet Union, had not Stalin annihilated the Finnish Communist party's best cadres so thoroughly that, when the hour of revolution struck and they were sorely needed, they no longer existed.

After the war, when a communist takeover in the manner of

Czechoslovakia could have been staged in Finland, nothing came of it because of the lack of skilled leaders.

It should be noted that, in declining to join the Terijoki government, I did not resign my post as secretary general of the Finnish Communist party. On the contrary, I emphasized that I still was the party's secretary general and continued to lead it. At my disposal were 2,500 thoroughly trained active members of the Finnish Communist party, as well as 250 specially trained saboteurs, skilled in blowing up bridges, railroads, and factories. As the former vice-chairman and long-time secretary general of the Central Federation of Finnish Trade Unions I also had considerable influence in the trade union movement.

It was not a question of a few thousand but of tens of thousands, perhaps a few hundred thousand Finns who had to decide their stand when the bombs began to drop.

I believe that if the secretary general of the Finnish Communist party backed by the membership of the party's central committee had given the order to support Otto Wille Kuusinen and his Terijoki government, a completely different situation would have developed than what actually did. It is very likely that a civil war would have erupted in Finland. Many would have refused to serve in the army, factories would have come to a halt, bridges would have been blown up and so forth. The situation might have become so chaotic that the Red Army along with its Terijoki government would have found it much easier to march toward Helsinki than it did under the conditions that actually prevailed.

Having refused to join the Terijoki government, I spread the word over my own network that we had to be on the alert. Whatever came from Moscow now was not to be trusted. The party was being directed from Stockholm, where the secretary general was. The members of the Central Committee in Finland supported the secretary general in the measures about to be undertaken. I mobilized the party into a more compact form.

Then, on November 30, I immediately notified the members of the Central Committee, the leaders of the district committees, and the leadership of the local committees—again over my own network—that now two fascist dictators, Stalin and Hitler, had decided to destroy the small nations. They already had destroyed Poland. Estonia, Lithuania, and Latvia were in danger. Now Finland's turn had come. Under no circumstances should the Finnish workers or the Finnish Communist party endorse this. All forces had to be mobilized against such an attack. Above all every Communist, who just then was suspected of being unpatriotic, had to make a special effort to show his patriotism. In short, the fatherland had to be defended when it was attacked. This was the progressive, justified war of which Marx spoke, a war in which a small nation defended its existence and sovereignty.

When the Finnish nation, as one man, fought its heavy, at times seemingly hopeless, battle, I was with it with every fiber of my being and tried to make my own contribution to the effort.

I expressed my opinions in a booklet printed at my own expense: "An Open Letter to a Finnish Fellow Worker." Through the efforts of certain labor organizations, large Finnish-language editions were printed and then distributed in Finland. Later I learned that its effect on that situation had been great.

In other words, I commanded my own "brigade" in the Winter War, and its name was the Finnish Communist party. Later, amazement was expressed at that fact and Field Marshal Mannerheim wondered why I didn't incorporate my brigade directly into the Finnish Army. I pointed out that I was not in the service of the Finnish Army or officials. I was the secretary general of the Finnish Communist party and fought with my own brigade, at least as effectively as it could have fought had it been subject to the command of the Finnish army.

Of course, this brigade of mine was distrusted during the early days of the war. But the military units with many active Communists were apt to fight even more courageously than the units consisting of Home Guards. And so the confidence that the Communists actually were taking part in the struggle grew day by day throughout the entire Winter War.

As I was doing this work and Finland's fate was being decided on her embattled soil, I continued to liquidate my own ideological insolvency. In becoming a supporter of communism I had believed that through it we would be freed of the horrors of war, exploitation, oppression, and uncertainty about the future; that it would guarantee personal inviolability to every citizen and higher intellectual and material standards for the entire nation, wipe out class distinctions and assure the freedom of nations both small and large.

I had believed that communism in itself encompasses a striving toward the scrupulous adherence to truth—in a word, toward a higher moral standard than heretofore has prevailed.

After theoretical study during my prison years in Finland I had the chance to study applied socialism and communism in the Soviet Union. In the beginning, between the years 1933–35, this study was rewarding and even pleasant. But then came a time that was neither socialism nor communism but actual dictatorship. I realized then that those beautiful ideals and ideologies had definitely collapsed; around me were only the ruins of my dreams.

In this situation I had the invaluable assistance of my wife, whose uncompromising sense of justice supported and strengthened my resolve to such a degree that my soul-searching was not limited to yearning and lamentation but grew into a public reckoning. I had joined in ideologically, she only technically. Not until I renounced communism and the Comintern did we pursue common lines. When I announced my refusal to join the Terijoki government my wife, who had said nothing about the matter either for or against, declared herself very happy about my decision.

"It may well mean," she added, "that your life and mine might be cut short, but anyway this was probably the wisest decision of your life."

And so I dared confess my errors and weaknesses in the letters and pamphlets that I wrote to my Finnish colleagues and the Moscow bosses during the Winter War and the weeks following, but I also dared say what I thought about Stalinist communism. In my booklet, "Stalin as the Keeper of Lenin's Legacy," I said about Stalin and Stalinism already in 1940 almost literally what the top communist leaders said about him some sixteen years later, notably Khrushchev in his famous speech at the Soviet Communist Party Congress of 1956.

I also condemned Comintern policies in my letter of April 4, 1940, to Secretary General Dimitrov that was published simultaneously in Finland and Sweden. In it I cited, point by point, how the Comintern had participated in and supported Stalin's policy.

I concluded my letter with the statement, "I have discussed the policy of the Soviet Government at such length because it is also the Comintern's policy, and because therein lies the crux of the matter which has prompted this letter and position report. If the

Comintern had wanted to be an organization for the world's workers, an organization for the oppressed and the abused, it should have taken a firm stand against such a policy, which conflicts sharply with the rights of all countries' workers and which, if it is allowed to continue, will cause—as it already has caused—untold suffering to the people of the Soviet Union as well as to those of other countries.

"Having seen the brutal destruction wrought in Finland by the Soviet Union, having seen the bleeding Finnish nation, the nation whose child I am and in which I am rooted with unbreakable bonds, having seen its distress and heard its anguished cry and been convinced that it has been the victim of a horrible injustice, and having affirmed that the Soviet Union as well as the Comintern have abandoned the policy of national freedom and peace and adopted this policy of injustice and destruction, I can no longer be silent. Hence I have had to effect this reckoning and dissociate myself from the policy that is contrary to my convictions and the basic principles of socialism."

Later I met hundreds of my old party comrades who told me that they were despairing in that situation and didn't know what to do. With the secretary general's command to fight, these vacillating people reached a new resolve. They realized that they were fighting with the blessing of the party and party secretary. And even though Kuusinen dropped countering leaflets from airplanes, they found it easy to ignore such leaflets because they were backed by the consent of the party secretary and the party.

Naturally they, too, were considerably shaken by the Hitler-Stalin pact. Already then they suspected—as did I—that perhaps Stalin had become completely demented. It was shocking to think that he actually could make an agreement with Hitler, against whom he had fought for many years and whom he had called the greatest and most monstrous terrorist and warmonger in history.

Actually, there was no sabotage to speak of in Finland, no strikes, no conscientious objectors, but rather the shaping of a truly 100 percent unified nation. Thus was born the "Winter War miracle," the rare integration of a people. Even today one can say that such a national consolidation into a unified homogeneous force is virtually unknown in world history, particularly when the people had been quite divided since the civil war of 1918.

Universal opinion manifestly helped the Finnish nation greatly, but had it been internally rent, not even universal sentiment could have saved it in that difficult situation.

Above all, the Finnish people's unified Winter War spirit was the factor that made possible the Finns' defense for 105 days against the Russians' overwhelming numerical and material superiority. When the war ended in an armistice on March 13, 1940, Finland lost about one-tenth of its territory, to be sure, but nevertheless not its independence.

The spirit of the Winter War assuredly was not merely an isolated, forgettable, fleeting miracle. As I see it, it was a great promise for the future. It was a diagnosis of the Finnish people's health, and it confirmed that Finland was essentially sound. Had it been decadent, it would not have withstood such a storm.

I realize that today's young people, who were not even born then, find it difficult to comprehend all this. But my conviction is that the spirit and miracle of the Winter War are the guarantee of our nation's future.

In reaching my difficult decision in November 1939 I was also helped by the legacy of my childhood home: my mother's sickle and my father's hammer, those objects that for me have symbolized honesty, truth, and righteousness. I repudiated absolutely and irrevocably the symbol of communist violence—the hammer and sickle—and adopted as the guiding star of my life my parents' productive tools: mother's sickle and father's hammer.

Index